An Introduction to
Classical
Evangelical
Hermeneutics

A Guide to
the History and Practice
of Biblical Interpretation

MAL COUCH
General Editor

PUBLICATIONS

Grand Rapids, MI 49501

An Introduction to Classical Evangelical Hermeneutics: A Guide to the History and Practice of Biblical Interpretation

© 2000 by Mal Couch

Published by Kregel Publications, a division of Kregel, Inc., P.O. Box 2607, Grand Rapids, MI 49501.

Library of Congress Cataloging-in-Publication Data
Couch, Mal.
   An introduction to classical evangelical hermeneutics: a guide to the history and practice of biblical interpretation / by Mal Couch, general editor.
   Includes bibliographical references and index.
     p.   cm.
   1. Bible—Hermeneutics. I. Title.
BS476C66   2000   220.6'01—dc21   99-33767
                                      CIP

ISBN 978-0-8254-2367-3

Printed in the United States of America

4 5 6 7 / 12 11 10

In honor of
The Conservative Theological Society
whose purpose is to call
evangelical Christians
to a renewed love of biblical truth.

For information about the organization
or its publication
The Conservative Theological Journal, contact
The Conservative Theological Society
6800 Brentwood Stair
Fort Worth, TX 76112

Contents

Part 3: Interpreting the Church

Part 4: Interpreting Prophecy

Acknowledgments for material previously published may be found at the end of a
chapter. The permission of other copyright holders to include their material in
this work is gratefully acknowledged by the editor. Unless so noted, chapters in
this work are the collaborative effort of the contributors; therefore, no individual
contributor is acknowledged as the author of such chapters.

Contributors

Mal Couch, M.A., Th.M., Th.D., Ph.D., is founder and president of Tyndale Theological Seminary in Fort Worth, Texas, and general editor of the award-winning *Dictionary of Premillennial Theology*.

Larry V. Crutchfield, M.A., M.Phil., Ph.D., is a freelance writer and Professor of Early Church History and Culture at Columbia Evangelical Seminary, Longview, Washington.

Thomas O. Figart, Th.M., Th.D., is Distinguished Professor of Biblical Education at Lancaster Bible College, Lancaster, Pennsylvania.

Bobby Hayes, M.A., Ph.D. candidate, is an associate professor at Tyndale Theological Seminary and Biblical Institute, Fort Worth, Texas.

Ron M. Johnson, M.B.A., D.Min., Ph.D. candidate, is senior pastor of Indian Trail Community Church in Spokane, Washington.

Russell L. Penney, M.A., D.Sc., Th.D., is a missionary teacher at Seminario Teológico Hebrón (Hebron Theological Seminary) in Santa Cruz de la Sierra, Bolivia.

Paul Lee Tan, Th.M., Th.D., is founder and president of Bible Communications, Dallas, Texas. Dr. Tan is the compiler of the popular *Encyclopedia of 7700 Illustrations*.

PART 1

God Has Spoken

CHAPTER 1

God Has Spoken

Almost all Christians believe that the Bible is the Word of God. They believe that the Lord has spoken and revealed Himself, His will, and the way of salvation in the revelation of the Old and New Testaments. Disagreements exist, however, about the interpretation and meaning of some areas of the biblical message.

A great many within the evangelical camp hold strongly to the doctrines of revelation, inspiration, and even inerrancy of the original texts of Scripture. Since the Reformation, evangelicals as a whole claim to take the Word of God literally, reading the prophets and apostles in a literal manner and accepting the historicity of the Scriptures at face value.

Where, then, is the greatest area of disagreement among Christians? And is the disagreement minor or major? Does it affect the overall thrust of the biblical message?

Among evangelicals there are generally two major camps regarding how prophetic passages should be read. Amillennialists will generally allegorize large portions of the prophetic Word, especially passages that speak of the Second Advent of Christ and the establishment of the one-thousand-year literal Davidic kingdom. In contrast, premillennialists, following the teaching of the early church, treat the Second Coming with the same literal hermeneutic as they would the First Coming of Jesus. They hold that the Bible, from Genesis to Revelation, should be understood literally from a normal reading unless typology or poetry is clearly used. And even then, premillennialists believe that "literalness" is implied behind the figure of speech or illustration used.

<u>Amillennialism</u> may be defined as follows:

> The amillennial view holds that the kingdom promises in
> the Old Testament are fulfilled spiritually rather than liter-
> ally in the New Testament church. Those who hold this view
> believe that Christ will literally return, but they do not be-
> lieve in His thousand-year reign on the earth.[1]

Though the amillennial scholar Berkhof claims to hold to an overall literal approach to the Bible, in the area of future prophecy he
does not. Without elaboration, he writes on the subject of prophecy,

> Under the guidance of the Holy Spirit, "the prophets occa-
> sionally transcended their historical and dispensational limi-
> tations, and spoke in forms that pointed to a more spiritual
> dispensation in the future." In such cases the prophetic ho-
> rizon was enlarged, they sensed something of the passing
> character of the old forms, and gave ideal descriptions of
> the blessings of the New Testament Church.[2]

Berkhof's view indicates a major difference between prophetic
allegorists and literal premillennialists. There is a clear difference
in how the Word of God is interpreted between allegorists and those
who take all of Scripture in a literal sense. Berkhof is saying that
the prophecies of blessing in the Old Testament are turned into
blessings in the New Testament church. He applies kingdom blessings to the present church age. Berkhof seems to connect the church
with promises made specifically to the Jewish people relative to
their promised restoration, which he foresees as happening by
miracle in some prophetic future day.

The allegorizing trend was also advocated by A. A. Hodge, who
writes,

> The Old Testament prophecies, . . . which predict this
> [Davidic] kingdom, must refer to the present dispensation
> of grace [the church], and not to a future reign of Christ on
> earth in person among men in the flesh.
>
> The spiritual interpretation of this difficult passage (Rev-
> elation 20:1–10) is as follows: Christ has in reserve for his
> church a period of universal expansion and of pre-eminent
> spiritual prosperity.
>
> The New Testament is entirely silent on the subject of any

such return [of the Jews to the land of their fathers]. . . . the literal interpretation of these [Old Testament] passages is inconsistent with what the New Testament plainly teaches as to the abolition of all distinctions between the Jew and Gentile; . . .

. . . the spiritual interpretation of these Old Testament prophecies—which regards them as predicting the future purity and extension of the Christian church, . . . is both natural and accordant to the analogy of Scripture.[3]

The Interpretative War

The views of Berkhof and Hodge clash strongly with the beliefs of premillennialists. Premillennialism can be described as follows:

In its simplest form, the premillennial view holds that Christ will return to earth, . . . literally and bodily, before the millennial age begins and that, by His presence, a kingdom will be instituted over which He will reign. It is during this reign that Israel will see the fulfillment of its covenants that were unconditionally promised in the Old Testament. Prophecies given to Israel are for Israel and cannot be usurped by the church. In this present age, Israel has been set aside, its promises held in abeyance. . . . God's promises have been made to Israel, and they will find their fulfillment in the Millennium.[4]

Which view is correct? One cannot argue that the issues are unimportant. While one's salvation is not contingent upon one's millennial beliefs, how one sees the future prophetic plan stated in Scripture is a monumental doctrinal issue.

From what has been stated thus far, it might seem that this book is simply about the hermeneutics of prophecy. Though this is not the case, the crucial elements of Bible interpretation must be applied carefully to Bible prophecies and the question of their future fulfillment. Will they take place in the normal sense in which they are expressed in both Old and New Testaments? Or should we allegorize a large portion of the Bible with a spiritualized system of hermeneutics?

Though it is certainly not true that all amillennialists have turned toward a more liberal orientation regarding the Bible, it may be seen in history that amillennialism opened the doors for denying great doctrines of Scripture. If one can allegorize the literal promises of a future millennial kingdom, why not the Virgin Birth, the Atonement, the Resurrection, or any other critical doctrine?

A premillennialist who takes all of the Word of God at face value would be one of the last to drift from taking the Scriptures in its most literal sense. Thus, the acceptance of Scripture as the inspired Word of God is a must for the premillennial view as well as the necessary starting point of historical and literal interpretation.

This book, then, is really about method. How is the Bible to be interpreted? Is there a standard method or reliable system in determining the message of Scripture? It is not possible in the present work to make a complete examination of biblical doctrine. Since it is necessary to limit the range of study and since eschatology is so controversial, it will become the central area of investigation.

Before discussing the science of interpretation and its application to prophecy, however, several larger questions must be addressed. Can we really know truth? Is the Word of God reasonable? Can human beings truly know that God has spoken?

Thus, before examining the subject at hand, a larger question must be addressed: Is the Bible actually the written Word of God? Thus, a look at the inspiration of Scripture is in order.

CHAPTER 2

The Evangelical Doctrine of Inspiration and Inerrancy—Restated

This I have learned to do: to hold only those books which are called the Holy Scriptures in such honor that I finally believe that not one of the holy writers ever erred.

Letter from Augustine to Jerome

The Scriptures have never erred. The Scriptures cannot err. It is certain that the Scripture cannot disagree with itself. It is impossible for that Scripture should contradict itself, only ✳ that it so appears to the senseless and obstinate hypocrites.

Martin Luther

Many of the major denominations that for centuries have held to full inerrancy and inspiration of Scripture have already or are now abandoning their position. Many schools, the founders of which valiantly defended inerrancy, have caved in under academic pressure and now allow their professors to teach the ideas of higher and historical criticism. Although many Bible teachers and professors attempt to preserve belief in the doctrine, they find themselves up against not only a culture that is hostile to such a belief, but also growing disbelief from their own congregations and students. James Draper writes,

There are people among us today, teaching in our institutions, laboring in our denominations, pastoring in our churches, who have not departed all that far from classic biblical doctrine. They still believe that Jesus is God. They still believe in the bodily resurrection of Christ. They still believe in the virgin birth. But, they do not believe that everything in Scripture is necessarily accurate and without error. They have started over the ledge.[1]

Today the Word of God is under attack more than at any time in the history of the church. In 1984, in his book *The Great Evangelical Disaster*, Dr. Francis Schaeffer wrote,

> Holding to a strong view of Scripture or not holding to it is the watershed of the evangelical world. The first direction in which we must face is to say most lovingly but clearly: evangelicalism is not consistently evangelical *unless there is a line drawn* between those who take a full view of Scripture and those who do not.[2]

The bottom line is, <u>if Scripture cannot be trusted in some areas, it cannot be trusted in any area</u>. Once full inspiration is denied, man determines what is inspired and what is not. Once there is a "crack in the dam" in our belief in full inspiration, the flood is imminent. Dr. Schaeffer understood that once the flood begins,

> there is no end. . . . The Bible is made to say only that which echoes the surrounding culture at our moment of history.[3]

Our belief in inspiration and inerrancy has a very practical effect on our daily life. As Dr. Schaeffer states, "Compromising the full authority of Scripture eventually affects what it means to be a Christian theologically and how we live in the full spectrum of human life."[4] With so much at stake, we must be very clear on what the Scriptures themselves teach about inspiration and inerrancy. Why is inerrancy so questioned today after being held in such high esteem for almost eighteen hundred years? What did the early church fathers and the apostles say about inerrancy? Does the loss of belief in inerrancy make a difference or is it a minor doctrine not worth debate? The answers to these questions will support the importance of the doctrine of inerrancy and inspiration.

Definitions

Norman Geisler and William Nix give us a good working definition of inspiration in their excellent book *A General Introduction to the Bible.* They state, "Inspiration is that mysterious process by which the divine causality [God] worked through the human prophets without destroying their individual personalities and styles to produce divinely authoritative and inerrant writings."[5]

And Young writes,

> By this word [inspiration] we mean that the Scriptures possess the quality of freedom from error. They are exempt from the liability to mistake, incapable of error. In *all their teachings* they are in perfect accord with the truth.[6] (italics added)

Paul D. Feinberg provides a solid definition of the evangelical view of inerrancy. He states, "Inerrancy is the view that when all the facts become known, they will demonstrate that the Bible in its original autographs and correctly interpreted is entirely true and never false in all it affirms, whether that relates to doctrine or ethics or to the social, physical or life sciences."[7]

Thus, in believing that the Bible is inspired and inerrant we hold that God divinely guided the apostles and prophets to write down exactly what He wanted, and that the Scriptures are totally without error and accurate. Evangelicals have historically held to this view, and it is often stated as a belief in *verbal* (the very words, not just thoughts and ideas), *plenary* (equally in every part of the Scriptures) *inspiration*. It should be stated, though, that only the original documents (hereafter referred to as autographs) are free from error. Geisler and Nix sum up the view as held by the church throughout the centuries. They write,

> Thus, the orthodox doctrine that the Bible is the infallible, inerrant Word of God in its original manuscripts has maintained itself from the first century to the present. This position holds that the Bible is without error in everything that it affirms. Indeed, according to the traditional teachings of the Christian church, what the Bible says, God Himself says. That includes all matters of history, science, and any other matter on which it touches. Any results of higher criticism that are contrary to this teaching are incompatible with the traditional doctrine of the inspiration and authority of Scripture as it has been held throughout church history. Being at variance with the traditional teaching of the Christian church in its broadest context, such contrary views of Scripture are actually unorthodox.[8]

Full and Limited Inerrancy

We have reached a point in the history of evangelicalism at which qualifying adjectives must be added to the term *inerrant* in order to communicate what is believed. Most conservative evangelicals now must use the term *full inerrancy*, which communicates the belief that all subject matter is inspired and correct. Certainly things in Scripture may confuse us, and we may have difficulties understanding some texts, but we know the problem lies within us—the interpreter—and not with what we are interpreting.

More and more "evangelicals," however, hold to the belief of *limited inerrancy*. The term *limited inerrancy* means that the Bible, when speaking of matters of faith and practice (i.e., salvation, principles relating to the Christian life, etc.), is free from error. But in matters of science, history, or biography, it can be supposed that there are mistakes. While God inspired the writers in matters of salvation and living for Christ, He left them on their own when it came to other matters. Characteristic beliefs associated with *limited inerrancy* are a dual authorship of the book of Isaiah; the book of Jonah is a novel rather than historical fact; the book of Daniel was written around 150 B.C. instead of 536 B.C.; Adam and Eve are not historical persons, but figures meant to reveal spiritual truths.

Implications of the Two Views

Plenary inspiration, defined above as full inspiration, tells us two things. First, every book of the Bible is equally inspired. God did not put forth more inspiration in John than He did in 2 Chronicles. Each book is important for the believer, and each must be given study and attention. Second, the whole Bible is the result of divine inspiration. One cannot pick and choose what is inspired and what is not. Inspiration applies to all Scripture, and we can rely on all information contained in the Bible. Such beliefs naturally lead to the doctrine of inerrancy. If God inspired the whole Bible and God cannot make mistakes, then the Bible has no mistakes.[9] We can confidently base our lives on the principles of Scripture knowing that they are objectively true.

On the other hand, the liberal interpreter has a problem. If only the *ideas* of Scripture are inspired, then how can he trust what he reads? It is illogical to assume that God, who is able to inspire the ideas, is not able to inspire the words. When we can't trust the very words, we are led to doubt and confusion. The liberal is not able to trust what he reads because there is no absolute truth. There is only observation of current value systems. As Schaeffer concludes,

The Bible is bent to the culture instead of the Bible judging our society and culture.[10]

Unfortunately, the liberal view increasingly is infecting the church. Pastors, influenced by liberal seminary professors, are departing from the doctrine of full inerrancy. Thus, the tolerance of seminary professors who hold to limited inerrancy causes a trickle-down effect. The infection goes from the liberal seminary professor, to the tainted pastor, to the laymen in the pew.

If we do not believe that the Word that we are studying is reliable, then how can it produce growth? Why then would the Bible admonish us to trust in the Word if it were fallible and not a trustworthy source on which to base our life and future hope? Yet the psalmist confidently stated,

> *How blessed is the man who does not walk in the counsel of the wicked, Nor stand in the path of sinners, Nor sit in the seat of scoffers! But his delight is in the law of the LORD, And in His law he meditates day and night. And he will be like a tree firmly planted by streams of water, Which yields its fruit in its season, And its leaf does not wither; And in whatever he does, he prospers. (Psalm 1:1–3)*

And Paul wrote,

> *All Scripture is inspired by God and profitable for teaching, for reproof, for correction, for training in righteousness; so that the man of God may be adequate, equipped for every good work. (2 Timothy 3:16–17)*

And again,

> *For whatever was written in earlier times was written for our instruction, so that through perseverance and the encouragement of the Scriptures we might have hope. (Romans 15:4)*

We would not be able to "delight in the law of the Lord" if we were continually questioning whether we could trust it. The liberal is put in such a position. He must decide what is fallible and what is infallible. When he decides what is fallible, he must decide to what extent it is fallible. Much time is spent trying to find the errors instead of enjoying the whole truth. For the limited inerrancy adherent, Scripture is held at the mercy of the interpreter.

But for those holding to full inspiration, the rules of interpretation assume that each word is inspired and retains the meaning it held in the culture and the historical context in which it was written. In this way, we can determine with a high degree of accuracy the meaning of God's Word. The liberal, however, has abandoned these rules of interpretation since to him the *words* are not inspired, simply *the ideas*.

What Caused Doubt to Creep In?

The view of limited inerrancy arose from liberal views of Scripture associated with the historical-critical approach to Scripture. Historical-critical interpretation in and of itself is not bad. It is an intelligent, research-oriented approach to the determination of Scripture. Many of the scholars who employed this method, however, held an anti-supernatural bias.

The seeds of historical-critical interpretation began in Germany among the rationalists who were infected by their cultural and intellectual settings. Their approach to the critical examination of Scripture was an attempt to answer and counteract the skepticism that arose from the French Enlightenment. The earlier "higher critics" included such men as Jean Astruc (1684–1766), who held that Genesis 1 and 2 were written by two different authors, based on the distinctions between such words as "Elohim," "Yahweh Elohim" (or "Jehovah Elohim"), and "El-Elyon." He was followed by Johann Semler (1729–1791), who believed that Jesus accommodated His language to the current opinions held by the Jews of His day regarding the Old Testament. Semler also denied that all parts of Scripture are equal in value.

The historical-critical trend continued until the latter half of the nineteenth century when Graf, Jeunen, and Wellhausen formulated the documentary hypothesis. This hypothesis, based on the names used for God in each section, held that the Pentateuch was compiled from four different sources. The four sources were compiled from 850 to 400 B.C. When the last book, "D," was finished, someone allegedly put the books together and produced the Pentateuch. (Moses is not even given the credit for compiling it.)[11]

Geisler and Nix write,

> In recent times all of these trends have had their impact on the traditional doctrines of revelation, inspiration, and the

authority of Scripture. Some evangelical scholars have attempted to incorporate various insights into the framework of the historical-grammatical method of interpreting. Others *have not been able to avoid the adoption of an erroneous or untenable position in their endeavor.* For many of them an extensive use of the dialectical method is the vehicle employed to achieve their scholarly synthesis.[12]

An increasing number of evangelical professors in our traditionally conservative seminaries are unwittingly applying the reasoning of the liberal scholars' higher critical approach to the Scripture, and as Geisler states, "have not been able to avoid the adoption of an erroneous or untenable position in their endeavor."[13]

What Do the Scriptures Say for Themselves?

Like any historical piece of literature, the Bible should be given the benefit of a doubt as to the accuracy of its claims. The accuracy of what it says should be called into question only if there is clear proof against what it claims. So what does the Scripture say about its own nature?

The Mosaic Authorship of the Pentateuch

In Matthew 8:4, we read,

> *And Jesus said to him, "See that you tell no one; but go, show yourself to the priest, and present the offering that Moses prescribed, for a testimony to them."*

In light of this statement, if someone other than Moses had written the book, Jesus would be lying. (Some point to the accommodation theory. It states that Jesus was declaring what the people believed, though He knew otherwise. This, however, would still be dishonesty.) Since Jesus Christ was God and His very nature is Truth, He cannot lie. Thus, this is a contradictory assertion.

The book of Deuteronomy is attributed to an unknown source, according to the documentary hypothesis. The apostle Paul, however, would disagree with such a conclusion. He writes,

> *But I say, surely Israel did not know, did they? At the first Moses says, "I will make you jealous by that which is not a nation, by a nation without understanding will I anger you."*
> *(Romans 10:19)*

In his letter to the church at Rome, Paul quotes from Deuteronomy 32:21. He would not have a problem when answering, "Who wrote Deuteronomy?" He clearly states the author was Moses. Yet learned scholars of today reject such a notion. A. S. Van Der Woude, the general editor of *The World of the Old Testament*, writes that the Mosaic authorship of the Pentateuch is a hypothesis derived from "classical" sources. He states the following under the heading of "Hypothesis about the origin of the Pentateuch":

> For centuries "official" Judaism and "official" Christianity have regarded Moses as the writer of the entire Pentateuch. The reader should realize, however, that this view did not arise as a result of historical research into the question of the origin of these books. Rather, by presenting Moses, the confidant of God, as the writer of the Pentateuch, this position attempted to stress the divine origin and thus the authority of the Pentateuch. There was hardly any concern about questions involving the origin of these writings. The focus of interest in the Pentateuch was doctrinal and practical.[14]

Van Der Woude cites in his evaluation the reason why the New Testament writers and Jesus connected Moses with the Pentateuch:

> In the New Testament the name of Moses is variously connected with the Pentateuch (e.g., Mark 7:10; 12:26; Luke 24:27, 44; John 1:45). All these references except John 1:45 were quoted by Jesus. From such references one can infer only the type of thinking about the authorship of the Pentateuch that was current at the time of Jesus and the apostles.[15]

As mentioned before, Van Der Woude uses the accommodation theory to prove his claim. The people believed that Moses was the author, so Jesus and the apostles used that belief. There is nothing in all of Scripture, however, that would indicate that this is the case. Such dishonesty through accommodation would be a horrible blight on the Messiah and His mission.

The Authorship of Isaiah

The various methods of criticism have also opened a floodgate of speculation regarding the book of Isaiah. Many "evangelicals" hold to the idea that two different authors, and in some cases three, wrote the book of Isaiah. Van Der Woude claims,

> The book of Isaiah has two main parts, chapters 1–39 and 40–66. The first part contains mainly prophecies from the time of Isaiah himself. The second puts us in the period of the Babylonian captivity or later (Deutero–Isaiah). . . . Chapters 40–66 of Isaiah transport us to a different time than that of Isaiah. Whereas many prophecies in 1–39 go back to Isaiah and relate to his time, the subsequent chapters relate to situations and events more than 150 years later, namely, the time of the Babylonian captivity. . . . Yet not all prophecies in 40–66 are from one source. Particularly chapters 56–66 are attributed to another prophet, usually designated Trito-Isaiah (third Isaiah).[16]

Wilkerson and Boa comment,

> The unity of this book has been challenged by critics who hold that a "Deutero–Isaiah" wrote chapters 40–66 after the Babylonian captivity. They argue that chapters 1–39 have an Assyrian background, while chapters 40–66 are set against a Babylonian background. But Babylon is mentioned more than twice as often in chapters 1–39 as in chapters 40–66. The only shift is one of perspective from present time to future time. Critics also argue that there are radical differences in the language, style, and theology of the two sections. Actually, the resemblances between chapters 1–39 and chapters 40–66 are greater than the differences. These include similarities in thoughts, images, rhetorical ornaments, characteristic expressions, and local coloring. It is true that the first section is more terse and rational, while the second section is more flowing and emotional, but much of this is caused by the different subject matter, condemnation versus consolation. Critics often forget that content, time, and circumstances typically affect an author's style. . . . Another critical argument is that Isaiah could not have predicted the Babylonian captivity and the return under Cyrus (mentioned by name in 44–45) 150 years in advance. This view is based on the mere assumption that divine prophecy is impossible, rejecting the predictive claims of the book (42:9). The theory cannot explain the amazing prophecies of Isaiah that were literally fulfilled in the life of Christ. . . ."[17]

Many arguments refute the theory of two or three authors of Isaiah. Ryrie comments,

> To claim two or more authors for this book is also to contradict the evidence of the New Testament. Quotations from chapters 40–66 are found in Matthew 3:3; 12:17–21; Luke 3:4–6; Acts 8:28; Romans 10:16, 20 and all are attributed to Isaiah. Moreover, in John 12:38–41, quotations from Isaiah 6:9–10 and 53:1 appear together and both are ascribed to the Isaiah who saw the Lord in the Temple vision of chapter 6. . . ."[18]

And in the Scripture, both John and Paul allude to only one Isaiah:

> *. . . that the word of Isaiah the prophet might be fulfilled, which he spoke, "Lord, who has believed our report? And to whom has the arm of the Lord been revealed?" For this cause they could not believe, for Isaiah said again, "He has blinded their eyes, and he hardened their heart; lest they see with their eyes, and perceive with their heart, and be converted, and I heal them." (John 12:38–41)*

> *However, they did not all heed the glad tidings; for Isaiah says, "Lord, who has believed our report?" (Romans 10:16; quoting Isaiah 53:1)*

> *And Isaiah is very bold and says, "I was found by those who sought Me not, I became manifest to those who did not ask for Me." (Romans 10:20; quoting Isaiah 65:1–2)*

Thus, John and Paul affirm that only one Isaiah authored the book by his name.

One last proof to draw on is from the Dead Sea Scrolls. These scrolls have been an object of fascination for over five decades. Ancient copies of almost every Old Testament book have been found, along with commentaries on several of the books. A complete copy of Isaiah was found among the documents. In fact, "the Old Testament book of Isaiah was found in the first discovery of the Dead Sea Scrolls in Cave One, and it is one of the seven original manuscripts found. The book of Isaiah is contained in its entirety in this scroll."[19] Does the Isaiah scroll support one, two, or three authors for Isaiah? When the Isaiah Scroll was discovered, there was much hope on both sides for evidence of their respective positions. Randall Price writes,

When the *Isaiah Scroll* was examined it revealed no break or demarcation of any sort between the contested divisions. Chapter 40 begins on the very last line of the column that included Isaiah 38:9–40:8. The last words on the former column are "cry to her . . ." and the first words on the latter column are ". . . that her warfare is accomplished." It is evident that the scribe who wrote those words was not aware of a supposed change in situation or authorship beginning with chapter 40. Four samples of *Isaiah Scrolls* subjected to carbon 14 dating produced calibrated age ranges between 335–324 B.C. and 202–107 B.C., and the paleographic date range is between 125–100 B.C. The scribal evidence in these copies indicate that they were the results of at least several generations of copying. Yet even with a date sometime during the second century B.C., critical scholars cannot assign portions of Isaiah's prophecies to the Maccabean period, or claim that first-century insertions were added to the text. The second-century B.C. date should also establish the *Isaiah Scroll* as an early witness in favor of the unity of Isaiah, since it (or an earlier copy from which it was generated) accorded roughly with the time the Septuagint version of the prophets was written (the Septuagint also has no indication of a textual break between chapters 39 and 40). However, critical (and most conservative) scholars disallow this early evidence in favor of single authorship because it is claimed that the recognition of multiple authorship (along with final redaction of the book) came later than these Qumran copies.[20]

Thus the weight of evidence, if one enters this examination with an open mind, supports the claims of Scripture on the authorship of these books. Only a preconceived bias would cause someone to claim otherwise.

Biblical Passages on Inspiration and Inerrancy

Let us now return to Scripture and let it speak for itself on how it was recorded. As Feinberg states, "At the heart of the belief in an inerrant, infallible Bible is the testimony of Scripture itself."[21] Scripture itself has much to say about its inspired nature. The apostle Peter writes,

But know this first of all, that no prophecy of Scripture is a matter of one's own interpretation, for no prophecy was ever

*made by an act of human will, but men moved by the Holy
Spirit spoke from God. (2 Peter 1:20–21)*

This Scripture gives us insight into how inspiration took place.
The Greek verb translated "moved" here is *pherō*, meaning "to bear,"
"to carry," or "to bring forth." It is significant that the verb is passive. Therefore, it could be said that prophets were "carried along"
by the Holy Spirit as they wrote.

Another helpful verse is given in Paul's second letter to Timothy.
There he writes, "All Scripture is inspired by God and profitable for
teaching, for reproof, for correction, for training in righteousness"
(2 Tim. 3:16). Here the Greek word translated "inspired" is
theopneustos. This is a compound word meaning "God" *(Theos)* and
"to breath out" *(pneuō)*. Thus, Scripture is the out-breathing of God.
Geisler and Nix comment on the term *Scripture:*

> The use of the word *Scripture* has a distinct and technical
> sense in the New Testament, as may be readily seen by its
> specialized application. The term is reserved in its definitive
> and articular sense for only the authoritative and canonical
> books of Holy Writ. For the devout although converted Jews
> who wrote the books of the New Testament, to describe any
> other books by this technical word amounts to claiming in-
> spiration for them. As a matter of fact, that is precisely what
> Peter claims for Paul's epistles when he writes, "Our beloved
> brother Paul . . . wrote you . . . as also in all his letters . . .
> which the untaught and unstable distort, as they do also the
> rest of the *Scriptures*" (2 Peter 3:15–16). Here Paul's writings
> are considered Scripture in the same sense as the Old
> Testament writings referred to earlier in the same passage
> (2 Peter 3:5, 7–8). Although this passage does not claim that
> all the New Testament books are Scripture, it does include
> many of them. In 1 Timothy 5:18 the apostle Paul quotes
> from Luke, placing it on the same level with the rest of
> Scripture, using the introduction "for the Scripture says"
> (with reference to Luke 10:7). Certainly if Paul's and Luke's
> writings were considered Scripture, then the epistles of the
> apostles of Jesus, and particularly those of the "inner circle"
> (Peter and John), which traditionally make up most of the
> remainder of the New Testament, cannot logically be ex-
> cluded from the category of inspired Scripture.[22]

So if all "Scripture" is inspired (2 Tim. 3:16)—here referring to the "sacred writings" or the Old Testament which Timothy had known from childhood (3:15)—and the New Testament is also "Scripture" (1 Tim. 5:18; 2 Peter 3:16), then the New Testament is inspired.

The Bible is its own best witness to the truthfulness of the Word. The Scriptures are replete with verses stating the truthfulness of God's Word and how we may depend on them. Psalm 19 gives us six observations on the trustworthiness of God's Word:

> *The law of the LORD is perfect, restoring the soul; the testimony of the LORD is sure, making wise the simple. The precepts of the LORD are right, rejoicing the heart; The commandment of the LORD is pure, enlightening the eyes. The fear of the LORD is clean, enduring forever; the judgments of the LORD are true; they are righteous altogether. (Psalm 19:7–9)*

God has handed down to us His word as revealed through the Scriptures. In that Word is truth to help us live holy lives dedicated to Him. The Word is declared to be perfect, despite the claims of those who hold to limited inerrancy. Jesus states,

> *For truly I say to you, until heaven and earth pass away, not the smallest letter or stroke shall pass away from the Law, until all is accomplished. (Matthew 5:18)*

Jesus assures His followers that the entire text of the Old Testament is vital and useful. From the smallest letter in Hebrew *(yodh)* to the strokes that make up the letters, they are all important. Not only are the words important but the letters as well.

> *If he called them gods, to whom the Word of God came (and the Scripture cannot be broken), . . . (John 10:35)*

Jesus informs His listeners as to the force of Scripture. He used the phrase "the Scripture cannot be broken" to disprove anyone claiming that the Scripture was in error. In other words, the Word will come to pass as written.

> *For the Scripture says, "You shall not muzzle the ox while he is threshing," and "The laborer is worthy of his wages." (1 Timothy 5:18)*

In his writings to Timothy, Paul quotes from the Old Testament (Deut. 25:4) and from the New Testament (Luke 10:7). Both of these passages are called Scripture. Paul maintains that both Testaments are to be considered equal and accepted as material from God.[23] Peter states,

> . . . and regard the patience of our Lord to be salvation; just as also our beloved brother Paul, according to the wisdom given him, wrote to you, as also in all his letters, speaking in them of these things, in which are some things hard to understand, which the untaught and unstable distort, as they do also the rest of the Scriptures, to their own destruction. (2 Peter 3:15–16)

Peter elevates the writings of Paul to a level equal with the Old Testament. His proclamation linking Paul's writings to Scripture also gives us insight into what the early church used for a canon. *The Bible Knowledge Commentary* says,

> The fact that Peter referred to Paul's letters and then to "the other Scriptures" indicates that Paul's writings were then considered authoritative Scripture. Such behavior—twisting the Scripture to suit their own purposes—is met with God's judgment which, in this case, the ignorant and unstable bring on themselves in the form of destruction (*apoleian;* cf. 2:1, 3). Believers may not fully understand all the Scriptures, but they certainly ought not twist their obvious meanings.[24]

It can be seen that Scripture itself makes strong claims to be inspired and inerrant. It also gives us insight into how inspiration occurred. Those who, without showing good proof, cast doubts on these facts are in a sense questioning the very nature of God and the claims of Jesus Christ.

Does Science Support the Bible's Claim to Inspiration and Inerrancy?

An open and honest approach reveals abundant scientific evidence that verifies claims of Scripture. Note the following two claims related to the fields of medical science and archaeology.

Medical Science

Most people today take for granted the knowledge of germs and their effects on the body. Yet as little as one hundred years ago, such knowledge would have been considered more superstition than fact. Many doctors affirmed that people became sick by chance, not by microbes. Ancient Egypt, which many uphold as the most advanced civilization at the time of Moses, utilized curious methods of disease control. A book entitled *An Ancient Egyptian Herbal* by Lise Manatee details the common ingredients in most Egyptian cures. The ingredients differ according to the animals from which they are obtained, but they contain one constant—*dung*.[25] These "cures" created with such an ingredient would relieve the patient of pain—because the patient would die!

As the Egyptian's literally revered dung as the miracle drug, the Bible warned of dangers from dung. Easy steps were given to prevent diseases that occur from improper sanitation.

> *You shall also have a place outside the camp and go out there, and you shall have a spade among your tools, and it shall be when you sit down outside, you shall dig with it and shall turn to cover up your excrement. (Deuteronomy 23:12–13)*

The book of Leviticus provided us guidelines on how to treat those who are infected with disease. Much of Leviticus details how to avoid contracting disease, such as forbidding the people to eat an animal that had died naturally or had been eaten by wild animals.

> *Also the fat of an animal which dies, and the fat of an animal torn by beasts, may be put to any other use; but you must certainly not eat it. (Leviticus 7:24)*

Any animal carcass found would be dangerous. If it died of a disease, the germs would still be on the corpse. Infectious germs would also develop within hours of the creature's death. God's command saved many of the Jews from making a fatal mistake.[26]

These instructions were a solution to a problem that plagued mankind for centuries. The Bible delivers to us in plain, literal language a method that would have saved untold lives.

Archaeology

For many years the Hittites have been a major stumbling block in Old Testament history. Until the twentieth century, no evidence other than the Old Testament could be cited for their existence. Renowned archeologist and author C. W. Ceram writes,

From these [Josh. 3:10; Num. 13:29] and a few other mentions in the Bible, the Hittite people would seem to have
been a tribe inhabiting Syria, and of no particular distinction. There is one passage, however, which would have given
historians pause long before Sayce if nineteenth-century
science had not been so wary of the Bible as a source of
history. This was Kings II: 7, 6: "For the Lord had made the
host of the Syrians to hear a noise of chariots, and a noise of
horses, even the noise of a great host: and they said one to
another, Lo, the King of Israel hath hired against us the kings
of the Hittites, and the kings of the Egyptians, to come upon
us." In contrast to all previous Biblical references, where
the Hittites are coupled with tribes which never made any
impression upon history, the Hittite kings are here named
in one breath with the most powerful monarch of the ancient world; the Hittite kings are, in fact, even given prece-
dence over the Egyptian pharaohs.[27]

The Bible not only gives the Hittites a place in history, but places
them above the mighty Egyptians. For years scholars scoffed at the
biblical accounts. They assumed that since archeology had found
no trace of the Hittites, they did not exist and the Bible was in error.
Nineteenth- and twentieth-century archeology provided the answers
to the Hittite problem. Unger writes,

It is now known that the center of Hittite power was in Asia
Minor. There an empire that once vied with Egypt and
Assyria, but had long been forgotten, has been discovered
by modern archaeologists. A missionary at Damascus named
William Wright and the orientalist A. H. Sayce were among
the first scholars to piece together the picture of this ancient
imperial people. . . . Many scholars consider the Hittites to
be the third most influential of ancient peoples in the Middle
East, rivaling the Egyptians as well as the Mesopotamians.
Hebrews dreaded them as well as the empires on the Tigris
and Euphrates. About 1750 they destroyed the Babylonian
capital of the great Hammurabi. Their aggressiveness is
demonstrated also in their commercial activities, which
included an extensive trade in horses with Solomon. . . . The
Hittites also kept secret their iron-smelting formula when
iron was regarded to be almost as valuable as silver and gold.
Not until two centuries later did the Philistines come into

this knowledge and not until the Saul-Davidic era did Israel learn it.[28]

The Bible is once again proven true. An old axiom says, "with every turn of dirt by an archeologist's spade, the Bible is proved over, and over, and over." In fact, the Bible testified not only to the Hittites, but a Hittite nation. Many laughed, but in the end, the Bible was proven true.

Conclusion

The above arguments are only a few of the hundreds of proofs that God's hand was upon the Holy Scriptures. Internally, the Bible claims to be inspired by God and without error. Externally, there is yet to be one shred of proof that it is anything other than what it claims. In a statement quoted earlier in this chapter, Francis Schaeffer notes the importance of the doctrines of inerrancy and inspiration; it bears repeating here: "Compromising the full authority of Scripture eventually affects what it means to be a Christian theologically and how we live in the full spectrum of human life."[29]

The doctrines of inspiration and inerrancy of Scripture having been addressed, the subject of interpreting the Bible naturally follows. Since God has spoken, how do we know what He has said?

This chapter was adapted from Bobby Hayes, "The Evangelical Doctrine of Inspiration—Restated," *The Conservative Theological Journal* 1, no. 2 (August 1997): 163–80.

CHAPTER 3

Systematic Theology and Hermeneutics

Theologians depend upon sound biblical exegesis, which they achieve by way of a valid hermeneutic. _Exegesis means to expose all that the biblical text contains_ in its grammatical, historical, cultural, and literary context. Packer calls interpreting Scripture from the foregoing contexts as using the "'natural' or 'literal' sense."[1] _Hermeneutics is the art and science by which one interprets the biblical text._

The goal of a sound hermeneutic is to capture what has been described as a _"pure biblical theology, which is an isolation and presentation of the unchanging biblical teachings which are valid for all of times."_[2]

> _Biblical theology_ is simply theology which is biblical, that is based upon and faithful to the teachings of the Bible. In this sense, systematic theology of the right kind will be biblical theology. It is not simply based on biblical theology; it is biblical theology.[3]

The hermeneutic, then, will determine the system of theology.

Systematic theology therefore must begin with divine revelation in its entirety, engaged by the Spirit-illuminated mind, drawing out the teachings of Scripture via sound grammatical-historical exegesis, respecting provisionally developed doctrine while ordering the results in a coherent whole and applying them to the full scope of human behavior.[4]

As J. I. Packer observes:

Ever since Karl Barth linked his version of Reformation teaching on biblical authority with a method of interpretation that at key points led away from Reformation beliefs, hermeneutics has been the real heart of the ongoing debate about Scripture. Barth was always clear that every theology stands or falls as a hermeneutic and every hermeneutic stands or falls as a theology.[5]

Two Systems of Theology

Covenant theology, contrary to the strong protest of the Reformers, interprets Scripture by *allegorizing* and *spiritualizing* portions of the biblical text.

Dispensational theology, or dispensationalism, results from a natural, normal reading of Scripture, consistently taken in context and at face value. Such a reading is the logical and obvious way to read any body of literature.

But a conflict regarding these two approaches to systematic theology exists within evangelical circles.

Dispensational theology and covenant theology take their respective forms as a result of the hermeneutic they employ. In the case of dispensational theology, a consistent, literal hermeneutic and a normal reading of Scripture are used to interpret all sixty-six books of the Bible.

When it comes to non-eschatological literature, covenant theologians usually begin with a literal, grammatico-historical method of interpretation, referred to below as a normal reading of Scripture. There are exceptions, however, especially when it comes to Israel and the church. Often in covenant theology, Israel does not mean Israel; it is *spiritualized* to mean the church. Regarding prophetic literature, the hermeneutic of covenant theologians is even more inconsistent, in that they consistently mingle an allegorical or spiritual method of biblical interpretation with a normal reading of Scripture.

A Normal Reading of Scripture

A *normal* reading of Scripture is synonymous with a consistent *literal, grammatico-historical* hermeneutic. When a literal hermeneutic is applied to the interpretation of Scripture, every word written in Scripture is given the *normal* meaning it would have in its *normal* usage. Proponents of a consistent, literal reading of Scripture prefer the phrase *a normal reading of Scripture* to establish the difference between *literalism* and *letterism*. Bernard Ramm addresses this issue:

To interpret Scripture literally is not to be committed to a "wooden literalism," nor to a "letterism," nor to a neglect of the nuances that defy any "mechanical" understanding of language. Rather, it is to commit oneself to a starting point and that starting point is to understand a document the best one can in the context of the normal, usual, customary, tradition range of designation, which includes "facit" understanding.[6]

A *normal* reading of Scripture recognizes figures of speech and symbolism used in eschatological literature and other books of the Bible. For example, consider Revelation 20:1–3:

> *And I saw an angel coming down from heaven, having the key of the abyss and a great chain in his hand. And he laid hold of the dragon, the serpent of old, who is the devil and Satan, and bound him for a thousand years, and threw him into the abyss, and shut it and sealed it over him, so that he should not deceive the nations any longer, until the thousand years were completed.*

A *normal* reading of Scripture recognizes the symbolism in this text, wherein a *key* and *chain* are used by the angel to bind Satan for one thousand years. These words do not mean that Satan will be imprisoned behind a locked, physical door that can only be opened by a physical key. Clearly, it's symbolic language used to describe a very real, secured holding place where Satan will be confined for a time. Nor is this passage saying that Satan, a spirit, will be bound by a great iron chain. Leon Morris notes,

> The angel had *the key* of the abyss . . . and a *great chain*. Both are clearly symbolical, for there cannot be a key to the abyss, nor can a spirit be shackled with a chain. But they show that the angel had authority over the abyss and that he could restrain Satan.[7]

Another example of symbolic, or figurative, language is Revelation 22:15. Here,

> The angel describes conditions outside the Eternal City, saying: "For outside are dogs, sorcerers, and whoremongers, and murderers, and idolaters." One must not suppose that actual, literal dogs, however, loyal to man in life, will follow

their evil masters to a godless eternity. The angel uses *dogs* as a figure to make more repelling and repulsive the character of evil men.[8]

From these illustrations one may conclude,

> The key to determining the figurative from the non-figurative lies in ascertaining whether a given word or act is at variance with the essential nature of the subject being discussed. <u>If a word or act, taken in the literal sense, fails to harmonize with either the flow of thought in the text or context, or with the analogy of Scripture, it is to be understood as figurative.</u> Otherwise, it is non-figurative. To know the context and the flow of thought in the text under study, as well as in the totality of prophetic Scripture is to understand the distinction between what is figurative and nonfigurative in prophecy.[9]

When this definition of *figurative* is applied to Morris's commentary on Revelation 20, three questions will determine whether *key* and *chain* should be understood literally or figuratively:

1. Are the words *key* and *chain*, taken in their literal meaning, at variance with the essential nature of the subject being discussed? Yes, Satan is spirit; the words describe material things.
2. Do the words, taken in their literal, natural meaning fail to harmonize with the flow of thought in the context of the text? No, the flow of thought is the imprisonment of Satan. The words *key* and *chain* are in harmony with the flow of thought.
3. Do the phrases, taken in their literal meaning fail to harmonize with the analogy of Scripture? Yes, Satan is a spirit and a spirit cannot be constrained by a material enclosure or an iron chain. It is correct to understand the words *key* and *chain* as figurative just as Morris has done.

Those who oppose the consistent use of a *normal* reading of Scripture, a *literal* hermeneutic, accuse its practitioners of "letterism." For example, consider Psalm 18:6–7:

> *In my distress I called upon the Lord,*
> *And cried to my God for help;*
> *He heard my voice out of His temple,*
> *And my cry for help before Him came into His ears.*

Then the earth shook and quaked;
And the foundations of the mountains were trembling
And were shaken, because He was angry.

Literalism *does not* understand that God has ears and a physical body. That's letterism. Such an accusation is nothing more than a straw man, which opponents use in an effort to discredit a consistent, natural reading of Scripture. A *normal* reading of Scripture recognizes the anthropomorphisms used here in Psalm 18 and throughout the Scriptures.

Those who are committed to a *normal* reading of Scripture offer at least three reasons: *First,* the obvious purpose of language is to enable effective communication between intelligent beings. Words have meaning and in their normal usage are intended to be understood. Languages also have rules of grammar that further define the literal meanings of words as they are linked together to express a complete thought. God is the originator of language. When He spoke audibly to man, He expected man to understand Him and respond accordingly. Likewise, when God speaks to man through the inspired writings of His apostles and prophets, He expects man to understand and respond accordingly. Jesus said this very thing in Luke 16:27–31, where man is directed to the written Word of God, Moses, and the Prophets.

And he said, "Then I beg you, Father, that you send him to my father's house—for I have five brothers—that he may warn them, lest they also come to this place of torment." But Abraham said, "They have Moses and the Prophets; let them hear them." But he said, "No, Father Abraham, but if someone goes to them from the dead, they will repent!" But he said to him, "If they do not listen to Moses and the Prophets, neither will they be persuaded if someone rises from the dead."

A *second* reason for a *normal* reading of Scripture concerns the historical fulfillment of prophecy. All the prophecies of the Old and New Testament that have been fulfilled to date have been fulfilled literally. That they have been literally fulfilled establishes God's intent that the prophecies were to be understood literally at the time they were given. Thus, it is not only reasonable to expect, but highly probable, that all prophecies which are yet to been fulfilled will be fulfilled literally.

The *third* reason concerns logic. If an interpreter does not use the normal, customary, literal method of interpreting Scripture, interpretation is given over to the unconstrained imagination and presuppositions of the interpreter. With all objectivity removed, only the imagination limits the hidden meanings of a word. When the words of the Bible cease to have objective meaning, so does the Word of God itself.

An Allegorical Reading of Scripture

Those who interpret Scripture allegorically assign to the literal words in the text secondary meanings that are not expressly taught by the words. "Allegorical interpretation believes that beneath the letter *(rhete)* or the obvious *(phanera)* is the real meaning *(hyponoia)* of the passage."[10] Allegorical interpretation determines whether the secondary, or hidden, meaning was an intended meaning of the original writer or merely something imported by the interpreter.

Allegory Described

When the original writer identifies the passage as an allegory, as does the apostle Paul in Galatians 4:24–26, the interpretation is not difficult. Paul is not *allegorizing* the text; he is using a literary device known as allegory to illustrate his point. Therefore it must be interpreted as an *allegory*, not *allegorized*.

> *This contains an allegory: for these women are two covenants, one proceeding from Mount Sinai bearing children who are to be slaves; she is Hagar. Now this Hagar is Mount Sinai in Arabia, and corresponds to the present Jerusalem, for she is in slavery with her children. But the Jerusalem above is free; she is our mother. (Galatians 4:24–26)*

Paul is discussing the contrast between grace and law, faith and works. In order to illustrate and contrast grace and law, the apostle applies a common Old Testament story. Paul is not using an allegorical method of interpretation, as F. F. Bruce asserts, but rather a literal, historical account analogous to and illustrative of the spiritual truths relating to law and grace.[11]

The story of Abraham, Hagar, and Sarah is historical. Paul is simply using elements in the story to teach a spiritual truth. Allegory, "attempts to express immaterial truths [here grace and law] in pictorial forms . . ., employing . . . a point-for-point comparison between the intangibles under discussion [grace and law], and specified representations which are recognizable to the intended audience."[12]

Allegorical Interpretation

The literary device of allegory is quite distinct from the allegorical method of interpretation, which looks for deeper meaning in the literal words of a text. Allegorical interpretation allows the exegete to manipulate the text to support his or her presuppositions. Morris, in his commentary on Revelation 20:1–7, offers an excellent example of allegorizing the text:

> The angel proceeded to tie him up for a *thousand years*. It is likely that we should take this symbolically. One thousand years is the cube of ten, the number of completeness. We have seen it used over and over again in this book to denote completeness of some sort, and this is surely the way we should take it here. Satan is bound for the perfect period.[13]

Using the three questions suggested earlier, it can be determined if text should be considered figurative or nonfigurative: (1) Are the words *thousand years* at variance with the essential nature of the subject being discussed? No. All agree the passage teaches that Satan, a spirit, will be imprisoned for a period of time. The question is, will it be one thousand years as the text reads, or a *spiritualized* measure of time? (2) Do the words, taken in their literal, natural meaning, fail to harmonize with the flow of thought in the context? No. The flow of thought is the imprisonment of Satan. A measure of time harmonizes with the flow of thought. (3) Do the words, taken in their literal meaning, fail to harmonize with the analogy of Scripture? No. A thousand years harmonizes with an analogy of a long period of time.

Because the answer to all three questions in this case is no, the words *thousand years* are to be understood according to their natural, customary usage. Morris, however, is compelled to allegorize the text, forcing the words *thousand years* to harmonize with his theological presuppositions. Morris's example above is illustrative of the inconsistent hermeneutic utilized by covenant theologians. When a passage, phrase, or word fails to harmonize with their theological presuppositions, covenant theologians have no other option but to allegorize the text.

The allegorization of Scripture forces the text and results in a false harmony between the text and the theological presupposition. Ryrie pinpoints the reason for this:

> Hermeneutics is the science that furnishes the principles of interpretation. These principles guide and govern anybody's

system of theology. They ought to be determined *before* one's theology is systematized, but in practice the reverse is usually true. At least in the awareness of most people, hermeneutics is one of the last things to be considered consciously. Most people know something of the doctrines they believe but little of the hermeneutics on which they have been built. Principles of interpretation are basic and preferably should be established before attempting to interpret the Word so that the results are not only correct interpretations but a right system of theology growing out of those interpretations.[14]

Dispensational Theology

The word *dispensation* is found in various forms some twenty times in the New Testament. "The Greek word οικομονια comes from the verb that means 'to manage, regulate, administer and plan.' The word itself is a compound whose parts mean literally to divide, apportion, administer or manage the affairs of an inhabited house. In the papyri, the officer *(οικονομοσ)* who administered a dispensation was referred to as a steward or manager of an estate, or as a treasurer. Thus, the central idea in the word *dispensation* is that of managing or administering the affairs of a household."[15]

The masculine noun οἰκονόμον is translated "steward" in Luke 16:1 by the NASB. The NIV translates the noun "manager." Another more detailed translation is "household manager." The feminine noun οἰκονομίας in Luke 16:2 is translated "stewardship" by the NASB, and "management" by the NIV. In Luke 16:2, the verb οἰκονομεῖν, a present active infinite, is translated "to steward" by the NASB and "be manager" by the NIV. Again in Luke 16:3 the masculine noun οἰκονόμος is translated "steward" by the NASB and "manager" by the NIV. The natural, literal meaning of the word is readily seen in a reading of Luke 16:1–4 from the NIV, where human stewardship or management is illustrated.

Jesus told his disciples: "There was a rich man whose manager was accused of wasting his possessions. So he called him in and asked him, 'What is this I hear about you? Give an account of your management, because you cannot be manager any longer.' The manager said to himself, 'What shall I do now? My master is taking away my job. I'm not strong enough to dig, and I'm ashamed to beg—I know what I'll do so that, when I lose my job here, people will welcome me into their houses.'"

For many years the term *dispensation* has been associated more with an age, or period of time, than understood by its biblical definition, *the management of a household,* or *stewardships.* This likely is due to "the well-known definition that appears in the notes of the original *Scofield Reference Bible:* 'A dispensation is a period of time during which man is tested in respect of obedience to some *specific* revelation of the will of God.'"[16] While *dispensations* and *age* are related terms, they are not synonymous. Ephesians offers an example:

> . . . *and to bring to light what is the* administration [οἰκονομία] *of the mystery which for* ages [αἰώνων] *has been hidden in God, who created all things. (Ephesians 3:9, emphasis added)*

The words *dispensation* and *age* are related in that dispensations operate throughout an age or period of time. The focus, however, is on the *management of the household (dispensation)* within a given period of time rather than on the *age,* or *period of time* itself. The apostle Paul mentions at least three different *divine stewardships,* or *dispensations,* that occurred in different periods of time.

> *He made known to us the mystery of His will, according to His kind intention which He purposed in Him with a view to an administration suitable to the fulness of the times, that is, the summing up of all things in Christ, things in the heavens and things upon the earth. (Ephesians 1:9–10)*

This passage speaks of the future "summing up" of all things in Christ, in the heavens and upon earth. Clearly, all things are not summed up in Christ at the present time. Presently, not every knee bows to Christ. Yet in the future, "at the name of Jesus every knee [will] bow, of those who are in heaven, and on earth, and under the earth" (Phil. 2:10–11). At the present time the universe is marked by corruption, war, and division. In the future, Christ will unify the entire universe to Himself (see Ps. 2; Heb. 1:8–13). Satan is now "the ruler of this world," but in that day he "shall be cast out" (John 12:31).

The second passage, Ephesians 3:1–10, addresses the present "stewardship of God's grace" concerning the Gentiles.

> *For this reason I, Paul, the prisoner of Christ Jesus for the sake of you Gentiles—if indeed you have heard of the steward- ship of God's grace which was given to me for you; . . . which*

in other generations was not made known to the sons of men,
as it has now been revealed to His holy apostles and prophets
in the Spirit; to be specific, that the Gentiles are fellow-heirs
and fellow-members of the body, and fellow-partakers of the
promise in Christ Jesus through the gospel, . . . and to bring to
light what is the administration of the mystery which for ages
has been hidden in God, who created all things; in order that
the manifold wisdom of God might now be made known
through the church to the rulers and the authorities in the
heavenly places. (Ephesians 3:1–2, 5–6, 9–10)

The apostle Paul explains that men of previous generations were not informed as they are now in the "stewardship of God's grace," which was given to Paul. To be specific, the Gentiles would be blessed as fellow heirs through the gospel. While previous generations may have had a glimpse of the truth, it was in a different "stewardship of God," or dispensation, than the one God later made fully known.

This third passage indicates there was also a "dispensation" or "stewardship" of God that *precedes* the present "dispensation or stewardship of God."

Of this church I was made a minister according to the stew-
ardship from God bestowed on me for your benefit, that I might
fully carry out the preaching of the word of God, that is, the
mystery which has been hidden from the past ages and gen-
erations; but has now been manifested to His saints, to whom
God willed to make known what is the riches of the glory of
this mystery among the Gentiles, which is Christ in you, the
hope of glory. And we proclaim Him, admonishing every man
and teaching every man with all wisdom, that we may present
every man complete in Christ. (Colossians 1:25–28)

The apostle Paul notes that he is a minister according to the "stewardship from God," bestowed upon him and that was hidden from past *ages* and generations but now has been made known to the saints. This passage also establishes that *dispensations* and *ages* are not synonymous, but are related in that "dispensations" or "stewardships" of God occur within periods of time.

Covenant theologians acknowledge there are at least two dispensations—or administrations—of God in different ages or periods of time. Berkhof writes,

On the basis of all that has been said it is preferable to follow the traditional lines by distinguishing just two dispensations or administrations, namely, that of the Old, and that
of the New Testament.[17]

Dispensational and covenant theologians can agree that there
are a certain number of dispensations in the Bible. The real debate
seems to be over hermeneutics.

Covenant Theology

Covenant theology understands the whole of Scripture and history through three covenants: the covenant of works, the covenant
of redemption, and the covenant of grace. Not all covenant theologians, however, embrace all three covenants.

Covenant theology was not systematized until the sixteenth to
seventeenth centuries. Berkhof writes,

> The history of the doctrine of the covenant of works is com-
> paratively brief. In the early Church Fathers the covenant idea
> is seldom found at all, though the elements which it includes,
> namely, the probationary command, the freedom of choice,
> and the possibility of sin and death, are all mentioned.[18]

Berkhof also notes,

> In the scholastic literature and in the writings of the Re-
> formers, too, all the elements which went into the construc-
> tion of the doctrine of the covenant of works were already
> present, but the doctrine itself was not developed. The de-
> velopment of the doctrine of the covenant of grace preceded
> that of the doctrine of the covenant of works and paved the
> way for it.[19]

It should be noted that the three covenants are theologically constructed and not biblical, as are the Abrahamic, Davidic, Mosaic,
Palestinian, and new covenant. The covenants of grace, works, and
redemption are assembled from Scripture solely on the basis of
deductive reasoning. Deductive reasoning starts with the general
and moves to the particular and is therefore *a priori* (prior to looking at the facts). Inductive reasoning, on the other hand, starts with
the particular and moves to the general and is therefore *a posteriori*
(*after* seeing the evidence). One studying the Bible using inductive

reasoning gathers all the facts before drawing a conclusion. J. I. Packer speaks to the importance of this method:

> Evangelicalism's theology, with all its local and in-house variants, is (at least in intention and idea, if not always in perfect achievement) a body of tenets, attitudes, and approaches drawn from the biblical documents by allowing them to speak for themselves in terms of their own interests, viewpoints, and emphasis; in other words, by a method that is thoroughly and consistently a posteriori. The method has been called 'grammatico-historical', as a pointer to the techniques involved; it could equally well be called the a posteriori method, in virtue of its purpose of reading out of Scripture what is there in each author's expressed meaning and of avoiding reading into it at any point what is not there in that sense. Use of this method over four and a half centuries has produced a relatively stable form of theology that centers on the sovereign, speaking God; the divine sin-bearing, risen, reigning, returning Christ. . . ."[20]

Thus, the difference between inductive and deductive reasoning frames the major differences between dispensational theology and covenant theology: ①Dispensational theology is *a posteriori:* the Scriptures declare that God used different dispensations, or methods of divine household management, to manage the affairs of His creation. While covenant theology acknowledges this as demonstrated, its espousal of the three covenants is *a priori:* Scripture does not specifically declare the covenant of works, grace, and redemption. ② Dispensational theology never *allegorizes* or *spiritualizes* the Scriptures. Covenant theology not only practices *allegorization* but also attempts to justify the allegorical method of interpretation, which has been soundly rejected since the Reformers. Covenant theology survives only because covenant theologians continue to *allegorize* and *spiritualize* certain portions of Scripture.

A Natural Reading of Scripture Will Result in Dispensational Theology

A natural reading of Scripture requires that a distinction be made between the ethnic nation Israel and the church. When Scripture speaks of Israel, the word *Israel* is understood in its natural, customary meaning, namely, the ethnic Jewish nation. Likewise, when the Bible refers to the church, it means just that—the church. God has different purposes for Israel and the church. He has made promises to Israel that do not apply to the church and promises to the church that do not apply to Israel. (God also has a different purpose for the angels that is separate from His plans for Israel and the church. He likewise has a purpose and plan for all of mankind who reject Him.)

A *natural* reading of Scripture will also result in a premillennial view of eschatology. The word *millennium* is Latin in its derivation, *mille,* meaning one thousand. Theologically speaking, the Millennium refers to the thousand-year reign of Jesus Christ on earth, during which time all the Old Testament prophecies made to Israel that have not been fulfilled will be fulfilled. Those who hold to a premillennial eschatology believe the Lord Jesus Christ will return bodily to earth where He will rule the world for one thousand years. At the end of the thousand years, the millennial kingdom and reign of Christ will merge with God's eternal kingdom. A *normal* reading of Scripture, i.e., a literal hermeneutic, will necessarily result in a premillennial eschatology. Oswald T. Allis, an ardent amillennialist agrees: "Old Testament prophecies if literally interpreted cannot be regarded as having been yet fulfilled or as being capable of fulfillment in this present age."[21]

Floyd Hamilton, another amillennialist agrees with Allis:

> Now we must frankly admit that a literal interpretation of the Old Testament prophecies gives us just such a picture of an earthly reign of the Messiah as the premillennialist pictures. That was the kind of Messianic Kingdom that the Jews of the time of Christ were looking for, on the basis of a literal kingdom interpretation of the Old Testament prophecies.[22]

A Call to Consistency

Theoretically, the acceptance and importance of a *normal* reading of Scripture, a literal hermeneutic, is not an issue or even debated between dispensational and covenant theologians. All credible evangelical exegetes and theologians of both camps agree there are certain essentials to the art and science of interpreting Scripture: each word should be understood in the original language and immediate context and by considering its etymology, usage, and cultural and historical setting; it is imperative to consider rules of grammar and common usage of the word in parallel passages relating to the same general topic; the analogy of Scripture must be the arbiter of interpretation. Scripture must interpret Scripture.

In reality, however, the amillennial/covenant theologian departs from these essential hermeneutical principles, most prominently when interpreting eschatology, and is, therefore, inconsistent in utilizing a valid hermeneutic. When it comes to eschatology, the covenant theologian routinely utilizes an allegorical (spiritualized) method of interpreting Scripture (see Leon Morris, *Revelation of St. John,* on Revelation 20:1–7, p. 235).

Berkhof attempts to justify this *spiritualization* of Scripture: "The books of the prophets themselves already contain indications that point to spiritual fulfillment."[23] He cites the following Old Testament passages as "indications" that point to *"spiritual* fulfillment": "Isa. 54:13, 61:6; Jer. 31:31–34; Hos. 14:2; and Mic. 6:6–8."[24] Likewise, Berkhof asserts the New Testament contains "abundant indications of the *spiritual* fulfillment of the promises given to Israel, Matt. 21:43; Acts 2:29–36, 15:14–18; Rom. 9:25–26; Heb. 8:8–13; 1 Peter 2:9; Rev. 1:6, 5:10."[25] A careful study of these passages utilizing a *normal* reading of Scripture, however, reveals there is no compelling reason to spiritualize the texts. Berkhof's attempt to justify an *allegorical method* of interpretation by use of these passages is flawed. When Scripture does point to a *spiritual* fulfillment it so notes, but the passage should be interpreted using a *normal* reading of Scripture. An example is John 6:51–63:

> *"I am the living bread that came down out of heaven; if any one eats of this bread, he shall live forever; and the bread also which I shall give for the life of the world is My flesh." The Jews therefore began to argue with one another, saying, "How can this man give us His flesh to eat?" Jesus therefore said to them, "Truly, truly, I say to you, unless you eat the flesh of the Son of Man and drink His blood, you have no life in yourselves. He who eats My flesh and drinks My blood has eternal life; and I will raise him up on the last day. For My flesh is true food, and My blood is true drink. He who eats My flesh and drinks My blood abides in Me, and I in him. As the living Father sent Me, and I live because of the Father, so he who eats Me, he also shall live because of Me. This is the bread which came down out of heaven; not as the fathers ate, and died, he who eats this bread shall live forever." These things He said in the synagogue, as He taught in Capernaum. Many therefore of His disciples, when they heard this said, "This is a difficult statement; who can listen to it?" But Jesus, conscious that His disciples grumbled at this, said to them, "Does this*

cause you to stumble? What then if you should behold the Son of Man ascending where He was before? It is the Spirit who gives life; the flesh profits nothing; the words that I have spoken to you are spirit *and are life." (emphasis added)*

There are many examples where the Lord Jesus Christ asserts His expectation that the Scriptures must be fulfilled just as they were written. Only a few are offered here. In them one clearly sees the consistency with which Jesus asserts a literal fulfillment of Scripture just as it is written. Not only did He affirm the literal fulfillment of prophetic events that had already taken place, but He also assured His disciples there would be a literal fulfillment of prophetic events that lay ahead.

> *This is the one about whom it was written, "Behold, I send My messenger before Your face, Who will prepare Your way before You." (Matthew 11:10; cf. Luke 7:27)*

> *And He took the twelve aside and said to them, "Behold, we are going up to Jerusalem, and all things which are written through the prophets about the Son of Man will be accomplished." (Luke 18:31)*

> *. . . because these are days of vengeance, in order that all things which are written may be fulfilled. (Matthew 26:24)*

> *For I tell you, that this which is written must be fulfilled in Me, "And He was classed among criminals"; for that which refers to Me has its fulfillment. (Luke 22:37)*

> *Then Jesus said to them, "You will all fall away because of Me this night, for it is written, 'I will strike down the shepherd, and the sheep of the flock shall be scattered.' . . . Or do you think that I cannot appeal to My Father, and He will at once put at My disposal more than twelve legions of angels? How then shall the Scriptures be fulfilled, that it must happen this way?. . . But all this has taken place that the Scriptures of the prophets may be fulfilled." Then all the disciples left Him and fled. (Matthew 26:31, 53–54, 56)*

> *And He said to them, "O foolish men and slow of heart to believe in all that the prophets have spoken. . . . And beginning with*

Moses and with all the prophets, He explained to them the things concerning Himself in all the Scriptures." (Luke 24:25, 27)

Now He said to them, "These are My words which I spoke to you while I was still with you, that all things which are written about Me in the Law of Moses and the Prophets and the Psalms must be fulfilled." Then He opened their minds to understand the Scriptures. (Luke 24:44–45)

The Lord Jesus Christ consistently interpreted Scripture literally. He made it clear that every word of God is essential to the life of the individual. He states in Matthew 4:4, "It is written, 'Man shall not live on bread alone, but on every word that proceeds out of the mouth of God.'"

Since the time of Luther, Calvin, Zwingli, and others, the allegorical method of biblical interpretation has been soundly rejected. Kaiser reasserts that the same is true today as it was with the Reformers:

The allegorical method cannot be established as a legitimate means of interpreting Scripture. While Scripture itself sometimes uses allegory (e.g., Prov. 5:15–19), such cases are clearly marked by the writer's intention and not the interpreter's wish, however sincere.[26]

Regarding biblical interpretation, Barth was right: systematic theology *is* the hermeneutic. Every theology stands or falls as a hermeneutic and every hermeneutic stands or falls as a theology.[27] It would be well, therefore, to reexamine covenant theology. As has been shown, the allegorical method of interpretation it employs creates difficulties in interpreting Scripture.

This chapter was adapted from Ron Johnson, "Systematic Theology Is the Hermeneutic," *The Conservative Theological Journal* 1, no. 3 (December 1997): 220–34.

Theological and Prophetic Systems Throughout History

It is important to understand how hermeneutics and interpretation were applied through the centuries. Early on, various systems tried to explain the overall plan and message of the Bible. The Jews of the Old Testament period looked at the promises and prophecies in their Scriptures as literal. In other words, they took the thoughts of the prophets at face value. By using common sense, they understood the difference between recorded biblical history, predictive prophecy, and poetry.

Orthodox Jewish View

Characteristics:
- Belief in the inspiration and authority of Scripture
- Normal interpretation of prophecy with historic fulfillment
- Generally, consistent hermeneutics
- Israel as a nation distinct from the Gentile nations
- Righteous Israelites distinct from righteous Gentiles
- Because of sin, the kingdom reign of the Messiah was postponed

Amillennial View

The early church and how it understood Scripture was profoundly influenced by Origen's tendency to spiritualize and allegorize Scripture. Augustine, too, greatly influenced the acceptance of amillennialism. Thus, the interpretation of the Word took a different turn. Amillennialists believe that the kingdom reign of Jesus started with

His first advent and that the Lord now simply reigns in the heart of the Christian. From Revelation 20, most amillennialists believe Satan was bound at Christ's first coming. The kingdom is allegorized and spiritualized. Though some see differences between Israel and the church, many amillennialists hold that the differences are only slight. They see one redeemed people of God with very few historical distinctions.

Characteristics:

- Belief in the inspiration and authority of Scripture
- Use of inconsistent or "mixed" principles of hermeneutics
- Uses literal interpretation on Christ's first coming but allegorical on His second coming
- Plays down any future for the nation of Israel
- Replaces Israel with the church
- Spiritualizes second coming events in order to make the church the prophesied millennial kingdom
- Ignores or plays down sharp distinctions in doctrines like the rapture and the tribulation

Postmillennial View

Like amillennialism, postmillennialism uses spiritualized, allegorical interpretation. It believes the church is the kingdom, that it is encompassing the world, and soon will cause the whole world to become one. The church will perfect the kingdom concept with a final golden age. The Lord will then come after (post) the church is victorious and has firmly established His kingdom and earthly authority. Postmillennialism was popular prior to World War I, with optimistic theologians believing that the advancement of technology and medicine was heralding the final stages of the church as it broke open the new kingdom age. Some liberal denominations as well as various conservative groups also embraced postmillennialism. But World War I brought about disillusionment, and postmillennialism waned in popularity.

[Postmillennialism] is built on the unsteady hermeneutic of spiritualization. It is an unfounded optimism that is not based on a realistic view of what has happened over the last two thousand years or on what is presently going on now. The world is not becoming morally and spiritually better, nor it is being dominated by Christianity. This basic reality forces postmillennialists to place their golden age well in the future, giving the church plenty of time to "shape up" and get on with kingdom business.[1]

Characteristics:

- Conservatives believed in the inspiration and authority of Scripture
- Positive about the success of the church and denied an ecclesiastical apostate decline
- Believed the church would grow mightily and the gospel would spread worldwide
- Replaced Israel with the church
- Denied any future for the nation of Israel
- Allegorized the kingdom and believed the church was bringing in the Millennium

Amillennialism/Covenant View

For the last several hundred years, covenant theology has dominated amillennialism, especially among the Dutch and Presbyterian Reformed. Covenant theology sees all of Scripture controlled by two or three covenants. (1) The covenant of redemption was made in eternity past between Christ the Son and God the Father, whereby the Son agrees to provide salvation for man at the Cross. (2) The covenant of grace started with Abraham, though some say Adam, and is ongoing until Jesus returns. Some covenant theologians see grace and redemption as one covenant rather than two, the grace/redemption covenant being in place in history as the great redemptive agency of God in elective salvation for the world. (3) The covenant of works was made with Adam. If Adam obeyed God, there was life; if he disobeyed, then death would follow. As the head of humanity, Adam failed and condemned his children to death and separation from God.

Characteristics:

- Holds to the inspiration and authority of Scripture
- Creates covenants that cannot be biblically substantiated
- Makes all of history to be redemptive
- In hermeneutics, spiritualizes some prophetic portions of the Word and other portions remain as literal
- Sees no distinction between Israel and the church
- Simplifies the Scriptures and sees only limited historic distinctions in the Bible

Classic Dispensational View

Dispensationalism is Calvinistic in its belief that God will, through a variety of economies, sovereignly work out glory to Himself in history. Dispensationalists hold that the student of the Word of God must use a normal, literal hermeneutic in interpreting Scripture and that interpretation does not shift from normal to allegorical. Dispensationalism proclaims a scriptural plan based on the biblical covenants: Mosaic, Abrahamic, Davidic, Palestinian, and new.

Dispensationalism proclaims that salvation through all the ages has been by faith alone, though God may change the object of that trust. For example, Abraham simply believed the promises God made to him, and that belief was counted for righteousness (Gen. 15:6). But the object of faith in the age of grace is clearly a personal trust in the Lord Jesus Christ as one's own Savior. "Dispensations are not ways of salvation but different ways God administers His rule in this world."[2] Dispensationalism is planted firmly on the doctrines of the inspiration and inerrancy of Scripture. It also holds to progressive revelation, the distinction between Israel and the church, to Christ's second coming as literal and historical just as His first coming. Classic dispensationalism generally holds to the pretribulational rapture of the church, i.e., Christ's coming before the seven-year tribulation period begins.

Characteristics:

- Holds strongly to the inspiration and authority of Scripture
- From Genesis to Revelation holds to a consistent, literal, and normal system of hermeneutics
- Believes that God will receive glory in all of the outworkings of His plans, not simply in the plan of salvation
- Holds to progressive revelation distinctively
- Believes that both the first and second comings of Christ will be literal
- Does not believe that the kingdom is the church and holds that God's purposes for Israel are different from His purposes with the church

CHAPTER 5

Principles of Hermeneutics

This chapter pulls together the major principles of interpretation agreed upon by most evangelicals. These rules have been compiled from writings on hermeneutics by prominent Christian authors. While most students of the Bible would agree that these principals represent important interpretive norms, many are not consistent in applying these guidelines to all doctrinal and interpretive issues.

Spiritual Attitude of the Interpreter

1. No one can believe the deep spiritual message of the Bible unless grounded in faith. That foundation is the testimony of God Himself speaking His Word and is authenticated as divine by the testimony of the Spirit with and by the truth in the heart of the believer.[1]

> *But when He, the Spirit of truth, comes, He will guide you into all the truth; for He will not speak on His own initiative, but whatever He hears, He will speak; and He will disclose to you what is to come. (John 16:13)*

2. The interpreter must recognize the Scriptures to be the Word of God and the work of One divine mind, and must understand from the biblical revelation that the Holy Spirit divinely guided and inspired the human writers—the prophets of the Old Testament and the apostles of the New Testament. The original writings were given by plenary and verbal inspiration.[2]

And I will bring upon that land all My words [plural] which I have pronounced against it, all that is written in this book, which Jeremiah has prophesied against all the nations. (Jeremiah 25:13)

[Jeremiah] speak to all the cities of Judah, . . . all the words [plural] that I have commanded you to speak to them. Do not omit a word! (Jeremiah 26:2)

All Scripture is inspired [God-breathed] by God and profitable for teaching, for reproof, for correction, for training in righteousness. (2 Timothy 3:16)

3. The interpreter must understand that the Scriptures, in their original autographs, were given as infallible and inerrant.

The sum of Thy word is truth, and every one of Thy righteous ordinances is everlasting. (Psalm 119:160)

4. One must interpret under the guidance of the Holy Spirit, which guidance is to be humbly and earnestly sought.[3]

Now we have received, not the spirit of the world, but the Spirit who is from God, that we might know the things freely given to us by God. (1 Corinthians 2:12)

5. Individual believers in the Lord Jesus Christ have the privilege, right, and duty to search the Word of God for themselves in seeking godly truth and guidance.[4]

Search the Scriptures, because you think that in them you have eternal life; and it is these [the Scriptures] that bear witness of Me. (John 5:39)

6. The interpreter must be as objective as possible and set aside subjective preconceptions; prejudices; doctrinal, traditional, or denominational biases.[5] Though sincere, the Jews kept their traditional biases and missed out on the truth concerning Jesus, their promised Messiah. Speaking of the Pharisees, Jesus said,

Neglecting the commandment of God, you hold to the tradition of men . . . thus invalidating the word of God by your tradition which you have handed down. (Mark 7:8, 13)

And Paul added,

I bear [the Jews] witness that they have a zeal for God, but not in accordance with knowledge. (Romans 10:2)

[7] The interpreter approaches the Bible realizing that it speaks to the issues of the soul, spirit, and mind. It is a spiritual Book but not mystical. It speaks reasonably, logically, and for distinct purposes.[6]

For the word of God is living and active and sharper than any two-edged sword, and piercing as far as the division of soul and spirit, of both joints and marrow, and able to judge the thoughts [mental processes] and intentions [plans, concepts] of the heart. (Hebrews 4:12)

[8] The interpreter must believe the Word of God is capable of yielding meaningful theological interpretation. Jesus claimed His doctrine was from God, and Paul speaks of obeying doctrine from the heart. The first proof of the Scripture is doctrine. Ramm notes,

[Jesus] was in His own ministry a "doctrinal" teacher. We note that people were astonished at His teaching (Matthew 7:28); He claimed His doctrine was from God (John 7:16); and He invited men to discover its divine origin (John 7:17).[7]

All Scripture is inspired by God and profitable for teaching [doctrine], . . . (2 Timothy 3:16a)

[9] The interpreter must realize that all of the Word of God points to the revelation of Jesus Christ. Redemption is a central theme of Scripture, but it is not the only one. The Bible also contains a vast storehouse of other truths and revelations that God wishes to convey to mankind.

As to this salvation, the prophets who prophesied of the grace that would come to you made careful search and inquiry, seeking to know what person or time the Spirit of Christ within them was indicating as He predicted the sufferings of Christ and the glories to follow. (1 Peter 1:10–11)

It is He who reveals the profound and hidden things; He knows what is in the darkness. (Daniel 2:22)

. . . there is a God in heaven who reveals mysteries, and He has
made known to King Nebuchadnezzar what will take place in
the latter days. This was your dream and the visions in your
mind while on your bed. (Daniel 2:28)

O king, . . . [God] who reveals mysteries has made known to
you what will take place. (Daniel 2:29)

He who forms mountains . . . declares to man what are His
thoughts, . . . the Lord God of hosts is His name. (Amos 4:13)

10. The interpreter must know, as much as he is capable, the original languages. The Bible in Hebrew and Greek *is* the Word of God. Everything else is a translation.

Luther accepted the primacy of the original languages. He felt that the original revelation of God could not be truly recovered until it was recovered from the Hebrew and Greek Testaments. His advice to preachers was, "While a preacher may preach Christ with edification though he may be unable to read the Scriptures in the originals, he cannot expound or maintain their teaching against the heretics without this indispensable knowledge."[8]

When the Jews returned from Babylon to Jerusalem, few of them knew the Hebrew language that was spoken by their grandparents, who had been taken in the three deportations. Those who came back (from 538–438 B.C.) were three and four generations removed from those captured and put into exile by the Chaldeans. According to Unger, they were speaking the vernacular Aramaic of Babylon and did not understand the Hebrew language native to Judah.[9] Thus, when Ezra the priest had the Law read in the hearing of the gathered crowd, a new generation apparently had never heard it. Those words of Moses had to be translated.

And they read from the book, from the law of God, translating
to give the sense so that they understood the reading.
(Nehemiah 8:8)

Therefore, the pastor today needs to know the original languages in order to make the Word of God clearer to the layman. English translations, or any other language versions, have a limited meaning. To be able to give the full sense of the Word of God is an extremely important component of effectively communicating the truth of Scripture.

[11] Interpreters should have some understanding of human behavior, ancient history, sociology, geography, the sciences, and the liberal arts. Knowledge in these areas lends a broad understanding of the world and of human behavior.

Ramm reminds us that the great scholars of but a few generations past, "insisted that liberal arts, history, and geography were basic to exegesis. History and geography especially form the natural background for literal exegesis. Literal exegesis gave rise to doctrine."[10]

[12] Students of Scripture need to sharpen their observation skills. Since every word in the Bible is inspired and placed there by divine inspiration, interpreters must work hard to discover what is being said and why. Keen observation and detailed analysis is required to learn what every detail of a passage has to say.

[13] Students of Scripture must use inductive reasoning. Using the scientific approach, one must perceive, compare, combine, remember, and infer. One must rely on the certainty of scriptural truths, which are not learned from experience but are given in the constitution of our nature.

[14] The interpreter has not finished until there is meaning and adequate practical application gleaned from the passage studied. Application has two stages, "direct" and "indirect" application. (a) Direct application asks, "What did this passage mean to those to whom it was written?" (b) Indirect application asks, "What does this passage mean to me now?"

For example, Nehemiah 7:5–73 gives a long listing and genealogy of those who returned back to Israel from Babylon under Zerubbabel.

a. Relative to direct application, what was the importance and value of that listing to that generation that had just made the long journey from the land of Chaldees? In the list they could see, for at least several generations past, the names of their families and their grandfathers. Thus, "the return" was a miracle from God and a historic fact that the Jews could understand because they could verify God's work in their midst and with their immediate ancestors.

b. Relative to indirect application, we can appreciate the historic nature of that return. We can understand that God keeps good records! The listings verify for us, many generations away, the truthfulness of the Word of God and that His working is stamped upon the pages of history. The return of the Jews from Babylon is not fiction, it actually happened. History tells us that the Word of God, even for our times, is a faithful record.

Nehemiah writes,

Then my God put it into my heart to assemble the nobles, the officials, and the people to be enrolled by genealogies. Then I found the book of the genealogy of those who came up first in which I found the following record: These are the people of the province who came up from the captivity of the exiles. (Nehemiah 7:5–6a)

15. Students of Scripture must learn to study with discipline. They must be patient and realize that Bible study both accumulates knowledge and becomes more incisive with time. Both knowledge and wisdom should be the goal of the interpreter of God's Word.

Thy testimonies are wonderful; therefore my soul observes them. The unfolding of Thy words gives light; it gives understanding to the simple. (Psalm 119:129–30)

Foundational Principles of Interpretation

1. The interpreter must understand that Scripture interprets Scripture. God cannot teach in one place anything that is inconsistent with what He teaches in another.[11]

For example, as far as can be ascertained, few if any of the Jewish rabbis saw the resurrection of the Messiah in Psalm 16, especially verse 10. But Peter recognized this prophecy and its meaning after the resurrection of Jesus. Peter interpreted this Davidic psalm as fulfilled before the eyes of his generation.

For Thou wilt not abandon my soul to Sheol; neither wilt Thou allow Thy Holy One to undergo decay. (Psalm 16:10)

Peter remarks,

And so, because [David] was a prophet, and knew that God had sworn to him with an oath to seat one of his descendants upon his throne, [David] looked ahead and spoke of the resurrection of the Christ, that He was neither abandoned to Hades, nor did His flesh suffer decay. (Acts 2:30–31)

The Scripture-interprets-Scripture principle led Calvin to strongly emphasize grammatical exegesis, philology, the necessity of examining the context, and the necessity of comparing Scriptures that treated common subjects.[12]

[2.] One must realize that Scripture cannot contradict Scripture. If a passage admits of different interpretations, the correct one should agree with what the Bible teaches elsewhere on the same subject.[13]

For example, nowhere in the New Testament does it teach that one person can be baptized as a substitute for a believer who had died. But the wording of 1 Corinthians 15:29, even in the Greek text, seems to imply this. The passage reads,

> *Otherwise, what will those do who are baptized for the dead?*
> *If the dead are not raised at all, why then are they baptized for*
> *them?*

Though this is admittedly a difficult passage, the *Bible Knowledge Commentary* handles the problem with sound reasoning:

> Up to 200 explanations have been given of this verse! Most of these interpretations are inane, prompted by a desire to conform this verse to an orthodox doctrine of baptism. It is clear from the context, however, that Paul distinguished his own practice and teaching from that described here. He merely held up the teaching of being "baptized for the dead" as a practice of some who denied the Resurrection.
>
> How the false teachers came to this view may never be known, but just across the Saronic Gulf, north of Corinth, lay Eleusis, the center of an ancient mystery religion lauded by Homer . . . and widely popular. . . . Part of the rites of initiation into this pagan religion were washings of purification in the sea without which no one could hope to experience bliss in the life hereafter (cf. Pindar Fragment 212; Sophocles Fragment 753). A vicarious participation in the mysteries was not unknown either (cf. Orphica Fragment 245). Given the Corinthian propensity for distortion in matters of church practice (11:2–14:40), it was likely that some in Corinth (possibly influenced by the Eleusinian mystery) were propounding a false view of baptism which Paul took up and used as an argument against those who denied the Resurrection. No interpretation of this text is entirely satis-

factory, but this view has as its chief strength the natural reading of the Greek verse, an asset singularly lacking in other explanations. Also it is noteworthy that Paul referred to "those" (not "we") who are "baptized for the dead."[14]

If this explanation is correct, it demonstrates how a knowledge of ancient history and the practices of other religions give us external information that, in turn, sheds light on what is happening in the biblical text. Also, since the teaching of believer baptism is clearly the New Testament pattern, this Corinthian passage must be interpreted in the light of that particular doctrinal truth.

[3.] One must take the words in their normal, literal, plain, historical sense. Literal would imply the natural or usual construction and implication, following the ordinary and apparent sense of words rather than an allegorical or metaphorical sense.

A perfect example of this principal is Luke 1:31–33. The angel Gabriel says to Mary,

> *And behold, you will conceive in your womb, and bear a son, and you shall name Him Jesus. He will be great, and will be called the Son of the Most High; and the Lord God will give Him the throne of His father David; and He will reign over the house of Jacob forever; and His kingdom will have no end.*

No evangelical argues (not even amillennialists) that the first coming of Christ was not literal and historical. Mary bore the promised Son, He was named Jesus, and He was called the Son of the Most High! But amillennial allegorists suddenly shift in their interpretation and apply the second part of these verses to a spiritualized kingdom, i.e., the church. Israel is left out, and there is no future and literal kingdom for the Jewish people. How could and why would a passage mean something in one half and something else in the other half?

Mary would have taken the entire promise literally. Why would the angel Gabriel have two distinct things in view and not explain this to Mary? As the prophecies of the Messiah's birth and reign were given in a literal, normal, and historic framework, so their fulfillment would take place in the same way (Isa. 7:14; Mic. 5:2; Isa. 9:6–7). A perfect example of a shift into allegorical interpretation (with the attendant distortion of meaning of the text) is the comments of Lenski:

"The House of Jacob" denotes all his descendants, not merely the Jewish nation as such, but the spiritual descendants on through the ages (Rom. 9:6–8). We need not be reluctant about accepting the angel's word in its full reality that Jesus should rule forever over the spiritual House of Israel, believing Jews and Gentiles alike. He does so rule now, . . . We are, however, told that we should not let the Old Testament prophecies control our New Testament exegesis! Thus the kingdom is where the king is, where he exercises his blessed rule of eternal grace, whether on earth or in heaven. Not the people as subjects make up the kingdom—there are really no subjects, for all in whom Christ rules are themselves kings and rule with him, and in this sense he is the King of kings (of us whom he has made spiritual kings by his spiritual rule).[15]

When thinking of the literal, one must emphasize the "natural," "proper," "obvious," and "normal." This is not "letterism," which fails to recognize nuances, plays on words, hidden metaphors, figures of speech, and lamination of meanings in a word. Nor is it the alleged "wooden literalism" that is supposed to characterize conservative hermeneutics.

The literal method of interpretation is the usual practice in the interpretation of literature. Whenever we read a book, an essay, or a poem we presume the literal sense in the document until the nature of the literature forces us to another level. This is the only conceivable method of understanding literature of all kinds.[16]

[4] Allegorical interpretation must be rejected as an overall interpretative system. No specific doctrinal area, such as eschatology, is to be interpreted by the allegorical system. The whole of the Bible, and all specific doctrines, are to be studied with the normal and historic sense in mind. Of course it is understood that within the framework of literal interpretation, there is room for illustration, symbols, figures of speech, and poetry. But to recognize these literary devices does not mean that literal interpretation is being abandoned.

Luther rejected allegory. He calls allegorical interpretation "dirt," "scum," and "obsolete loose rags." Calvin also rejected allegorical interpretation, saying it led men away from the truth of Scripture.[17]

The books of Daniel and Revelation are full of symbolic language. But in both books, keys are given as aids in seeing the literalness behind the symbols. For example, God explained to Daniel the symbolism of Nebuchadnezzar's dream of the great statue (Dan. 2:31–36). In the king's dream, he saw the statue with a golden head, breast and arms of silver, and stomach and thighs of bronze. Daniel explains that the head represents Nebuchadnezzar and his kingdom. The other metals portray lesser and inferior kingdoms that would follow (vv. 37–43). Behind the symbolic is the literal.

Over one hundred times in Revelation the symbolic is explained by the Greek words *hos* and *homoios*. They are translated "as," "as if," "as it were," "seemed to be," and "like." To illustrate, "The sun became black *as* sackcloth" (6:12), "the whole moon became *like* blood" (v. 12), "The [asteroids] of the sky fell to the earth, *as* a tree casts its unripe figs" (v. 13), "Something *like* a great mountain burning with fire was thrown into the sea" (8:8), "The appearance of the locusts *was like* horses" (9:7).

Granted, these particles are not always used with every illustration that could be labeled symbolic. But since the above phrases are used in such an overwhelming number of verses, this is a key to understanding Revelation. It is clear, however, that John's use of such illustrations demonstrates the apostle's struggle to communicate what he saw with comparative language. Where he does not use comparative language, more than likely the passage can be taken literally without much confusion. For example, "A third of the earth was burned up, and a third of the trees were burned up" (8:7). There would be no reason not to accept this as literal.

[5.] Interpreters can assume that all literary devices depend on the literal, normal stratum of language. Parables, types, allegories, symbols, and figures of speech presume a level of understanding in the audience. For example, the parable of the sower is understood only within the context of literal "farm" language. The symbolism of a lion is based upon what is asserted about lions in literal speech.

The typological or perhaps allegorical way Paul speaks of Abraham, Sarah, and Hagar in Galatians 4:21–31 is based upon the historical and factual statements about these people, which in turn reflects the literal stratum of language. This Galatians paragraph is the only passage in the Word of God that is specifically designated as allegorical. The apostle gives the reader a clear warning that he is "creating" an allegory in order to make a comparison between works and faith.

[6.] The interpreter must approach the Word of God logically and systematically. The task of the theologian is to systematize the teachings of Holy Scripture the best he can.[18] The writer of Hebrews tells us,

God, after He spoke long ago to the fathers [by means of] the prophets in many portions and in many ways, . . . (1:1)

Though the writer does not say so, the various ways would include the laws, prophecies, judges, ceremonies, etc. given in the Old Testament. Few would question that Peter and Paul "systematized" or put all of this information together to form a theology or system of doctrine. This systemization can be seen in Peter's great discourses in Acts (2:14–4:31), in which he created a theology about Christ and an Old Testament prophetic doctrinal chronology. The same systematized theology can be seen in Paul's writings, especially his book of Romans.

We can take lessons from this and continue to analyze scriptural truth in like manner.

Beginning the Process of Interpreting the Scriptures

[1] Careful attention must be paid to the contextual whole of the Bible when studying a given verse or paragraph of the Word of God.

a. That is, the overall biblical context must be taken into account. The Word of God creates a context of itself. This becomes the larger setting from which a given passage is studied.

b. The Old or New Testaments form contexts in themselves. If the passage of Scripture under study is in the New Testament, that becomes the contextual framework of that verse of Scripture.

c. A given book or section of books form a context. If the passage under study is in Luke, then the Gospels become a context for the framing of Luke. Or, if the passage under study is 1 Timothy, the pastoral letters (1 and 2 Timothy, Titus) become the framework for that study.

d. The specific chapter in which the verse or verses come from is the more immediate context. The chapter before and the chapter following play a role in context.

e. The same is true of the few verses before and after those being studied. They also form the most immediate context.

[2] Extra-biblical history also forms a context. For example, in Matthew 24, Jesus refers to the coming destruction of Jerusalem. This disastrous prophecy took place under the Roman general Titus in A.D. 70 and throws a great deal of light and understanding on Matthew 24.

[3] The historical and grammatical principle must be used in

interpretation. This is inseparable from the literal principle. The interpreter must give attention to grammar; to the times, circumstances, and conditions of the writer of the biblical book; and, as already shown, to the context of the passage.[19]

In this, the interpreter must be aware of

a. The origin and root meaning of words. Words are the units of thought in most of our thinking and writing; they are the bricks of our conceptual formulation. Though meaning can shift by time and usage, it is still important to know the root idea behind words.[20]

b. The etymology of words. We attempt to understand words by the way they are formed. Words may have prefixes and suffixes, and sometimes are made up of a combination of other words. Again, because of shifting meaning or the evolution of how a word is used, the etymological approach must be used carefully.[21]

c. The comparison of words. By this means, and using a Hebrew or Greek concordance, all the occurrences of the word in Scripture may be discovered. By how many times a word is used and by how it is used in a given context, we can begin to get the "feel" of the word. Noting what word a writer considers as a synonym for another word also gives us a clue about what the writer understood the first word to mean.[22]

d. The cultural use of words. Behind a word in the New or Old Testaments is a practice of the culture. To know the richness of the word, we must know the cultural practice. Today, students of the Word have available to them many details of history and cultural practice that give a cultural context to specific thoughts and words.[23]

e. The cognitive comparison of words. By studying other words that belong to the same family of languages, one can plumb the depths of a word's meaning. For example, since the Bible was often translated in an ancient language, we can see how that translator understood specific Hebrew and Greek words. Since he lived closer to the times of the Scriptures, we can gain a further understanding of how certain words were used.[24]

f. The grammar of sentences. All languages must be approached through the science of syntax. How a word is analyzed through declining and parsing becomes the basis of translating any sentence in all languages. Nouns must be analytically examined through case, number, and gender. Verbs are dissected apart analytically by tense, mood, voice, number, and person.[25]

g. The principle of cross-referencing. Since Scripture interprets Scripture, cross-referencing is important to see how words and sentences are used in other portions of the Word of God. Cross-references help us see the importance of thoughts, concepts, and doctrines, which may be expressed in other passages verbally, i.e., word for word, or with an apparent verbal coincidence. One can cross-reference concepts alone, or cross-reference exact ideas. By cross-referencing we can understand how and why ideas are borrowed and repeated, especially from the Old into the New Testament.

4. The interpreter must consider progressive revelation. In many prophecies of Scripture, God did not reveal everything at once concerning a specific truth or doctrine. Over years and even centuries, a doctrine may be progressively expanded upon.

For example, not everything in regard to the doctrine of the Trinity is told in Scripture all at once. This doctrine is revealed over the pages of both Old and New Testaments, and from the pages of Genesis all the way to Revelation. One has to put together all the passages that allude to the Trinity in order to gain a full and comprehensive picture of the subject. Progressive revelation is especially important in gaining a full understanding of eschatology as the prophetic plan unfolds through the Word of God.

5. The interpreter must appreciate the principle of human commonality. Though we will never understand completely the thoughts and feelings of ancient people, we can to a large degree identify with their pains, sorrows, and joys. In many ways, the people of the past are just like us today. They wept over the death of a loved one; they grieved as they struggled with the pains of life. As an illustration, David writes,

> I am weary with my sighing; every night I make my bed swim, I dissolve my couch with my tears. My eye has wasted away with grief. (Psalm 6:6–7a)

Human commonality can be calculated into passages that are addressing strong emotional issues. This may help the student of Scripture better comprehend the human drama taking place emotionally within the lives of the personalities of the Bible.

6. Interpreters must study the Bible dispensationally, looking for

clues that indicate God is doing something different in biblical history that is important for the unfolding of a plan. After Adam had sinned and disobeyed the Lord, God began a new and different dispensation with our ancient parents. They were driven forth from the protection of the garden to begin a new life in a hostile world. Similarly, something new began following the crucifixion and resurrection of Jesus. The dispensation of the church age would begin in Acts 2. Without noting dispensational distinctions, the interpreter misses the important changes in the plan that God Himself is setting forth. Overlooking changes in dispensation often leads to interpretative problems that distort and dull the full message of Scripture.

It is clear, for example, that the apostle Paul says we are now under the new dispensation of the church rather than Law. He writes,

> *Therefore the Law has become our tutor to lead us to Christ, that we may be justified by faith. But now that faith has come, we are no longer under a tutor [i.e., under the Law]. (Galatians 3:24–25)*

> *. . . you are not under law, but under grace. (Romans 6:14b)*

[7] The interpreter must realize that the rule of comprehension dictates that each passage of Scripture has but one meaning. Though a passage may also be quoted as an illustration, it still has one primary meaning in view. A multiplicity of senses and meanings makes comprehension difficult, if not impossible. Thus, the interpreter must give each passage of Scripture one interpretation.[26]

Tan points out that this rule is tested in respect to the Sermon on the Mount (Matt. 5–7). In this section, Jesus refers often to "the kingdom of heaven." Thus, its primary context is about behavior in the future kingdom, not the church age. The one interpretation then refers to that period when the Messiah rules personally on earth and enforces righteousness by His scepter of iron (Ps. 2:9; Rev. 2:27; 12:5; 19:15), and when law principles seem to be in force.

Seeing how puzzled His listeners were, Jesus replied, "Not everyone who says to Me, 'Lord, Lord,' will enter the kingdom of heaven; but he who does the will of My Father who is in heaven" (Matt. 7:21). The primary interpretation has to do with the coming King and His kingdom, though there are some practical and universal moral principles that have to be chosen carefully and that have practical application to any age. For example,

- Love your enemies, and pray for those who persecute you (5:44).
- Do not lay up for yourselves treasures upon earth (6:19).
- No one can serve two masters (6:24).
- Where your treasure is, there will your heart be also (6:21).
- Why are you anxious about clothing? (6:28).
- Whatever you want others to do for you, do so for them (7:12).

Dozens of moral precepts are repeated over and over throughout Scripture. For example, it is as wrong to commit murder in the dispensations of government (Gen. 9:6), of Law (Exod. 20:13), of grace (Rom. 13:4), and certainly in the dispensation of the kingdom (Isa. 11:4–5). Though such precepts are repeated, the dispensations still have distinct features and singular purposes in God's dealings with humanity.

Tan explains well single interpretation:

> Many interpreters see the Sermon on the Mount as directly and primarily applicable to Christians today. To do this, interpreters depend heavily on the method of spiritualization, for it is apparent that the laws and regulations found in the Sermon cannot be directly applied today without producing insurmountable problems and repercussions.
>
> Moreover, a casual reading of the Sermon reveals that it contains an embarrassing absence of church truths. Nothing is said regarding Christ's sacrifice for sin, . . . the faith which brings salvation, prayer in the name of Christ, the Holy Spirit, and even the church itself. These are all foundational truths taught by Christ during His early ministry (cf. John 14:13, 26; Matt. 16:18–19; etc.).[27]

8. If there seems to be a conflict in interpretation, the interpreter would choose the alternative that is the simplest. The student of Scripture should not choose simple alternatives for simplicity's sake. One should diligently investigate all alternatives, consider the logical and natural harmony of God's Word, and, after the consideration of the harmonized facts, embrace that which is most easily accepted.[28] Tan further states, "When alternative interpretations seem equally plausible and contain equally good sense, the general rule of thumb is to choose the one interpretation which imposes the least strain on credulity."[29]

Tan uses the rash vow of Jephthah in Judges 11 to illustrate the rule of the simplest alternative:

Interpreters marshal equally good reasons for seeing Jephthah's daughter offered up as a burnt offering or given up as a perpetual virgin in the sanctuary of Shiloh. The alternate views are so compelling that the result is pretty much a draw. In this case, the rule of the simplest alternate should be applied. Jephthah's daughter was offered up.[30]

[9] When the plain sense of Scripture makes common sense, seek no other sense; therefore, take every word at its primary, ordinary, usual, and literal meaning unless the facts of the immediate context, studied in the light of related passages and axiomatic and fundamental truths, clearly indicate otherwise.[31]

Referring to the millennial kingdom blessings, Isaiah says, "The wolf will dwell with the lamb, and the leopard will lie down with the kid, and the calf and the young lion and the fatling together; and a little boy will lead them" (Isa. 11:6). How is this to be taken? There is no reason not to take it literally. If the Messiah is ruling with complete authority and control over nature, why is this not to be seen as a literal happening? A second view might argue that this is hyperbole and poetry. But even then, the idea communicated is that nature is at rest and there is safety and peace in the King's realm.

Though a thorough dispensational literalist, Unger takes the second view but still remains in the camp of those taking Scripture at face value. He writes,

> This highly poetical passage vividly and dramatically paints a picture of the sublime tranquillity that will pervade the Messiah's earthly Kingdom, fulfilling the Davidic Covenant and the many prophecies of the Old Testament of this "golden age." . . . The creatures named are literal animals, not representative of men, and represent a partial lifting of the curse and a limited restoration of the state [of peace] in Eden.[32]

[10] As mentioned, the interpreter must realize there are types and symbols in Scripture, but this does not mean that they hold some mysterious and hidden interpretation. Types and symbols are literary devices that are part of an overall literal interpretive meaning of the text.

A type is fulfilled at a specific time by its antitype. A symbol does not have its symbolic meaning because of what it is in itself. A symbol means "a throwing together." A symbol is some object (real or imagined) or action that is assigned a meaning for the purpose of depicting, rather than stating, the qualities of something else.[33]

[11]. The interpreter must realize the Bible contains figurative language, but it, too, has a literal point of reference. If the literal meaning of any word or expression makes good sense, it should be taken as literal; but if the literal meaning does not make good sense, it is figurative. Since the literal is the most usual signification of a word, and therefore occurs much more frequently than the figurative, any term will be regarded as literal unless there is good reason for a different understanding.[34]

An example is God's judgment of the Assyrians as described in Isaiah 10:33–34: "The Lord . . . will lop off the boughs with a terrible crash; . . . He will cut down the thickets of the forest with an iron axe, and Lebanon will fall by the Mighty One." A literal interpretation of this passage does not, of course, make sense. Unger notes, however, the figurative sense of God "as an omnipotent woodsman, lopping off the branches of the tall trees (the proud Assyrians) with tremendous force. . . . These verses portray the sudden overthrow of Sennacherib at the pinnacle of his success."[35]

The Responsibility of the Interpreter

[1]. The interpreter has a responsibility to teach and share what he has learned from God's Word.

Paul writes,

The Lord stood with me, and strengthened me, in order that through me the proclamation might be fully accomplished, and that all the Gentiles might hear [through me]. (2 Timothy 4:17)

[2]. Interpreters should consider the discovery of spiritual truths from Scripture more precious than gold. We must see it as a blessing to study the Word of God!

David shouts out,

Deal bountifully with Thy servant, that I may live and keep Thy word. Open my eyes, that I may behold wonderful things from Thy law. (Psalm 119:17–18)

[3]. Interpreters must avoid making the study of God's Word an end in itself. Rather, the study must bring us and others with whom we share our knowledge closer to Jesus Christ. Spiritual maturity should be the goal of the student of Scripture.

From childhood [Timothy] you have known the sacred writings which are able to give you the wisdom that leads to salvation through faith which is in Christ Jesus. (2 Timothy 3:15)

All Scripture is inspired by God . . . that the man of God may be adequate, equipped for every good work. (2 Timothy 3:16–17)

4. The student of Scripture should avoid radical views or making a certain doctrine a hobbyhorse. The interpreter should strive for doctrinal balance.

But avoid worldly and empty chatter, for it will . . . spread like gangrene. Among them are Hymenaeus and Philetus, men who have gone astray from the truth . . . and thus they upset the faith of some. (2 Timothy 2:16–18)

5. The interpreter should not "create" doctrine or go beyond scriptural evidence. As what a scientist discovers must pass the test of logic and experimentation, in terms of the science of Bible study, what the interpreter discovers must pass the test of "Is it reasonable?" and "Can others find the same truths written in the pages of Scripture?" Disputes in theology often result from theologians extending themselves beyond the data of Scripture.

Where the Bible speaks, we may speak. Where Scripture has not spoken, we are wise to be silent.[36]

Now these [Bereans] were more noble-minded than those in Thessalonica, for they received the word with great eagerness, examining the Scriptures daily, to see whether these things were so. (Acts 17:11)

6. In order to be competent, the student of Scripture needs to assemble useful study tools. These reference works should be considered as "guides," for they are human resources and therefore imperfect in themselves. But a wise student will listen to the guidance of his "teachers." And in this case, it is our collected books that will help us in our task. A good library may take years to assemble. It should consist of

a. recognized commentary sets that explain the biblical languages and give excellent background material for the various books of the Bible

    b. at least one good classic single commentary on each book of Scripture that explains the biblical languages as well

    c. Bible encyclopedias, dictionaries, and English concordances

    d. books dealing with Bible chronologies, maps, and geography

    e. volumes dealing with biblical history and background references

    f. language lexicons, word study volumes, and concordances

    g. reliable evangelical theologies

    h. individual classic theology texts on such subjects as the Holy Spirit, the person of Christ, salvation, biblical prophecy, etc.

    i. sets and/or individual books on church history

7. Finally, students of the Word of God must examine themselves from time to time to see if they are living up to what they are learning. No one can accomplish this perfectly, but there must be a sincere desire to grow spiritually. The Bible is a personal book that speaks to each believer individually.

Paul says,

> *But let each one examine his own work, and then he will have reason for boasting in regard to himself alone, and not in regard to another. (Galatians 6:4)*

> *. . . holding fast the word of life, so that in the day of Christ I may have cause to glory because I did not run in vain nor toil in vain. (Philippians 2:16)*

CHAPTER 6

Symbols and Types in Prophecy

There are two categories of prophecy, each unique and requiring special consideration. These are symbolical and typical prophecies.

Symbolical Prophecy

Description of Symbols

A symbol is a graphic representation of an actual event, truth, or object. The lion in some prophecies, for example, symbolizes power and strength (cf. Rev. 5:5); the sword, the Word of God (cf. Rev. 19:15); and the sun-clad woman in Revelation 12, Israel in the tribulation.

Symbols can be *words* or *acts*. Symbolical *words* refer to objects and things seen by the prophets in their visions. Objects such as trees, figs, candlesticks, beasts, horses and riders, and people appear as symbols in many prophetic visions. It must be noted, however, that not every object seen in a vision is symbolic. Neither is it true that because some objects in a vision are symbolic, everything else in that vision must be symbolic.

Proper names are sometimes used as symbols in prophetic Scripture. The context and the analogy of prophecy will generally bring these out. Utmost care must be exercised before a proper name is interpreted as a symbol. For example, while the names *David* (1 Kings 12:16), *Babylon* (Rev. 17:5), and *Egypt* (Hos. 9:3) may well be symbolical, the name *Elijah* is not.[1]

Symbolical *acts* are actions performed symbolically by the prophet in order to convey specific messages to his contemporaries. Some

71

interpreters think that symbolical acts are not performed outwardly by the prophet but are enacted only in the prophet's mind. As E. W. Hengstenberg observes, "For as the sphere of the prophets, as long as they were in an ecstatic state, was not the outward world, but the inward, *every* action performed by them in this state of ecstasy must have been an *inward* action also" (italics added).[2] Interpreter Fairbairn thinks that symbolical acts performed outwardly are "exceptions."[3]

It is safer to assume that, as a rule, symbolical acts are enacted by the prophets under real life situations before spectators—not in their heads where no one but the prophets could see the performance and understand its meaning.

When Ezekiel is commanded by God to engrave the city of Jerusalem on a piece of brick and place a pan between himself and the engraved city (Ezek. 4:1–3), this symbolical act is truly performed before spectators and not simply imagined by the prophet. Similarly, when Zechariah is described as making crowns of silver and gold for the head of Joshua the high priest (Zech. 6:9–15), although the act is intended by the prophet to be symbolic, he truly makes the crowns. The context will generally indicate when a symbolical act is *not* performed outwardly. Thus, the symbol of the boiling caldron in Ezekiel 24:3–12 is not actual, because its context definitely labels it a parable.

Reasons for Symbols in Prophecy

There are at least two reasons why divine revelation makes use of symbols. First, future events must be manifested in some way in order to be perceived by the prophets. The prophets were not projected (as in a time machine) into eschatology; neither is the future advanced beforehand into reality. God uses *signs* to depict how the future will be worked out. As Revelation 1:1 reports, "God sent and signified it by his angel unto his servant John."

Second, prophecy sets forth the future, much of which relates to the rise and fall of nations, the outcome of wars and struggles, and the destinies of peoples and individuals. "Some of the events predicted are of such a nature, that the fate of nations depends upon them; and they are to be brought into existence by the instrumentality of men. If the prophecies had been delivered in plainer terms, some persons would have endeavoured to hasten their accomplishment, as others would have attempted to defeat it."[4]

Prophecy therefore must be expressed in symbolic language in order that only the faithful and the spiritually discerning might know. Symbols confuse unbelieving skeptics without unnecessarily frustrating believing Christians.

Sounding Out Symbols

Some interpreters see prophecy under a smoke screen of pervasive symbolism. This is the mistake of Fairbairn who states, "A large proportion of the communications of prophecy came in the guise of symbolical actions."[5] Floyd Hamilton suggests that "difficulties" are resolved by interpreting prophecy "as teaching spiritual truths in symbolical language, under the religious symbolism of the age in which the prophecies were written."[6]

Literal interpreters recognize that there are, of course, symbols in prophecy. But this is not saying that prophecy is predominantly or pervasively symbolic. Symbols are not hidden in every cranny and nook of the prophetic Scriptures, and the careful interpreter should not search for them with this assumption in mind. "Symbolic language is exceptional. . . . It is in no way characteristic of prophecy in general."[7] Even Louis Berkhof agrees: "Though the prophets often express themselves symbolically, it is erroneous to regard their language as symbolical throughout."[8]

The best solution to sounding out symbols is twofold. *First,* the interpreter should accept as symbolic that which is so designated in the context or seen under the harmony of prophecy. King Nebuchadnezzar's four sectional image (Dan. 2), Daniel's four beasts from the sea (Dan. 7), and the women-borne ephah (Zech. 5) are all symbols explainable from the context or the harmony of prophecy. "The Bible terminology is always the simplest of any literature," observes Lewis S. Chafer. "Where symbolism is employed in the text, it will, almost without exception, be so indicated."[9]

Second, the interpreter should accept as symbols those elements that are truly impossible in the realm of reality, taking care to note that eschatological times are real times. The sun-clad woman (Rev. 12), the beast with seven heads and ten horns (Rev. 17), and the lifting of Ezekiel from Babylon to Jerusalem "by a lock of mine head" (Ezek. 8:3) would be impossible in actuality.

Once a prophecy is found to contain symbols, interpreters often succumb to the temptation of treating everything else in that prophecy as symbolic. This error is reflected in Fairbairn's statement: "The figurative character of the description, in its general features, not less than in the particular images it employs, should be preserved *throughout* . . . since we cannot suppose that the vision shifted from a symbolical or ideal description in one part to a plain matter-of-fact description in another" (italics added).[10]

The presence of symbols in a prophecy, however, does not indicate that everything else in that prophecy is symbolical. The designation of symbols must be on an individual basis. Each symbol must be carefully examined, weighed, and adequately supported by strong evidence before a symbolical designation is made. Symbols are not cheaper by the dozen.

Thus, just because the "beast" in Revelation 19:19 is a symbol does not mean that the "kings of the earth and their armies" in the same verse are symbols. Just because the "sword" from Christ's mouth (Rev. 19:15) is a symbol does not mean that Christ and His saints in the same passage (Rev. 19:11–15) are symbols. Just because the book of Revelation contains symbols does not mean that the Millennium and the tribulational scenes described in the book are symbols.

When a Symbol Is Not a Symbol

Many interpreters err in seeing an inordinate amount of symbolism in Bible prophecy. For this reason, the interpreter should be conversant with the various situations in which symbols are not required by the text. These situations are as follows:

1. *When the "symbol" involves things possible.* The prophetic Scriptures contain many descriptions of the future that are possible or plausible. In such instances, the interpreter should not assign these to the realm of symbolism. By accepting these as literal descriptions, the interpreter gives the Scriptures the benefit of the doubt and honors God's written revelation. The locusts from the bottomless pit (Rev. 9) are not symbols of the Turks or Saracens. That these are actual locusts or locust-like creatures is a reasonable possibility.

Some prophecies appear impossible at first glance. But when these are given closer inspection, they will be found to contain plausible reasons for actual existence. For example, the prophecy of Isaiah 65:25 reads,

> *"The wolf and the lamb shall graze together, and the lion shall eat straw like the ox; and dust shall be the serpent's food. They shall do no evil or harm in all My holy mountain," says the* Lord.

Many interpreters reject the literality of this prophecy, commenting that for lions to eat straw like oxen, and snakes to eat dust like angleworms, would require radical changes in their digestive systems. On the basis of this and related passages, skeptics are prompted to comment that "it was an awe-inspiring faith that dared to paint so gorgeous a picture . . . so far above all possibility of realization."[11]

Due to the alleged impossibility of anatomical changes in animals, interpreters have concluded that the prophecy is merely "a poetic description"[12] or a figure of speech describing how "forces naturally antagonistic and at enmity with each other shall be gradually subdued" in a progressively Christianized world.[13] Saul of Tarsus, for example, "was a wolf ravening and destroying, but who was so transformed by the Gospel of Christ that he became a lamb."[14]

That this prophecy from Isaiah lies within the realm of the plausible is not hard to show. During the Millennium, miraculous situations such as the longevity of man, the fruitfulness of the earth, and the elevation of the Dead Sea will occur. Moreover, since "there could have been no carnivorous beasts on earth before the Fall," pre-Fall, Edenic conditions will be restored at the Millennium. It is natural to expect the restoration of the vegetarian diet of animals on the millennial earth.[15]

Even today, the giant Panda bear, which shares anatomical similarities with some of the most ferocious animals in existence, prefers a vegetarian diet, being more willing to munch on bamboo shoots than to stalk prey and feast on meat.

Another case of a *possibility* is found in the pearls of the New Jerusalem (Rev. 21:21). Some interpreters affirm that these pearls must be symbolical, for "it is out of all the order of nature to produce a pearl large enough to make a gate to such an immense city."[16] But the sacred record does not say that the gate-sized pearls will be produced by nature. The divine architect, who says that He will make "all things new" (Rev. 21:5), is able to create and form large pearls to beautify the heavenly city.

Let us consider a group of prophecies that belong to the realm of the possible and are therefore not symbolical. When the millennial prophecies are normally and literally interpreted, the conclusion is unavoidable that non-resurrected inhabitants of the Millennium and glorified saints and angels will mingle on the millennial earth. Many nonliteral interpreters object, however, saying that for mortals and immortals to mix on the earth is absurd and impossible and contrary to their concept of what millennial conditions should be.

Herman Hoeksema raises an objection: "[The literal method] involves itself in all kinds of absurdities. How can the glorified saints, in their resurrected bodies, which are spiritual and heavenly, still exist and manifest themselves and operate in the old world? . . . And how can sinners and saints, the former in their old and sinful body, the latter in their glorified state, stand in the presence of Christ, the glorified Lord?"[17]

In reply, we pose our own questions: How could heavenly angels enter and presume to lodge within sinful Sodom? How could the resurrected Christ eat fish and mingle freely with His disciples after His resurrection? How could Paul and Stephen look at the glorified Christ when both of them were still mortals? How is God's Son able to take the form of "sinful flesh" (Rom. 8:3) and "dwell among men" (John 1:14) if glorified saints could not mingle with earthly sinners?

On the basis of the Scripture and history, we conclude that during the Millennium the commingling of mortals and immortals, the resurrected and the non-resurrected, and the earthly and the heavenly, is possible and not symbolical. A real impossibility would be a prophecy that envisioned one thousand human beings in mortal bodies occupying a room ten feet square with an eight-foot ceiling.[18]

2. *When details superfluous to the "symbol" are given.* When a "symbol" is found, the interpreter must test its symbolic nature by asking whether it contains details unnecessary and incidental to the intended symbolism. If so, its symbolism should be denied and its nonsymbolical character affirmed.

The prophecy of the 144,000 in Revelation 7 contains so many incidental details such as the genealogies, tribal names, and subdivided memberships of that group that it cannot possibly be a symbol. Also, the two witnesses of Revelation 11 must be nonsymbolic persons, otherwise the details concerning their ministries, death, and resurrection, as well as the earthquake that killed seven thousand would be quite superfluous.

Perhaps the best illustration of the "no superfluous details" rule is found in Ezekiel's prophecy of the millennial temple (Ezek. 40–48). Nonliteral interpreters maintain that this prophecy is a symbol of the Christian church. This major prophecy in the book of Ezekiel, however, contains descriptions, specifications, and measurements of the millennial temple that are so exhaustive that one may actually make a sketch of it, just as one might make of Solomon's historic temple. In fact, F. Gardiner in Ellicott's *Commentary on the Whole Bible* succeeds in sketching the layout of the millennial temple, all the while denying it is possible.[19] This has prompted Alva J. McClain to comment that "if an uninspired commentator can make some sense out of the architectural plan, doubtless the future builders working under divine guidance should have no trouble putting up the building."

The temple vision of Ezekiel is simply too extensive and contains too many details for the entire prophecy to be set aside as a symbol.

If the entire vision were intended by God as a symbol of the church, what a strange and roundabout way for God to so express Himself.

3. *When the "symbol" separates from itself.* When handling symbols, the interpreter must judge as nonsymbolic that which is found separated or apart from it. Every symbol must behave as a composite unit and not be seen in action separated or apart from itself.

Thus, the twenty-four elders of Revelation 7 cannot be symbolical, because one of the elders is described as coming forward to talk with John (v. 13). If the twenty-four elders were a symbol, it would mean that one-twenty-fourth part of a symbol came apart to talk with John!

Another often alleged "symbol" that is found separated from itself is the millennial temple of Ezekiel. In that prophecy, the temple and the city (Ezek. 48:8, 15) are definitely differentiated and distinguished. If both the temple and the city in Ezekiel 40–48 were a symbol of the Christian church, this would mean that the church becomes separated from herself.

Interpreting Symbols

In the interpretation of prophetic symbols, interpreters must have the patience of Job. One must collect, sift through, and collate a large amount of prophetic data to set up a working "harmony" of prophetic symbols. Thomas Hartwell Horne calls the interpretation of symbols "almost a science in itself." Some helps for the interpretation of symbols are:

1. *The immediate context.* The best possible clues for the interpretation of symbols is the immediate context in which given symbols are found. Under the guidance of contextual studies, the guesswork is taken out of many Bible symbols.

Interpreters of prophetic symbols generally agree that the two most symbolical books of the Bible—Daniel and Revelation—contextually explain their own symbols. Regarding the book of Daniel, Milton S. Terry testifies, "The symbols employed in the book of Daniel are, happily, so fully explained that there need be no serious doubt as to the import of most of them."[20] And with regard to the book of Revelation, Gerald B. Stanton witnesses, "When a symbol or sign does appear in the Revelation, it is often plainly designated as such in the immediate context, together with what the symbol represents."[21]

The four ferocious beasts of Daniel 7 are explained as four earthly kingdoms in Daniel 2. "The dragon, that old serpent" in Revelation 20:2, is immediately identified as "the Devil and Satan." "Sodom and Egypt" in Revelation 11:8 is identified at once as the city "where also our Lord was crucified" (Jerusalem). And the star that fell from heaven (Rev. 9:1) is identified as symbolic of a personal being (v. 2, "he opened the bottomless pit").

(2) *The remote context*. When the immediate context does not give a clear meaning to a symbol, the interpreter should examine similar or analogous symbols used elsewhere in prophecy. Thus, the "sword" that goes out of the mouth of Christ at His second coming must be interpreted in light of Hebrews 4:12 ("the Word of God"); the "time and times and half a time" (Dan. 7:25; 12:7; Rev. 12:14) must be compared with "forty and two months" (Rev. 11:2; 13:5) and "a thousand two hundred and three score days" (Rev. 12:6), as well as with Daniel's prophecy of the seventieth week (Dan. 9:26–27).

Though such situations are rare, sometimes the meaning of a given symbol may not be readily understood from its near or far context. The common mistake of interpreters is to devise their own interpretation for it. This does not settle the case, for it never touches on the literal meaning that is behind the use of the symbol. Charles Ryrie cautions, "If a symbol does not represent an actual or literal truth, then it must be a symbol of another symbol, and the process goes on and on and becomes completely meaningless. Somewhere along the line, a symbol *must* represent something *literal* in order that it may have meaning."[22] As Nathaniel West puts it, "We are not to explain the symbol symbolically."[23] In instances where the meaning of a symbol is not readily understood, one must withhold a decision until contexts, parallel passages, and the harmony of prophetic symbolism have been consulted.

(3) *Some clarifications.* It must be noted that not every word-picture in prophecy is a symbol but is an everyday figure of speech. When the angel in Revelation 19 invites the fowls to "the supper of the great God," this is not symbolism but merely figurative language. When Isaiah exclaims that "in the last days, the mountain of the Lord's house shall be established in the top of the mountains . . . and all nations shall flow unto it" (Isa. 2:2–3), the prophecy is not a symbol of the Christian church and world evangelization. Rather, Isaiah is using figurative language to describe the glory of the Jerusalem temple at the Millennium.

An object or concept that may not be a symbol, however, can have symbolical *significance*. While the twenty-four elders in Revelation 7 are certainly twenty-four glorified, actual persons, they may also represent the saints in heaven; and while the "river of life" (Rev. 22:1) is a real and material river, it also corresponds to the abundance of spiritual life that will characterize those living in the eternal state. And the names of the apostles actually written on the walls of the New Jerusalem (Rev. 21:14) means that church saints are included in the eternal city.

Herman A. Hoyt comments regarding the New Jerusalem: "Every detail should be taken literally . . . [But] everything in this city speaks of something about the glories and virtues of God, indicating that the materials serve a twofold purpose: (1) they are the substance of construction; and (2) they provide symbolism for contemplation."[24]

Symbolical Numbers

Nonliteral interpreters often ascribe mystical significances or symbolical designations to numbers in prophecy. This is not justifiable. John J. Davis, after an extensive study of the symbolism of numbers in Scripture, states, "It is our conclusion that the mystical or symbolical interpretation of numbers has little place in a sound system of hermeneutics."[25]

Like prophetic words, prophetic numbers are to be accepted as actual and literal. In the book of Zechariah, a revealing angel asks the prophet what he sees. Zechariah replies, "I see a flying scroll; its length is twenty cubits, and its breadth ten cubits" (Zech. 5:1–4). When the angel then interprets the scroll, he ignores the numerical dimensions mentioned by the prophet. Apparently, the "twenty by ten cubits" of the flying scroll are the actual, nonsymbolical dimensions of the scroll.

Regarding Revelation 9, many interpreters consider a literal army numbered at "two hundred million" as preposterous. The entire world population at John's time did not approach this number. Never in the history of the human race until now has there been an army of this size. It is safe, however, to accept the size of this eschatological army, even though its number may be phenomenal.

Often, though, numbers given in Scripture also have symbolical significance. The number *seven* is an obvious example. In the book of Joshua there is significance in the seven priests blowing seven trumpets while marching around Jericho for seven days, and on the seventh day, they march seven times around. And consider the book of Revelation being addressed to the seven churches and unfolded through the seven seals, seven trumpet woes, and seven bowls of wrath. It is not unreasonable to see significance in the repetition of *seven*.

That some prophetic numbers do contain symbolical significances, however, does not negate the literality and actuality of the numbers.

As Charles Lee Feinberg states, "Prophetic numbers are symbols just because and only because they are literal. . . . It is true that the seven lampstands of the first chapter of the Revelation are symbolical of completeness, but this does not imply that there are six or five lampstands. There are literally seven and the symbolic significance is derivable from the literalness of the number."[26]

Typical Prophecy

The subject of typology is a most difficult one. Affirmations on typology contain so many exceptions that soon the exceptions begin to overrule the rules. Patrick Fairbairn exclaims in despair, "The landmarks that are set up today are again shifted tomorrow."[27] Oswald T. Allis says that typology is "very difficult; and it is easy to make mistakes, even serious mistakes, in dealing with it."[28] Special care is therefore necessary in the treatment of typical prophecy.

Description of Typology

The word τύπος *(tupos, type)* carries the basic idea of an impression, a blow, or a stamp. New Testament writers use it to designate a pattern, a model, or an example. The apostle Paul instructs young Timothy to be "an *example* of those who believe" (1 Tim. 4:12) and challenges the Thessalonians to be "an *example* to all the believers" (1 Thess. 1:7). The word can also be used in a more technical sense: "Adam, who is a *type* of Him who was to come" (Rom. 5:14).

Since the word *type* is thus used quite loosely in the New Testament, it is difficult to make an exact definition of a type based on the Scriptures. Donald K. Campbell's definition, however, is solid: "A type is an Old Testament institution, event, person, object, or ceremony which has reality and purpose in Biblical history, but which also by divine design foreshadows something yet to be revealed."[29]

A large group of things and events in the Old Testament are uniquely related to elements in the New Testament. These resemblances are divinely intended and beautifully exemplify the organic unity of the Word of God. As the *New Scofield Reference Bible* points out, typology "illustrates the principle that prophetic utterances often have a latent and deeper meaning than at first appears."[30]

The Messiah anticipated in the Old Testament becomes the New Testament's Christ (cf. Heb. 1), the Old Testament sacrificial system looks forward to the finality of the cross, and the requirement of faith as life-principle extends from the Old Testament to the New. It is these scriptural similarities and resemblances that give birth to the subject of Bible typology.

There are of course certain things in the Old Testament that do not relate directly to those in the New Testament and should not be interpreted under type-antitype relationship. The different peoples of God (Israel and the Christian church) are not identical concepts, and the kingdom prophesied in the Old Testament does not become the New Testament church.

As far as basic natures and characters are concerned, a type is no different from a prophecy. Prophecies and types both point to things future and are predictive in their natures. *Types*, however, are to be distinguished from *prophecies* in their respective forms. That is, a type prefigures coming reality; a prophecy verbally delineates the future. A type is expressed in events, persons, and acts; a prophecy is couched in words and statements. A type is passive in form, a prophecy active.

Some interpreters see an antithesis between typological interpretation and literal interpretation—the interpretation of types automatically rules out literal interpretation. They affirm that it is impossible to interpret typologically and literally at the same time. "It is difficult to understand how two such methods of interpretation as the *literal* and the *typological*—so completely opposite to one another as they appear to be—can not only be adopted by the same student of Scripture, but by that student pushed to their utmost limits!" exclaims a nonliteralist.[31]

Typological interpretation, however, is not a different method of interpretation. What is interpreted arises from the text and is shown to have a higher application of the same sense of that text. The historical reality and existence of the type is never denied. Its typical prefigurement springs from a literal, historical base. When we say that the Passover lamb of the Jews is a type of Christ (1 Cor. 5:7), we are not denying the historicity of Passover lambs vicariously slain in every Jewish home the night of the Exodus. We have projected a higher application of the Passover lambs to Christ, the Lamb of God.

Typological interpretation is, therefore, the unfolding of the literal base of the type, not the allegorization of that which is typified. Typological interpretation is the literal interpretation of types. When an Old Testament element is said to be a type of an element in the New, this does not mean that one *equals* the other. One element may prefigure another and the resemblance between the two may be very close, but a type never equals its antitype. The Old Testament sacrificial lamb typifies—but does not equal—Christ. "It is one thing to say that Israel *typifies* the Church, as premillennialists rightly do; it is quite another thing to say that Israel is the Church, as amillennialists wrongly teach."[32]

Extent of Typology

No one has been able to compile a comprehensive list of persons, events, and features in the Old Testament that have typical significances. It is extremely difficult to define which Old Testament persons, objects, and occurrences properly constitute a type.

Two extreme positions exist with regard to the extent of typology. The fanciful typologists see types lurking everywhere and anywhere in Scripture. Designation of types is by the imagination of the interpreter. This method of interpretation should not be tolerated. The other extreme declares that nothing in the Bible is a type unless the New Testament explicitly states it. That is, a type is not a type unless the New Testament specifically says so. "Whatever persons or things, therefore, recorded in the Old Testament, were *expressly declared by Christ or by His apostles* to have been designated as prefigurements of persons or things relating to the Old Testament," states Bishop Marsh, "such persons or things so recorded in the former are types of the persons of things with which they are compared in the latter" (italics added).[33]

We must be careful that extreme positions do not influence us in deciding the extent of typology, for it is between these two extremes that the real extent of biblical typology lies. It is safe to assume that a divinely designated type exists when ① the Scripture expressly states it, ② an interchange of name exists, and ③ there is an evident and manifest analogy. For instance, the Scripture indicates that Adam is a type of Christ (Rom. 5:14); the Passover is a type because Christ's name is interchanged with it (1 Cor. 5:7, "Christ our Passover"); and Joseph is typical of Christ because both lives are analogous in many respects.

Types must be based on either the explicit or the implicit teachings of Scripture. Imagination has no place in typology. One's sanctity is not gauged by the number of types one can see in Scripture. Areas of the Bible where most typical materials might be found are the Old Testament tabernacle with its priesthood and offerings and the wilderness wanderings of the Israelites.

Interpretation of Types

There are a few do's and don'ts that should be observed during typological interpretation:

1 *Use good sense*. Types are like wild flowers; their beauty is

spoiled by too much cultivation. The interpreter should refrain from poking into every nook and corner of the tabernacle or every facet of the patriarchs' lives in search of types. Interpreters must discipline themselves severely in this regard.

[2] *Base the interpretation on clear analogy.* The *Scofield Bible Correspondence* course cautions that "types are interpreted by their use in the New Testament and by their analogy with clearly revealed doctrines."[34] There should be a clear resemblance, connection, and design between type and antitype. Jonah's experience inside the fish is a type of Christ in the tomb (Matt. 12:40), and the Passover Lamb typifies the Savior, Jesus Christ (1 Cor. 5:7).

[3] *Do not teach doctrines by types.* It is legitimate for interpreters to illustrate doctrines by the use of types. Peter used the Noahic Flood to illustrate baptism (1 Peter 3:21), and Paul used the primeval creation of light to illustrate God's work of light in the heart (2 Cor. 4:6). Modern interpreters may also do this. It is never right, however, for modern interpreters to teach doctrines by types. Of course, the writer of Hebrews did use types to teach and prove doctrine, but Bible writers wrote under divine inspiration. We do not.

[4] *Do not limit the antitype to an unreal fulfillment.* Prefigurements of types are not necessarily always in terms of unreality, spirituality, and the heavenly. The madman Antiochus Epiphanes typifies the antichrist (Dan. 11), who will appear during the tribulation in person. The unfolding of the type into the antitype can be from the literal to the literal, not necessarily from the literal to the nonliteral. Louis Berkhof thus overstates the case when he says, "To pass from the type to the antitype is to ascend from that in which the carnal preponderates to that which is purely spiritual, from the external to the internal, from the present to the future, from the earthly to the heavenly."[35]

[5] *Be cautious with an expanded typology.* As Bernard Ramm says, "Whenever we draw out an ethical principle, a spiritual rule, or a devotional from the Old Testament which is not a matter of its literal expression we have made a typological interpretation."[36] Here we have left the area of typology proper and entered what we may call *applicational typology.* Typology is thus given its widest possible definition and application and enters the area of the nontechnical.

Messianic Prophecy and Typology

The coming of the Messiah and the redemption He shall bring is the theme of a group of Bible prophecies known as the *messianic prophecies.* A large percentage of these messianic prophecies come in the form of types.

Types of the Messiah are found not only in verbal prognostications but also in certain Old Testament offices and institutions, historical leaders, and individual happenings that prefigure Christ and His redemptive work. The Old Testament sacrifices; the Passover; the brazen serpent (John 3:14–15); the Jewish temple (John 2:19); the cities of refuge (Heb. 6:18); Jacob's ladder (John 1:45–51); aspects of the lives of Adam, Melchizedek, David, Solomon, and others all have divinely intended typical prefigurements in Christ.

The first coming of the great Antitype, Christ, is an event so stupendous that many Old Testament saints actually lived life patterns that would prefigure His earthly experience centuries later. David and his devouring zeal for God's house (Ps. 69:9, "The zeal of thine house hath eaten me up") prefigures Christ's zeal for the house of God. Israel's history of sorrow and tears (Jer. 31:15) looks toward Herod's slaying of the infants following the birth of the Messiah (Matt. 2:17–28).

Many messianic prophecies, especially in the Psalms and Proverbs, can be primarily applied only to Christ. Psalm 16:10 ("neither wilt thou suffer thine Holy One to see corruption") cannot fit the life of David, whose body saw corruption.[37] As Patrick Fairbairn observes, "The plain import of the words seems to carry us directly to Christ, while it requires a certain strain to be put upon them before they can properly apply to the case of David."[38]

On the other hand, one must not interpret the messianic prophecies separately from their respective historical contexts. Herein lies the genius of typological interpretation. While allegorists see deeper and "real" meanings under Old Testament events and lives, typologists rightly see both the historic and the messianic blended under divine designation and unfolded according to set time factors.

This chapter is adapted from Paul Lee Tan, *The Interpretation of Prophecy* (Dallas: Bible Communications, 1974), 152–74.

PART 2

Interpretive Systems
Throughout History

CHAPTER 7

The Early Church Fathers and the Foundations of Dispensationalism

For decades, dispensationalists have endured the charge that, prior to John Nelson Darby (1800–1882) and the Plymouth Brethren, there are no historical antecedents for their doctrine. Millard J. Erickson, for example, asserts flatly that "No trace of this theology can be found in the early history of the church."[1] And Clarence B. Bass declares that "No dispensational writer has ever been able to offer . . . a single point of continuity between what is today known as dispensationalism and the historic premillennial view."[2]

Such charges by non-dispensationalists are to be expected, but today the same charge is coming from within dispensational ranks. In his review of *Progressive Dispensationalism*, authored by Craig A. Blaising and Darrell L. Bock, Walter A. Elwell reports that "It is . . . nice not to be told that virtually everyone in church history was a dispensationalist. . . . Blaising and Bock maintain that dispensationalism is both recent and different from most of what went before it."[3]

Elwell's accusation that dispensationalists have claimed "everyone in church history" as their own is an exaggeration. But Blaising and Bock's attempt to detach dispensationalism from its historic roots requires a careful response. Dispensational premillennialism is neither as "recent" nor as "different from most of what went before it" as these two scholars claim.

Dispensationalists like Charles C. Ryrie, Arnold D. Ehlert, and many others rightly maintain that "features" or rudimentary concepts of dispensational theology were held by the fathers of the early church and later by certain individuals after the Reformation.[4] While Ryrie

87

and Ehlert readily acknowledge that *modern*, systematized dispensationalism must be traced to Darby,[5] they insist that historical and theological antecedents exist for this system of theology even in the patristic era.

The Theological Context

In order to evaluate the writings of the fathers for dispensational concepts, it is necessary to set forth the main features of "classic" or "normative" dispensational theology as presented by men like C. I. Scofield, Lewis Sperry Chafer, and Charles C. Ryrie. Perhaps the best recent definition of dispensationalism that incorporates the essential features of (1) the distinction between Israel and the church, (2) the hermeneutical principle of literal or normal interpretation, and (3) the purpose of God in history as the glorification of Himself is that formulated by Robert P. Lightner.[6] He defines dispensationalism,

> as that system of theology which interprets the Bible literally—according to normal usage—and places primary emphasis on the major biblical covenants—Abrahamic, Palestinian, Davidic, New—and sees the Bible as the unfolding of distinguishable economies in the outworking of God's major purpose to bring glory to Himself.[7]

In keeping with this belief that God's primary purpose is self-glorification, Ryrie suggests that the goal of history is the future millennial kingdom in which the glory of God will be uniquely manifested to all mankind.[8] It is clear that this system of theology is closely associated with and intimately involved in the study of eschatology.

In this regard, Ryrie sets forth the following as the salient features of dispensational eschatology: (1) *the hermeneutical principle of literal interpretation,* which leads to a belief in (2) *the literal fulfillment of Old Testament prophecies,* which in turn causes one to recognize (3) *a clear distinction between Israel and the church,* out of which the concept of (4) *the pretribulation rapture of the church* grows, and the belief in (5) *a literal, earthly millennial kingdom* during which the covenant promises to Israel will be fulfilled.[9]

The Rudimentary Features

Literal Interpretation

During the first centuries, the church's leaders were faced with a myriad of problems. With neither an established canon of either

Testament nor principles of interpretation other than those of the rabbinical schools, and with the three-pronged challenge of heresy from within and Judaism and paganism from without, it is not surprising that the practice of biblical exegesis was anything but uniform.[10] In varying degrees, the early fathers combined the allegorical method of interpretation—which had come down through the pagan Greeks and subsequently Alexandrian Jews like Philo—with the literal method.

With respect to principles of hermeneutics, the apostolic fathers seemed to pursue one of two lines: (1) either they followed a moderate, straightforward path between literalism and allegorism (e.g., Clement, Ignatius, Polycarp, *The Didache*), or (2) they leaned heavily upon the allegorical method (e.g., Barnabas, Hermas). In Barnabas' case, the practice was in opposition to the strict literalism of the Jews. On the whole, these earliest fathers simply interpreted the biblical text without any discussion of the method employed.

A new trend began early in the first century, however, and continued for the next one hundred and fifty years. Even though a fair amount of artificial exegesis was produced by Justin Martyr's practice of plundering the Old Testament for what he perceived to be its teachings concerning Christ, he nevertheless became one of the first to argue forcefully for a literal interpretation of prophecy. This trend to literalism became even more pronounced in Irenaeus and Tertullian. It was no coincidence that these fathers were all millenarians.

But what was to become of the literal method of interpretation and its progeny—the millennial expectation? With the rising popularity of the allegorical method, belief in a literal millennial reign of Christ seems to have reached a turning point in the middle of the third century. The Egyptian bishop Coracion, who succeeded Nepos, buckled under pressure from Alexandria and abandoned the staunch millennialism of his predecessor.[11] And Hippolytus, the pupil of Irenaeus, is said to have wavered in his stance as well.[12]

Israel and the Church

In the ante-Nicene age, the relationship between Israel and the church was expressed primarily in terms of faith in Christ and the seed of Abraham.[13] The prevailing view among the millenarian fathers was that Israel as a nation had been set aside by God because of her idolatry and unfaithfulness in Old Testament times and her rejection and crucifixion of Christ in the New Testament. Consequently, according to these early fathers, God's favor was transferred to those among the Gentiles who believed in Christ. Thus, as the "new Israel," the church inherited the promises made to the old Israel.

Lest covenant amillennialists claim support for their system from these fathers, we hasten to point out the following. In the first place, though not systematically presented, the early fathers recognized three categories of the *seed of Abraham* in Scripture: (1) the physical seed (descendants) of Abraham, particularly through Jacob; (2) the physical/spiritual seed of Abraham, i.e., those among the physical seed who like Abraham were justified by faith; and (3) the spiritual seed of Abraham who are not of his physical seed, i.e., Gentile believers also justified by faith like Abraham. With these distinctions in view, the fathers nowhere made Israel the church or the church national Israel.[14]

In the second place, in contrast to the covenant amillennial view, it was no strictly spiritual kingdom for which these early Christian leaders looked. Nor did they equate the church with the kingdom.[15] While the fathers certainly recognized the spiritual dimension of Christ's coming kingdom, at the same time they believed in a literal fulfillment of the covenants made with Abraham and David.

Dispensational Distinctions

In the writings of the fathers, it is possible to find distinctions and divisions of human history based upon God's dealings with humanity.[16] Non-dispensationalists freely admit that the fathers frequently employed the word *dispensation* and set forth multi-age schemes, but these were time-period divisions devoid of significant theological import. C. Norman Kraus's position is typical.

Kraus, a Mennonite author, notes that the word *dispensation* combines the two ideas of a time period—from the Greek word *aion* and translated "age" or "world"—with "something of the meaning of the New Testament word *oikonomia,* which means a plan, arrangement, stewardship, or dispensation." Kraus concludes from this that "dispensations, then, are periods of time which can be clearly discerned and marked off from other periods by the changing methods which God employs in dealing with mankind. They are stages in God's developing plan of the ages."[17]

Elsewhere, Kraus opines, "The age schemes which were developed by Christian scholars prior to the contemporary dispensationalist movement were generally historical in nature." In this regard, he points out the prevalence of the year-day theory in the early church.[18] The corollary for Kraus is that the divisions have little if any theological basis.

Several of the fathers set forth dispensational systems that had nothing to do with time periods. Their focus, rather, was on God's redemptive dealings with humankind. Justin Martyr, for example, presented a fourfold dispensational system (fivefold if the millennium is counted separately), which was based almost exclusively upon the failures of God's people.[19] With the failure in each economy, there was a corresponding institution of new rites to aid in the nurture of faith and in the quest for righteousness and justification before God. With slight variations, at least the bare outline of Justin's scheme was repeated by Irenaeus, Tertullian, Victorinus of Petau, and Methodius.[20]

We find ourselves in basic agreement, then, with Clarence E. Mason, who writes,

> The argument for dispensationalism is sustained by a multiple-age dealing of God with man in His progressive self-revelation. Men of the early church believed and wrote about these various eras. They spoke of various ages. That none of them codified these ages specifically as dispensationalists do today does not deny that they could have been so codified. It is simply not true that there are only two covenants and thus two ages.[21]

Mason continues, "Dispensationalism had its roots in the very theses of early church chiliasm."[22] Walvoord affirms the same when he contends that "dispensationalism should be considered not a new doctrine, but a refinement of premillennialism such as was held by the early fathers. A similar refinement can be observed in all major doctrines in the history of the church."[23]

Patristic Premillennialism

Belief in the premillennial return of Christ was a settled doctrinal principle in the ante-Nicene church. In summarizing premillennial teachings, Walvoord writes,

> Premillennialism generally holds to a revival of the Jewish nation and their repossession of their ancient land when Christ returns. Satan will be bound (Rev. 20:2) and a theocratic kingdom of righteousness, peace, and tranquillity will ensue. The righteous are raised from the dead before the millennium and participate in its blessings. The wicked dead are not raised until after the millennium.[24]

The early church regarded this millenarian expectation as one of the fundamentals of orthodox Christianity. So widely diffused was the doctrine that noted church historian Philip Schaff calls it "The most striking point in the eschatology of the ante-Nicene age."[25] Schaff's conclusion is supported by the testimony of many other dispensationalists and nondispensationalists alike.

A unique element of premillennial teaching is the belief that the resurrection of the dead will occur in two main stages. In preparation for the millennium, the resurrection of the righteous or just will take place when Christ returns at the end of the present age (1 Cor. 15:22–23; 1 Thess. 4:14–17; John 5:28; Rev. 20:4). The resurrection of the wicked or unjust, however, will occur at the conclusion of the millennium in preparation for the judgment at the Great White Throne (Rev. 20:13).[26] The twofold resurrection doctrine is clearly taught by some of the millenarian fathers.

Imminent Intratribulationism

Dispensationalists hold that the resurrection and rapture of the just will occur not only before the millennial kingdom but also prior to the seven-year tribulation period (see Dan. 9). The key element of this pretribulational doctrine is the imminence of Christ's return for the saints. Several church fathers admonished believers to live in daily expectation that the Lord could come for His people at any moment. Henry C. Thiessen summarizes early patristic views on the great tribulation this way:

> In the testimony of the early Fathers there is an almost complete silence on the subject. They frequently speak of tribulations, but very seldom of a future period known as "the" Tribulation. . . .
> Though on the whole the testimony of the Fathers is somewhat inconsistent, we seem to have in Hermas: The Shepherd, . . . a fairly clear indication of the fact that there were those who believed that the Church would be taken away before that period of judgment begins.[27]

With reference to the imminence of the Lord's second coming, Thiessen asserts that,

> It is clear . . . that the Fathers held not only the pre-millennial view of Christ's coming, but also regarded that coming as imminent. The Lord had taught them to expect His return

at any moment, and so they looked for Him to come in their day. Not only so, but they also taught His personal return as being immediately, with the exception of the Alexandrian Fathers, who also rejected other fundamental doctrines. We may say, therefore, that the early Church lived in the constant expectation of their Lord, and hence was not interested in the possibility of a Tribulation period in the future.[28]

Walvoord identifies imminence as the central feature of pretribulationism.[29] In fact, the position of the early fathers, says Walvoord,[30] was a type of imminent posttribulationism with an occasional pretribulational inference.[31] The term *imminent intratribulationism* is perhaps more descriptive of the tribulational views of the millenarian fathers, and at the same time precludes the inaccurate perceptions one might get from the term *posttribulationism*.

The reason for the fathers' peculiar hybrid view of the tribulation is, no doubt, attributable to their persistence, like the Israelites caught between God and Baal (1 Kings 18:21), in hesitating between two positions. On the one hand, Scripture clearly teaches that Christ's coming could occur at any moment and therefore the believer is to live his life in holiness and with an attitude of expectancy. On the other hand, until Constantine's Edict of Milan, which granted Christianity full legal toleration (A.D. 313), persecutions of every sort were a present reality for believers in the Roman Empire. For many, the persecutions, coupled with a belief that Christians must be tested and purified by fire (i.e., trials in the form of persecutions for Christ's sake) to make them fit for God's kingdom, led to something like the Thessalonian error. The church, it was reasoned, was already in the tribulation. Therefore, it could expect the any-moment return of the Lord.

Ryrie affirms that the church fathers were not dispensationalists in the modern sense to be sure, but "some of them enunciated principles which later developed into dispensationalism, and it may be rightly said that they held to primitive or early dispensational-like concepts."[32] Many biblical principles and concepts held by the millenarian fathers were in an embryonic state. And while elements of their teachings lack the sophistication and systematic presentation the modern scholar might like, it should be remembered that these "doctors" of the primitive church lived on the frontier of Christian theological formulation.

This chapter was adapted from Larry V. Crutchfield, "The Early Church Fathers and the Foundations of Dispensationalism—Part I," *The Conservative Theological Journal* 2, no. 4 (March 1998): 19–31.

CHAPTER 8

The Allegorists Who Undermined the Normal Interpretation of Scripture

In this chapter it will be shown that the early church was overwhelmingly premillennial. Many of the interpretative battles of today did not, of course, exist for the early church. Thus, they did not deal with the same hermeneutical issues. But they had philosophical wars that dealt with the deity and nature of Christ, the person of the Holy Spirit, and the nature of the Trinity. The church fathers argued, fought well, and won many doctrinal conflicts, thus establishing the teaching framework of the Word for generations to come. Allegory, however, became their Achilles heel. How did allegorical interpretation begin? Actually, it began before the church age.

Pagan Greek Allegory

By the time of Xenophanes in the sixth century B.C., the literature of Homer was under attack because the gods appeared too sinful and human. By the time of Plato, Homer's poems were taken as symbolic, to be read allegorically. Plato agreed but felt that the poems were too disgraceful to be read to children in their literal form.

By the first century A.D., Heraclitus taught the scandalous passages in Homer as allegory. To explain the behavior of the gods, Heraclitus wrote *The Homeric Problem*, in which he offers alternative poetic allegorical interpretations for the sexual affairs of Aphrodite and others.

For example, as Heraclitus saw it,

> The ribald laughter of the gods at the hapless pair (Aphrodite
> and her lover Ares) signifies their joy at the cosmic harmony
> that results from the union of love (Aphrodite) and strife
> (Ares, the god of war). The passage can also be interpreted
> metallurgically. Fire (Hephaestus) unites iron (Ares) with
> beauty (Aphrodite) in the blacksmith's art.[1]

With allegory the antics of the gods were purified, but who determined the allegorical interpretations? By whose authority were words and concepts changed? If there were no "guidelines" as to the meaning of the "new" message, how did readers know the authors' intentions? These problems consistently overshadow allegorical interpretation.

Alexandrian Jews Copy Allegorism

Following the Babylonian captivity, the Jewish rabbis fell into quasi-worship of even the letters of Scripture, adopting "letterism" as a springboard to allegorization and spiritualization. They committed the sin about which Paul later wrote: "The letter kills, but the Spirit gives life" (2 Cor. 3:6). To their credit, not all the rabbis fell into letterism or, later, allegory. The majority held to a sane literalism whereby they took the Old Testament promises in a natural and normal way. Tan writes,

> The Jewish rabbis did not really misuse the literal method.
> Literalism and letterism are two different things. It was the
> exclusion of any more than the bare letters of Scripture which
> set the rabbis on a tangent. Letterism is the premature (not
> extreme) form of literalism. The interpreter who is properly
> conversant with the literal method of interpretation can never
> be too literal in interpreting God's Word.[2]

Tan further explains that the Jews in Alexandria, Egypt, had daily contact with the Greek philosophers of the day and noticed how allegory cleaned up the uglier exploits of the Greek gods.[3] With distasteful portions of the Old Testament to deal with (such as Lot's incest, Noah's drunkenness, Jacob's many wives, etc.), the rabbis began to allegorize certain passages. "Allegorism enabled the Alexandrian Jews to make Moses speak the beautiful philosophy of Plato and other Greek sages."[4]

Who Was Philo?

The personality most cited for the change to allegorical interpretation is Philo (ca. 20 B.C.–A.D. 54), "A philosophical Jew who possessed both reverence for the Mosaic revelation and fondness for Grecian metaphysics, [who] aimed to explore the mystical depths of significances allegedly concealed beneath the Old Testament Scripture."[5]

Philo taught that the milk of Scripture was the literal but the meat was allegory. Thus, there was a hidden meaning. The Word of God had two levels: the literal was on the surface, but the allegorical represented the deeper, more spiritual meaning. Therefore, anyone who simply interpreted the Bible in its most natural, normal way was simple and missing the great meanings of the Scriptures. Ramm writes,

> Philo did not think that the literal meaning was useless, but it represented the immature level of understanding. The literal sense was the body of Scripture, and the allegorical sense its soul. Accordingly the literal was for the immature, and the allegorical for the mature.[6]

To reiterate, allegorical interpretation creates meaning through the interpreter. Accordingly, an allegorist believes the average person may be reading and interpreting wrongly without the help of a scholar or, in the case of Scripture, a wise, well-trained theologian. Often, even today, allegorists look down their noses at those who take the Bible at face value with a normal, literal hermeneutic.

In Philo's writings are thousands of examples of his allegorization of the Old Testament. Only a few will be cited here. In the creation of Eve, for example, when Adam's side was closed up (Gen. 2:21), Philo writes, "That is to say, he [God] filled up that external sense which exists according to habit, leading it on to energy and extending it as far as the flesh and the whole outward and visible surface of the body."[7]

Genesis 2:24 reads, "Therefore a man shall leave his father and mother and be joined to his wife, and they shall become one flesh." Philo says,

> On account of the external sensation, the mind, when it has become enslaved to it, shall leave both its father, the God of the universe, and the mother of all things, namely, the virtue and wisdom of God, and cleaves to and becomes united to

the external sensations, and is dissolved into external sensation, so that the two become one flesh and one passion.[8]

The Negative Effects of Philo

Philo was a mystic and a Platonist, whose "tampering" with the meaning of Old Testament texts would have long range negative effects on Christianity. His writings were preserved by some of the Church fathers because he had resisted Greek authors and Hellenistic thought. But he would have great influence on many of the Alexandrian church fathers.

Is There a Connection Today Between Philo and Amillennial Theologians?

Varner correctly notes in regard to Philo's legacy,

> The Alexandrian method greatly influenced medieval hermeneutics and resulted in the displacement of premillennialism with amillennialism after Augustine.
>
> While most of evangelical hermeneutics has abandoned the Alexandrian allegorical method as applied to the narrative portions of Scripture, it is still inconsistently applied to the prophetic portions of the Old Testament, resulting in spiritualized interpretation of such terms as Israel, Jerusalem, and Zion. On a more popular level, many sermons unconsciously reflect the Philonic emphasis or number symbolism and illegitimate spiritual interpretations of texts.[9]

Pentecost well concludes,

> The allegorical method was not born out of the study of the Scriptures, but rather out of a desire to unite Greek philosophy and the Word of God. It did not come out of a desire to present the truths of the Word, but to pervert them. It was not the child of orthodoxy but of heterodoxy.[10]

Who Was Origen?

Origen (ca. A.D. 185–254), often called "Mr. Allegorism," followed Philo in searching both Old and New Testaments for the deep and hidden spiritual meanings. Origen's work, *On First Principles,* argues that if no spiritual significance is found on the surface of a Bible passage, it may be concluded that the verses are to be taken symbolically. Allegory, which was a legacy from Greece, dominated much of Origen's biblical thought.

In a short time, Origen "made allegory the dominant method of biblical interpretation down to the end of the Middle Ages. . . . It took no genius to recognize that such allegory was a desperate effort to avoid the plain meaning of the text, and that, indeed, is how Origen viewed it."[11]

How Did Philo Influence Origen?

In time, Philo's approach to Bible interpretation fell out of favor with the rabbis. But it lived long enough to be transmitted down to many Christian interpreters who accepted it enthusiastically. Origen probably became familiar with Philo's works, of which he thoroughly approved, through Clement. Trigg further explains,

> The circumstances in which Christianity developed into a religious tradition independent of Judaism gave allegory from the very first a strong appeal to Christians. Christians retained the Old Testament, which for some time was their only Bible, as their sacred Scriptures, but they quickly found it appropriate to cease demanding literal observance of the commandments of the Torah. Allegory enabled Christians to justify their abandonment of the ceremonial law.[12]

Concerning biblical prophecy, Origen rejected the popular Christian hope of the coming earthly millennial reign of Jesus. As a result, he questioned the authenticity of Revelation, which so clearly speaks of such a millennium, and treated the book symbolically.[13] He wrote, in fact, that Christ's coming in the clouds, as described in Matthew 24:30, referred to the Lord's coming into the souls of the openhearted when they accepted the basic truths of doctrine. In Origen's thinking, "His [Christ's second] coming" occurred when the mature Christian found Jesus in the hidden meanings of Scripture.

On some of Origen's other prophetic views, Trigg makes this most interesting comment:

> The trials and tribulations the world must endure before the second coming symbolize the difficulties the soul must overcome before it is worthy of union with the Logos. The imminence of the second coming refers to the imminent possibility, for each individual, of death. Perhaps more radically, the two men laboring in a field, one of whom is taken

and the other left when the Messiah comes (Matt. 24:40), represent good and bad influences on a person's will, which fare differently when the Logos is revealed to that person. Although Origen did not openly deny the vivid apocalyptic expectations such passages originally expressed and still did for many Christians, he tended by psychologizing them to make them irrelevant. Although that was far from Origen's intention, the outcome of his work was to make the church feel distinctly more at home in the world.[14]

Trigg's last line has far-reaching implications. Crutchfield on Origen concludes,

Origen's allegorical interpretations, including his views on Bible prophecy, gained wide acceptance in the church of his day. His influence, followed by Constantine's acceptance of Christianity and Augustine's teaching in the fourth century, are usually cited as the principal causes of premillennialism's eventual replacement by amillennial eschatology. Though he was broken by the persecution under Decius in 250 and died a few years later at the age of sixty-nine, Origen's exegesis still colors prophetic expectations in modern times.[15]

Who Was Augustine?

Augustine (A.D. 354–430) was a godly, sincere follower of Christ. His most well-known works, *The City of God* and *Confessions* , have inspired believers for centuries. Despite good intentions, however, Augustine followed Origen into the crevice of allegorical interpretation. By Augustine's day, though, many had already adopted the pagan Greek system of approaching the meaning of Scripture. But this saintly church father developed a compromise in dealing with certain truths.

That is, he interpreted the non-prophetic Scriptures literally and the prophetic Scriptures allegorically. This dualistic method of interpretation represents a new twist to the allegorical interpretation then on a rampage. Unfortunately for the church, Augustinian dualism was accepted without much debate into the Roman Catholic church, and later also by the Protestant reformers.

Augustine, while rejecting the earthly, millennial kingdom accepted the literality of the 1,000 years of Revelation 20

and expected the second coming of Christ to occur around
A.D. 650. This inconsistency in spiritualizing portions of Revelation 20 while literalizing its 1,000 years is an evidence
that the church father did not give a reasonable exegesis to
this subject.[16]

Augustine, despite his interpretative shortcomings, systematized
the study of sacred Scripture by developing principles for approaching the Word of God. Ramm summarizes twelve of Augustine's most
important guidelines:

1. A genuine Christian faith was necessary for the understanding of the Scriptures.
2. Although the literal and historical are not the end of Scripture, we must hold them in high regard.
3. Scripture has more than one meaning and therefore the allegorical method is proper.
4. There is significance in biblical numbers. The entire world of
   logic and numbers are to be regarded as eternal truths, with
   numbers playing a special role in human knowledge.
5. The Old Testament is a Christian document and is full of prophetic references concerning Christ.
6. The task of the expositor is to derive meaning from the Bible,
   not bring meaning to it. The expositor is to express accurately
   the thoughts of the writer.
7. The analogy of faith, the true orthodox creed, must be consulted when interpreting. If orthodoxy represents Scripture, then
   no expositor can interpret Scripture contrary to orthodoxy.
8. No verse is to be studied as a unit in itself. The context of the
   verse must be noted, i.e., what the Bible says on the same
   subject somewhere else.
9. If an interpretation is uncertain, nothing in the passage can
   be made a matter of orthodox faith.
10. The Holy Spirit cannot substitute for the necessary learning
    to understand Scripture. The able interpreter must know He-
    brew, Greek, geography, natural history, music, chronology,
    numbers, history, dialectics, natural science, and the ancient
    philosophers.
11. The obscure passage must yield to the clear passage.
12. No Scripture is to be interpreted so as to conflict with any
    other—the harmony of revelation.[17]

Augustine and the Book of Revelation

The Alexandrian school of theology, represented by Clement and Origen, took an allegorical or nonliteral view of the final book of inspired Scripture. Walvoord notes,

> The more moderate form of allegorical interpretation, following Augustine, has achieved respectability and regards the book of Revelation as presenting in a symbolic way the total conflict between Christianity and evil or, as Augustine put it, the City of God versus the City of Satan.[18]

But Augustine also espoused the preterist (or past) view of Revelation. Walvoord calls preterist interpretation similar to allegory, yet it considers Revelation as a symbolic *history* rather than prophetic. But it is Lange who ascribes preterism to Augustine. "This theory is so styled as it was first propounded by the great Augustine in his *Civitate Dei (The City of God)*, xx. 7–9 [of Revelation]. It has been upheld in all ages of the Church since its first promulgation."[19] Lange summarizes Augustine on Revelation:

1. The period [of Revelation] began at the first Advent [of Christ], when Satan was bound and cast out of the hearts of true Christians and their reign over him . . . began.
2. The Beast symbolizes the wicked world.
3. The first resurrection is that of dead souls to spiritual life, a resurrection continued in every true conversion throughout the period.
4. The thousand years is a symbolic expression of completeness appropriately indicating the entire period of the Messiah's reign.
5. This period [is] to be followed by a new persecution of the Saints under Antichrist; . . . [then] the general judgment; after which will begin, in heaven, the glorious period of the New Jerusalem.[20]

The Literal Millennial Kingdom Discredited

Cohn shows that with Augustine the interpretative climate would be finally and completely changed.

> Early in the fifth century St. Augustine propounded the doctrine which the new conditions demanded. According to *The City of God* the Book of Revelation was to be understood as

a spiritual allegory; as for the Millennium, that had begun with the birth of Christianity and was fully realized in the Church. This at once became orthodox doctrine.[21]

Crutchfield aptly concludes,

Augustine abandoned the premillennial position for the superficial reason that some millenarians had envisioned a kingdom age of unparalleled fruitfulness featuring banquet tables set with excessive amounts of food and drink (*The City of God* 20.7). He favored instead the position of his contemporary, the Donatist and lay theologian Tyconius who offered a spiritualized interpretation of the Apocalypse. Proceeding from this position, Augustine articulated an amillennial view in which no future thousand-year earthly millennium was expected.[22]

CHAPTER 9

Calvinism, Dispensationalism, and Later History

Some in the Reformed tradition have difficulty reconciling Calvinism and dispensationalism, the belief being that a Calvinist cannot be a premillennialist, and all dispensationalists are, of course, premillennialists. The argument may be, "If Calvin didn't believe it, it's just not true!"

What a shame if Calvinists—and for that matter dispensationalists—follow a doctrinal system rather than the Word of God. For all believers in Christ, the ultimate authority is the Bible, not the teachings of a man, no matter how brilliant and spiritual that man may be.

But some staunch Calvinists give no quarter on dispensationalism, considering it almost cultish. Such an attitude is not only unfair, it reflects a lack of knowledge about what dispensationalists historically and doctrinally believe.

At the risk of seeming to cast a stone for a stone, many dispensationalists sense a certain elitism or superior air among our Reformed friends: "We are Reformed and covenant in our theology, and you are but a dispensationalist." Although this attitude is not exhibited in all who are theologically Reformed, in some instances a certain arrogance does indeed come through. Neither camp is correct in adopting such a superior outlook.

Early Dispensationalists Were Calvinists

Almost all of the early dispensationalists were Calvinists. Dispensationalism matured after the beginning of the nineteenth century in many Calvinistic circles. All who perceived the premillennial

104

message of Scripture, however, still held to distinctive Calvinistic theology. Those early scholars clung to the doctrines of inspiration of
Scripture, salvation by grace alone, eternal security, the sovereignty
and providence of God, divine election and predestination apart from
divine foreknowledge, and the sinfulness and total depravity of man.
These beliefs are still held by a majority of dispensationalists. Neither have dispensationalists cast off the doctrines of the Trinity, the
person and work of Christ, and the dynamic work of the Holy Spirit.

Though there are some minor differences and shades of belief,
the greatest doctrinal variations between covenant and dispensational advocates concern the rapture of the church, the issue of the
seven-year tribulation, and the prophesied premillennial coming of
Christ to reign on earth. Since history shows that a multitude in the
early church held to some of these beliefs, especially in reference to
premillennialism, dispensationalism cannot be the greatest of theological sins.

Though dispensationalism may be embraced by some of the
Arminian persuasion, including many charismatics and Pentecos-
tals, the distinctives of the system have nothing to do with Armin-
ianism or Calvinism per se.

In terms of American dispensationalism, George Mardsen, in "Introduction: Reformed and American" from the book *Reformed Theology in America: A History of Its Modern Development*, writes,

> Dispensationalism was essentially Reformed in its nineteenth-
> century origins and had in later nineteenth-century America
> spread most among revival-oriented Calvinists. Strict Old
> School confessionals were, however, uneasy with
> dispensationalist's separation of the Old Testament dispen-
> sation of Law from the era of Grace in the church age.
> Dispensationalism, accordingly, was accepted most readily
> by Reformed Christians who had a more New School, or
> revivalist-evangelical, emphasis than among the various Old
> School, or doctrinalist, groups.[1]

Mardsen further states that after World War II,

> The new evangelicals were largely Reformed in leadership
> and had moved away from strict dispensationalism. Institu-
> tionally they gained strength at centers such as Wheaton
> College, Fuller Theological Seminary, Trinity Evangelical
> Divinity School, and Gordon-Conwell Theological Seminary.[2]

This statement may be true for the 1970s and on, but earlier, Wheaton, Moody Bible Institute, and dozens of other dispensational schools that hired dispensational faculty, were clamoring for more men of the same mind-set who could best explain the Bible to their young students. These schools let it be known that they were seeking dispensational professors who, by their theology, would make the Bible clear and understandable. Too, dispensational instructors could be counted on to hold the line on inspiration and inerrancy of Scripture. As the urgency of teaching strong doctrine began to fade, and as many of the old dispensational schools developed a certain "sophistication," dispensational theology was no longer "in." Adding to the decline of academic interest in dispensationalism was a growing lack of interest in the return of the Jews to Palestine and biblical prophecy in general.

Pioneers of Normal, Consistent Bible Interpretation

The Reformation initiated a more consistent interpretation of Scripture and called for a literal and normal meaning of the biblical text. But old habits and thoughts die slowly. It must be remembered that the theological thinking of Catholicism was saturated with allegory, mysticism, hidden revelation, triple meaning of a passage, and the almost Godlike authority of the writings of the Church fathers.

The Reformers had to slice away at scholasticism and learn anew how to be objective. They had to overcome the theological accretions of hundreds of years of one interpretative system, forced upon all from the single doctrinal viewpoint of the medieval church.

The godly interpreters of the Reformed movement both succeeded and failed. They brought the Protestant churches back to a more sane, literal interpretation as a guiding theory, but they failed to be consistent. Seeming to have a blind spot in their spiritual vision, they continued to allegorize biblical prophecy.

For example, though the Old Testament clearly predicted a rebirth of the Jewish people, some Reformers loathed the Jews of their own generation and could never accept the return of the Jews to Palestine, much less their conversion to Christ. Thus, most biblical prophecy was couched in terms of fulfillment within their period of history. Prophetic truth was garbled, becoming so confusing, in fact, that Calvin refused to write a commentary on Revelation, feeling it was too mysterious and beyond his grasp.

A New Generation

But as the Reformation matured in its scope and impact, there arose men who pioneered a more consistent system of hermeneutics.

They were basically Calvinistic in persuasion, but many saw the prophecies as future events. They no longer interpreted biblical passages that spoke of the Jews returning to the land as applicable to the church. They envisioned a kingdom yet to be fulfilled where the Messiah-Savior would physically reign and rule in Jerusalem.

Nevertheless, these changes came slowly. The men who poured such energy into their Bible studies were still products of the Reformation, and most remained staunch Calvinists. But with the publishing of their renewed findings, a chasm would widen and soon separate those who retained allegory in prophecy and those who became premillennialists.

The premillennialists came to see the mistakes of the past. As if blinders dropped from their eyes, they understood the final chapter of world history that included a terrible future tribulation and a regathering of Israel, who would believe in Jesus their Messiah.

These premillennialists generally remained within their own associations and denominations. But they refreshed the church at large by quenching the thirst among laymen to learn more. In the eighteenth and nineteenth centuries, they fostered a support for the Jewish people that fostered a favorable attitude for their return to Palestine.

At the beginning of the twentieth century, *The Scofield Reference Bible* promoted sane and sensible Bible study. Prophecy was explained and history was better understood. Popular evangelism was given an impetus. And since prophecy must be based on revelation, the doctrine of the inspiration and authority of Scripture was given new meaning and respect.

Of course mistakes were made in the refining of premillennialism. Not all the pioneering scholars agreed on every prophetic point. For example, some held to only a few dispensations; others claimed upwards of seven dispensations. Some became extreme in their views. Others provided a balance that made for clearer Bible interpretation.

A Return to the Full Meaning of Scripture

It is appropriate here to list some of the humble and godly Bible teachers who aided the cause of literal and consistent interpretation of the Scriptures. We may not agree with everything each man taught. Some were unsure where they were going. But all groped forward with a love of and thirst for the Word of God.

Keep in mind the names included here are just a sampling. Certainly some men are left out who made even a greater impact than those listed below, but their contribution is lost in the silence of history. Only at the judgment of Christ will their efforts be weighed and rewarded.

John Bale (1495–1563)

Educated at Jesus College in Cambridge, England, Bale became a dramatist and a theologian of some reputation. Using drama, he showed the failure of the papacy and called for church reform. He was one of the first to divide world history into seven stages that closely parallel the seven dispensations. Bale also compared the seven ages of church history to the seven seals of Revelation.[3]

Joseph Mede (1586–1638)

Born in Essex, England, Mede is often called the father of English premillennialism. Holding his M.A. from Cambridge, he was one of the leading intellectuals of his day. A professor of Greek, Mede knew Hebrew well and was noted for his skills as a mathematician and logician. Applying his discipline to the study of prophecy, Mede focused his studies on the book of Revelation and held to the literal return of Christ and the reign of the Lord for a thousand years. Mede also saw in Scripture two judgments separated by the thousand-year kingdom. In his time, he was the outstanding millennial scholar in England.[4]

The Mathers

The Mathers, a seventeenth-century Puritan New England family, clearly held a premillennial viewpoint. Richard (1596–1669) immigrated to America in 1635. He later became an Oxford scholar who held a great interest in prophecy. He was a popular pastor, holding that office in Dorchester, Massachusetts, from 1636 to 1669. His son, Increase (1639–1723), was educated at Harvard and Dublin, Ireland. The most famous Mather was the son of Increase, Cotton (1663–1728). Educated at Harvard, Cotton joined his father in the pastorate in Boston and later took over the church when his father died.

John Davidson writes, "Historians are probably most familiar with the eschatological opinions of Increase and Cotton Mather, who have generally been cast in the roles of archetypical premillennialists of the period before the Great Awakening." Premillennialism is woven throughout the writings and sermons of the Mathers.[5]

Isaac Watts (1674–1748)

Born in Southampton, England, and the eldest of nine children, Watts became one of the most brilliant scholarly minds of his day.

He knew well Hebrew, Greek, Latin, grammar, hymnology, logic, the ancient classics, philosophy, and best of all, the Scriptures. He was ordained as a Puritan pastor in 1702. Because of his poetry and hymn writing, he influenced the singing and worship of churches for generations to come.

A controversy surrounded Watts about the doctrine of the Trinity, yet most believe he held firm to that doctrine to the end of his life. Watts may be one of the first clearly stated dispensationalists, believing there were seven running through the history of the Bible.[6]

John Gill (1679–1771)

Born in Kettering, Northamptonshire, Gill was raised in a pious family. John was forced to leave the local school at an early age because the schoolmaster insisted that all the school children attend prayer services in the local Anglican church. Because the family were members of the Particular Baptist congregation, this was impossible to do. Gill was an ardent student, mastering Latin and Greek at an early age, and later, he taught himself Hebrew with the help of a secondhand grammar and lexicon.[7]

Gill worked his way up from a deacon in his church to being recognized by friends and foes alike as one of the most respected teachers of the Word. He became pastor of the Horsleydown church in London and became a force to be reckoned with among the religious leaders of his day. A strong Calvinist, he became one of the most able scholars in reference to the ancient rabbinical writings of the Jews. In his commentaries, he quotes Jewish references more than any writer before or after him.

Because of his knowledge of the Jewish commentaries, Gill adopted a premillennial view of prophecy. But one must quickly note that this change was by degree, and it was certainly neither uniform nor consistent. He often allegorized one prophetic passage but took the next quite literally. In this, he was a product of his day, surrounded by amillennial views that were not easy to abandon. He also had growing and developing ideas about the rapture of the church. Gill wrote,

> The place whither he shall come, is the earth: . . . he shall stand on the earth in the latter day; though he shall not descend upon it at once; when he appears from the third heaven, he shall descend into the air, and there stay some time, until the dead saints are raised, and the living ones changed; and both are brought unto him there; and till the

new earth is made and prepared for him and them; when he and they will come down from heaven to earth, and they shall reign with him on it a thousand years; and he shall reign before his ancients [Old Testament Jews] gloriously.[8]

On the restoration of the Jewish people, Gill notes,

> . . . and since the blindness of the Jews is not yet removed, it seems plain that the full number of God's chosen ones among the Gentiles is not yet completed in regeneration; for as soon as ever they are all called and brought in, the vail [sic] will be taken away from the Jews, and they will be turned unto the Lord.
>
> . . . since there are a number of people among the Jews whom God has loved, and has chosen to everlasting salvation, and has in covenant promised to them, and secured and laid up gifts for them, and has determined to call them by his grace; and since all these are unchangeable and irreversible, the future call and conversion of these persons must be sure and certain.[9]

Jonathan Edwards (1703–1758)

Considered one of America's foremost thinkers, philosophers, and theologians, Edwards began his theological journey as an amillennialist. Eventually he converted to postmillennialism, seeing the millennium as the end of all of literal history. He believed that the days of glory would probably begin in America.

The millennial views of Edwards were a major factor in shaping the social events in New England that contributed to and resulted in the American Revolution. He saw Rome as the Antichrist and the millennium arriving around 1866. He believed the Great Awakening, along with technological advance, would herald the advancing kingdom. Following the millennium, there would be a great apostasy, a tribulation, and then the second coming of Christ.[10]

Morgan Edwards (1722–1792)

Born in Wales, Morgan was educated at Bristol College in England. Later he served several small Baptist congregations before ending up in Cork, Ireland. Later, he migrated to America and became pastor of the Baptist church in Philadelphia, having been recommended by John Gill. Edwards taught a developing premillennialism and, with Gill and others, refined the views about the rapture of the church. He saw correctly, as did Gill, the first resurrection, with the rapture in 1 Thessalonians 4:17. He wrote of believers meeting the Lord in the air and returning to the Father's house (John 14:2).

He saw the tribulation lasting only three and a half years, however, rather than seven. Many believe Edwards truly saw first, and in a most clear fashion, the proper biblical teaching on the rapture of the church.[11]

Robert Haldane (1764–1842)

Robert studied at Edinburgh University and was converted after brief careers in the British navy and as a successful landscape gardener. In 1795 he began funding mission work in India. Though the authorities stopped this mission work, he continued in ministerial work by establishing small theological seminaries in Scotland. He spent three years teaching in Geneva, where he had a profound influence on the Swiss and French churches. His commentary on Romans is considered one of the best ever written.

Though Reformed in theology, Haldane in his commentary on Romans 9–11 advocates a premillennial and literal return of Christ to establish the kingdom with literal Israel. He writes,

> And though Israel has for a long time departed from Him, yet thither at length will the Redeemer return, and make His word and law powerful to restore them unto Himself. "He shall set up an ensign for the nations, and shall assemble the outcasts of Israel, and gather together the dispersed of Judah from the four corners of the earth," Isa. xi. 12.
>
> In this prophecy, in the fifty-ninth chapter of Isaiah, God is represented as doing two things. One is, to reproach the Jews with the multitude and enormity of their transgressions; the other, to promise to them the redemption of the Messiah, and by Him an everlasting covenant.
>
> The Apostle [Paul] grounds his conclusion from the prophecy on the fact that God in these words speaks of a time when He would take away the sins of Israel as a body, and so all Israel shall be saved.
>
> Israel, then, shall be restored to their own land, which God gave to Abraham for an everlasting possession. . . . at the destruction of Jerusalem the whole Jewish nation was not exterminated: "Except," said our blessed Lord, "those days should be shortened, there should no flesh be saved;

but for the elect's sake those days shall be shortened," Matt. xxiv.22. The term elect here cannot be applicable to those Jews who had then embraced the Gospel, for the tribulations of those days, even had they not been shortened, would not have caused their destruction, scattered as they were through many countries. It must refer to the elect of God in that future age, when all Israel shall be saved. It was for their sakes, who were to descend from the Jewish people, that the destruction of that people was limited, and for which God was pleased to preserve a part of them, and continues to preserve them to this day.[12]

John Nelson Darby (1800–1882)

One of the most brilliant premillennialists and dispensationalists, Darby was born in London of wealthy Irish parents. He graduated from Trinity College, Dublin, with high honors and planned to enter law. But after a spiritual struggle, which led to his conversion, he gave up the law to become in 1826 a priest in the Church of England. But from 1827 to 1833, his ecclesiology and eschatology were formed, which led to his disenchantment and departure from the state church of England.

Having joined the Plymouth Brethren, the mature period of his life was spent as a missionary to Germany, France, New Zealand, and the West Indies. He made teaching tours also and somehow found time to translate the New Testament into English, French, and German. He also assisted in translating the Old Testament into French and German. As part of his teaching tours, he came to America and Canada seven times. Altogether, he wrote thirty-four volumes of theological notes and commentaries. One small volume included poems, meditations, and hymns.

Over time, through study of the Scriptures, Calvinist Darby could see dispensations becoming distinct. Using a normal, literal approach to hermeneutics throughout Scripture, Darby's mature understanding of the Word of God was formed.[13] For him, a dispensation was an economy, any order of things that God has arranged on the earth. Dispensations dealt with nations, laws, Israel, and the Gentiles. It also had to do with the failure of peoples and judgments. Darby clearly laid out an eschatological chronological pattern: (1) the rapture and first resurrection; (2) postrapture events in glory; (3) postrapture events on earth; (4) the return of Christ and the millennial kingdom; (5) postmillennial events; and (6) the eternal state.

John Charles Ryle (1816–1900)

Ryle was an evangelical minister in the low-church Anglican tradition. Educated at Eton and Christ Church, Oxford, he pastored several churches, was made dean of Norwich, and appointed first bishop of the new diocese of Liverpool. A strong evangelical, he wrote more than one hundred tracts and pamphlets on doctrinal and practical issues. He was somewhat of a dispensationalist and certainly a strong premillennialist. Concerning prophetic issues, he was a careful conservative; yet he held firmly to the premillennial return of Christ to establish His earthly kingdom.

In his book *Coming Events and Present Duties* (1867), Ryle wrote what has become an important list of articles that should govern the study and the attitudes of those who teach the prophetic message. One may not agree with all of them, but the eleven articles should cause all students of the Scriptures to ponder the centrality of the second coming.

1. I believe that the world will never be completely converted to Christianity by any existing agency, before the end comes.
2. I believe that the widespread unbelief, indifference, formalism, and wickedness, which are to be seen throughout Christendom, are only what we are taught to expect in God's Word.
3. I believe that the great purpose of the present dispensation is to gather out of the world an elect people, and not to convert all mankind. All mankind will not turn to Christ!
4. I believe that the second coming of our Lord Jesus Christ is the great event which will wind up the present dispensation, and for which we ought daily to long and pray.
5. I believe that the second coming of our Lord Jesus Christ will be a real, literal, personal, bodily coming; and that as He went away in the clouds of heaven with His body, before the eyes of men, so in like manner He will return (Acts 1:11).
6. I believe that after our Lord Jesus Christ comes again, the earth shall be renewed, and the curse removed; the devil shall be bound, the godly shall be rewarded, the wicked shall be punished.
7. I believe that the Jews shall ultimately be gathered again as a separate nation, restored to their own land, and

converted to the faith of Christ, after going through the great tribulation.

8. I believe that the literal sense of the Old Testament prophecies has been far too much neglected by the Churches, . . . and that under the mistaken system of spiritualizing and accommodating Bible language, Christians have too often completely missed its meaning (Luke 24:25–26).

9. I do not believe the preterist scheme of interpreting the Apocalypse, which regards the book as almost entirely fulfilled, or the futurist scheme, which regards it as almost entirely unfulfilled.

10. I believe that the Roman Catholic Church is the great predicted apostasy from the faith, and is Babylon and the Antichrist.

11. Finally, I believe that it is for the safety, happiness, and comfort of all true Christians, to expect as little as possible from churches or governments under the present dispensation, to hold themselves ready for tremendous convulsions and changes of all things established, and to expect their good things only from Christ's Second Advent.[14]

James Robinson Graves (1820–1893)

Born in Chester, Vermont, Graves was raised a Congregationalist but later became a Baptist. Completing the equivalent of a college degree on his own in four years, he also mastered four languages in the process. Before the Civil War, he formed the Southern Baptist Sunday School Union and a publishing house. He became an accomplished writer and editor as well as a popular speaker, preacher, and skilled debater.

Spending much study time on his own, Graves became a strong premillennialist and probably should be classified as a dispensationalist as well. He held to a strong, consistent, literal hermeneutic. His most important work is entitled *The Work of Christ Consummated in Seven Dispensations*. Around 1878, he held two very successful prophecy conferences in both New York and Chicago, with the newspapers paying attention and suggesting that prophetic studies were gaining in interest. In these meetings he gave a dispensational scenario and was attacked afterward for his literal interpretation of the Bible. For decades, Graves' premillennialism influenced Baptists across America through his conferences and lectures. He came along at a time when premillennialism was gaining ground and during the period of much discussion about the Jews returning to the land of Israel.[15]

Joseph A. Seiss (1823–1904)

Seiss was one of the most able and popular of Lutheran preachers in America. He held several important pastorates and was in demand as an able speaker and author. He wrote over a dozen books and edited two magazines, *The Lutheran* and *Prophetic Times*. His classic work, *The Apocalypse*, is one of the most important studies on the book of Revelation, and it is called "an exhaustive, premillennial exposition." Seiss survived as a Lutheran under much criticism from his church, probably because of his high visibility as a conservative yet able scholar of the Word of God.

Seiss answered criticism by writing, "There is widespread prejudice against the study of the Apocalypse. . . . there are religious guides, sworn to teach 'the whole council of God,' who make a merit of not understanding [Revelation], and of not wishing to occupy themselves with it."[16]

Elijah Richardson Craven (1824–1908)

Craven received a B.A. from the College of New Jersey and then Princeton Seminary in 1848. He also studied law. When many Presbyterian ministers shifted from postmillennialism to premillennialism, Craven led the way. He held several pastorates but settled into a longtime ministry with the Third Presbyterian Church in Newark (1854–87). As well as being pastor, he held many important posts in the Presbyterian Church North.

Craven was a strong Calvinist who fought against the rising tide of liberalism in his denomination. He seems to have felt that the proclamation of the return of the Lord would help in that struggle. He was a speaker at the famous 1878 prophecy conference in New York City at which he spoke on "The Coming of the Lord in its Relations to Christian Doctrine."

Craven worked tirelessly to demonstrate the normal and literal interpretation of Scripture as preferable to the spiritual method of his day. With other great premillennial godly teachers like James H. Brookes and Nathaniel West, Craven made premillennialism synonymous with evangelicalism.[17]

George N. H. Peters (1825–1909)

Not a lot is known about Peters. He remains one of the most mysterious and fascinating premillennial scholars of the nineteenth century. Why, as a Lutheran, he was driven to hold strongly to premillennialism is not fully understood. Peters graduated from Wittenburg College and took pastorates in Xenia and Springfield, Ohio. Taking many years to produce, Peters turned out what is called the "grandfather" work on Bible prophecy, the 2,100 page *The Theocratic Kingdom*. Why, when, and how he became so interested in the full and complete doctrine of eschatology is not clear. The "author lived and worked in an oblivion that seems almost mysterious, and experienced so little recognition at the time of the [first] publication of his work that one must almost believe that there was an organized determination to ignore its appearance."[18]

Some conjecture that Peters was inspired to study premillennialism because of the influence of two Lutheran prophecy scholars, Dr. S. S. Schmucker and Dr. Seiss. He endured criticism from other Lutheran pastors, and his motives, piety, and private life were abused and doubted. His character was demeaned, and his abilities and even mental state questioned.

Peters's work includes over four thousand quotes, which took possibly twenty years to compile. Thousands of verses are cited, and hundreds if not thousands of individual quotes from the church fathers are listed. Clearly, his research proves premillennialism was far more accepted than its critics would have us believe.

Peters writes about his *Theocratic Kingdom* effort:

> The Millenarian views of the ancient and modern believers, and paving the way for a more strict and consistent interpretation of the kingdom, this itself would already be sufficient justification for its publication.[19]

Nathaniel West (1826–1906)

Though born in Sunderland, England, West came to America and received a B.A. and M.A. from the University of Michigan. Later, he earned a doctorate from Allegheny Seminary. West quickly became a popular prophetic and interpretative scholar. Pastoring eight churches in his lifetime, he also became a noted speaker at popular prophecy conferences. His unsurpassed work, *The Thousand Year Reign of Christ*, is considered a classic on the return of Christ to rule on earth. In it he has strong words for amillennial thinking:

> A false spiritualizing, allegorizing, and idealizing, interpretation has contributed to rob the predictions concerning Israel of their realistic value. . . . The church does not understand

the present age, nor its relation to the coming age, nor Israel's relation to both, and to the Nations, and to the church itself. And this blindness will continue until the false systems of interpretation, by which it has been caused, are rejected.[20]

James Hall Brookes (1837–1897)

From his Presbyterian pulpit in St. Louis, Brookes became one of the leading proponents of dispensational premillennialism. The son of a Presbyterian minister, he was born in Pulaski, Tennessee. Though his father died when James was young, he was raised by a godly mother. As a young man, James entered Princeton Seminary but was unable to complete the first year.

Brookes was ordained a Presbyterian minister and held several important pastoral positions. He served as commissioner to the denomination's general assembly and in 1874 was state clerk for the Missouri Synod. But it was in his writings that he gained national attention. In the early 1870s, he published *Maranatha*, a huge volume on eschatology. In the magazine *The Truth or Testimony for Christ*, which he edited, Brookes became an influential premillennial authority. As a great Bible teacher, he introduced thousands to the subject of the return of the Lord. One of his most visible pupils was C. I. Scofield, who would later edit *The Scofield Reference Bible.*

Brookes was a master teacher of the pretribulational rapture. Though not a date setter, he argued for the imminence of the return of the Lord. Brookes also argued strongly that his prophetic views came through his own reading and the study of Daniel and Revelation.[21]

E. W. Bullinger (1837–1913)

Born in Canterbury, England, Bullinger was a direct descendent of Johann Heinrich Bullinger, a covenant theologian who succeeded the great reformer Zwingli in Zurich in 1531. Educated at King's College, London, he was recognized as an outstanding scholar in biblical languages. In 1881, he was awarded an honorary Doctor of Divinity by the Archbishop of Canterbury for his superb biblical scholarship.

Though he taught the pretribulational and premillennial rapture of the church, his influence for the Christian church at large is marred by some extremes. He was an annihilationist who believed in the extinction of the souls of the lost after death. He was also an ultradispensationalist who taught that the church age actually began under Paul's ministry after Acts 28:28. Despite these doctrinal blemishes, he had a strong influence upon his own and later generations.[22]

Dwight Lyman Moody (1837–1899)

To illustrate the importance of Moody, within one year after his death on December 22, 1899, fourteen biographies were written about this highly respected preacher. Primarily self-taught, Moody was not articulate and systematic, but very early espoused premillennialism and dispensationalism, with scriptural inerrancy also a central tenet of his theology.

Around the period of the Civil War, Moody became concerned for the poor children who filled the streets of Chicago. He began Sunday school work with them and soon was completely committed to evangelism. Not a sophisticated preacher, Moody was simple and down to earth, and his sincerity was respected by all who heard him. Active as an international evangelist until the last few years of his life, Moody kept the imminent return of Christ at the center of his message.

James M. Gray, a former president of Moody Bible Institute, wrote "the pervading life of his theology [was] . . . namely the hope of the coming of the Lord—His personal and visible appearing. . . . He was looking for His coming every day."[23]

Samuel H. Kellogg (1839–1899)

Kellogg helped turn the tide among evangelicals from post-millennialism to premillennialism between the Civil War and World War I. He was a highly respected Presbyterian scholar, linguist, professor, missionary, and pastor. Home-schooled as a youngster, Kellogg graduated from Princeton College (1861) and Seminary (1861) and was ordained as a missionary to India. Kellogg taught at the seminary in Allahabad and completed a monumental grammar on the Hindi language in 1875.

Upon the death of his wife, he returned to the U.S., took a Presbyterian church in Pittsburgh, then was called to chair systematic theology at Allegheny Presbyterian Seminary in Pittsburgh. In addition to his contribution to the Hindi language, his second greatest contribution was as an Old Testament scholar who specialized in eschatology. He wrote several outstanding works on prophecy including *Are Premillennialists Right?* In the book he answers postmillennialism, especially the claim that premillennialism blunts evangelism.

Partly because of his influence, toward the end of the nineteenth century missions were dominated by premillennialism. Kellogg himself was said to have been motivated to go to the mission field because of his anticipation of the return of the Lord. Kellogg's premillennialism was developed by what he saw prophetically in the Old Testament. His

understanding of a future for the Jews and a yet-future, literal fulfillment to them as a nationally distinct people drove him to the only
possible eschatology to which such an understanding leads.[24]

Sir Robert Anderson (1841–1918)

Born into an influential Dublin family, Anderson's father served
as crown solicitor for the city and was also a distinguished elder in
the Irish Presbyterian Church. Converted during the great Irish
Revival, Anderson became a lay preacher and was used of the Lord
to win many to Christ.

After receiving his law degree from Trinity College, Dublin (1863),
Anderson worked for a while drawing up legal briefs on a traveling
circuit and ended up in London, working with the city police. After
serving as chief of the criminal investigation department, he re-
tired with distinction and, with his investigative training and ability to think logically and succinctly, began studying the Scriptures.
He published many books including the prophetic works *Unfulfilled Prophecy and The Hope of the Church* and *The Coming Prince*.

In *The Coming Prince,* Anderson examines Daniel's seventy weeks.
Though more recent work in Bible chronology may shed new light
on Anderson's prophetic calculations in Daniel, his work stands as
a classic in its attempt to understand the prophet's datings.
Anderson's books highlight the dependable authority of the Bible,
the deity of Jesus, the necessity of the new birth, and the blessed
hope in the premillennial return of Christ.[25]

Cyrus Ingerson Scofield (1843–1921)

Born in Lenawee County, Michigan, Scofield was one of seven
children. After Cyrus's mother died, a stepmother raised him and
the other children. Little is known of his education. During the Civil
War, he fought for a short time with the Confederacy but was re-
leased, being "an alien" from Michigan. He studied law following
the war, and with his law degree, entered into politics in Kansas.
He later was appointed to the office of District Attorney for Kansas
by President Grant. Hounded by political scandal and drunkenness,
and forlorn at the loss of his wife and children, he fell into a life of
thievery.

But in 1879, the Lord touched his heart, and he turned to Christ.
Almost immediately Scofield became active in Christian work, in-
cluding helping out in some of the campaigns of Dwight Moody in
St. Louis. In 1882 Scofield was called to a mission church in Dallas,
Texas, where he was ordained in 1883. With Moody's help, Scofield

acquired a large pastorate in Northfield, Massachusetts, where he also presided over Moody's Northfield Bible Training School. After teaching on the Bible Conference circuit, he settled down at one conference center, the Sea Cliff Bible Conference, on Long Island. There, along with the input by some other godly men, the idea for his reference Bible was born. The project was supported financially by John T. Pirie.

The Scofield Reference Bible was first published in 1909. It advocated a pretribulational rapture and a literal return of the Jews to their homeland, as well as premillennialism and dispensationalism. Because of Scofield's research on the Scriptures, he felt that, with a literal hermeneutic, there could be no other positions. After the Bible was published, he was wanted worldwide as an evangelist and Bible teacher.

Scofield also helped found the Southwestern School of the Bible, presided over the Northfield School, founded the New York School of the Bible, and established the Philadelphia School of the Bible. Also, he helped found the Central American Mission, published many booklets and leaflets, and began the Scofield Bible Correspondence Course.

Scofield may be the most single influential Bible teacher and writer of the twentieth century. His reference Bible cut across denominational lines and was read and studied by thousands. Though *The Scofield Reference Bible* was often publicly scorned by denominational leaders and liberal seminary teachers, it continued to change lives and to educate and mature the larger Christian public about doctrinal and prophetic matters.

One such matter concerns the Jews. Allegorists and amillennialists saw no future conversion for Israel.[26] Because *The Scofield Reference Bible* gave hope for the return of the Jews to their homeland, it created a sympathy and support for the Jewish people.

Clarence Larkin (1850–1924)

Born in Chester, Pennsylvania, Larkin was an ambitious young man. He worked hard in his father's feed store and later took a position in a bank. He was a member of the Episcopal church but was converted to Christ through the local YMCA. In 1873 he graduated with a bachelor's degree in mechanical engineering from the Polytechnic College of Philadelphia. In 1882, at the age of thirty-three, he joined the Baptist church, and he was ordained two years later. He took pastorates in his home state.

Based on his own study, he became a premillennialist and

dispensationalist, putting to good use his engineering skills by draw-ing charts and maps of Bible prophecy. One of his first published works was *Dispensational Truth or God's Plan and Purpose in the Ages*. He also produced illustrated commentaries on Revelation and Daniel. In his book *Dispensational Truth*, some of his historical facts about the Reformers and others are flawed, which led to some criti-cism of his work. But his time-line illustrations helped millions to visualize the Scriptures and the outline of biblical history. Even today most prophecy charts are modeled after the original work of Larkin. Though by now his artwork is somewhat dated in style, many readers are still blessed by his work.

Though frequently ridiculed by critics today as too intricate or sensational, his charts were popular prior to the advent of contem-porary audiovisual technology, especially in the years between the First and Second World Wars.[27]

James Martin Gray (1851–1935)

Not a lot is known about Gray's early life. At the age of twenty-two, however, while in seminary training for a ministerial career in the Protestant Episcopal Church, he was converted to Christ. Trans-ferring his denominational ties, Gray apparently completed his edu-cation in the Reformed Episcopal Church and was ordained in 1877. In his earlier ministerial years, he served in several pastorates and taught in several Bible schools, including the Reformed Episcopal Seminary in Philadelphia (1894).

Gray became associated with Moody around 1893, lectured at Moody Bible Institute, became its dean, and finally its president in 1925, a position he held until his death in 1935. He played a key role in the fundamentalist-modernist controversy in the 1920s, staunchly defending the verbal inspiration of Scripture. He was also a contributor to *The Fundamentals* (1910–15).

Gray's contributions to Moody Bible Institute, to the Bible insti-tute movement in general, to the growth of the fundamentalist movement, and to the popularization and propagation of dispensa-tional premillennial theology is incalculable. His theological foci were bibliology, Christology, soteriology, pneumatology, and eschatology, and were due in part to the demands of the era and in part to his personal interest.[28]

David Baron (1855–1926)

Born in a strict orthodox Jewish home in Russia, Baron studied Hebrew under rigorous rabbinical training. After an independent search of the Scriptures, he became a Christian. Immediately he set out to explain Christianity to the Jews and to help Christians understand prophecy and the future restoration of Israel. To do this, Baron founded an organization called Hebrew Christian Testimony to Israel, which along with his writings, became one of the greatest testimonies of God's working in the lives of the Jewish people.

Baron published several classic premillennial works including *The Servant of Jehovah* and *Types*. His *Commentary on Zechariah* is considered a classic among expositions of this Old Testament book. Because so many American churches allegorized and spiritualized the Scriptures, in his preface to *Zechariah* he writes, "Almost all the existing works on this prophetic book are in one way or another defective, and some of them misleading. The older commentaries are commendable for their reverent spiritual tone . . . but they more or less are vitiated by the allegorizing principle of interpretation, by which all references to a concrete kingdom of God on earth, a literal, national restoration of Israel, and the visible appearing and reign of Messiah, are explained away."

Baron also wrote that he attempted "to unfold . . . prophetic events which center around the land and the people of Israel—events the rapid fulfillment of which men may now begin to see with their own eyes."[29]

William Bell Riley (1861–1947)

Born in Green County, Indiana, Riley attended Southern Baptist Seminary in Louisville in 1885 and pastored several small churches in Kentucky, Indiana, and Illinois. In his mid years, Riley was considered a pastor, revivalist, civic reformer, educator, and ecclesiastical politician. Seeing liberalism creeping into the Northern Baptist Convention, he and others attempted to halt the departure from the faith. Though Riley was sometimes controversial, he stood strongly for the inerrancy of Scripture and dispensational premillennialism. He taught a coming apostasy, the premillennial rapture of the church, the Tribulation, the Antichrist, Armageddon, and the coming kingdom reign of Christ.

Because he was so well known as a scholar, he was asked by C. I. Scofield to contribute to *The Scofield Reference Bible*, but he declined because of other pressing duties. He started the Northwestern Schools, from which, at the time of his death, over seventy percent of Baptist pastors in Minnesota were alumni. At one time he turned those scattered schools over to a young Billy Graham, but Graham did not stay long as the head of these institutions.

Harry Ironside called Riley one of the greatest leaders ever in Christian circles. Though modernism had already taken hold of the educational process and denominational power, Riley had the most influence, at least for a while, with the people and the pastors. By his strong teaching of premillennialism, he established the love of prophecy for many decades among Baptists and others in the Northern states.[30]

Arno Gaebelein (1861–1945)

Gaebelein was born in Thuringia, Germany, and came to America at age eighteen. Ordained in the Methodist Episcopal church, he held pastorates in Baltimore and New York City. In New York he began an important ministry to reach the Jewish population, and he published a magazine entitled *Our Hope*. Around 1887, while in New York, he became a premillennialist. He wrote, "This attempt to bring the Gospel to the Jews led me deeper into the Old Testament Scriptures. I began to study prophecy. Up to this time I had followed in the interpretation of Old Testament prophecy the so-called 'spiritualization method' (allegorical)." He realized that only with literal interpretation would *Israel* mean Israel and not the church. He realized that a promise of redemption back to the land of Palestine still held for the Jews.

Though not formally trained, Gaebelein was a remarkable scholar who knew biblical Hebrew and Greek as well as many Middle Eastern languages. He wrote nearly fifty books and many pamphlets on prophecy and lectured widely at Bible conferences. Adhering to a grammatical-historical interpretation, he taught the pretribulational rapture of the church, the Tribulation, and the thousand-year reign of Christ. About the love of prophecy, he wrote, "the Old Testament is practically a sealed book to every person who does not believe in a literal restoration of Israel to their land."[31]

W. H. Griffith Thomas (1861–1924)

Thomas was born in Oswestry, Shropshire, near the border of Wales. Through the influence of several friends, he became a believer in Christ at the local WMCA. He achieved an excellent record at King's College and Oxford, where he was awarded the Doctor of Divinity in 1906, and later served as vicar of one of the most influential evangelical Anglican congregations in London. Thomas became an international speaker on the Scriptures, lecturing at leading institutions not only in England but also in America and Canada.

Early on, Thomas influenced England with regard to premillennialism but expressed it more emphatically when he came to

America. In a sermon entitled "Our Lord's Second Coming" given in 1918, he proclaimed the Lord's second advent would be personal and premillennial, giving a standard premillennial view of biblical prophecy including the pretribulational rapture. As did many premillennialists of his day, he held to Calvinism and the doctrines of total depravity, predestination, and irresistible grace.[32]

William T. Pettingill (1866–1950)

An educator, pastor, and author, Pettingill was closely associated with Scofield, served as dean of the Philadelphia College of Bible, and served on the editorial staff of *The Scofield Reference Bible*. He also spent twenty-five years as a pastor in Wilmington, Delaware, wrote many books, and was the editor of several periodicals including *Serving and Waiting* and *Just a Word*. Through his many writings and as a popular Bible teacher at prophecy conferences, Pettingill was known as a conservative, premillennial, and dispensational interpreter of the Word of God.

A highly effective minister of the gospel, Pettingill showed an acquaintance with the biblical languages as well as the great world classics. He traveled widely and taught in England, Europe, Central America, Canada, and throughout the U.S. He was scholarly, spiritually deep, quick to the point, and persuasive in his messages and writings.[33]

Henry Allan Ironside (1876–1951)

Having come up through the ranks of the Salvation Army, Ironside early on had a heart for serving God. But the theology of the Salvation Army troubled him, and in time, he left and discovered real peace and security through a biblical view of the teaching of the grace of God. Ironside was basically self-taught in the Scriptures, though Wheaton College honored him with a doctorate (Litt.D.) for his great accomplishments in writing and speaking.

Through speaking at prophecy conferences and Bible study retreats, Ironside traveled much, yet he taught extensively at Moody Bible Institute and the Evangelical College in Dallas. His legacy was left to us in sixty books, including his devotional commentaries on the whole Bible. His style (1) encompassed devotional exposition, (2) consisted of simple outlining of complicated material, (3) utilized fresh wording and simple illustrations aimed at warming the heart, and (4) encouraged a continuation of Bible reading.

In the end, Ironside was known as a beloved teacher dedicated to the literal interpretation of prophecy and the resultant belief and hope in the pretribulational premillennial coming of Jesus Christ.[34]

John Frederick Strombeck (1881–1959)

Born in Moline, Illinois, of a pioneering Swedish family, Strombeck early on trusted in Jesus as his Savior. After graduating from Northwestern University (1911), he founded the Strombeck-Becker Manufacturing Company, specializing in wood products. Having become a successful business entrepreneur, Strombeck was then free to study, research, and teach the Bible.

Strombeck became popular at Bible conferences nationwide, but he also excelled at publishing his biblical books and booklets. Among his most helpful works were *So Great Salvation* and *First the Rapture*. Having acquired wealth in business, he contributed to many Christian institutions including Moody Bible Institute. His book on the rapture helped thousands understand not only that doctrine but also to comprehend God's plan of the ages. Also in *First the Rapture,* he answered posttribulational views and led many to understand the difference between the present spiritual body of Christ and the nation of Israel.

Having helped multitudes awaken to the message of the Word of God and prophecy, Strombeck lamented the poor quality of Bible teaching in this century. Whether teaching Bible prophecy or any other truth from the Word of God, Strombeck's guiding rule was "What do the Scriptures say?" [35]

Harry Bultema (1884–1952)

Born in Holland, Bultema came to America with his family of six siblings in the early 1900s. Being nurtured by strong spiritual parents, it was only natural that Bultema would attend seminary or Bible school. After graduating from Calvin College and Calvin Seminary in Grand Rapids, Michigan, he held pastorates in several states within the Christian Reformed Church.

Through his own study, he concluded that there was a difference between Christ being the present head over the church and His coming to reign over the restored kingdom of Israel. Becoming premillennial, pretribulational, and dispensational, he felt the need to leave the Reformed Church. Having set to writing, he penned several classic works including his *Commentary on Isaiah, Commentary on Daniel,* and *Maranatha.*

Bultema wrote, "In all of Scripture there is not a semblance or shadow of justification for the identification of Israel as a nation with the church as the body of Christ. In the New Testament the word Israel appears seventy times, but it must always be taken in its literal historical meaning."[36]

M. R. DeHaan (1891–1965)

DeHaan received his M.D. degree from the University of Illinois Medical School. But after practicing medicine for several years, he returned to his first love of teaching the Scriptures. He studied Bible and theology at Western Theological Seminary and began his teaching career via public meetings, radio, and writing. He wrote twenty-five books and countless daily devotionals and tracts, and wrote for and edited *Our Daily Bread*, the popular daily devotional book read across America. Probably because of his medical training, DeHaan often taught on Bible themes that touched on medicine or science and evolution.

DeHaan's most important subject, however, was Bible prophecy, concerning which he was thoroughly dispensational and premillennial. He continually reminded his audiences of the difference between Israel and the church, and following the events of World War II, he realized that God was moving providentially in the Middle East by bringing the Jews back to their homeland.

Using lay terms, DeHaan reminded his audiences of basic Bible interpretation. He emphasized that (1) all Scripture has but one primary interpretation, (2) all Scripture has several practical applications, (3) most Scripture passages or books generally have something to do with prophecy. He wisely noted, "To ignore the primary . . . and to be occupied only with its practical applications may result in fanaticism and losing the real purpose for which the revelation was given."[37]

René Pache (1904–1979)

Raised in a godly home in Switzerland, Pache received a doctorate in law from Lausanne University. As a twenty-four year old lawyer, he met Christ in Basle while reading the Bible. Though attending Bible school for only one year, he went on to teach himself the Scriptures. He was greatly influenced by *The Scofield Reference Bible* and later was instrumental in having it published in French. In terms of organizational influence, he served as vice-chairman of the International Fellowship of Evangelical Students, was director of Emmaus Bible and Missionary Institute in Lausanne, and lectured at the Aix-en-Provence Theological Seminary in France.

Pache was a conservative, a dispensationalist, a premillennialist, and held to the doctrine of the rapture but was unsure about the pretribulational rapture. Although Pache authored fourteen books that appeared in ten languages, in reading his material it is unclear where he stood on the Lord coming for His church. Possibly he took a midweek pretribulationalism, since his writing indicates a belief in a three-and-a-half year tribulation.

On most other eschatological issues, he was typical of mainstream dispensational, premillennial, pretribulationalism. He distinguished between Israel and the church and saw a future for national Israel. As well, he took a strong futurist view of Revelation 4–22.[38]

Conclusion

Though all the premillennial and dispensationalist teachers listed above did not hold to the same views on every detail, there are some very important points they held in common: they all endorsed a literal view of hermeneutics; they were Calvinistic in their convictions or inclinations; they believed in the distinct difference between Israel and the church; they held generally to the same position on the rapture, though a few had differing opinions; they seemed to have a common love of prophecy and taught often on the blessed hope and the return of Christ; they saw the kingdom as distinct from the church today; they looked for a regathering of Israel and a spiritual awakening of the Jews to their Messiah; they looked for a literal return of Christ to reign a thousand years.

Clearly, the commonly held views of these influential teachers outweighed their differences.

CHAPTER 10

The Dispensations of Charles Hodge

Charles Hodge (1797–1878) was a leading American theologian during the nineteenth century. He graduated from Princeton seminary in 1819.

> He became a instructor at Princeton Seminary in 1820, and remained there for the rest of his life, except for two years' study in France and Germany (1826–28). He was a professor of oriental and biblical literature (1822–40), then professor of theology. His own theology was mainly that of the Westminster Confession with obvious traces of scholastic Calvinism. . . . His thought was governed by a high view of verbal inspiration and infallibility.[1]

Charles was the father of Archibald Alexander Hodge, who succeeded his father as Princeton's systematic theologian in 1877. Charles Hodge listed four dispensations, concerning which dispensationalists hold similar views but disagree in some particulars.

First Dispensation: From Adam to Abraham

Hodge writes,

> Although the covenant of grace has always been the same, the dispensations of that covenant have changed. The first dispensation extended from Adam to Abraham. Of this period we have so few records, that we cannot determine how far the truth was revealed, or what measures were adopted

for its preservation. All we know is, that the original promises concerning the seed of the woman, as the Redeemer of our race, had been given; and that the worship of God by sacrifices had been instituted.[2]

Dispensationalists would basically agree, although they maintain that there is no biblical evidence whatsoever of the covenant of grace. Even Berkhof admits the same.

Second Dispensation: From Abraham to Moses

Hodge continues,

The second dispensation extended from Abraham to Moses. . . . By the selection of the descendants of Abraham to be the peculiar people of God. They were chosen in order to preserve the knowledge of the true religion in the midst of the general apostasy of mankind. To this end special revelations were made to them, and God entered into a covenant with them, promising that He would be their God, and that they should be his people.[3]

Again, dispensationalists would basically agree but they would wonder why Hodge, who was a godly, pioneering theologian, would leave certain important factors out. He does not mention, for instance, that the covenant he refers to is actually the Abrahamic covenant, which was inaugurated by the Lord in Genesis 12:1–3.

Hodge's last sentence quoted above contains problems that would bother many dispensationalists. Referring to the Abrahamic covenant, Hodge writes, ". . . promising that He would be their God, and that they should be his people." That quote actually comes from Jeremiah, who is referring to the new covenant: "And they shall be My people, and I will be their God" (Jer. 32:38). Although Hodge would probably not agree, dispensationalists hold that the new covenant arises from the Abrahamic covenant or at least is an extension of it. With this in view, dispensationalists might give Hodge a little leeway on this point.

It is interesting, though, that Hodge did not finish the verses in the larger paragraph in Jeremiah 32. The Jeremiah passage continues, "I will faithfully plant them in this land with all My heart and with all My soul" (v. 41). Along with that omission, and in an apparent attempt to avoid any messianic kingdom ideas, Hodge also left out key new covenant passages from Ezekiel 37. The Ezekiel verses

(21–23, 25, 27) quote the "their God, My people" verses in a literal kingdom context:

> *I will take the sons of Israel from among the nations where they have gone, and I will gather them from every side and bring them into their own land; and I will make them one nation in the land, on the mountains of Israel; and one king will be king for all of them; and they will no longer be two nations, and they will no longer be divided into two kingdoms. . . . I will cleanse them.* And they will be My people, and I will be their God. . . . *And they shall live on the land that I gave to Jacob My servant, in which your fathers lived; and they will live on it, they, and their sons, forever; and David My servant shall be their prince forever. . . . My dwelling place also will be with them; and* I will be their God, and they will be My people. *(emphasis added)*

Hodge creates more confusion by calling this second dispensation the church. He writes, "Besides thus gathering his Church out of the world, and making its members a peculiar people, distinguished by circumcision from the Gentiles around them, the promise of redemption was made more definite."[4] Again, the covenant is made with Abraham and later confirmed to his sons. But more importantly, the children of Abraham are never referred to as the church.

Third Dispensation: From Moses to Christ

With this dispensation, Hodge becomes even more unclear. He correctly writes that this period is based upon the Mosaic covenant, which was a national covenant with the Jewish people. He then speaks of what he calls the "evangelical character" of the Mosaic Law, a legal covenant, and that it is "a renewed proclamation of the original covenant of works."[5] There is no biblical evidence, however, for this statement since there is no biblical covenant called the covenant of works.

In a weak statement, Hodge attempts to explain the difference between law and grace. He writes,

> If a man rejects or neglects the gospel, these are the principles [from the Mosaic Law], as Paul teaches in the opening chapters of his Epistle to the Romans, according to which he will be judged. If he will not be under grace, if he will not

accede to the method of salvation by grace, he is of necessity under the law.[6]

Concerning this Mosaic Law dispensation, Hodge could have pointed out from the book of Galatians that the purpose of the law was to lead men to Christ:

> For if a law had been given which was able to impart life, then righteousness would indeed have been based on law. But the Scripture has shut up all men under sin, that the promise by faith in Jesus Christ might be given to those who believe. . . . Therefore the Law has become our tutor to lead us to Christ, that we may be justified by faith. (3:21–22, 24)

Fourth Dispensation: The Gospel

Though he does not emphasize the point, Hodge does seem to understand that this dispensation rests upon the new covenant that is prophesied in Jeremiah 31 as well as other important Old Testament passages. According to dispensationalists, the new covenant also is an extension of the Abrahamic covenant. And dispensationalists would point out that, technically, this period is specifically called in Scripture the stewardship (NASB) (i.e., dispensation) of the church (Col. 1:24–25), or the stewardship (NASB) (i.e., dispensation) of grace (Eph. 3:2).

About this gospel dispensation, Hodge writes,

> The gospel dispensation is called new in reference to the Mosaic economy, which was old, and about to vanish away. It is distinguished from the old economy. . . . It is more spiritual. . . . It is more purely evangelical. . . . The Christian economy is specially the dispensation of the Spirit. The great blessing promised of old, as consequent on the coming of Christ, was the effusion of the Spirit on all flesh, i.e., on all nations and on all classes of men.[7]

Dispensationalists would basically agree with the above, but they would also point out that the features concerning the Spirit that Hodge refers to come from the new covenant. With this dispensationalist argument in mind, Hodge writes, "The old dispensation was temporary and preparatory; the new is permanent and final."[8] Dispensationalists would clarify the sentence this way: "The old dispensation of the Mosaic Law was temporary and preparatory; the new dispensation of the church rests upon the new covenant. The church will be raptured away someday and, following the seven year period of tribulation, its dispensation will be finally replaced by the dispensation of the kingdom."

But in his final paragraph on this fourth dispensation, and apparently aware that some believed in a final earthly kingdom dispensation, Hodge closed his chapter on the dispensations by making his gospel economy the last in God's program. Thus, he ignored the verses throughout the Bible that predicted a blessed period of peace on the earth with Christ reigning and ruling. In fact, it appears that Hodge did more than simply ignore the kingdom issue—he closed the curtain on any possibility of the millennial reign taking place.

> This dispensation [of the gospel] is, therefore, the last before the restoration of all things; the last, that is, designed for the conversion of men and the ingathering of the elect. Afterwards comes the end; the resurrection and the final judgment. In the Old Testament there are frequent intimations of another and a better economy, to which the Mosaic institutions were merely preparatory. But we have no intimation in Scripture that the dispensation of the Spirit is to give way for a new and better dispensation for the conversion of the nations. When the gospel is fully preached, then comes the end.[9]

Hodge's Rules of Interpretation

Charles Hodge listed three interpretative rules he felt were essential in determining what the Word of God teaches:

1. The words of Scripture are to be taken in their plain historical sense.

   That is, they must be taken in the sense attached to them in the age of and by the people to whom they were addressed. This only assumes that the sacred writers were honest and had meant to be understood.

2. If the Scriptures be what they claim to be, the word of God, they are the work of one mind, and that mind divine.

   From this it follows that Scripture cannot contradict Scripture. God cannot teach in one place anything that is inconsistent with what He teaches in another. Hence Scripture must explain Scripture. If a passage admits of different interpretations, the true interpretation is that which agrees with what the Bible teaches elsewhere on the same subject.

3. The Scriptures are to be interpreted under the guidance of the Holy Spirit, which guidance is to be humbly and earnestly sought.

The ground of this rule is twofold: First, the Spirit is promised as a guide and teacher. He was to come to lead the people of God into the knowledge of the truth. And secondly, the Scriptures teach that "the natural man receiveth not the things of the Spirit of God: for they are foolishness unto him" (1 Cor. ii. 14). The unrenewed mind is naturally blind to spiritual truth.[10]

Though rule 1 is a common hermeneutical directive, dispensationalists note that allegorists and covenant theologians violate this most obvious and sacred of principles. We must understand Scripture in the plain and ordinary sense, just as the people to whom it was addressed understood it. Amillennialists agree that the Old Testament saints and the people of the period of the Gospels believed in a coming earthly messianic kingdom. But, they argue, the sages of old, later the disciples and others of the time of Christ and Paul, misunderstood. They simply were wrong in holding to a primitive physical view of that promised kingdom. The amillennialist would contend that the Jews of the early New Testament period, whether pious believers or not, failed to comprehend that the prophesied kingdom was simply spiritual in nature, not historical and physical.

A good example of Hodge's misunderstanding of the intent of the biblical text is found in *The Preacher's Homiletic Commentary* notes on Ezekiel 37:22–25. The passage is quoted by the commentary this way:

I will make them one nation, and one king shall be king to them all. David My servant shall be king over them, and they all shall have one shepherd. My servant David shall be their prince for ever.

The commentary then says,

It was plainly revealed that the coming Messiah-King was to be a descendant of David, the Jewish hero, and both prophets and people expected that he would restore the kingdom on the lines of its ancient constitution, for they knew nothing higher. The conception of a purely spiritual kingdom was altogether beyond the range of human thought, and was not dreamed of till proclaimed by the lips of our Lord. Even then the idea was but slowly comprehended by the best-instructed Jewish minds; and the rejection of the true Messiah by the bulk of the Jewish nation shows how unwilling or incapable they were to take in the sublime notion. It is only by the light of the New Testament that a later age has been able to realise the far-reaching significance of the prophetic vision. The true Israel is not a political but a spiritual community gathered out of all nations under heaven, compacted and unified into a spiritual kingdom.[11]

The commentary quotes Patrick Fairbairn on 37:15–28:

That there has been no adequate fulfillment of this prophecy in what may be called the literal sense of its terms is too plain to require any lengthened proof. The most characteristic part of the description—the cementing, strengthening, . . . rule of David—had not even the appearance of a literal fulfillment in the post-Babylonian history of Israel; and, with so strong and prominent a feature of an ideal sort as the eternal presidency of David, it seems amazing that any one should expect it to be realised after that manner in the ages to come.[12]

In the two paragraphs above, violations in common sense are heaped upon the most basic hermeneutical principles. And if the thoughts reflected are true, then all language fails us as to the meaning. For example, because a prophesied literal kingdom has not come about, Fairbairn assumes that a historic reign of the son of David, Christ, cannot come about.

As well, the commentary notes confuse the idea of a spiritual kingdom with the idea of a "spiritualized" or allegorical reign of the Messiah. The dispensationalist believes whatever God brings about will be spiritual in nature. But amillennialists assume that the kingdom cannot be spiritual and earthly at the same time. This is incorrect. Again, the commentary notes maintain that everyone in the Old Testament was fooled about the nature of the kingdom, that inspired words were misunderstood, and that the nature of the kingdom was completely misrepresented in the prophetic Word.

Intellectual Dishonesty?

Though both amillennialists and dispensationalists claim that, in principle, they faithfully believe in Hodge's rule 1, only dispensationalists and premillennialists are consistent in applying that rule. In other words, the saints of the Old Testament and the disciples had interpreted the kingdom promises of the prophets correctly. They were neither fooled nor intellectually and spiritually blinded. What they looked for will come to pass. The Davidic and messianic kingdom is yet to arrive and be established here on earth in the future.

The amillennialists are both hermeneutically and intellectually incorrect in their approach to future prophetic truth. All hold to Christ's first coming as literal and historical. But when there is any promise that may smack of literalness about His second coming, they switch into an allegorical mode and claim that the kingdom is really only a spiritualized concept and not to be taken as literal.

Additional Interpretive Rules

Benware sets forth five rules of interpretation that expand on Hodge's rules:

1. *Interpret the Prophetic Passage Literally.* But to interpret literally includes everyday life renderings of language and meaning. Our "literal" expressions are loaded with symbols and figures of speech that are part of ordinary conversation. Benware cites two illustrations:

   . . . if I were to say to you, "I was sitting in the back yard the other evening, and there were millions of mosquitoes out there," you would immediately recognize "millions" as a figure of speech (in this case, a hyperbole), realizing that I did not count the mosquitoes but was simply saying that there were a large number of them. You would interpret my statement within the normal use of language. If a person declares, "I'm freezing!" we take that statement normally. We do not assume that their body temperature has dropped to 32 degrees but, rather, that they feel very cold.[13]

Benware continues by adding, "It is essential, therefore to have this literal mind-set as we approach the prophetic Word of God."[14] The basic approach to the prophetic Word must be literal, though symbols are valuable communication tools. Far more often than not, symbols and figures of speech represent something literal. Benware notes further,

> Those (such as amillennialists) who resist this principle of literal interpretation adhere instead to the spiritualization of prophecy. A spiritual (or allegorical or mystical) approach treats the literal sense as secondary to a deeper, more spiritual meaning. Those who spiritualize prophecy work on the principle that these portions of the Bible have a hidden meaning. They assume that the literal approach obscures the real, deep meaning of the passage. However, abandoning the literal as the primary meaning is a terribly arbitrary way to approach the prophetic Scriptures.[15]

2. *Interpret by Comparing Prophecy with Prophecy*. Benware notes that many amillennialists cite Revelation 20 as the only section of Scripture that refers to a millennium. "The prophets of the Old Testament have spoken volumes on the subject of the millennial kingdom, and, in order to understand Revelation 20 correctly, it is essential to visit Isaiah, Daniel, Jeremiah, and others to learn what they have said [about a future prophetic kingdom]."[16]

To gain the complete picture on any doctrine, the interpreter must compare Scripture with Scripture.

3. *Interpret in Light of Possible Time Intervals*. The ancients did not calculate time as we do today. Though they placed several prophetic messages side by side, this does not mean they fully understood the full sequence of events nor the time of fulfillment. They spoke prophecy under inspiration but they also spoke of the distant future. Often events were stacked one upon another in the prophet's narration.

> This telescoping phenomenon is found a number of times in the prophets and reveals gaps in prophetic fulfillment. . . . Daniel 9:24–27 contains a gap that is critical to a proper interpretation of that prophecy. It is, of course, only in the

progress of God's revelation that we can see such intervals of time between prophetic fulfillments.[17]

4. *Interpret in Light of Double Reference.* Benware writes, "It is also true that one prophecy may have more than one fulfillment. An earlier, partial fulfillment may be coupled with a later complete fulfillment."[18] Many interpreters today question the truthfulness of double reference, sometimes also called "double fulfillment." In interpretative history, double reference was first devised by liberal scholars who felt that many New Testament fulfillments were but prophetic devices used by the New Testament writers to "create" prophecy connections. Their purpose in quoting some ancient passage was to show that certain events in their books were actually Old Testament prophecies coming to pass.

But again as stated, more study is needed. Benware gives an appropriate warning concerning double reference:

Of course, great care must be exercised by the prophetic interpreter to make sure that such a phenomenon does exist in a particular passage. It is obvious that the New Testament will be the key to seeing such a double reference.[19]

5. *Interpret Figurative Language Scripturally.* Benware observes,

Since the prophets did not include charts and graphs in their prophecies, and since they did not have overhead transparencies, they had to rely on the language that they used. . . . The use of symbols as a communication device became quite important to the message they were giving. As already mentioned, figures of speech and symbols represent something literal.[20]

But symbols must be interpreted *in light of the immediate context and in light of the larger context.* Often figures of speech may be used in one place in the Scriptures and then in another place by another writer. One should not be surprised to find Daniel using a symbol found in Isaiah, who clearly used that same symbol over a hundred years earlier. "The symbols found in Scripture and then used by other writers of Scripture do set parameters for interpretation. Symbols do not give an interpreter freedom to apply any meaning he wants to a text."[21]

Benware concludes, taking into consideration these rules of interpretation, "We believe that Jesus Christ will literally return to this earth and reign at His second coming because He literally came to this earth the first time, being born of the virgin Mary at Bethlehem."[22]

CHAPTER 11

Hermeneutics and the Covenants of Scripture

Unlike covenant theology, which actually "creates" three covenants that are not in the Scriptures, dispensationalists allow their theology to develop along the lines of the scriptural theological covenants that are obvious in the Word of God. Though there may be a debate on the number, dispensationalists also recognize the importance of scripturally observable historic dispensations. And, as has already been noted, many of these dispensations are even admitted as biblical by many amillennialists and postmillennialists.

Though well meaning, covenant theologian Berkhof confuses "imagined" covenants with actual biblical covenants. He also admits of dispensations that dispensationalists can agree on. For example, he calls the promise in Genesis 3:15 of the Seed of woman crushing the head of the serpent a covenant. There is no evidence for this. Berkhof admits that this "protoevangel" gospel "certainly does not refer to any formal establishment of a covenant. The revelation of such an establishment could only follow after the covenant idea had been developed in history."[1]

Berkhof continues to confuse biblical revelation when he labels the Abrahamic covenant the covenant of grace, which he has already admitted has no verification in Scripture. He adds that the establishment of the grace covenant with Abraham "marked the beginning of an institutional Church."[2] He does state correctly that the Sinaitic covenant (or the Mosaic covenant) neither took away nor supplanted the Abrahamic covenant, though still calling the Abrahamic the covenant of grace.[3]

As dispensationalists speak of a New Testament dispensation, so does Berkhof. But he makes another hermeneutical mistake by writing, "The covenant of grace, as it is revealed in the New Testament, is essentially the same as that which governed the relation of the Old Testament believers to God."[4] After reading his views on the covenants and dispensations, one comes away feeling confused as to what he actually believes on the subjects.

What Are the Biblical Covenants?

Below is a summary of the covenants that are indeed labeled covenants in the Scriptures themselves. This section is not meant to be an exhaustive study of the covenants. Peters's *Theocratic Kingdom* and Pentecost's *Things to Come* as well as many other works have plumbed the depths of each of these covenants. But a recognition and study of the covenants is important to sound hermeneutics. It is enough to note here that the covenants form the axis of the Bible. If they are ignored, one's conclusion about the message and thrust of the Word of God will be skewed and distorted.

The Noahic Covenant

Following the trauma of the great global flood (Gen. 6:13–8:19) and after the ark had landed safely upon mount Ararat, the Lord established an everlasting covenant between Himself "and every living creature of all flesh that is on the earth" (9:16). The rainbow forming in the clouds is "the sign of the covenant which I have established between Me and all flesh that is on the earth" (v. 17). The Lord added, "While the earth remains, seedtime and harvest, and cold and heat, and summer and winter, and day and night shall not cease" (8:22).

As long as earth history remains in its present physical state, this covenant is in effect.

> God not only gave [men] a fresh start; He also gave them an unconditional promise or covenant. He promised not to destroy the earth with a flood no matter how evil Noah's descendants got. . . . God unilaterally promised to uphold the rhythms of the earth in order to sustain human life—even though humans had rebelled against Him, their Creator.[5]

The Mosaic Covenant

Though the Abrahamic covenant comes before the Mosaic, for the purpose of emphasis in this chapter, the Mosaic will be dealt with here. In actuality, the Abrahamic covenant was given to this patriarch around 2090 B.C., and the Mosaic covenant was given over a period of time to Moses, around 1444–1410 B.C. (though this dating cannot be absolute).

The purpose of the Mosaic covenant is important to note. The Law was given to Israel and not to the church or mankind in general. God entered into this covenant with the Jews whom He had "brought out . . . of the land of Egypt" (Exod. 20:2). It was Israel's constitution, given to guide the people through life (31:12–17).

> . . . The law given at Mount Sinai was designed to be temporary. It would exist as a rule of life for Israel until the Messiah came (Gal. 3:23–4:5). The law was never designed to save anyone but was given to protect Israel from the terrible sins of the Gentiles and to teach them about their God.[6]

The Law was imperfect because of the weakness of humans to keep its demands, but it was perfect because it reflected the righteousness of God and His holy demands. The Law was also based on "fulfillment" in that people had to keep it in order to be blessed (Deut. 28:1–14). If they failed to do so, there was nothing left but a curse (28:15–22). Interestingly, in this same chapter (Deut. 28), Moses predicted that the nation of Israel would ultimately depart from God morally and spiritually and be scattered worldwide for their sins (vv. 64–68).

Because of a promise and a warning, that is, a blessing and a curse, it is clear that the Mosaic covenant was *conditional* in that if the covenant was not kept, there would be the curse and the scattering. The only portraits of grace in the Mosaic law was sacrifice. If the Jew who had sinned offered an atoning sacrifice with a true heart of conviction and repentance, the Lord would forgive and the relationship was restored. But because of the sinfulness of the Jewish people, sacrifices were continued on an ongoing basis for all of the people. In time, the sacrifices were being offered, but the heart of the people was far from the Lord. But what about the New Testament period? Writing of the two covenants, the new and the Mosaic, Benware notes,

> The two cannot be mixed; you must choose which system you want to live under. If you choose the law, then you "fall from grace" ([Gal.] 5:4). The law has no role in a person's justification or sanctification. The church has not been given

the commission of taking Israel's law code and mixing it with the gospel message of grace and imposing this mixture on the nations of the earth.[7]

With the death of Christ, the Law was made null and void. "Christians are not under the law but under the new covenant and the teachings of Jesus Christ."[8]

Paul argues for this dispensational change in Galatians 3:23–25: "Before this faith came, we were held prisoners by the law, locked up until faith should be revealed. So the law was put in charge to lead us to Christ that we might be justified by faith. Now that that faith has come, we are no longer under the supervision of the law" (see also Gal. 3:19–22; 4:1–11; 5:16–18; Eph. 2:15–16; Heb. 7:11–22).[9]

But this is getting ahead of the covenantal issues. It is important first to look at the Abrahamic covenant and the three sub-covenants that spring forth from it. Again remember, the Abrahamic covenant came before the Mosaic covenant in time sequence.

The Abrahamic Covenant

McAvoy writes,

God's covenant with Abraham is first set forth and initiated in Genesis 12:1–3. It is later reiterated in Genesis 13:14–17, ratified in Genesis 15, and signified in Genesis 17. It is again reiterated in Genesis 22:15–18. In each case it is enlarged upon. It is later confirmed to Isaac (Gen. 26:3–5, 24) and Jacob (Gen. 28:13–15; 35:9–12; cf. 46:1–4), and is subsequently spoken of as God's "covenant with Abraham, Isaac, and Jacob" (2 Kings 13:23).[10]

He further notes,

A unilateral covenant was binding only on one party, the one making the pledge. The Abrahamic covenant is a unilateral covenant, a divine covenant in which God alone pledges Himself to a course of action through Abraham and his seed, which cannot be reversed (else God would prove untrue) and cannot be annulled by the failure of either Abraham or his seed, for the existence and continuance of the covenant depends not upon the fidelity of Abraham or his seed, but on God alone.[11]

What is also important, McAvoy points out, is that to the people of Abraham's day, making such a covenant was extremely important and "irreversibly binding."[12] One's word, honor, and very life were at stake when the covenant was finally initiated. This is why Moses, the author of Genesis, makes sure the reader understands the historic nature and significance of the covenant.

Why Is the Abrahamic Covenant Important to Hermeneutics?

McAvoy further states,

From an interpretative standpoint, the Abrahamic covenant is the single most important event in the Old Testament. It governs God's entire program for Israel and the nations and is thus determinative of God's program in history. The Abrahamic covenant is foundational to all of Scripture. It is the key to both the Old and New Testaments and is foundational to the whole program of redemption. All subsequent revelation is the outworking of this covenant. This covenant, and the subsequent covenant framework, is the key to understanding Scripture.[13]

How Does the Abrahamic Covenant Govern the Plan of Scripture?

Dispensationalists see the Abrahamic covenant as the driving force of the Word of God. So much of the Bible unfolds from the key chapter, Genesis 12. From this important chapter, one can see a plan unfolding all the way to the book of Revelation. As the story of Abraham begins, he is told by the Lord to leave his country of origin and travel far from his father's house and his relatives to a land that God would reveal to him.

In that land, Canaan, the Lord gave promises to make of him a great nation and to give him a blessing. God said, "in you all the families of the earth shall be blessed." In sum, this covenant speaks of (1) a nation (the children of Abraham); (2) a land—Canaan or Palestine and even beyond; (3) a blessing, ultimately to all families of the earth.

This covenant is without question a binding agreement in that God tells Abraham to walk through the land that he and his children would receive (Gen. 13:15–18). The Lord too speaks of literal children that will be so many they are uncountable (16:10). The covenant promises are eternal as well: "I will give [the land] to you and to your descendants forever" (13:15).

Finally, the Abrahamic promises are unconditional in that God put Abraham asleep when He further assured him of the final fulfillment of the agreement: "A deep sleep fell upon Abram" (15:12). "Though a covenant is between two individuals, God sovereignly finalized the promise Himself."[14]

What Other Features Characterize the Abrahamic Covenant?

Couch summarizes the outstanding additional features of the covenant:

> The Lord confirmed the promises with Abraham's son Isaac. "I will be with you and bless you, for to you and to your descendants I will give all these lands, and I will establish the oath which I swore to your father Abraham" (Gen. 26:3). To Jacob the covenant was also repeated as a future national promise (Gen. 35:10–12). The Abrahamic covenant is affirmed as a literal, eternal agreement. Genesis closes with Joseph referring to it. "I am about to die, but God will surely take care of you [the tribal families], and bring you up from this land [Egypt] to the land which He promised on oath to Abraham, to Isaac and to Jacob" (Gen. 50:24).
>
> Two of the most striking things about the Abrahamic covenant is that it is seen as a *forever* promise and also literal. It was not spiritualized or allegorized. The patriarchs understood the promises in a literal context: a literal land and actual descendants, or children, who would receive the promises. Some say, for sin the nation of Israel was cut off from the promises. Though a specific generation would be scattered from the land (Deut. 28:64), a future generation would be regathered by the Lord to the promised region. "The LORD your God will restore you from captivity . . . and will gather you again from all the peoples where the LORD your God has scattered you. . . . The LORD your God will bring you into the land which your fathers possessed" (Deut. 30:3, 5). This cannot be allegorized to a spiritual Gentile generation or to the church age. This clearly means Jewish descendants of Abraham—literal children returning to a literal land![15]

The Land (Palestinian) Covenant

This covenant comes under the Abrahamic covenant. It is an expansion, an extension, and a further revealed promise as to what God had in mind, in regard to what He told Abraham.

Now lift up your eyes and look from the place where you are, northward and southward and eastward and westward; for all the land which you see, I will give it to you and to your descendants forever. (Genesis 13:14–15)

Arise, walk about the land through its length and breadth; for I give it to you. (Genesis 13:17)

The eternal nature of the land promise tells us that, though the Jews today are unfaithful to God, they still hold the everlasting deed to the land. The Lord added,

And I will establish My covenant between Me and you [Abraham] and your descendants after you throughout their generations for an everlasting covenant, to be God to you and to your descendants after you. And I will give to you and to your descendants after you, the land of your sojournings, all the land of Canaan, for an everlasting possession; and I will be their God. (Genesis 17:7–8)

Though the Jews will be unfaithful and will be scattered worldwide, this covenant stands firm. It will intertwine with the new covenant to spiritually and physically restore a remnant back in the land. This ultimate restoration of course will have to do with the kingdom of the Messiah. Ezekiel predicts,

Behold, I will open your graves and cause you to come up out of your graves, My people; and I will bring you into the land of Israel. Then you will know that I am the LORD, when I have opened your graves and caused you to come up out of your graves, My people. And I will put My Spirit within you, and you will come to life, and I will place you on your own land. (Ezekiel 37:12–14)

And they shall live on the land that I gave to Jacob My servant, in which your fathers lived; and they will live on it, they, and their sons, and their sons' sons, forever; and David My servant

shall be their prince forever. And I will make a covenant of peace with them; it will be an everlasting covenant with them. And I will place them and multiply them, and will set My sanctuary in their midst forever. (Ezekiel 37:25–26)

Is the Land Promise Truly a Covenant?

The answer is a resounding, yes! Pentecost points out a progression of verses:

To your descendants I will give this land. (Genesis 12:7)

For all the land which you see, I will give it to you and to your descendants forever. (Genesis 13:15)

And I will establish My covenant between Me and you and your descendants after you throughout their generations for an everlasting covenant, to be God to you and to your descendants after you. And I will give to you and to your descendants after you, the land of your sojournings, all the land of Canaan, for an everlasting possession; and I will be their God. (Genesis 17:7–8)[16]

Note that the word *covenant* is used in the singular. This is referring to the Abrahamic agreement, but the land promise is included. In this sense then the land restoration promise is an extension of the original promise God made with Abraham. One can see the land promise, then, as an extension or a mini-covenant that expands and explains in more detail what God promised to Abraham.

In a real sense, progressive revelation comes to play here. Progressively and by degree, God unfolds the more complete revelation He had in mind in regard to a future generation of Jews and their ultimate return to the promised land. Pentecost concludes,

From the original statement of the provisions of this covenant, it is easy to see that, on the basis of a literal fulfillment, Israel must be converted as a nation, must be regathered from her world-wide dispersion, must be installed in her land, which she is made to possess, must witness the judgment of her enemies, and must receive the material blessings vouchsafed to her. This covenant, then, is seen to have a wide influence on our eschatological expectation. Since these things have never been fulfilled, and an eternal and

unconditional covenant demands a fulfillment, we must provide for just such a program in our outline of future events.[17]

The Davidic Covenant

Enns explains the Davidic covenant,

> In God's original promise to Abraham, He promised to bless
> the patriarch, giving him an innumerable posterity. God
> promised to give Abraham a great name and make him a
> blessing through his posterity. It is the promise regarding
> these promised descendants in Genesis 12:2 that is ampli-
> fied in the Davidic Covenant of 2 Samuel 7:12–16. God prom-
> ised David that he would have a son, Solomon, who would
> establish his throne; moreover, David's lineage would be per-
> petuated, ultimately issuing in the kingdom rule of Messiah,
> who would have a political kingdom, an earthly rule that
> would endure forever. . . . The kingdom concept reaches its
> zenith in the Davidic Covenant, which predicts the future
> millennial reign of David's greater Son, the Messiah.[18]

Throughout the latter Old Testament, the prophets amplified and
expanded on the person of the Messiah. Other features would flesh
out the doctrine of the Messiah. For example, He would be called
the Son of God (Psalm 2) and the Son of Man (Daniel 7). He would
have a virgin birth (Isaiah 7:14) and be born in Bethlehem (Micah 5).
He would present Himself to Jerusalem riding upon the colt of a
donkey (Zechariah 9). He would substitute for sin (Isaiah 53), suffer,
and die (Psalm 22) but come forth from the dead (Psalm 16). As well,
the Messiah would carry forth David's lineage (Psalm 89). Coming to
the earth dramatically, He would split the Mount of Olives in Jerusalem (Zechariah 14) and be recognized by the surviving remnant of
Jews as the King whom their earlier ancestors had pierced (Zechariah
12). He would judge the nations (Psalm 110), rule over a restored
Jewish people (Isaiah 9), and be called "a righteous Branch of David"
(Jeremiah 33) exercising earthly righteousness (Isaiah 11).

One of the most dramatic prophecies mentioned over and over
in the New Testament is the fact that Jesus is the Son of Man who
will receive earth's final great kingdom, the fifth kingdom mentioned
in Daniel 7:22–28. Now, as New Testament verses repeat over and
over, He sits at the right hand of God, waiting for His enemies to be
subdued (Ps. 110:1). But someday He will come to Zion (the regathered Israel) (110:2) with the "clouds of heaven" (Dan. 7:13) and

be given "dominion, glory and a kingdom, that all the peoples, nations, and men of every language might serve Him" (v. 14).

The allegorists, of course, turn all of this into a nonliteral scenario that is mostly applied to the church, though there are some who believe the Jews too will be saved at the end of the "kingdom" period, i.e., at the close of the church period. As in orthodox Jewish history, premillennialists take the above passages in a literal, consistent manner. This of course fits with a natural, normal reading of the Old Testament promises.

The New Covenant

This covenant clearly seems to be an extension of the Abrahamic covenant as mentioned in the seed promise in Genesis 12:3. God would someday, through the Abrahamic promise, bless "all the families of the earth." Since the promise of the land has already been given in verse 2 to the physical descendants of Abraham, this "blessing" promise would be more than likely spiritual blessings. Later prophecies about the new covenant would prove this to be so. But as well, Gentiles, or all families of the earth, would be blessed equally with the Jewish people but under a different time frame and with a dispensational change. Of the new covenant, Enns states,

> The prophet Jeremiah announced the impending invasion by Nebuchadnezzar and the subsequent captivity in Babylon. But Jeremiah envisioned a future day when God would restore the fortunes of Israel and bring them back into the land (Jer. 30:3). This would be an eschatological restoration for it would follow the time of great tribulation for Israel (Jer. 30:7). Jeremiah prophesied the rebuilding of Jerusalem in that future day (Jer. 30:18–24) and the resultant kingdom blessings (Jer. 31:1–12). The blessing of Israel in that future day would be based on the New Covenant that God would make with Israel (Jer. 31:31–34). That New Covenant is made with the nation Israel (Jer. 31:31) and will be in contrast with the Old Covenant, the Mosaic Covenant, which could not produce righteousness in the people.[19]

What Are Some of the Views About the New Covenant?

Covenant Theology. Surprisingly, Berkhof makes no reference to the new covenant in "Index of Subjects" in his *Systematic Theology.* Nor does he mention it by name in his book. Instead, he refers to it as the Covenant of grace and writes that it is a "renewal of the covenant [of grace], Jer. 31:33; 32:38–40."[20] Here he cites the actual biblical new covenant verses in Jeremiah, but fails to address it as such.

Dispensational Views. Among dispensationalists, there has been a progressive change that is in keeping with the realization that faithful interpreters must be cautious to practice consistent and normal hermeneutics. But earlier dispensationalists were afraid to commingle the new covenant—that which was prophesied in Jeremiah 31–32 and mentioned first of all to be for Israel—with the church. But it was said to Abraham that through him the Lord would bless all families of the earth (Gen. 12:3), and it appears that this instrument of blessing for the nations is the new covenant. But how this blessing would occur must be explained correctly and biblically.

The Two Covenant Position

Lewis Sperry Chafer and other early dispensationalists thought there were actually two new covenants inaugurated, one for Israel and one for the church. But Decker correctly argues,

> The basis for this view is the presupposition that there can be no common interest between God's purposes for Israel and for the Church. This position suffers two fatal flaws: Scripture never explicitly says that there are two new covenants nor does it ever juxtapose them in the same context, and second, it is built on a theological presupposition rather than on an exegesis of the text. Chafer's determination to maintain a complete separation between Israel and the Church has forced him to an exegetically indefensible conclusion.[21]

The Three Dispensational Views

1. The church has no part in the covenant. This view claims that the new covenant is for Israel only and will be fulfilled in the future messianic kingdom.

> The church enjoys similar spiritual blessings and promises as those that are specified for Israel but not on the basis of the new covenant. The only relationship between the church and the new covenant is that members of the church are united to the mediator of the new covenant—Jesus Christ.[22]

There are verses (Luke 21:20; 1 Cor. 11:25; 2 Cor. 3:6), however, that do indeed relate the new covenant to the church, and which will be examined later.

2. The church has some part in the covenant. In simple terms, "The new covenant will be fulfilled with Israel eschatologically but is enjoyed soteriologically by the church now."[23]

3. The church has a preliminary part in the covenant. This view is gaining acceptance because it is more consistent with normal and natural hermeneutics, and because there are so many verses that support it. The new covenant is not necessarily fulfilled by the church age, nor does this position commingle Israel with the church. Decker explains,

> The principle of authorial intent necessitates the fulfillment of what God promised Israel—a future fulfillment of the new covenant (including its territorial and political aspects) for the nation. Continuity comes into play when it is recognized that the church experiences a preliminary and partial fulfillment of some aspects of the new covenant. These include forgiveness and the indwelling of the Spirit.[24]

Decker's opinion makes sense in light of the promises to Abraham in Genesis 12:1–3. The children of Abraham would become a great nation (in influence and in God's purposes) and would receive a distinct land promise in Canaan (and even beyond to the river Euphrates). But through Abraham, the families of the earth, the nations, would receive a blessing. And of course that blessing would be salvation through the death and resurrection of Israel's Messiah.

The church's preliminary part in the covenant would be developed in Scripture as follows:

a. A new covenant is prophesied that will someday bless the descendants of the house of Israel and the house of Judah (Jer. 31:31).
b. It will contrast with the Mosaic covenant, which the Jews broke when they came out of Egypt (v. 32).
c. God will write His law in the hearts of His people, and they will experience a personal relationship with the Lord (v. 33).
d. The people will receive permanent forgiveness of iniquity and complete forgiveness of sin (v. 34).
e. Ezekiel further adds that the Lord will "sprinkle [slosh] clean water" on His people, and they will be cleansed from filthiness (Ezek. 36:25).
f. God will grant His people a new heart, a new spirit, and will replace a hardened heart with a heart of flesh (v. 26).

g. The Lord will place His Spirit within and cause His people to observe His ordinances (v. 27). "You will be My people, and I will be your God" (v. 28).

h. Jesus told His disciples that His body and blood would be for (ratification of) the new covenant. Of this sacrifice, He said at Passover in the Upper Room, "This cup which is poured out for you is the new covenant in My blood" (Luke 22:20).

i. As prophesied, the Holy Spirit comes upon the believers at Pentecost (Acts 2:4). This "coming" launches the new covenant.

j. Believers in Christ become "servants of the new covenant" (2 Cor. 3:6a). That is, they are responsible for sharing the good news that in Christ there is provision for the forgiveness of sins, as promised in the covenant.

k. The apostle Paul compares the new covenant with the Mosaic covenant. He writes that believers are the servants of the new covenant, "not of the letter [of the Law], but of the Spirit [of the new covenant]; for the letter [the Law] kills, but the Spirit [through the new covenant] gives life" (2 Cor. 3:6b).

One purpose of the book of Hebrews is to compare the new covenant with the weaknesses of the Mosaic covenant. The author of Hebrews repeatedly quotes Jeremiah 31 and the new covenant promises. As well, he continually makes a comparison of the two covenants and shows the superiority of the new because of the finished work of Christ as a living sacrifice.

In chapter 8, the Hebrews author makes a lengthy contrast between the two. He says Jesus is the mediator "of a better covenant, which has been enacted on better promises" (v. 6), and that it is the superior "second" covenant that would replace the first covenant (the Mosaic), which had "faults" (v. 7).

After quoting Jeremiah 31:31–34, the writer of Hebrews says God gave a new covenant because He made "the first obsolete, and [it was] growing old . . . ready to disappear" (v. 13). He adds that the spilling of Christ's blood was necessary to make this new covenant (9:15–28).

The church now benefits in these spiritual blessings of the coming of the Holy Spirit and the forgiveness of sins. The new covenant replaces the law as promised back in Jeremiah 31, but the prophecy of the new covenant, in its direct and "first and foremost" purpose, is yet to be applied to Israel. The new covenant will be applied, however, when the eyes of the Jewish people are opened and the remnant returns to the land to greet their Messiah. Thus, in the Millennium, the new covenant is ultimately fulfilled.

How Then Should the New Covenant Be Understood?

Lindsey states,

> The truth is that the New Covenant is partially in force in this present age. But nowhere does the book of Hebrews teach that there will be no future fulfillment to natural Israel, to whom the promise was originally made.
>
> The Christian is only allowed into the covenant's blessing through union with Christ, who, as a son of Abraham, inherited the blessings of the covenant.
>
> The major purpose of the Epistle to the Hebrews is to prove four things from Old Testament prophecy: (1) that the conditional Mosaic Covenant has been replaced by the partial institution of the promised New Covenant; (2) that the New Covenant could not be instituted at all until it was made possible through the vastly superior sacrifice of the Messiah; (3) that the Messiah is the Son of God; (4) that Jesus is the only one who could be the Messiah.[25]

Benware correctly summarizes how dispensationalists and others should see the new covenant:

> Provision for the blessing of Gentiles was made in the Abrahamic covenant ("in you all the families of the earth shall be blessed," Gen. 12:3). The salvation and blessing of Gentiles was always part of God's plan and concern. In the Old Testament, the book of Jonah reveals much of the heart of God for the Gentiles. It is not surprising that, after the Cross, Gentiles in the church are seen as the recipients of salvation and blessing because of the Abrahamic covenant (cf. Gal. 3:14; Rom. 11:11–20). Because the church (now made up primarily of Gentiles) receives blessings of the new covenant does not mean that Israel will not receive these same blessings, and more, in the future.
>
> The church does partake in the blessings of the new covenant, but not all of them. As members of the Body of Christ we, like Israel in the future, are regenerated, indwelt, forgiven, and taught by the Holy Spirit. These blessings, however, are unrelated promises having to do with restoration to the land and the blessings related to that land. Israel alone will receive those.
>
> The church, then, is a partaker of the spiritual blessings

of the new covenant, enjoying regeneration, the forgiveness of sin, and the presence and ministry of the Holy Spirit. The church is primarily Gentile in its makeup—those who have been graciously grafted in by God *until* their number is complete. Multitudes of Gentiles experience the wonderful blessings of the new covenant. But the church is not national Israel, the people with whom God made this covenant. The church does not and cannot fulfill the new covenant. Its fulfillment awaits the arrival of Jesus the Messiah. When He returns at the Second Coming, all the spiritual and material blessings promised Israel will be received.[26]

PART 3

Interpreting the Church

CHAPTER 12

Covenant Theology and the Doctrine of the Church

It is surprising that covenant theologians are not more critical of their own system of theology. A close examination of the Bible reveals that the covenant approach to the Word of God is lacking and flawed. Granted, some covenant theorists may have overlooked a point or two in the development of the system, but the system taken together is inadequate to properly explain the way the Word of God is structured. As James Orr writes, the system of covenant theology is flawed hermeneutically:

> It failed to seize the true idea of development, and by an artificial system of typology, and allegorizing interpretation; sought to read back practically the whole of the New Testament into the Old. But its most obvious defect was that, in using the idea of the Covenant as an exhaustive category, and attempting to force into it the whole material of theology, it created an artificial scheme which could only repel minds of simple and natural notions. It is impossible, e.g., to justify by Scriptural proof the detailed elaboration of the idea of a covenant of works in Eden, with its parties, conditions, promises, threatenings, sacraments, etc.[1]

Covenant theology minimizes important and obvious biblical covenants that are clearly outlined in the Word of God: the Abrahamic covenant and, arising from this, the Palestinian (land) covenant, Davidic covenant, and new covenant. To be fair, some covenant theologians occasionally refer to the new covenant, but usually in such a New Testament context that its Abrahamic covenant origin is all but missed. It is important to note, however, that most covenant theologians, in agreement with dispensationalists, would hold to the Noahic covenant and to the Mosaic covenant, or the covenant of Law.

It is particularly disturbing, though, that the leading proponents of covenant theology admit that there is no scriptural evidence for the two most important covenants in their system—the covenant of works and the covenant of redemption (and/or grace). Covenant theologists admit that these covenants were likely revealed in time, specifically, that they were made in eternity past and outside of the framework of Scripture. Yet they claim that there is substantial evidence that they indeed are legitimate biblical covenants.

A case in point is the outstanding and well-known covenant theologian Berkhof, who admits throughout his covenant discussion that the system is based on weak biblical evidence. He writes in regard to the covenant of works, "It must be admitted that the term 'covenant' is not found in the first three chapters of Genesis, but this is not tantamount to saying that they do not contain the necessary data for the construction of a doctrine of the covenant."[2] "It may still be objected that we do not read of the two parties as coming to an agreement, nor of Adam as accepting the terms laid down [for a covenant], but this is not an insuperable objection."[3] "Some deny that there is any Scripture evidence for such a promise. Now it is perfectly true that no such promise [as the covenant of works] is explicitly recorded."[4] "There may still be some doubt as to the propriety of the name 'Covenant of Works,' but there can be no valid objection to the covenant [of works] idea."[5] "They who deny the covenant of works generally base their denial in part on the fact that there is no record of such a promise in the Bible. And it is perfectly true that Scripture contains no explicit promise of eternal life to Adam."[6] "We have no definite information in Scripture respecting the sacrament(s) or seal(s) of this covenant [of works]."[7]

Berkhof admits that some Reformed teachers "question whether, and in how far, the covenant of works can be considered as a thing of the past; or whether and in how far, it must be regarded as still in force."[8] In reference to the covenant of redemption, which some have labeled the "counsel of peace," Berkhof further notes, "The Scriptural character of the name cannot be maintained, but this, of course, does not detract from the reality of the counsel of peace."[9]

And Charles Hodge further agrees concerning the issue of God entering into this covenant of works with Adam that "this statement does not rest upon any express declaration of the Scriptures."[10] And "Although the word covenant [as in works] is not used in Genesis, and does not elsewhere, in any clear passage, occur in reference to the transaction there recorded, . . . it is plain that the Bible does represent the arrangements made with Adam as a truly federal transaction."[11]

The History of Covenant Theology

Buswell points out that covenant theology can be traced from Heinrich Bullinger (1504–1575) to Johannes Cocceius (1603–1669), a German theologian who taught at Bremen, Franeker, and Leiden. Many regard him as the founder of covenant theology.[12] From Cocceius, the system was refined by Hermann Witsius (1636–1708), through whom it reached its final development. These men saw the Bible develop along the lines of two main covenants, that of works and grace. Some covenant theologians say that there are three covenants and hold to a covenant of redemption as well. A split in opinion exists, however, as to whether the covenant of redemption is really also the covenant of grace or whether it is a separate covenant.

The Covenant of Works

Berkhof's candid statements quoted above demonstrate that the covenant of works rests on suppositions. It is stated, however, as follows:

> The covenant is an agreement between God and Adam that he would obey the Lord in regard to not eating of the tree of good and evil. This obedience incumbent upon Adam shows that it is a covenant, though sovereignly initiated by God alone. In a sense, this was a salvation by works. Covenant theologians argue as to whether this covenant has been revoked and annulled or not. When Adam sinned "Spiritual death entered instantly, and the seeds of death also began to operate in the body. The full execution of the sentence, however, did not follow at once, but was arrested, because God immediately introduced an economy of grace and restoration."[13]

Dispensationalists respond that nowhere does the Bible call Adam's obedience a kind of covenant. Nor would they agree that obedience was a form of works salvation. According to the biblical evidence gleaned from the limited verses about Adam in Genesis, dispensationalists consider the pre-Fall a period of innocence in which Adam was sinless and was commanded not to eat of a certain tree. God related to Adam in this innocent condition. But in no way can this be called a covenant relationship in the normal sense of the words. Dispensationalists have far more evidence for calling the period the dispensation of innocence than do covenant theologians for calling it the covenant of works.

About the covenants of works and grace, Ryrie notes,

> . . . they are ideas that are not systematized, formalized, and stated by Scripture as covenants. At least the dispensationalist finds the word *dispensation* used of one or two of his specific dispensations (Eph. 1:10; 3:9); the covenant theologian *never* finds in the Bible the terms *Covenant of Works* and *Covenant of Grace*.[14]

Ryrie further writes,

> The existence of the covenants is not found by an inductive examination of passages. . . . Now, if it is permissible for the covenant theologian to base his entire system on a deduction rather than on a clear statement of Scripture, why can he not permit the dispensationalist to deduce the existence of various dispensations, especially when certain of the dispensations are specifically named in Scripture? The dispensationalists has more inductive evidence for the existence of the specific dispensations than does the covenant theologian for his covenants of works and grace.[15]

The Covenant of Grace

In presenting the covenant of grace, an immediate conflict arises between the various covenant theologians. Charles Hodge says there are two distinct covenants, of grace and redemption. But Berkhof insists,

> Though this distinction (between the covenant of redemption and the covenant of grace) is favored by Scripture statements, it does not follow that there are two separate and independent covenants. . . . The covenant of grace and redemption are two modes or phases of the one evangelical covenant of mercy.[16]

Hodge argues,

> Both [covenants] are so clearly presented in the Bible that
> they should not be confounded. The latter, the covenant of
> grace, is founded on the former, the covenant of redemp-
> tion. Of the one Christ is the mediator and surety; of the
> other He is one of the contracting parties.[17]

Hodge also admits, "The Westminster standards seem to adopt
sometimes the one and sometimes the other mode of representation."[18] The larger catechism would also say that the covenant of
grace was signed and sealed by Christ, the second Adam. As the second Adam, in Him are the seed of those who are elected to salvation.
Hodge would say that the covenant of redemption was made between the Father and the Son concerning man's salvation.[19] The gospel is the offer of salvation to all men. "In this sense, the covenant of
grace is formed with all mankind."[20] Through this covenant,

> . . . salvation is offered to all men on the condition of faith in
> Christ. And therefore to that extent, or, in a sense which ac-
> counts for that fact, the covenant of grace is made with all
> men. The great sin of those who hear the gospel is that they
> refuse to accept of that covenant, and therefore place them-
> selves without its pale.[21]

Ryrie points out,

> There is not one reference from Scripture . . . that deal[s]
> directly with the establishment of the covenant of grace or
> its characteristics. There are references concerning the bless-
> ings of salvation but none to support the covenant of grace.
> What is missing is rather significant and revealing.[22]

Dispensationalists assert that salvation comes through the new
covenant that was ratified by the shed blood of Jesus. The Lord told
His disciples before His arrest and ultimate death, "This cup which
is poured out for you is the new covenant in My blood" (Luke 22:20).
This new covenant was in seed form when God prophesied to
Abraham that all the nations would be blessed through him (Gen.
12:3). This new covenant was meant first for Israel, but the Gentiles would benefit from it during the dispensation of the church.
Gentiles who now accept Christ as Savior become spiritual sons of

Abraham (Gal. 3:7), and with the believing Jew, become the spiritual body of Christ, the church. Throughout Paul's presentation of the gospel, he does not refer to the covenant of grace but makes reference to the Abrahamic covenant. He writes,

> *Be sure that it is those who are of faith that are sons of Abraham. And the Scripture, foreseeing that God would justify the Gentiles by faith, preached the gospel beforehand to Abraham, saying, "All the nations shall be blessed in you." So then those who are of faith are blessed with Abraham, the believer. (Galatians 3:7–9)*

Paul sees believers now as responsible for sharing the new covenant. He says that God "made us adequate as servants of a new covenant, not of the letter, but of the Spirit; for the letter kills, but the Spirit gives life" (2 Cor. 3:6). The new covenant is the key factor for the dispensation of the church. And in 2 Corinthians 3, Paul makes a contrast between this dispensation and that of law, which he says was "the ministry of death, in letters engraved on stones, . . . so that the sons of Israel could not look intently at the face of Moses because of the glory of his face" (v. 7).

Paul shows the difference between the dispensations of law and church (or grace). He nowhere refers to a man-made covenant of grace or redemption. Paul clearly saw the law as done away with, and yet he points out it had a moment of glory. According to Paul, this dispensation would be hailed as the period of "the ministry of righteousness." "For if the ministry of condemnation [Law] has glory, much more does the ministry of righteousness [new covenant] abound in glory. For indeed what had glory [the Law], in this case has no glory on account of the glory that surpasses it [new covenant]" (vv. 9–10).

Summary

No one concludes the issues better than Ryrie when he writes,

> If it is permissible for the covenant theologian to base his entire system on a deduction rather than on a clear statement of Scripture, why can he not permit the dispensationalist to deduce the existence of various dispensations, especially when certain of the dispensations are specifically named in Scripture? The dispensationalist has more inductive evidence for the existence of the specific dispensations than does the

covenant theologian for his covenants of works and grace; and the dispensationalist has as much, if not more, right to deduce his dispensational scheme as does the covenant theologian his covenant scheme.

What the covenant theologian does to make up for the lack of specific scriptural support for the covenants of works and grace is to project the general idea of covenant in the Bible and the specific covenants (like the covenant with Abraham) into these covenants of works and grace. . . . But there remains still the reality that nowhere does Scripture speak of a covenant of works or a covenant of grace as it does speak of a covenant with Abraham or a covenant with David or a new covenant.

Allis calls the revelation of this important covenant in Genesis 3:15 cryptic. This is all very strange and hard to swallow, especially when the biblical covenants with Abraham, Israel, David, and others are so clearly and specifically revealed. Abraham had no doubt that a covenant was being made when God Himself passed between the pieces of the sacrifice (Gen. 15:17–21).

And yet we are asked to believe in the existence of a covenant of grace that was scarcely revealed, although it is the fountainhead out of which even the Abrahamic covenant came![23]

This chapter is adapted from Mal Couch, "The New Dispensation: The Church," in *A Biblical Theology of the Church,* ed. Mal Couch (Grand Rapids: Kregel, 1999), 29–43.

CHAPTER 13

Dispensational Hermeneutics and the Doctrine of the Church

If there are no covenants of works and grace, how does God bring about salvation? What is the true nature of the church? Is there just one people of God, who, as a thread, connect the Old Testament to the New Testament? Is there one (or two) covenants that determine the salvation for this one people of God? Is the church the Israel of God? When did the church begin? Is the church simply the New Testament version of the Israel of the Old Testament? Which system—covenant theology or dispensational theology—best explains ecclesiology and the doctrine of the church?

The answers hinge on how one interprets the Bible, and interpretation is formulated under the term *hermeneutics*. By the science of hermeneutics, the entire Bible, all specific Scriptures, and each doctrine should be interpreted with the same consistent, linguistic approach. The laws of interpretation should be applied equally in every part of the Bible.

One's view of the church should be determined by this scientific method of linguistic study. Dispensationalists and covenant theologians agree on many areas of the scientific approach to interpretation. And while covenant theologians claim to be consistent in interpretation, their writings indicate otherwise.

Is it possible to be biased, unscientific, inconsistent, and subjective when trying to understand God's Word? In a word—yes. Interpreters must, however, put aside their preconceived notions about a specific passage or particular truth when attempting to discern the will of God from the Bible.

Thus, it is important to examine the basic definitions concerning hermeneutics and to compare how, from the two systems of hermeneutics, the church is set forth and viewed by both covenant and dispensational theologies.

Definition of Hermeneutics

Ramm writes,

> The word hermeneutics is ultimately derived from Hermes the Greek god who brought the messages of the gods to the mortals, and was the god of science, invention, eloquence, speech, writing, and art. As a theological discipline hermeneutics is the science of the correct interpretation of the Bible. It is a special application of the general science of linguistics and meaning. It seeks to formulate those particular rules which pertain to the special factors connected with the Bible. It stands in the same relationship to exegesis that a rule-book stands to a game. . . . Hermeneutics proper is not exegesis, but exegesis is applied hermeneutics. Hermeneutics is a science in that it can determine certain principles for discovering the meaning of a document.[1]

Zuck notes that Hermes was responsible for transmitting what is beyond human understanding: "The verb *hermeneuō* came to refer to bringing someone to an understanding of something in his language (thus explanation) or in another language (thus translation). The English word *interpret* is used at times to mean 'explain' and at other times 'translate.'"[2] A. A. Hodge adds,

> Hermeneutics, or the scientific determination of the principles and rules of Biblical Interpretation, including (1) the logical and grammatical and rhetorical principles determining the interpretation of human language in general, (2) the modification of these principles appropriate to the interpretation of the specific forms of human discourse, e.g., history, poetry, prophecy, parable, symbol, etc.[3]

At the heart of the rules for interpretation is the *literal method*. A literal reading is the starting point for explaining a passage of Scripture, *unless* there are clues by word usage or context that would indicate a verse or sentence should be taken figuratively or as an illustration. Tan notes,

The literal method of interpreting God's Word is a true and honest method. It is based on the assumption that the words of Scripture can be trusted. It assumes that since God intends His revelation to be understood, divine revelation must be written based on regular rules of human communication. To "interpret" means to explain the original sense of a speaker or writer according to the normal, customary, and proper usages of words and language. Literal interpretation of the Bible simply means to explain the original sense of the Bible according to the normal and customary usages of its language.[4]

In summary, "hermeneutics is this: It is the science (principles) and art (task) by which the meaning of the biblical text is determined."[5] Hermeneutics is scientific in its method for unlocking the meaning of language, particularly of the Scriptures. At the heart of that method is literal interpretation or normal meaning. Hermeneutics is also an art in that the interpreter must acquire experience and skill. It is not an art, however, in the sense that it is subjective. Biblical truth is not found in the personal taste of a specific pastor or teacher. As much as is humanly possible, all bias and prejudice must be put aside when interpreting the Word of God. In understanding the nature and function of New Testament ecclesiology, one must begin with orderly and consistent interpretation of key passages.

Principles of Hermeneutics

Though not meant to be exhaustive or detailed, the principles below are accepted by most Bible scholars as the laws for governing sound hermeneutics. Buswell lists some of the most important principles for interpretation (more on these principles is found in chapter five, "Principles of Hermeneutics"):[6]

1. Scripture interprets Scripture. The Bible is a closed volume of literature, having a cohesive historical context that is obviously differentiated from all other writings. In interpreting the Bible we do not ignore what are considered the proper rules for reading any serious literature.

2. The meaning of words is to be established by their usage. The Holy Spirit chose human language to convey the Word of God. Thus, an ordinary use of language conveys to us what God wants us to know.

3. Context must be taken into account. Words and thoughts must be understood within the setting, the time frame, the mood of the moment, the culture, etc.

4. A grammatico-historical interpretation must be used. A mastery of the historical setting and of the grammar used is imperative to comprehending the sense of a given sentence or paragraph. Thus an understanding of the biblical languages is imperative for the interpreter.

Other important rules and principles follow:

5. The interpreter must begin assuming literal or normal interpretation in a passage unless otherwise indicated by common linguistic sense. To read "the hills skipped like lambs" is obviously poetic. From a literal picture of a frisky lamb playfully jumping about, one can imagine the joy of creation expressing itself in worship to God. In other words, behind the poetry are literal concepts that in turn give meaning to the poetic language.

6. Thus, as in interpreting all languages, the Bible interpreter must use common sense in interpreting figurative language, i.e., poetry, figures of speech, metaphors, similes, illustrations, etc. But again, even these literary devices attempt to convey very actual, even literal concepts.

7. The "human drama" must be allowed to come forth. The interpreter should avoid "wooden-headed literalism" that follows so stiff and rigid an interpretation that all normal human expression is destroyed.

8. As part of context, factors such as culture, historical background, social setting, and geography all play a part in interpretation.

9. The Bible must be studied dispensationally in order to see how God dealt with people and nations differently at different time periods. The student of Scripture must observe carefully the context of a specific period in Bible history to ascertain how God worked in different ways.

For example, the Lord dealt with Abraham differently than with Moses and the Jews as they came out of Egypt. He now deals with the nations by grace, but someday He will pour forth His wrath upon the world in the period known as the Tribulation. The Jews under the Law did not know of the full revelation of the death, burial, and resurrection of their Messiah. The test of their faith was simply "Do you believe in God?" Now the test of faith in this grace dispensation is "Do

you believe that Jesus is your Savior and that He died for
your sins?" To see this difference one must study context
carefully and also "observe" the different message for a different period.

10. Progressive revelation is also important in dispensational
hermeneutics. Not everything is revealed at the beginning of
the Bible. Not only does each successive book presuppose the
books that went before, but many passages in the earlier books
clearly point to Scripture that was yet to come. God progressively, generation to generation, revealed new truth. Some
things, such as the church, were mysteries and not previously
revealed in the Old Testament. That God would save Gentiles
was prophesied in the Old Testament, but how, when, and by
what means was not revealed. Thus the church, its nature,
and its structure were revealed from Pentecost (Acts 2) and
forward. And that revelation, too, was progressive. It began
with the principal apostle Peter, who observed through the
unfolding of the book of Acts how the Holy Spirit was operat-
ing and building the church. But the full and complete revelation was given exclusively to the apostle Paul:

*You have heard of the [dispensation] of God's grace which
was given to me for you; that by revelation there was made
known to me the mystery, . . . to be specific, that the Gentiles
are fellow-heirs . . . and fellow-partakers of the promise in Christ
Jesus through the gospel. (Ephesians 3:2–3, 6)*

Kaiser adds,

11. "Under the strong impetus of the Reformation there was a
renewed emphasis that there is only one sense or meaning to
be gleaned from every passage if the interpreter is true to his
mission."[7] There are a few cases when the New Testament
writers quote an Old Testament passage as an illustration. But
the original meaning of the passage is still honored and this
rule still remains applicable.

12. The process of hermeneutics is threefold: (1) Students of the
Word are to *observe* everything they can about a given passage, using all the tools available. (2) Students are then to *interpret* all the data collected as to the meaning and message of
the verses under study. (3) Finally there must be *application*
of the truths and doctrines discovered in the material. That
application is twofold: (a) What did the passage mean to those

to whom it was written? (b) What does the passage mean now
to present day believers?

Requirements for the Interpreter

Ramm lists some essential spiritual and intellectual qualifica-
tions necessary for the student of the Word of God.[8] Note, however,
that one can possess these essentials yet have a blind spot as to how
to properly interpret or apply hermeneutics.

1. The interpreter must be born again.
2. The interpreter must have a passion for God's Word.
3. The interpreter must depend on the direction of the Holy Spirit.
4. Interpreters should have a basic, solid educational background.
   They must know something of history, literature, logic, and
   geography.
5. The interpreter should be competent in the biblical languages.
6. The interpreter must have adequate tools to work with: lexi-
   cons, grammars, language commentaries, an atlas, volumes
   on biblical background, and geography texts.
7. Though this has already been stated, the interpreter must come
   to the Bible as open as possible, without any theological bias
   or presuppositions.

The Bible student must also approach the Scriptures with
sound judgment and reason, seeking to be as objective in
his approach to the Bible as possible, without coming to the
Scriptures with prejudice or preconceived notions.[9]

8. It is the interpreter's job to represent the text, "not the prejudices, feelings, judgments, or concerns of the exegete. To in-
   dulge in the latter is to engage in eisegesis, 'a reading into' a
   text what the reader wants it to say."[10]

In conclusion, Ramm notes,

Matters of fact cannot be settled solely by spiritual means.
One cannot pray to God for information about the authorship of Hebrews and expect a distinct reply. Nor is it
proper to pray for information with reference to other
matters of biblical introduction expecting a revelation about
the revelation.[11]

Dispensationalism and Hermeneutics

Technically, there is no such thing as dispensational hermeneutics. Dispensationalists hold strongly to the hermeneutical principles given above and argue that if they are consistently followed, one will arrive at dispensationalism. Concerning the doctrine of ecclesiology, the church and Israel will be clearly seen in Scripture as separate bodies. It will be clearly seen as well that the Lord has two distinct plans for the church and for Israel.

The etymology of the word *dispensation* is from the Greek word *oikonomia*, a compound of two words, *oikos* meaning "house," and *nomia* meaning "law." The word implies how one manages and organizes the affairs of a household. The English word "economy" comes from this Greek term. On the biblical usage of the word, Ryrie states,

> The various forms of the word *dispensation* appear in the New Testament twenty times. The verb *oikonomeo* is used once in Luke 16:2, where it is translated "to be a steward." The noun *oikonomos* appears ten times (Luke 12:42; 16:1, 3, 8; Rom. 16:23; 1 Cor. 4:1, 2; Gal. 4:2; Titus 1:7; 1 Peter 4:10) and is usually translated "steward" or "manager" (but "treasurer" in Rom. 16:23). The noun *oikonomia* is used nine times (Luke 16:2, 3, 4; 1 Cor. 9:17; Eph. 1:10; 3:2, 9; Col. 1:25; 1 Tim. 1:4). In these instances it is translated variously ("stewardship," "dispensation," "administration," "job," "commission").[12]

"A concise definition of a dispensation is this: *A dispensation is a distinguishable economy in the outworking of God's purpose.*"[13] Mason defines a dispensation as,

> . . . a divinely established stewardship of a particular revelation of God's mind and will which is instituted in the first instance with a new age, and which brings added responsibility to the whole race of men or that portion of the race to whom the revelation is particularly given by God.[14]

Couch adds,

> A dispensation is an obvious historical division in Scripture in which God deals in a specific way with mankind on earth, during a specified period. Rather than controlling

history, dispensations reflect how God sees human beings by mirroring His view and testing man. . . . All dispensations end in moral failure. . . . To see the overall thrust of the Scriptures, in a literal and consistent sense, leads to a dispensational approach to the Word of God. This is the only way to study the Bible that allows it to make sense in its message to us. A dispensation is not a way of salvation nor is it iron clad with rigid walls. It is simply a way of evaluating God's dealing in a period of history.[15]

The dispensations that most dispensationalists would probably agree upon today are the

- dispensation of innocence (Gen. 1:28–3:6)
- dispensation of conscience (Gen. 3:7–8:14)
- dispensation of government (Gen. 8:15–11:32)
- dispensation of promise (Gen. 12:1–Exod. 18:27)
- dispensation of the Law (Exod. 19:1–Acts 1:26)
- dispensation of the church (or grace) (Acts 2:1–1 Thess. 4:18)
- dispensation of the kingdom (Matt. 24–25; Rev. 19:11–22:21)

For the purpose of this chapter, only the dispensations of Law and the church will be compared:

Dispensation of Law: Will the people of Israel be faithful to their God, following a moral and judicial legal code? Will they obey the Ten Commandments and other laws that govern their relationship with God and man?

The People's Response: "'All that the LORD has spoken we will do.' And Moses brought back the words of the people to the LORD" (Exod. 19:8).

The Failure: As a nation and as individuals, the Israelites could never keep the Law. In time, even in their failure, many Jews began to see the Law as a way of salvation—something it was never intended to be. By the time of Christ, the people of Israel were hypocritically fooling themselves concerning their ability to be law keepers.

If you bear the name "Jew," and rely upon the Law, and boast in God . . . you therefore, who teach another, do you not teach

*yourself? . . . Through your breaking the Law, do you dishonor
God? (Romans 2:17, 21, 23)*

*We maintain that a man is justified by faith apart from works
of the Law. . . . since indeed God who will justify the circumcised [the Jews] by faith, and the uncircumcised [the Gentile]
through faith is one. (Romans 3:28, 30)*

Dispensation of the Church—the Promise: By the message of
personal salvation through the death and resurrection of Jesus
Christ, God graciously offers personal forgiveness of sins, the indwelling of His Spirit, and eternal life. The dispensation of the
church is made possible because of the new covenant.

The Problem: The heart of men will grow cold and, in time, will
even reject the personal offer of salvation.

The Failure: This period will end with the apostasy, the outright
personal rejection by men of the offer of salvation. There will be a
great company who appear to be Christian and outwardly religious,
but they will be apostate. The dispensation of the church closes
with the rapture of the church from earth just prior to the coming
seven-year period of world tribulation.

The Essentials of Dispensational Theology

Benware points out that there are three indispensable elements
(sine qua non) of dispensational theology. "These three essentials
are (1) a consistent literal approach to interpreting the Scriptures,
(2) a clear distinction between the church and the nation of Israel
in God's dealings, and (3) the glory of God as God's ultimate purpose of history."[16]

Enns demonstrates that dispensationalism will always lead the
student of Scripture to premillennialism, noting that dispensational
premillennialism has two important features:

1. Literal hermeneutic. Literal interpretation refers to "normal" interpretation—understanding words and statements in
their normal, customary way. Because prophecies concerning Christ's first coming were fulfilled literally, one can expect
that the prophecies concerning His second coming were intended to be interpreted literally. Furthermore, if prophecy
can be spiritualized, all objectivity is lost. Dispensational

premillennialists emphasize consistency in interpretation by interpreting prophecy literally.

2. Distinction between Israel and the church. The term *Israel* always refers to the physical posterity of Jacob; nowhere does it refer to the church. Although nondispensationalists frequently refer to the church as the "new Israel," there is no biblical warrant for doing so. . . . Israel was given unconditional promises (covenants) in the Old Testament that must be fulfilled with Israel in the millennial kingdom. The church on the other hand, is a distinct New Testament entity born at Pentecost (1 Cor. 12:13) and not existing in the Old Testament, nor prophesied in the Old Testament (Eph. 3:9).[17]

Theologically, the word *oikonomia* is used four times—Ephesians 1:9–10; 3:2–3, 9; Colossians 1:25—in a specific, interpretative way to (1) show that a new dispensation of grace (or the church) has come and (2) to make a distinction between the dispensation of Law and the dispensation of grace. By using all the interpretative principles cited above, it can be demonstrated that there are other dispensations in Scripture besides law and grace. Note carefully the main verses:

Ephesians 1:9–10

He made known to us the mystery of His will, . . . with a view to an administration [dispensation] suitable to the fullness of the times, that is, the summing up of all things in Christ.

Mystery means something not previously revealed, "which He purposed in Him [Christ]" (v. 9) "[with the result] that we who were the first to hope in Christ should be to the praise of His glory" (v. 12). In Christ, we who heard the gospel and believed "were sealed in Him [Christ] with the Holy Spirit [who was] promise[d]" that we would be "to the praise of His glory" (vv. 13–14). Nicoll writes extensively on Ephesians 1:10:

God had His reason for the long delay in the revelation of the "mystery." That reason lay in the fact that the world was not ripe for the dispensation of grace which formed the contents of the mystery. In classical Greek the word *oikonomia* had the two meanings of (a) *administration,* the management of a house or of property, and (b) the *office* of administrator or steward. It was used of such things as the arrangement of the parts of a building, . . . the disposition of the parts of speech, . . . and more particularly of the financial administration of a city. . . . It has the same twofold sense in the NT—an *arrangement* or *administration* of things (in the passages in the present Epistle and in I Tim. 1. 4), and the office of administrator—in particular the stewardship with which Paul was entrusted by God (I Cor. ix. 17; Col. i.25).

The idea at the basis of the statement here, therefore, as also in the somewhat analogous passage in Gal. iv. 1–11, is that of a great household of which God is the Master and which has a certain system of management wisely ordered by Him. . . . God has His household, . . . with its special disposition of affairs, its *oikonomos* or steward (who is Christ), its own proper method of administration, and its gifts and privileges could not be dispensed in their fullness while those for whom they were meant were under age (Gal. iv. 1–3) and unprepared for them. A period of waiting had to elapse, and when the process of training was finished and the time of maturity was reached, the gifts could be bestowed in their completeness. God, the Master of the House, had this fit time in view as the hidden purpose of His grace. When that time came He disclosed His secret in the incarnation of Christ and introduced the new disposition of things which explained His former dealings with men and the long delay in the revelation of the complete purpose of His grace. . . . This "economy of the fullness of the seasons," therefore, is that stewardship of the Divine grace which was to be the trust of Christ, in other words, the dispensation of the Gospel, and that dispensation as fulfilling itself in the whole period from the first advent of Christ to the second.[18]

How different this dispensation is compared to the dispensation of Law with all its heavy demands of legal requirements! The writer of Hebrews demonstrates how weak and useless the dispensation of the Law had become:

Now if perfection [completeness] was through the Levitical priesthood . . ., what further need was there for another priest to arise according to the order of Melchizedek? (7:11)

*For, on the one hand, there is a setting aside of a former com-
mandment because of its weakness and uselessness (for the
Law made nothing perfect), and on the other hand there is a
bringing in of a better hope, through which we draw near to
God. (7:18–19)*

*But now He [Christ] has obtained a more excellent ministry,
by as much as He is also the mediator of a better covenant
[the new covenant], which has been enacted on better promises. For if that first covenant [the Law] had been faultless,
there would have been no occasion sought for a second [cov-
enant]. (8:6–7)*

*When He [God in Jeremiah 31:31–34] said, "A new covenant,"
He has made the first [the Law] obsolete. But whatever is becoming obsolete and growing old is ready to disappear. (8:13)*

Ephesians 3:2–3

*. . . if indeed you have heard of the stewardship [dispensation]
of God's grace which was given to me for you; that by revelation there was made known to me the mystery.*

This "mystery" is concerning Christ (v. 4) and was not revealed
previously to the sons of men as now revealed by the Spirit to God's
holy apostles (v. 5), specifically, that Gentiles are fellow heirs "of
the body" and fellow partakers "of the promise in Christ Jesus
through the gospel" (v. 6). To Paul this grace was granted "to preach
to the Gentiles the unfathomable riches of Christ" (v. 8).

Could Paul be any clearer? Without question he is referring to the
church age or dispensation of grace. The larger context goes back to
Ephesians 2:11–22, where Paul writes of the Gentiles "now in Christ"
(v. 13) brought near by His blood. Jesus is the peace who has united
Jew and Gentile "into one new man" (v. 15) and reconciled "them
both in one body [body of Christ] to God" (v. 16), and together "we
both [Jew and Gentile] have our access in one Spirit to the Father"
(v. 18) and are now in Christ "God's household" (v. 19).

Ephesians 3:9

*. . . to bring to light what is the administration [dispensation]
of the mystery which for ages has been hidden in God, who
created all things.*

Paul wraps up his great dispensational teaching by pointing out that the church shows forth the "manifold wisdom of God" (v. 10) and how He had "eternal purpose[s] which He carried out in Christ Jesus our Lord" (v. 11), whereby we have "access through faith in Him" (v. 12). Paul's final verses constitute an anthem to what God is doing in this new church dispensation: ". . . to Him be the glory in the church and in Christ Jesus to all the generations forever and ever. Amen" (v. 21).

Colossians 1:25

> Of this church I was made a minister according to the stewardship [dispensation] from God bestowed on me for your benefit, that I might fully carry out the preaching of the word of God.

This Colossians verse is similar to Paul's teaching in Ephesians. He speaks of the church as a mystery (v. 26) "hidden from the past ages and generations." But to the saints, "God willed to make known what is the riches of the glory of this mystery among the Gentiles, which is Christ in you, the hope of glory" (v. 27). Out of this Paul wishes to present "every man complete in Christ" (v. 28).

Ryrie summarizes,

> Though emphasizing the distinctiveness of the church, the dispensationalist also recognizes certain relationships that the church sustains. . . . He recognizes believers in this age as the [spiritual] seed of Abraham but not the only seed. He seeks to be a realist concerning the course of this age and the church's program in the midst of increasing apostasy. All his viewpoints stem from what he feels to be a consistent application of the literal principle of interpretation of Scripture.[19]

Consistency in Interpretation

Although in truth there is but one hermeneutic, this study has focused on the phrase *dispensational hermeneutics* to call attention to the need for consistency in interpretation. Dispensationalists believe that covenant theologians fail at consistency. They call Israel the church and the church Israel without any objective, biblical evidence. Enns sums up the most important principles of dispensational hermeneutics:

Dispensationalists use a consistent, literal, normal system of interpretation. This approach is applied to all the disciplines of theology. By using literal interpretation on Old Testament prophecies about Christ's first and second coming, dispensationalists anticipate His literal return just as His first advent was historic and actual, not spiritualized! Dispensationalists hold to the fact that God has made unconditional promises to Israel through the Abrahamic Covenant (Gen. 12:1–3). These promises are both physical fulfillments as well as having to do with a spiritual revival for the Jewish people. Nondispensationalists "spiritualize" or allegorize most of these prophecies and relegate them to the church.

Dispensationalists never confuse Israel with the church nor call the church "the new Israel." Dispensationalists can show that God has distinct programs for future Israel with the coming Messianic Kingdom but He also has a specific program now for the body of Christ, the church. Dispensationalists emphasize the unifying theme of the Bible is God's glory, where in covenant theology, salvation is the unifying theme. In every dispensation God has shown His glory. This is the unifying theme of all of the Bible.[20]

The Greek Word *Ekklesia*

Ekklesia is the common Greek word for church. Often it is translated as assembly and congregation. Generally, it is referring to a religious or even a political gathering. Technically, the word means "the called out ones." *Ekklesia* is many times used in the Greek Septuagint (LXX) to refer to different assemblies within the Old Testament. In Acts (7:38; 19:32) the word can simply mean a crowd or gathering. Most often in the New Testament, however, the word *ekklesia* is used to describe the entire body of believers, the universal church, or the assembly of Christians in the local church.

The Church: Universal Spiritual Body of Christ

Many think that the use of the word *universal* advocates the heresy of "universalism," when instead the word is simply referring to a worldwide fellowship of true believers. The word *universal* here, however, is used in the sense of a universal spiritual body of Christ. A man in India who has trusted Christ as Savior, for instance, is a spiritual brother, though he may not speak the same language nor belong to the same local church as you or I.

"You are the Christ, the Son of the living God," (Matt. 16:16). Upon hearing these confirming, rock solid words from the apostle Peter, Jesus responds that He will build His church; and the gates of Hades shall not overpower it (v. 18). Note, it is a single church. But this would not be a single denomination with a governmental hierarchy. It would not be an outward, overwhelming, exclusive system such as the Roman Catholic Church.

This church would be encompassed by a period of time in which all who place personal faith in Christ would constitute a spiritual unity, i.e., one body. Christ is the head of this body, and in fact, the church is the body of Christ (1 Cor. 12:12–13). But there will also be a local church—a localized cell or community of believers who are a part of the whole body of those who have trusted Jesus. As well, the local church would have a visible leadership, a distinct purpose for local fellowship, and a moral mandate for individual discipline. The New Testament church letters reflect both this spiritual body and the local cell of Christians.

The apostle Paul speaks of the whole body of Christ when he writes, "with all who in every place call upon the name of our Lord Jesus" (1 Cor. 1:2). He likens all believers in Christ, who are many, to the one body, Christ's (12:12). The apostle adds, "whether Jews or Greeks, whether slave or free," all were made to drink from one Spirit. "For the body is not one member, but many," (12:14). Though most of Paul's letters are addressed to local churches, for the most part, what he says is applicable to all those in Christ.

For example, Paul writes, "Do you not know that all of us who have been baptized into Christ Jesus have been baptized into His death?" (Rom. 6:3). He adds, "by one Spirit we were all baptized into one body" (1 Cor. 12:13). And, "He saved us, not on the basis of deeds which we have done in righteousness, but according to His mercy, by the 'again-birthing' of regeneration and the 'remaking' of the Holy Spirit" (Titus 3:5, Greek). This universal body of believers, Paul calls the "household" (Eph. 2:19), the building growing into a holy temple (2:21), "in whom you [believers in the local church at Ephesus] also are being built together into a dwelling of God [by] the Spirit" (v. 22).

Further, Paul writes in Ephesians that Christ is the head and Savior of the church (5:23), that He loved it and gave Himself for it (v. 25). In an almost anthem-like verse, Paul summarizes, "And He [God] put all things in subjection under His [Christ's] feet, and gave Him as head over all things [relating] to the church, which is

His body . . ." (1:22). The New Testament continually emphasizes the singularity—or wholeness—of the church: while Peter was in prison, prayer for him was "being made fervently by the [whole] church of God" (Acts 12:5); overseers (plural) are to "shepherd the [whole] church of God which He purchased with His own blood" (20:28); "I [Paul] persecuted the [whole] church of God" (1 Cor. 15:9).

The New Testament emphasizes the church as an organism, a living union of all true believers in Christ. This is the distinctive truth that is presented beginning with the day of Pentecost, with the advent of the Spirit, and concluding with the coming of Christ for His church, at which time it will be caught up out of the world and taken to heaven.[21]

The Church: The Local Congregation

The church, the living organism and the organized cell of believers, is in this dispensation God's way of doing business in local communities. This is a unique period in divine time. In terms of the local church, believers of a given age must see themselves as having a special calling to serve the Lord in their own generation. As surprising as this may sound, the local church itself is never instructed in Scripture to evangelize. That is the job of the individual believer. The purpose of the local cell is to arm, equip, and train Christians to speak out and witness within their circles of influence. But more on this issue later. Chafer further notes,

> It is obviously true that a person may be a Christian and not be a member of a local organized church. In fact, all should be saved before they join a church; and, if saved, it is normal for the individual to choose the fellowship of the people of God in one form or another. On the earth, the church is seen to be a pilgrim band of witnesses. They are not of this world even as Christ is not of this world (John 17:16), and as the Father has sent the Son into the world, so has the Son sent these witnesses into the world.[22]

In his letters, Paul continually addresses the local congregations, the body of believers who are struggling in a given city or region. Almost all he writes is applicable for today.

In 1 Corinthians (1:2), the apostle makes a separation between the entire church of the Lord and the local body. He writes "to the church of God which is at Corinth." He then adds "with all who in every place call upon the name of our Lord Jesus Christ, their Lord and ours." At the end of this Corinthian letter, Paul says, "The churches of Asia greet you" (16:19), and then also mentions the local church that meets in the house of Aquila and Priscilla (v. 19). In 2 Corinthians he writes about the regional churches "throughout Achaia" and the church there in Corinth (1:1).

The Dispensational Nature of the Church

God had a distinct dispensational purpose for the nation of Israel in the Old Testament. Through that people, the Lord's perfect and righteous demands would be displayed through the Law. The temple and all its ceremonies would reflect and foretell the coming of the Redeemer, Jesus the Messiah. And through the Jewish nation, Jesus Himself would be born. But as a whole, the Jews would reject their king. God would temporarily set aside His work with the Jewish people as a nation and would create a new era called the age of grace, or the church age. In this new period, individuals—both Jew and Gentile—would be saved worldwide and placed into this new body called the church.

Both Jew and Gentile now have a common ground. Both are said to be under sin (Rom. 3:9) and needing a common Savior. When the Holy Spirit came at Pentecost, the Lord began a new divine program, away from the recognition of a specific people, to an appeal to individuals, Jews and Gentiles alike. The Jews had trouble understanding that their covenants were set aside for a time but would someday still be fulfilled. (The writer Luke shows this struggle in the book of Acts.)

As a people and as a nation, the Jews will in part remain blind until the church is called home (Rom. 11:25). Then the Deliverer, the Messiah, will return and restore the Jews to their land and ungodliness will be turned away from this people when He removes their sins (Rom. 11:26–27). Yet now, individual Jews and Gentiles who respond to the proclamation of the gospel are added to this new "thing," the church.

That God is now forming this one new body (Eph. 2:15) was a mystery not previously revealed. That God had purposes for the Jewish people, and that He would someday touch the Gentiles was no secret. The Old Testament prophesied that Gentiles would someday find Jehovah, but how the Lord would accomplish this was "hid in God."

This chapter is adapted from Mal Couch, "Dispensational Hermeneutics and the Doctrine of Ecclesiology," in *A Biblical Theology of the Church*, ed. Mal Couch (Grand Rapids: Kregel, 1999), 13–28.

CHAPTER 14

Dispensation of the Law Replaced by the Dispensation of the Church

The new covenant is the driving force of the church. The principles of this covenant actually create the church. To understand how all this works, one must go back to the Abrahamic covenant (Gen. 12:1–3). Therein, God promised to Abraham a land, a great physical seed, and a blessing to his children and to all families of the earth. The Gentiles, or all the families of the earth, are not given the land promises, but it is prophesied that they will someday receive the blessings.

As the Old Testament unfolds by progressive revelation, the new covenant is revealed. This covenant will be first for Israel, and it involves an agreement with all the house of Israel (Jer. 31:31). It will contrast the conditional Mosaic Law (v. 32), and it will be written on the hearts of the Jews. As well, the Lord promises to indeed be their God and they will be His people in a close and very personal way (v. 33). At some future point, it can be said that "they all know the Lord" (v. 34). But one of the most dramatic promises is "I will forgive their iniquity, and their sin I will remember no more" (v. 34). This would certainly imply that the temple sacrifices will no longer be needed for atonement, and that once and for all God has reconciled with the problem of sin. Of course, this would be fulfilled with Christ being the final solution for sin.

This new covenant is also called "an eternal covenant," with God never again turning away from the Jews. The covenant, launched at Pentecost (Acts 2), will have its ultimate completion and fulfillment in the kingdom. The principal condition of the new covenant is faith in the death, burial, and resurrection of the Messiah. But

Gentiles will also be blessed and can receive the benefits of the covenant by the same faith. In this way, Gentiles partake of the blessing promised them through Abraham.

Ezekiel and Joel continue, by progressive revelation and the inspiration of the Holy Spirit, to give more details about the new covenant. The Lord will slosh *(zarach)* clean water on the Jews whereby "I will cleanse you from all your filthiness and from all your idols" (Ezek. 36:25). Since water would not cleanse away idol worship, the cleansing referred to would be a spiritual one. As well, the Lord promises a new, soft heart that would be obviously responsive to Him (v. 26). And most importantly, He will place His Spirit within (v. 27; 37:14). Mixed together and swirling around the new covenant is the Palestinian covenant that promises God would someday "gather you from all the lands, and bring you into your own land" (36:24). As dead bodies, Israel will be spiritually resurrected and returned to their own land (37:12). "Behold, I will open your graves and cause you to come up out of your graves, My people and I will bring you into the land of Israel."

The tangible promises of a return and restoration to the land are a unique blessing for the Jews by which their kingdom promises are restored. The intangible promises of permanent forgiveness of sins and the indwelling of the Holy Spirit would be granted to both Jew and Gentile. Again, forgiveness and indwelling originate from the blessing portion of the Abrahamic covenant. This blessing would fall upon both the physical children of Abraham and "all families of the earth" (Gen. 12:3).

Concerning the new covenant and its promise of the coming Spirit, the prophet Joel continues, "I will pour out My Spirit on all mankind" (Joel 2:28). In the same paragraph Joel predicts the display of wonders in the sky: "blood, fire, and columns of smoke . . . before the great and awesome day of the LORD comes" (vv. 31–32). In Acts 2, Peter refers to this entire paragraph when he speaks of the outpouring of the Holy Spirit. He certainly did not understand the issue of the separation of time between the coming of the Spirit and the beginning of the "day of the LORD," the tribulation (Acts 2:14–21). Many dispensationalists and nondispensationalists believe that when Peter said, "This is what [the coming of the Holy Spirit] was spoken of through the prophet Joel" (v. 16), he was simply saying "this is 'like' what was spoken by Joel."

But after the coming of the Spirit at Pentecost, throughout the book of Acts, the Spirit continues to fall upon Jew and Gentile alike. When Peter visited Cornelius's house and the Gentiles there, "all the circumcised believers who had come with Peter were amazed, because the gift of the Holy Spirit had been poured out upon the Gentiles also" (Acts 10:45). In looking at Joel 2:28 and how Peter quotes it, it is clear the Spirit is meant for both Jew and Gentile. In 2:28 it is written that God's Spirit would come upon "all mankind." The Hebrew text reads "upon all *basar.*" *Basar* is a metaphor for the human race. In Acts 2:16 the Greek quote of the Joel passage reads *upon pasan sarka,* or "every kind of humanity."

Thus, when the new covenant was launched at Pentecost, the Spirit descended upon Jew and Gentile equally, i.e., the blessing portion of the promise to Abraham would come on all. Dispensationalists believe the new covenant was promised first for Israel. And although its ultimate fulfillment is in the future kingdom, Gentiles are presently benefiting from it. As a whole, the Jews are not now benefiting from the new covenant promises unless of course they are part of the body of Christ, the church, by faith. Only those who now trust Christ as Savior are receiving the blessings of the covenant promised them. As a nation, the Jews rejected the work of salvation and the blessings of the new covenant, though it was given first to them.

As to the words of Joel in Acts 2:16–21, Kistemaker, though not a dispensationalist, notes,

> Luke reports that Peter quotes [of the signs and wonders] from Joel's prophecy, but Luke fails to give its application. . . . Luke does not indicate that at Pentecost God fulfilled Joel's prediction of the signs and wonders. He relates that the outpouring of the Holy Spirit occurred in Jerusalem. . . . God opens the way of salvation to all people, both Jew and Gentile. He makes his promise to individual persons and asks them to respond individually. These believers as members of Christ's body constitute the Christian church.[1]

On "this is that which was spoken" Alexander writes,

> The sum of it is: this is not intoxication, it is inspiration, and the fulfillment of a signal prophecy. . . . *All flesh* is an idiomatic Hebrew phrase, . . . more usually [meaning] all mankind (Gen. 6, 12).[2]

Hackett also believes Joel's prophecy is being fulfilled here in Acts 2. He writes,

The Greek identifies this prophecy with its fulfillment. . . . Yet the prophecy has indirectly a wider scope. It portrays in reality the character of the entire dispensation. Those special manifestations of the Spirit at the beginning marked the Economy as one that was to be eminently distinguished by the Spirit's agency.[3]

On "this is that which was spoken" dispensationalist Toussaint notes,

This clause does not mean, "This is like that"; it means Pentecost fulfilled what Joel had described. However, the prophecies of Joel quoted in Acts 2:19–20 [blood, and fire, and vapor of smoke] were not fulfilled. The implication is that the remainder would be fulfilled if Israel would repent.[4]

To conclude, although sometimes they may not be clear in their arguments, most dispensationalists assert that the church is presently "benefiting" from the blessings promised in the new covenant. But they would say that the ultimate fulfillment of those promises for Israel will take place in the kingdom.

The New Covenant Will Replace the Old Mosaic Covenant of Law

The book of Galatians was written to show that the new covenant has come to replace the Law. This is the only time in Scripture that *allegory* is mentioned, by which technique the apostle is trying to make a point. Paul writes, "allegorically speaking" (4:24) the "two covenants" are like Abraham's two sons, Ishmael born of Hagar, the slave, and Isaac born of Sarah, his wife. Mount Sinai, where Moses received the Law, is the place where the children were born who are in slavery to the Law (v. 24). Hagar conceived by Abraham, who through self-works tried to have children through his own efforts. But the Lord by His sovereign grace brought forth Isaac through Sarah apart from human effort. God simply made promises and then kept them.

One of the most outstanding promises in the new covenant is the giving of the Holy Spirit to dwell within. And as well, by faith in Christ's sacrifice, Jew and Gentile can become heirs and sons of God (4:7). Paul explains, "And the Scripture, foreseeing that God would justify the Gentiles by faith, preached the gospel beforehand to Abraham, saying, 'All the nations shall be blessed in you.' So then those who are of faith are blessed with Abraham, the believer" (3:8–9). Then those who receive Christ as Savior "receive the promise of the Spirit through faith" (3:14). The giving of the Spirit was promised in Ezekiel 36–37 as part of the new covenant. But the land promises are certainly not given to the church. The Holy Spirit and those kingdom earthly blessings will come upon the Jews in the future.

Paul emphasizes that the Law was but a tutor "to lead us to Christ, that we may be justified by faith. . . . But . . . we are no longer under a tutor" (Gal. 3:24–25). And by faith "if you belong to Christ, then you are Abraham's offspring, heirs according to promise" (v. 29).

To be "born again" is a concept prophesied by Ezekiel in his vision of the dry bones (Ezek. 37:1–14). The prophet sees a desert full of scattered bones into which the Lord breathes life (v. 5). Skin and flesh come on the bones, and the Jews come alive "and you will know that I am the Lord" (v. 6). When this army of those born again stand up, they are led back into the land of Israel. "And I will put My Spirit within you, and you will come to life, and I will place you on your own land" (v. 14).

At this point, the new covenant is applied to the Jewish people whereby they are born again and return to the land as the Messiah institutes the kingdom. In fact, the new covenant will be the spiritual driving force for the messianic reign. But it was instituted at Pentecost and applies to the church age now. The new covenant and the work of the Holy Spirit are the spiritual driving forces in this age, or dispensation, of the church. They will also be the spiritual dynamic for the dispensation of the kingdom. It must be emphasized, however, that the new covenant promises were first for Israel but with an attendant benefit for the church.

Is the Church a New Israel?

It is not difficult to understand that Gentiles who become "Abraham's offspring" are not his physical children. Gentiles become Abraham's spiritual seed, which God makes happen because of trust in Christ. Equally so, believers become "adopted sons of God" (Gal. 4:5–6), an event also understood as spiritual. Nowhere in Scripture is the church seen as the extension of Israel. Neither is the church nominated Israel. Some theologians, however, claim that in Galatians 6:11–18, Paul refers to the church as Israel. A careful examination proves otherwise. Eadie gives the most convincing arguments:

The apostle is not in the habit of calling the church made up of Jews and Gentiles—Israel. Israel is used eleven times in Romans, but in all the instances it refers to Israel proper; and so does it and *Israelites* in every other portion of the New Testament. In the Apocalypse, the 144,000 sealed of Israel stand in contrast to "the great multitude which no man can number," taken out of the Gentile or non-Israelitish races. . . . the apostle never in any place so uses the name, never gives the grand old theocratic name to any but the chosen people.[5]

But for some reason the old covenant divines, as far back as Puritan theologians, did just that. To them, almost everything in the Old Testament is labeled with one word, "church." The Puritan teacher William Ames (1576–1633) wrote the classic theological work, *The Marrow of Theology*, which became the basic instruction text in the new world. It was considered the only book, except the Bible, a student of theology needed, and it was read by all undergraduate freshmen at Harvard and Yale. It was highly recommended by Thomas Hooker and Increase Mather to be sound in theological principle. In *Marrow*, Ames wrote,

> From the time of Abraham the church chiefly consisted of his family and his posterity. . . . The church of the Jews instituted by Moses, . . . was only one because the whole solemn communion prescribed at that time depended upon one temple and was exercised by public profession and rites. . . . Therefore, the church of the Jews was a national church—though in some respect catholic or universal, insomuch as the believing proselytes of every nation under heaven were bound to join themselves to that one church.[6]

The Dispensation of the Law Must Pass Away

The book of Hebrews is one of the most "Jewish" of the books in the New Testament. Some see it as almost evangelistic in that its purpose is to convince the Jews that Christ is better than anything or any person in the Mosaic legal system. Though the debate continues, it is certain that the author of Hebrews writes that the new covenant will replace the Mosaic covenant of Law. He points out, ". . . so much the more also Jesus has become the guarantee of a better covenant" (7:22), that is, the new covenant. This is because as "the Son of God, he abides a priest perpetually" (v. 3).

The dispensation of the Law had so many limitations that it could make no one mature (or perfect) (v. 11). Neither could all the gifts and sacrifices offered up by the sinner make that worshiper mature in conscience (9:9). The Levitical priesthood was hindered in that the human priestly order was made up of sinful men who had moral and physical limitations. But Jesus was of the superior priesthood of Melchizedek that goes back to the period of Abraham (7:1). It was an eternal, unending order that was not confined to any human limitations. In other words, Jesus could be an independent, sinless, priest, representing man to God and God to man. And of course the most profound priestly work He performed is that "He offered up Himself (once) for the sins of the people" (v. 27).

Many fail to understand that the Mosaic Law had passed its usefulness. "For, on the one hand, there is a setting aside of a former commandment because of its weakness and uselessness" (v. 18). Neither could the animal blood sacrifices of bulls and goats sanctify the sinner or make his flesh clean from sinning (9:13). Christ became "the mediator of a better covenant [the new], which has been enacted on better promises. For if that first covenant had been faultless, there would have been no occasion sought for a second" (8:6–7). Following these verses, the author of Hebrews then cites Jeremiah 31:31–34, wherein the promised new covenant is prophesied. Chapter eight is concluded by noting, "When He said, 'A new covenant,' He had made the first obsolete. But whatever is becoming obsolete and growing old is ready to disappear" (8:13). The teaching on the new covenant in Hebrews is then concluded: Christ is "the mediator of a new covenant" that "those who have been called may receive the promise of the eternal inheritance" (9:15).

The Church Is Not Simply Added to Israel

Covenant theologian Berkhof defines the kingdom of God as the church and the Israel of the Old Testament as not only that kingdom but, more specifically, the church simply in an older form. Most covenant teachers would agree, thus blurring clear and important distinctions. Dispensationalists, however, are true to the biblical text; otherwise we are interpreting God's plans instead of listening to what He tells us He is doing in the outline of history.

A further error made by covenant advocates is that of reading New Testament truths back into the Old Testament. That is, they interpret the Old Testament by the New Testament. Instead, the New Testament should be seen as a fulfillment of, or progressing from, the Old Testament. Though they would dispute it, covenant theologians become sloppy in their observations of covenant and dispensational issues, especially in the areas of eschatological and ecclesiastical doctrine. For example, Berkhof writes, "The fundamental ideal of the Kingdom in Scripture is not that of a restored theocratic kingdom of God in Christ—which is essentially a kingdom of Israel—, as the Premillenarians claim."[7] He admits, however, that some church fathers "regarded [the kingdom] as the coming millennial rule of the Messiah."[8]

Berkhof looks to Augustine for his confirmation and notes that he "viewed the kingdom as a present reality and identified it with Church."[9] As well, Berkhof points out, "The Roman Catholic Church frankly identified the Kingdom of God with their hierarchical institution, but the Reformers returned to the view that it is in this dispensation identical with the invisible Church."[10] And finally concerning the church, he writes, "It is impossible to be in the Kingdom of God without being in the church as the mystical body of Jesus Christ."[11]

But can Berkhof prove that all these contentions are biblical? Does the Bible really see the kingdom as the church? And in particular, can Berkhof especially demonstrate that the Israel in the Old Testament was just the church in an older form?

Many covenant theologians believe that Ephesians 2:11–22 says that the church was joined to Israel. For example, Nicoll believes the expression "brought near" (v. 13) means the Gentiles are brought into the camp of Israel by Christ's blood. He writes, "It is probably to be taken, therefore, in the large sense of being brought into the Kingdom of God, made near to God Himself."[12] Although Gentiles are brought near to God, Nicoll misses Paul's point: The new body, the church, is comprised of both Jew and Gentile.

Verse 14 says, Christ "is our peace, who made both groups into one." This is not an argument for saying the new body, the church, is simply an extension of Israel. Charles Hodge, though a covenant teacher, understands this passage as referring to the church as something new. It is not warmed over Israel, even in some reconstituted form.

Several verses in this Ephesians passage speak to the church as separate from Israel. Paul writes that the Gentiles were "excluded from the commonwealth of Israel, and [were] strangers to the covenants of promise, having no hope and without God in the world" (v. 12). Paul adds, "now in Christ Jesus you who formerly were far off have been brought near by the blood of Christ" (v. 13). Jesus is the peace between the two groups, abolishing the enmity, which is the Law of commandments (vv. 14–15).

The apostle then points out that God makes something new with the two groups of people, Jews and Gentiles. He does not simply plug Gentiles into the body of Israel. God "made both groups into one" (v. 14), and He made "the two into one new man" (v. 15). He "reconcile[d] them both in one body [the church] to God through the cross" (v. 16).

A new "household" of God is formed whereby we are fellow citizens with believing Jews. This household has,

> . . . been built upon the foundation of the apostles and prophets, Christ Jesus Himself being the corner stone, in whom the whole building, being fitted together is growing into a holy temple in the Lord; in whom you also are being built together into a dwelling of God in the Spirit. (vv. 20–22)

In Ephesians 3:2, 9 the word dispensation, is oikonomia, "house law." In 2:19–22 above, the word for "house" appears five times.

- Household—oikeioi: plural—the saints are the "housing ones"
- Having been built—epoikodomeō: "upon house, constructed"
- Building—oikodoma: "constructed house"
- You are being built together—sunoikodomeō: "together house, constructed"
- Dwelling—katoikatarion: "down housing, to settle down"

The words above (three of which utilize prepositional prefixes) describe the dispensation of the church. God dwells on earth in this new body, the church, the spiritual body of Christ. As mentioned, Hodge describes the church in similar terms as do the dispensationalists. On this Ephesians passage, he writes,

> By abolishing the law of commandments, i.e. the law in both its forms, the apostle says, Christ has, first, of the twain made one new man, v. 15; and secondly, he has reconciled both unto God in one body by the cross, v. 16. . . . The reconciliation itself is expressed by saying, "He made the two one, having removed the wall or enmity between them." The mode in which this was done, is expressed by saying, "He abolished the law." . . . The design of Christ in thus abolishing the law was two-fold. First, the union of the Jews and Gentiles in one holy, Catholic [universal] church. And, Secondly, the reconciliation of both to God. . . . "In order that he might

create the two, in himself, one new man, making peace." . . . They are created anew, so as to become one body of which Christ is the head. . . . The distinction between Jew and Gentile is abolished. . . . There is now one fold and one shepherd. Since the abrogation of the law there is neither Jew nor Greek, there is neither bond nor free, there is neither male nor female; for all believers are one in Christ Jesus. . . . The subjects of this reconciliation are the Jews and Gentiles united in one body, i.e. the church.[13]

The apostle Paul further explains in Ephesians 3:2 that this new thing, the dispensation of the church, is a mystery (something not previously revealed), the mystery concerning Christ (v. 4), and that it was a unique revelation given exclusively to him (v. 3). In fact, it was hidden from previous generations (v. 5). What, then, is now revealed? "To be specific, that the Gentiles are fellow [together] heirs [with the Jews] . . . of the body, and fellow partakers of the promise in Christ Jesus through the gospel . . ." (v. 6). This was grace "preach[ed] to the Gentiles . . ." (v. 8). To Paul it was given "to bring to light what is the [dispensation] of the mystery which for ages has been hidden in God . . ." (v. 9).

In the salvation provided in this new dispensation, the Lord and His wisdom is glorified in the heavenlies. Angels are rejoicing over those now saved who are added to the body of Christ, the church, ". . . in order that the manifold wisdom of God might now be made known through the church to the rulers and the authorities in the heavenly places" (v. 10).

Conclusion

The new covenant is linked to the Abrahamic covenant in that it is the promised blessing to be given for "all families of the earth." In that sense, the Abrahamic covenant is in operation through this new covenant. The new covenant replaces the Mosaic covenant, which could never bring anyone to maturity because it depended on the obedience of the flesh. The new covenant provides the spiritual dynamics for personal salvation, forgiveness of sins, the placing of the Holy Spirit within, and the placing of the believer in the spiritual body of Christ. The dispensation of the church is then the outward manifestation of God's work today. It forms the historic mode by which God is at work in the world. Thus, God has annulled (i.e., made legally void) the dispensation of Law.

CHAPTER 15

Salvation in the Dispensation of the Church

The title of this chapter may be disturbing. Has not salvation always been by grace through faith? Is salvation different in the dispensation of the church than in the Old Testament (or in future dispensations for that matter)? In spite of clarification through the writings of dispensationalists, the controversy persists concerning whether dispensationalists teach a different method of salvation for past dispensations than for the present dispensation. As Ryrie states,

> Without a doubt the most frequently heard objection against dispensationalism is that it supposedly teaches several ways of salvation. In particular, dispensationalists are said to teach salvation by works in some dispensations and salvation by grace in others. This is a very serious charge and must be examined carefully.[1]

Thus, it is important to clarify the similarities and differences by which salvation is attained in past dispensations versus in the present dispensation.

Past Misstatements of Dispensational Thought

Dispensationalists have not always accurately presented their case. In the 1917 second edition of *The Scofield Reference Bible*, for instance, the note summarizing the doctrine of grace (p. 1115) contains a statement that is easily misunderstood:

(2) As a dispensation, grace begins with the death and resurrection of Christ. . . . The point of testing is *no longer legal obedience as the condition of salvation,* but acceptance or rejection of Christ with good works as a fruit of salvation.[2] (emphasis added)

While this appears to be a contradiction, a study of C. I. Scofield's position on salvation reveals that he did not advocate salvation by the works of the Law (as can be seen in the paragraph in *Scofield* that immediately precedes the one excerpted above). In the 1967 edition, Scofield's statement was expanded and revised to read as follows:

(2) In its fullness, grace began with the ministry of Christ involving His death and resurrection, for He came to die for sinners. . . . Under the former dispensation, law was shown to be powerless to secure righteousness and life for a sinful race (Gal. 3:21–22). Prior to the cross man's salvation was through faith (Gen. 15:6, Rom. 4:3), being grounded on Christ's atoning sacrifice, viewed anticipatively by God; . . . now it is clearly revealed that salvation and righteousness are received by faith in the crucified and resurrected Savior with holiness of life and good works following as the fruit of salvation.[3]

In 1945 Dr. Oswald T. Allis, renowned professor of Old Testament at Westminster Seminary in Philadelphia and a confirmed amillennialist, wrote *Prophecy and the Church,* in which he attempted to discredit dispensationalism in general, and *The Scofield Reference Bible* in particular. Though Allis did not quote the note mentioned above, he alluded to it in his statement that dispensationalists insist on the unconditional nature of the Abrahamic covenant:

As regards the New Testament they are concerned to make the promise unconditional, with a view to proving that obedience was a condition of the Mosaic age only, and that obedience is as little a condition under the dispensation of grace as it was under the dispensation of promise.[4]

Of his many attacks upon *The Scofield Reference Bible,* Allis's harshest comment fell on Scofield's note on Revelation 14:6 concerning the gospel:

Scofield places his clearest and most significant statement regarding the "four forms" of the gospel in his notes on the Book of Revelation. While mentioning four, he distinguishes most emphatically between *two* forms of the gospel: the "gospel of the kingdom" and the "gospel of the grace of God"; and between two "preachings" of the former. We have seen that the definition of the "gospel of the kingdom" makes no mention of the cross.[5]

Again, a careful reading of the entire note along with the expanded note in the 1967 edition, will clear up any misconceptions.

What Have Dispensationalists Traditionally Taught About Salvation?

Although dispensationalists occasionally have made statements that created confusion regarding their stand on salvation, a thorough study of dispensational theology reveals its true position. Ryrie, for instance, summarizes the heart of dispensational theology regarding salvation: "[Dispensationalists teach that] the *basis* of salvation in every age is the death of Christ; the *requirement* for salvation in every age is faith; the *object* of faith in every age is God; the *content* of faith changes in the various dispensations."[6]

C. I. Scofield, Lewis Sperry Chafer, and other theologians agree with Ryrie. Dispensationalists have never believed that one is saved by the Law, always maintaining that the basis of salvation was the death of Christ. Chafer writes,

Are there two ways by which one may be saved? In reply to this question it may be stated that salvation of whatever specific character is always the work of God in behalf of man and never a work of man. This is to assert that God never saved any one person or group of persons on any other ground than that righteous freedom to do so which the Cross of Christ secured. There is, therefore, but one way to be saved and that is by the power of God made possible through the sacrifice of Christ.[7]

Chafer also stated, "The law was never given as a means of salvation or justification."[8] Scofield wrote, "Law neither justifies a sinner nor sanctifies a believer." Covenant theologians have difficulty understanding the dispensational teaching of one dispensation as Law and one as grace, believing this communicates ways of salvation, and they cannot understand how dispensationalists see Law and grace relating to each other. Ryrie concisely explains the relationship:

> [The] . . . dispensationalist answer to the question of the relation of grace and law is this: the requirement for salvation in every age is faith; the object of faith in every age is God; the content of faith changes in the various dispensations. It is this last point, of course, that distinguishes dispensationalism from covenant theology, but it is not a point to which the charge of teaching two ways of salvation can be attached. It simply recognizes that obvious fact of progressive revelation. When Adam looked upon the coats of skin with which God had clothed him and his wife, he did not see what the believer today sees looking back on the cross of Calvary. And neither did other Old Testament saints see what we can see today. There have to be two sides to this matter—that which God sees from His side and that which man sees from his.[9]

Thus, during the dispensation of Law, each person who was justified was justified by faith in God; yet the content of the faith was different. Ryrie adds,

> It is entirely harmonious to say that the means of eternal salvation was by grace and that the means of temporal life was by law. It is also compatible to say that the revelation of the means of eternal salvation was through the law and that that revelation (though it brought the same results when believed) was not the same as the revelation given since the incarnation of Christ. Thus, the revelation concerning salvation during the Mosaic economy did involve the law, though the basis of salvation remained grace.[10]

The Content of Faith

Dispensationalists agree that the *basis* of salvation, *requirement* for salvation, and *object* of faith for salvation in every age has stayed and will stay constant. But the content of faith has changed in various dispensations. As Enns states,

> God's revelation to man differs in different dispensations, but man's responsibility is to respond to God in faith according to the manner in which God has revealed Himself.

Thus when God revealed Himself to Abraham and promised him a great posterity, Abraham believed God, and the
Lord imputed righteousness to the patriarch (Gen. 15:6).
Abraham would have known little about Christ, but he responded in faith to the revelation of God and was saved.
Similarly, under the law God promised life through faith.
Whereas the Israelite under the law knew about the importance of the blood sacrifice, his knowledge of a suffering
Messiah was still limited—but he was saved by faith (Hab.
2:4). Dispensationalists thus emphasize that in every dispensation salvation is by God's grace through faith *according to
His revelation.*[11] (italics added)

To argue that the content of the gospel has remained constant is to
completely deny progressive revelation. Dispensationalists assert that,
although salvation has always been and always will be by faith, the
amount of knowledge one had of the future death of Christ was limited, and thus the content of faith was different at different stages of
God's progressive revelation. As Enns notes, dispensationalists understand that the *content* of the message in which believers place
their faith is affected by the stage of redemptive history or the progress
of revelation. Thus, most dispensationalists believe that the distinctions made by C. I. Scofield between the several messages contained
in the "good news" or the "gospels" are accurate and should be maintained, especially Scofield's distinction between the "gospel of the
kingdom of God" and the "gospel of the grace of God":

1. The Gospel of the kingdom. This is the good news that
God purposes to set up on the earth, in fulfillment of the
Davidic Covenant (2 Sam. 7:16 . . .), a kingdom, political,
spiritual, Israelitish, universal, over which God's Son, David's
heir, shall be King, and which shall be, for one thousand
years, the manifestation of the righteousness of God, in human affairs. . . .

Two *preachings* of this Gospel are mentioned, one past,
beginning with the ministry of John the Baptist, continued
by our Lord and His disciples, and ending with the Jewish
rejection of the King. The other is yet future (Matt. 24:14),
during the great tribulation, and immediately preceding the
coming of the King in glory.

2. The Gospel of the grace of God. This is the good news
that Jesus Christ, the rejected King, has died on the cross

for the sins of the world, that He was raised from the dead for our justification, and that by Him all that believe are justified from all things. This form of Gospel is described in many ways. It is the Gospel "of God" (Rom. 1:1) because it originates in His love; "of Christ" (2 Cor. 10:14) because it flows from His sacrifice, and because He is the alone Object of Gospel faith; of "the grace of God" (Acts 20:24) because it saves those whom the law curses; of "the glory" (1 Tim. 1:11; 2 Cor. 4:4) because it concerns Him who is the glory, and who is bringing the many sons to glory (Heb. 2:10); of "our salvation" (Eph. 1:13) because it is the "power of God unto salvation to every one who believeth" (Rom. 1:16); of "the uncircumcision" (Gal. 2:7) because it saves wholly apart from forms and ordinances; of "peace" (Eph. 6:15) because through Christ it makes peace between the sinner and God, and imparts inward peace.[12]

Most dispensationalists hold to these distinctions because of their commitment to a normal, natural hermeneutic, which forces a recognition of the distinction between God's program for Israel and His program for His church. And as noted above, dispensational theologians keep in mind progressive revelation. Thus, to be hermeneutically consistent, one must see a different content of faith in various dispensations.

Conclusion

No better summarizing statement can be made regarding the belief of most dispensationalists on dispensationalism and salvation than that quoted previously by Ryrie: "[Dispensationalists teach that] the *basis* of salvation in every age is the death of Christ; the *requirement* for salvation in every age is faith; the *object* of faith in every age is God; the *content* of faith changes in the various dispensations."[13] The church age, however, makes it clear that in which those who would be justified must place their faith is the death, burial, and resurrection of Jesus Christ (1 Cor. 15:1–4).

Ryrie summarizes the dispensational perspective in this way:

To show that dispensationalism does not teach several ways of salvation, we emphasized that (1) the law was brought in alongside and did not abrogate the promises of the Abrahamic covenant and (2) there were many displays of grace under the law. Dispensationalism alone among theological systems teaches both the antithetical nature of law and grace and the truth of grace under the law (and, incidentally, law under grace). Grace was shown to be displayed in several ways, but the crux of the matter was the display of grace in salvation.

In examining salvation under the Mosaic Law the principal question is simply, How much of what God was going to do in the future did the Old Testament believer comprehend? According to both Old and New Testament revelation it is impossible to say that he saw the same promise, the same Savior as we do today. Therefore, the dispensationalists' distinction between the content of his faith and the content of ours is valid. The basis of salvation is always the death of Christ; the means is always faith; the object is always God (though man's understanding of God before and after the incarnation is obviously different); but the content of faith depends on the particular revelation God was pleased to give at a certain time. These are the distinctions the dispensationalist recognizes, and they are distinctions necessitated by plain interpretation of revelation as it was given.

If by "ways" of salvation is meant different content of faith, then dispensationalism does teach various "ways" because the Scriptures reveal differing contents for faith in the progressive nature of God's revelation to mankind. But if by "ways" is meant more than one basis or means of salvation, then dispensationalism most emphatically does not teach more than one way, for salvation has been, is, and always will be based on the substitutionary death of Jesus Christ.[14]

This chapter is adapted from Mal Couch, "The New Dispensation: The Church," in *A Biblical Theology of the Church*, ed. Mal Couch (Grand Rapids: Kregel, 1999), 34–42.

CHAPTER 16

The First Reference to the Church: Matthew 16:13–20

Though it would be through the apostle Paul that the full meaning and revelation of the church would be taught, Jesus first uses the word *church* in Matthew 16:18. Not only is *church* (Greek, *ekklesia*) first used here in the New Testament, in this particular context the word is used in the technical sense, i.e., of the coming of the new dispensation of grace that would replace the dispensation of Law.

In Matthew 16:21, the Lord is preparing His disciples for His coming death: "From that time Jesus Christ began to show His disciples that He must go to Jerusalem, and suffer many things from the elders and chief priests and scribes, and be killed, and be raised up on the third day." But just prior to that, He had asked His disciples, "Who do people say that the Son of Man is?" (v. 13). The phrase "the Son of Man" means "The Son related to mankind," and it is a powerful description of the Messiah who would represent humanity before the presence of God the Father.

Peter answered the Lord first, and said, "Thou art the Christ, the Son of the living God" (v. 16). Peter's words confirmed his understanding that Jesus was the Anointed King (the Christ) and that He was somehow related to deity ("the Son related to God," Psalm 2). The Lord then called Peter "blessed" because the Father in heaven had revealed these truths to him (v. 17).

Jesus then speaks these important words:

And I also say to you that you are Peter, and upon this rock I will build My church; and the gates of Hades shall not overpower

199

> *it. I will give you the keys of the kingdom of heaven; and what-*
> *ever you shall bind on earth shall have been bound in heaven,*
> *and whatever you shall loose on earth shall have been loosed in*
> *heaven. (vv. 18–19)*

Before examining the various parts of these two verses, it is important to note that there are two different topics in the passage. The
first relates to Christ building His church, the second to another
subject—the kingdom of heaven. Grammatically, these two nouns
can be separated: "'church' in Matt. 16:18 and 'kingdom' in verse 19
may not be identical in meaning."[1] "The question is raised at once if
Jesus does not here mean the same thing by 'kingdom' that he did by
'church' in verse 18."[2] "These words become clear when we note that
'the keys' belong to 'the kingdom of heaven,' and that this kingdom is
not identical with 'my church' in v. 18."[3] "Jesus' 'church' is not the
same as his 'kingdom': the two words belong to different concepts,
the one to 'people' and the other to 'rule' or 'reign.'"[4]

By examining the passage carefully, it can be seen that two distinct topics are in view: "I will build My church"; and "I will give
you the keys of the kingdom of heaven." If the two topics were the
same, the passage might read something like, "I will build My church
and give to you Peter its keys." Or, "My church is the kingdom I
have been teaching about all along." Or, "Peter, you will be the head
over My kingdom, the church." But no such hint that *church* and
kingdom are the same is given in this context or in the history of the
founding of the church recorded in the book of Acts.

For a complete understanding in regard to this passage of Scripture, it is helpful to ask a series of questions:

- Who or what is the "rock"?
- Who had a greater role in reaching the Gentiles at Rome?
- What does "kingdom of heaven" mean?
- What does the binding and loosening mean?
- What are the views about this passage of Scripture in the early
  church?
- What has been Roman Catholicism's most common view of
  Matthew 16?
- What are Roman Catholicism's changing views on Matthew 16?

Who or What Is the "Rock"?

Peter's name, *Petros,* is a masculine word in Greek. But *upon this
the rock,* "petra," is a feminine phrase. Jesus was not calling Peter

"the girl rock." The feminine, "this the," must, therefore, be referring to something already said, rather than to the disciple Peter. It is true that the feminine form of *rock* can be referring to something said or indicated that in itself is not feminine, but the most logical explanation is that it refers to Peter's statement, "Thou art the Christ, the Son of the living God" (v. 16). Jesus acknowledges Peter's words with "flesh and blood did not reveal this to you, but My Father who is in heaven" (v. 17).

> Jesus purposely uses two Greek words which, though not identical, are closely related in meaning. What he said was, "You are petros, and upon this petra I will build my church," meaning, "You are a rock, and upon the rocky ledge (or cliff) of the Christ, 'the Son of God the living' who was revealed to you and whom you confessed, I will build my church." If Jesus had intended to convey the thought that he was going to build his church on Peter he would have said, "and on you I will build my church."[5]

Thus, by extension the church is built upon the person of Christ in whom Peter and the disciples have declared their faith.

Who Had a Greater Role in Reaching the Gentiles at Rome?

Since Rome was the capital of the Gentile world, one must question the primacy of Peter in that city. Paul makes it clear in his writings that he was the apostle sent to the pagan world. This of course does not mean that Paul and Peter ministered exclusively to the two different groups, Jews and Gentiles. Many times in the ministry of Paul, he witnessed to his Jewish brothers. Likewise, Peter often shared the gospel with Gentiles.

But since the early church was made up of more Gentiles than Jews, one would expect Paul to be the head of the church, if God had so appointed a human figure to hold that position. After Paul's first missionary journey, he shares with the church at Antioch how God used him to open a "door of faith to the Gentiles" (Acts 14:27), and that by his mouth the Gentiles "should hear the word of the gospel and believe" (15:7).

When the Jews refused the truth at Corinth, Paul swore that from then on he would go to the Gentiles with the truth of Jesus (18:6). The Lord Himself had told the apostle "I will send you far away to the Gentiles" (22:21), making it clear that Paul was indeed the apostle to the Gentiles (Rom. 11:13). In contrast, Peter makes it clear that his primary role was to be the apostle to the Jews, "aliens, scattered throughout Pontus" (1 Peter 1:1).

If Peter was to be the head of the church, as Roman Catholicism contends, why is this not mentioned elsewhere in the development of the New Testament? Paul writes of Christ as the head of the church: "He makes no mention of any visible head; had one been appointed by Christ he would have been of necessity compelled to mention here the fact."[6]

> St. Paul throughout his teaching as to the Unity of the Body, which is the Church, never in the remotest way alludes to any necessity for there being a visible head to that portion of the mystical Christ which is here on earth.
>
> Further, that St. Paul, *the* Apostle, as he is designated by the Fathers, for example, by St. Augustine and St. Chrysostom, was entirely ignorant of the existence in the Church of any office superior to that which he held himself.
>
> Moreover, when the Acts of the Apostles is examined there is no reference, explicit or implicit, to any visible Head of the Church, who as Supreme Pastor governed the Church.[7]

What Does "Kingdom of Heaven" Mean?

In almost all instances, the expressions "kingdom of God" and "kingdom of heaven" refer to the coming millennial reign of Christ on earth. That a form of this kingdom then goes on into eternity following the one-thousand-year reign of Christ is agreed upon by most dispensationalists. The focus of the kingdom of God lies in the Gospels. John, Mark, and Luke use the expression "kingdom of God" exclusively. Matthew used the phrase "kingdom of heaven" some thirty times and "kingdom of God" only three times.

In the view of most premillennialists and dispensationalists, the two expressions clearly point to the Davidic covenant and the millennial reign of the Son of David, Jesus the Messiah. David himself says, "[The Lord] has chosen my son Solomon to sit on the throne of the kingdom of the LORD over Israel" (1 Chron. 28:5). And Christ came through Solomon's line. Though it is the Lord's kingdom (29:11), it is still bequeathed to David's sons and established forever (28:7–8).

Since Peter will help launch the church in Acts 2, what does it mean that he will be given the keys to the kingdom of heaven, especially since that kingdom is not the church? Isaiah 22:20–23, although a passage not directly related to the issue, may hold the key to the answer.

As Israel faces the terror of the Assyrians during the reign of Judah's king Hezekiah (approx. 701 B.C.), Isaiah the prophet tells Israel that God has placed a servant, Eliakim, in Jerusalem, who has prophetic spiritual authority: "He will become [like] a father to the inhabitants of Jerusalem and to the house of Judah. Then I will set the key of the house of David on his shoulder, when he opens no one will shut, when he shuts no one will open" (vv. 21–22).

Like Eliakim, Peter would be given authority over the city of Jerusalem and the people of Judah in regard to judgment based on their acceptance or rejection of the gospel message. This authority, if it can be called that, also extends over the house of David and the kingly line. After all, it was Israel's king who was crucified by His own people for their own sins. As Peter preached, the people made judgments about the kingdom and their king. For example, Peter cried out to the people of Jerusalem, "Repent, . . . that your sins may be wiped away, in order that times of refreshing may come from the presence of the Lord; and that He may send Jesus, the Christ appointed for you, whom heaven must receive until the period of restoration of all things about which God spoke by the mouth of His holy prophets" (Acts 3:19–21).

This is clearly a kingdom offer, though Peter certainly did not know God's timetable for the coming millennial reign. In theory, Peter was unlocking or opening. He was living out the prophetic word. And before the Sanhedrin, Peter cried out, "[Jesus] is the one whom God exalted to His right hand as a Prince and a Savior, to grant repentance to Israel, and forgiveness of sins" (5:31). Note how Peter focuses on the Messiah's work as Savior for Israel, the Jewish people.

In time, the message of Christ will slip away from the Jews. Peter's work of judgment against the people will be over. The gospel message will then go to the Gentiles, and Israel will be cut off and scattered.

What Does the Binding and Loosening Mean?

While the meanings of "bind" and "loose" in the context of Matthew 16:19 have been partly explained above, a closer examination of the verse is needed. The text is best read, "I will [future tense] give you the keys of the kingdom of heaven; and whatever you should bind [Aorist, active, subjunctive] on earth shall itself have been bound [Perfect, passive, participle] in heaven, and whatever you should loose [Aorist, active, subjunctive] on earth shall itself have been loosed [Perfect, passive, participle] in heaven."

By the use of two perfect, passive participles, the Lord seems to be saying that what Peter does here on earth is but carrying out what God has already determined in heaven. In other words, Peter is but an instrument of judgment that has been previously determined by the Lord. Thus, Peter is the Lord's visible instrument of judgment, but the final active authority still rests with God. Peter, then, really does not have authority in the way most would think. He is but a providential instrument against the Jews and their view of the kingdom of heaven. Once they have been judged through the "instrument" Peter, the work of the Lord through the church increases, as evidenced in the book of Acts.

Is this interpretation correct? Though there are some differences of opinions, many great Bible scholars think so.

> . . . And when the perfect participle is given its full force in the Matthean passages, the periphrastic future perfect in 16:19 becomes 'whatever you bind on earth shall have been bound in heaven, and whatever you loose on earth shall have been loosed in heaven' (similarly for 18:18). Thus, as [the grammarian] Mantey insisted, there is no evidence for "sacerdotalism or priestly absolution" in the NT.[8]

Thus, the church on earth carries out heaven's decisions. Heaven is not ratifying the church's decisions.

Views About Matthew 16:13–20 in the Early Church

Seventeen of the early church fathers—including Origen and Jerome—felt the passage means that the church was built on Peter. Another group of church fathers felt that the church was built on all the apostles, not simply upon Peter. But a majority—forty-five—of the church fathers felt

> . . . that these words are to be understood of the Faith which St. Peter had confessed, that is, that this Faith, this profession of faith, by which we believe that Christ is Son of the living God, is the eternal and immovable foundation of the Church.[9]

This interpretation is by far the most customary, and it is attested to by the Eastern church fathers Gregory of Nyssa, Cyril of

Alexandria, Chrysostom, Theodoret, and Theophylact. It is supported as well by the Western fathers Hilary, Ambrose, Augustine, and Gregory the Great.

That the rock was Peter would not be fully espoused until Siricius, bishop of Rome, wrote a letter in A.D. 385 to the bishop Himerius of Tarragona, Spain, arguing for the primacy of Peter.

Though a faulty hermeneutical argument, Denney believes that the interpretation that Christ is the Rock does not take away from the third interpretation—held by the majority of the Fathers—that it is upon Peter's confession of faith that the church rests. In fact, some feel that both views are acceptable.

> Hence Dionysius the Carthusian gives the two interpretations as equally expressing the meaning of the words, saying, "And upon this rock, that is, upon the firmness and foundation of his Faith [i.e. upon that of Peter], or upon this Rock which thou hast confessed, that is Myself, the chief corner-stone, the lofty mountain of which the Apostle says other foundation can no man lay, etc."[10]

A major rule of biblical interpretation, however, is that there is almost always one meaning for a given passage. It is rare that two distinct ideas are embedded in one sentence or short paragraph.

Thus, the weight of early church history demonstrates that the church fathers believed Christ's statement in regard to the rock has to do with Peter's confession of who Jesus really is. It is upon that confession that the church will be built.

The Most Common View
of Roman Catholicism on Matthew 16

Since around 1860, the Catechism of Father Joseph Deharbe has been recognized as the most important doctrinal statement for Catholics throughout North America. Thousands of Catholics cut their teeth on this little volume that carried the imprimatur of John Farley, the Archbishop of New York. This book proclaims that, on the basis of Matthew 16, Christ appointed Peter to be the supreme head of His church.[11] Deharbe notes,

> We learn [this fact] from this, 1. That Christ built His Church upon Peter, as upon the true foundation-stone; 2. That He gave him in particular the keys of the Kingdom of Heaven; and 3. That He commissioned him alone to feed His whole flock.[12]

206   Classical Evangelical Hermeneutics

In the catechism the question is then asked, "Who followed Peter upon his death?"

> The Councils, as well as the Fathers of all ages individually have unanimously and most decidedly, by word and deed, acknowledged in the Roman Popes the Primacy and Supremacy of St. Peter. The Ecumenical Council of Florence (1438) referred to "the Decrees of the General Councils, and the Ecclesiastical Statutes," when it declared "that the Bishop of Rome (the Pope) possessed the Primacy over the whole universe; that he was the Successor of the Prince of the Apostles, St. Peter, and the true Vicegerent of Jesus Christ, the Head of the whole Church, . . . and whoever refused to recognize the Pope as the Head of the Church was at all times considered by all the faithful as an apostate."[13]

The Catholic Church is serious about the Matthew 16 passage of Scripture. Upon it is built a powerful system that controls the religious life of all who are under the Church's purview. This power starts with Peter and is bequeathed to every pope ever placed in office.

The Catechism of Father Deharbe notes that it is easy to find the visible Church because perceptible marks have been left that the world can see. Because of these perceptible marks, all who deny the Church are "under pain of eternal damnation" if they do not listen to her.[14] "Non-Catholic Religious Societies" (Protestant denominations) are not true because they have no common Head (such as the pope), and because their founders are not holy."[15] As well, they "have rejected many articles of faith and means of sanctification, as, for example, the Sacrifice of the Mass and most of the Sacraments."[16] The people in these groups are lost "because they cannot produce from among themselves one Saint, confirmed as such by his miraculous power."[17]

Father Deharbe's catechism warns that all must adhere to the decisions of the Church. And when the pope speaks for the Church, he speaks infallibly: "The General Council of the Vatican, in 1870, defined that the Pope is infallible when he teaches the Church *ex cathedra*."[18]

Contrary to what the Catholic Church tries to convey today, in reality their doctrine maintains that all non-Catholics are likely outside of salvation unless they come back into the fold of the Mother Church.

From the beginning whoever obstinately refused to accept and believe a doctrine of Catholic Faith, when so declared *ex cathedra* by the Pope, was always cut off from the communion of the Church, and condemned as a heretic.[19]

And Who Is a Heretic?

All those who by their own fault are Heretics, i.e., 1. who profess a doctrine that has been condemned by the Church; or who are Infidels—that is, who no longer have nor profess any Christian faith at all; and 2. All those who by their own fault are Schismatics—that is, who have renounced, not the doctrine of the Church, but their obedience to her, or to her Supreme Head, the Pope.[20]

Further, one becomes a heretic by one's own fault, knowing about the Catholic Church, convinced of her truth, but not joining her. But more, one could know her, if one searched, but through indifference and other culpable motives, neglects to do so.[21]

And finally, apart from the Church there is no salvation. "Every one is obliged, under pain of eternal damnation, to become a member of the Catholic Church, to believe her doctrine, to use her means of grace, and to submit to her authority."[22]

From the words of Jesus in Matthew 16, the Catholic Church has constructed a system that confines its followers to its own deadly path. Through Peter, power was transferred down the centuries, from bishop to bishop, and has created a mountain of belief from which there is neither room for challenge nor is there an escape. Those who do not believe all that the Church says are lost. And there are changes in the wind that will prove to be a deeper and more subtle trap for those not familiar with Catholic strategy.

What Are the Changing Views of Roman Catholicism on Matthew 16?

After the first three or four centuries, developing Roman Catholicism held that the Church is the kingdom of heaven, or kingdom of God. Theologically, this is amillennialism. But in the theological writings of the modern Church, there is an attempt to change this kingdom idea. How far this change will go is not certain. In the 1286-page work, *Catholicism* (1994), by Father Richard P. McBrien, new thoughts emerge about a kingdom yet future that is related to, yet separate from, the present earthly Church. McBrien writes, "Insofar as the Church offers a credible witness to the truth, it will arouse the world to a 'living hope' in the coming of the Kingdom of God."[23]

He then quotes Catholic theologian Karl Rahner, who states, "The Church is not itself the Kingdom of God."[24] Another Catholic theologian, Edward Schillebeeck, writes, "The Church is committed to the coming Kingdom of God, but it is not yet in possession of the Kingdom. The Church is still on the way, in history, searching tentatively for solutions to the problems of human existence."[25] He says further that when the Church finds the solutions, the world can then be fully "humanized."

To many more recent Catholic theologians, the Church is seeking a parallel path to the world, "critically involved in the building of the world and the progress of the nations."[26]

McBrien further writes,

> The Church is necessary for the world as a sacrament, an efficacious sign and instrument of God's redemptive activity in Jesus Christ, leading toward the final Kingdom of God. . . . The Church is necessary for those individuals who are in fact called by God to acknowledge the Lordship of Jesus and to collaborate with him in the coming Kingdom of God.[27]

McBrien also admits that it was Augustine who first identified the Church with the kingdom.[28] But twentieth-century Catholic theology insists that the Church and the kingdom are not the same. The kingdom, they say, will be the product of divine and human initiative and collaboration. It will have political and social dimensions, and it will be fully manifested in the future.[29] In the meantime, the Eucharist represents the kingdom and even "anticipates" it.

> The Catholic Church has never officially defined the meaning of the Kingdom of God. The Second Vatican Council overcomes the separation between general and individual eschatology, links the present and the future, and establishes a fundamental unity between the earthly and the heavenly.[30]

By what has been written by McBrien, it is possible that the current view of the Church could evolve into an imminent and near millennial view of a coming kingdom. If this happens, a clash could occur between the promised Jewish millennial kingdom and the kingdom of the Catholic Church on earth, thus precipitating the open warfare described in the book of Revelation between the false prophet—who could be the pope—and the people of God. The pope would be loyal to and standing behind the "political and social dimensions" of the kingdom of the antichrist.

It can be concluded that the keys to the kingdom given to Peter refer to his role in the judgment of the Jewish nation and their notion of the reign of the Messiah. Wherever Peter went, he convicted the Jewish leaders about their rejection of Jesus as their Savior and Messiah. Peter was but the instrument in the hands of a sovereign God for carrying out the spiritual opening and closing of doors (loosening and binding) for that generation of the Jewish people.

The church is not that kingdom, but the church is built upon the declaration of Peter concerning the divine person of the Lord. New Testament history seems to best support these views.

In great error, the Catholic Church has created a primacy of Peter from the Matthew 16 passage to support their political structure.

This chapter is adapted from Mal Couch, "The New Dispensation: The Church," in *A Biblical Theology of the Church*, ed. Mal Couch (Grand Rapids: Kregel, 1999), 42–48.

CHAPTER 17

Matthew 13: The Church or the Kingdom?

Matthew 13 stretches the minds and the imaginations of all students of Scripture. Jesus suddenly makes a shift in His teaching and, using a series of parables, begins speaking about the "mysteries of the kingdom of heaven."

Key questions for interpreters are (1) Why did the Lord change His manner of teaching by using so many parables? (2) In relation to the kingdom of heaven, what do the parables mean? (3) Do the parables refer to something beyond the kingdom, such as the church?

These mysteries and parables cannot refer to the coming church age. If they do, then basic hermeneutics would be terribly torn and violated, and the meaning of the text would lose all shape and substance. If the people and the disciples were still hearing with their ears "the kingdom of heaven" and "the kingdom of God," what message were they receiving?

Was Jesus just fooling them? Did He sneak in a new message about this new thing, the church, when they did not notice? Is the church what John the Baptist and Christ were proclaiming all along? And were the crowds simply tricked into believing that both were still speaking of the prophesied messianic Davidic kingdom?

What Is One of the First Rules of Interpretation?

According to Charles Hodge,

The words of Scripture are to be taken in their plain historical sense. That is, they must be taken in the sense attached to them in the age and by the people to whom they were addressed. This only assumes that the sacred writers were honest, and meant to be understood.[1]

Jesus taught openly and honestly. He would not have tried to fool His disciples or the people.

The Three Views on the Mysteries of the Kingdom

1. Allegorical/Amillennial view. This view claims that from the beginning the Lord was referring to the church as He spoke about the kingdom. Since the people could not understand the revelation of this new era, Jesus simply taught in coded language and in terms they understood, that is, still in reference to a kingdom. Ellicott, an amillennialist, notes in reference to the parable of the mustard seed (13:31),

> The interpretation of the parable lies almost on the surface. Here again the sower is the Son of Man; but the seed in this case is not so much the "word," as the Christian society, the Church, which forms, so to speak, the firstfruits of the word.[2]

On the parable of the leaven (13:33), he says,

> The parable sets forth the working of the Church of Christ on the world, but not in the same way as that of the Mustard Seed. There the growth was outward, measured by the extension of the Church, dependent on its missionary efforts.[3]

On the parable of the good seed sown (13:37),

> Primarily, we must remember that the parable refers to the kingdom of heaven—i.e., to that new order of things which the Christ came to establish, and which is conveniently described as the Church which owns Him as its Lord. [The parable] offers, accordingly, as explanation of the presence of evil in that Church.[4]

On the tares sown by the Devil (13:39), he comments,

> [The passage deals with] many problems in the history and policy of the Church of Christ. (1) The enemy sowed the tares

"while men slept." The time of danger for the Church is one
of apparent security. Men cease to watch. Errors grow up and
develop into heresies, carelessness passes into license, and
offenses abound. (2) The "servants" are obviously pastors of
the Church. Their first impulse is to clear the kingdom from
evil. . . . To seek for the ideal of a perfect Church in that way
may lead to worse evils than those it attempts to remedy.[5]

Is this the message the disciples received from Christ's words? Is
this how they understood that something new was coming? "Oh,
Lord, when You speak of the kingdom, You no longer mean the messianic earthly rule over the government of restored Israel, do You?"
There is not the slightest evidence that they took His words as
referring to a new entity, a new dimension about the kingdom they
had not conceived of.

2. "New program of the kingdom" view. This view is held by the
premillennialist J. Dwight Pentecost and others, and it claims that
there was an added dimension to the kingdom not revealed in the
Old Testament. The kingdom would be seen in a new spiritual form,
specifically including the church age. Caution must be taken in attempting to understand this position, because those who advocate
it are not saying that the church replaces the millennial kingdom.
They argue that the church is a kind of spiritual prelude, and that
this new spiritual essence will continue on into the earthly kingdom era. Pentecost writes,

. . . We come to see that the time period covered by the
parables in Matthew 13 extends from Israel's rejection until
its future reception of the Messiah. Thus this new program
began while Christ was still on the earth, and it will extend
until His return to the earth in power and great glory.

This period includes within it the period from Pentecost
in Acts 2 to the Rapture, that is, the age of grace (which we
can also call the age of the Holy Spirit, or the age of the
church). Although this period includes the Church Age, it
extends beyond it, for the parables of Matthew 13 precede
Pentecost and extend beyond the Rapture. Thus these
parables do not primarily concern the nature, function, and
influence of the church. Rather, they show the previously
unrevealed form in which God's theocratic rule would be
exerted in a previously unrevealed age, made necessary by
Israel's rejection of Christ.[6]

This view comes very close to saying that the parables are about the church. But then Pentecost retreats from that idea.

A similar view is given by Fruchtenbaum, who states,

> The Mystery Kingdom covers the age between the two comings of the Messiah, between the first and second coming. More specifically, it begins with the rejection of the Messiahship of Jesus in Matthew 12–13 and continues until the acceptance of the Messiahship of Jesus by Israel just before the second coming. Perhaps the best single word to define the Mystery Kingdom is the term "Christendom." It describes conditions on this earth while the King is absent from the earth and is in heaven. These mysteries of the kingdom relate truth to the eternal purpose of God in relationship to His eternal kingdom program.[7]

3. "To reveal new truths concerning the messianic kingdom" view. This view is most consistent with normal and literal hermeneutics and allows the continuity of words and thoughts to continue through the Gospels without suddenly having to shift to a new meaning for the idea of the kingdom of heaven.

Toussaint says,

> This view states that the King is giving new revelation concerning the kingdom promised to the Jews. The truths relate to the time of the establishing of the kingdom, the preparation for it, and other such material which had never before been revealed. This approach is the best for several reasons.
>
> First, it is consistent with the uniform New Testament concept of the kingdom.
>
> A second advantage of this view is its agreement with the Old Testament prophecies of the kingdom. The Old Testament expected a judgment to precede the establishment of the kingdom (Daniel 7:21–27); the parables concur (Matthew 13:30, 41–42, 49–50). The Old Testament prophet foresaw the giving of rewards to the righteous which would be manifested in the kingdom (Daniel 12:2–3); the parables present the same truth (Matthew 13:30, 41–42). Daniel's prophecy of the stone "cut out without hands" indicates that the coming of the kingdom was to be supernatural (Daniel 2:34); the parables state the same fact (Matthew 13:30, 40–41). The kingdom was to come suddenly (Isaiah 46:13; Daniel 2:34,

44–45; Malachi 3:1); again the parables agree (Matthew 13:30, 40–41, 48–49). The authority of the prophesied Messianic kingdom was to be universal (Psalm 2:8); the [future] kingdom presented in Matthew 13 likewise extends throughout the world (Matthew 13:38–41). The conclusion is patent: the nature of the kingdom portrayed in the parables is the same as that pictured by the Old Testament prophets.

This view has the further advantage of being consistent with the New Testament concept of a mystery. Because of the Jewish rejection of the Messiah, the promised kingdom is now held in abeyance. The parables of Matthew 13 reveal new truths involving the preparation for the establishment of the kingdom during this time of postponement which was not predicted in Daniel's seventy weeks or other Old Testament prophecies.[8]

In his commentary introduction to Matthew 13, Glasscock concurs:

> . . . It would appear that the kingdom of heaven, the messianic reign on the throne of David, was postponed for the time being. This is not to imply that the kingdom had been lost to Israel, but that the gospel would be sent to the Gentiles, and the universal work of Messiah will be the focus until Israel is brought back in repentance. Like the postponement of entrance into the Promised Land while Israel wandered in the wilderness for forty years, so now, once again, Israel's joy was postponed by her rebellion.[9]

What Is Matthew 13 Actually Teaching?

First, in the context of Matthew 13, which includes the previous chapter, Jesus pronounces a judgment on the hardheartedness of the Pharisees and the people. Everything in chapter 12, continuing into chapter 13, is Jewish and has to do with Israel. In chapter 12, the Lord calls Himself the Son of Man, who is Master of the Sabbath (v. 8). He refers to Isaiah 42:1, where God calls the Messiah "My Servant whom I have chosen; My Beloved in whom My soul is well-pleased" (12:18). Again, all this sets the stage for Matthew 13. In chapter 12 the people call Him "the Son of David" (v. 23). The Lord curses the leaders and labels them evil and a "brood of vipers" (v. 34), and He speaks of their judgment to come (v. 37). When the Pharisees ask for a sign (v. 38), Jesus answers with an illustration about Jonah in the stomach of the fish: "Something greater than Jonah is here" (v. 41). Finally, three times He refers to this evil generation that must someday face a judgment for rejecting Him (vv. 41–42, 45). The entire section preceding chapter 13 is Jewish and has to do with Israel not the church.

Second, it must again be noted that the expressions "kingdom of heaven" and "kingdom of God" are clearly messianic kingdom concepts not referring to the church. Jesus uses both expressions when He gives the discourse on the mysteries of the kingdom as recorded in the synoptic gospels: "To you it has been granted to know the mysteries of the kingdom of heaven . . ." (Matt. 13:11); "To you has been given the mystery of the kingdom of God . . ." (Mark 4:11); "To you it is granted to know the mysteries of the kingdom of God . . ." (Luke 8:10).

Third, in Matthew 13, when the Lord spoke about the spiritual blindness and deafness of Israel, He quotes Isaiah 6:9–10, which prophesies the judicial dullness placed upon Israel because they would have a stubborn heart against the truth. Christ nowhere in these verses hints that a new "church" form of the kingdom is about to come that would make void the Davidic kingdom.

Fourth, in Matthew 13 the Lord speaks of "the righteous [who] will shine forth as the sun in the kingdom of their Father" (v. 43). Jesus paraphrased Daniel 12:3, in which Daniel speaks of the righteous shining as stars in the heaven forever. The context of Daniel refers specifically to "your people" the Jews, not the Gentiles, or to some new body, the church.

Fifth, in Matthew 13 Jesus uses in more than one place the messianic term "the Son of Man" and "His kingdom" (vv. 37–41). Again, this is purely Jewish, and there is no way to insert the church into the context of Matthew 13.

Why Did Christ Speak of the Kingdom in Parables and Mysteries?

From chapter 13 in Matthew and forward, Jesus would begin speaking more to the crowds in parables in order to hide from the people the truths about the kingdom. He told His disciples that to the people of Israel "it has not been granted" (13:11) for them to know anymore about the promised Davidic kingdom. In a sense, the offer of accepting His kingdom to that present generation was being rescinded and postponed until a far later generation.

But to the disciples, these "mysteries" about the kingdom of heaven/God would be revealed (v. 11). The word "mystery" means "something not before revealed in regard to the nature of the kingdom." Many opinions have been expressed about this, but the most plausible answer is that the Lord is speaking about the spiritual sensitivities of the kingdom, those multidimensional and deeply spiritual truths not conveyed in the Old Testament.

It was revealed that the millennial kingdom would be spiritual, even having God's very presence in the midst of the people. But the Jewish people had trouble understanding. Many of them only saw the kingdom as earthly and political, though this theory has often been overworked.

There were many godly and righteous Jews who were spiritually mature and longed to see the blessed Messiah come and reveal the glory of God. But there were also those who thought they would enter into the messianic age simply because they were Jews. In Matthew 13, Jesus confounded the crowds with parables but was also going deeper with spiritual truth for the sake of His disciples. He was making it clear, as He taught, that to come into that promised blessed state of the earthly kingdom, the Jews had to believe in Him, repent of their sins, and have a genuine thirst for the Lord and for spiritual truth.

Christ's words in chapter 12, *evil treasures* (12:35) and *evil hearts* (9:4), served as a prelude to His teaching in chapter 13. When the Jews then told the Lord they were blessed simply because they were the physical children of Abraham, He replied that if God simply wanted bodies for His offspring, He was "able from these stones to raise up children to Abraham" (Luke 3:8).

The teaching of chapter 13 and the parables show that the kingdom will take place on earth in time and history. It will be physical and geographical, and its capital will be Jerusalem in Israel. But it will also exist as a spiritual kingdom. A spiritual dynamic will govern this kingdom through the presence of the Messiah, and He determines its citizenship.

What Do the Parables Teach?

Beacham points out,

> The subject matter of these kingdom parables, then, was new revelation with regard to the prophesied kingdom. The mysteries of the kingdom ... was [not] a new revelation that confuted, overruled, or redefined previous kingdom prophecies. These were not truths that were found in the Old Testament but not yet fully realized or understood. . . .

In this revelation was something new and something old (Matt. 13:52).[10]

Summary of the Parables

The parable of the sower, Matthew 13:3–9, 18–23. When truth is spread forth, like a farmer scattering seed, no one knows for sure what the crop will be like. Some of the seed is scorched, and some is choked by thorns. But some seed yields many bushels of grain. In like manner, this is how the truth of the kingdom will be accepted. Some do not understand the "word of the kingdom" (v. 19). Some hear about the kingdom and rejoice, but the rocky soil gives no firm footing for the truth. Immediately, because of persecution or affliction caused by the teaching about the kingdom, the hearer "falls away" (vv. 20–21).

The parable of the wheat and tares, Matthew 13:24–30. After the land owner sows good wheat seed, at night an enemy comes and sows tares. Probably the tares were something like darnel or rye seed that in its early growth stages may look like wheat. As the crops grow, there is the mixture of the good with the bad. Only at harvest time can the two grains be separated. The kingdom of heaven is like this, Jesus says. As the grains grew, the landowner and his servants could see the difference but waited until the harvest and gathered the crops into barns (v. 30). At that time, the tares would be separated.

In Matthew 13:34–43, Jesus gives the explanation for this parable. He tells the disciples that the good seed are the sons of the kingdom, and the tares represent the sons of the evil one (v. 38). "The harvest is the end of the age; and the reapers are angels" (v. 39). The end of the age takes place just before the Son of Man begins His kingdom (vv. 40–41). The actual wording says the angels "gather out of His kingdom all stumbling blocks, and those who commit lawlessness, and will cast them into the furnace of fire; in that place there shall be weeping and gnashing of teeth" (vv. 41–42).

At first glance, the passage seems to teach that the separation of wheat and tares takes place at the beginning of the king's reign. But looking more closely at this parable in light of Matthew 24–25, it appears that the Messiah comes to earth (24:30–31), the righteous elect are gathered (v. 31), and then the evil are removed from their places and brought before the Master, the King (vv. 40–50), who tries and judges the kingdom impostors and orders them cast forth into outer darkness (v. 51). Chapter 13:42 and 24:51 read the same:

"There shall be weeping and gnashing of teeth." Then 13:43 reads: ". . . the righteous will shine forth as the sun in the kingdom of their Father."

To reiterate, none of these parables could be referring to the church age.

The parable of the mustard seed, Matthew 13:31–32. The mustard seed is the size of a grain of sand, but when fully grown, its branches and leaves are larger than that of most any other plant. The kingdom of heaven is like the mustard seed. The truth about the kingdom appears so small that men pay no attention to it. But when the seed matures, or when the kingdom actually comes, it will be all-pervasive and dominate everything.

The parable of the leaven, Matthew 13:33. The kingdom of heaven is also like the leavening that rapidly spreads throughout the bread dough when it is left to rise. It will cause the entire loaf of bread to rise or swell up. Again, when the kingdom arrives, it will quickly dominate the whole earth.

The parable of the hidden treasure, Matthew 13:44. The truth of the kingdom of heaven should be most precious. When a man finds a valuable treasure buried in a field, he sells all he has to purchase the field in order to secure the riches for himself. The glories of the kingdom should be to the Jews and all who love Christ a most valuable and consuming spiritual truth. It should be anticipated and eagerly prayed for.

> The anticipation of the coming glories of the kingdom of heaven is a treasure so inestimably precious that one who obtains it is willing to surrender for it whatever could interfere with having it. It is the supreme treasure because it fully satisfies the needs of the heart. It brings inner peace and satisfaction.[11]

The parable of the pearl of great price, Matthew 13:45–46. This parable is similar to that of the hidden treasure. The kingdom of heaven is like a valuable pearl that one will give everything one has to possess.

The parable of the dragnet, Matthew 13:47–50. This parable is similar to that of the wheat and the tares. The kingdom of heaven is like a fishing net that sweeps into it both good and bad fish. At the end of the age, or at the beginning of the kingdom, the wicked are removed from among the righteous (v. 49) and are cast into the furnace of fire, where there is "weeping and gnashing of teeth" (v. 50).

When the kingdom comes to earth with the king, He will begin His reign only with His righteous subjects.

The parable of the householder, Matthew 13:51-52. In this parable, Jesus said that the scribe of the kingdom of heaven, or the student of kingdom truth, would bring out of his storehouse (vault of safekeeping) valuable things (treasures) that are both new and old. The old treasures are things already described about the messianic kingdom from the Old Testament. The new treasures are the intangible and spiritual truths about that kingdom, which are at least in part taught in these parables. And they were meant to be understood by the disciples (13:11).

Though not everyone agrees as to the interpretation of the parables of the kingdom, there can be little question that the major subject is the kingdom of heaven, which is the future millennial reign of Christ.

The Parables and the Importance of Consistent Hermeneutics

Though the quote is lengthy, Beacham's conclusion on the parables sums up well the issues involved. Using proper and consistent hermeneutics, there can be no other meaning to the parables. Beacham writes,

A comparison of Matthew 25:31-46 with Matthew 13:38-43 clarifies many issues regarding the kingdom parables. It is clear, for example, that the kingdom out of which the offenders are gathered in Matthew 13:41 is not some kingdom that exists during the absence of the King or during the era of the church. Rather, the offenders are cast out of the prophesied kingdom that Christ establishes at His coming (Matt. 25:31-32, cf. 24:30-31). These are discriminatory judgments, one for Jews (Ezek. 20:33-38; 34:17-22) and one for Gentiles (Matt. 25:32-46), which probably take place in the transitional days following Daniel's Seventieth Week as alluded to in Daniel 12:11-12. The comparison of Matthew 25 with Matthew 13 also makes it clear that the kingdom parables cannot refer exclusively to the Jews and the millennial period, as some assert. The sowing of the good seed and the bad (Matt. 13:38) cannot take place during the Millennium, for the discriminatory judgment at the end of the age is clearly tied to the Second Advent, which begins the millennial reign (Matt. 24:30-31; 25:31-32). The parallel contexts, terminology, and descriptions in these passages (Matt. 13:38–43; 24:27–31; 25:31–46) present a unified account. The kingdom parables must be descriptive of a period prior to the Second Advent, yet the actual establishment of the kingdom in these parables is entirely future, immediately following the Second Advent.[12]

CHAPTER 18

The Postponement Theory

Most dispensationalists hold to a kingdom postponement theory, but amillennialists do not. Dispensationalists believe that the kingdom was set aside, the Jews suffered the final dispersement, and the church, which was not mentioned in the Old Testament, was given to reach the Gentile nations. But dispensationalists also hold that the earthly Davidic kingdom will yet come when Jesus returns. On this position Pentecost writes,

> . . . when Jesus Christ came as the anointed Messiah to offer the covenanted kingdom to Israel, He called on the people to repent, to put faith in His person, and to show the genuineness of their faith by their works. This the nation as a nation refused to do, with the result that Messiah's offer of the kingdom was withdrawn and its establishment postponed until some future time when the nation would repent and place faith in Jesus Christ.[1]

Does Postponement Mean God Is Not in Control?

Amillennialists believe that the church replaced the nation of Israel. They hold that the idea of a postponement sounds as if God is not in control, that a mistake was made, and that God had to revise His plans. To the amillennialist, all the promises in the Old Testament must be reinterpreted allegorically or abandoned and forfeited by Israel. On the disciples' question in Acts 1:6, "Lord, is it at this time You are restoring the kingdom to Israel?" McGarvey answers,

"The form of the question, 'restore the kingdom to Israel,' shows that they still retained their former misconception, that Christ's kingdom was to be a restoration of the old kingdom of David, and not a new and different institution."[2] Notice how quickly the kingdom concept is so easily dismissed. Observe also the standard amillennial argument that the disciples were simply misled.

Did God Make a Mistake?

Regarding postponement, the Bible shows that the kingdom was a legitimate offer to Israel because Christ the king was present. When the Jews finally rejected Him, the final stage of their scattering took place. Dispensationalists may agree that the word *postponement* is not the best one, and they would be delighted for a better term. But dispensationalists also hold to the sovereignty of God in all of His affairs. Since most dispensationalists are Calvinists, they do not believe there was a "mistake" in God's plans, or that He was caught unawares by the Jewish rejection of His Son. Peter tells us that when the Lord went to the cross, the Jewish people along with the Gentiles were gathered "to do whatever Thy hand and Thy purpose predestined to occur" (Acts 4:28). But some raise the question, "What about God's foreknowledge?" Larkin addresses the question of God's foreknowledge:

> God's foreknowledge that the Jewish nation would not at that time heed the announcement that the Kingdom of Heaven was at hand and repent, does not militate against the sincerity of the announcement any more than the offer of spiritual salvation by a preacher of the Gospel to an audience of sinners who he has every reason to believe will refuse his offer, is not a sincere and "bona fide" offer.[3]

Larkin adds,

> God's foreknowledge did not require or compel the Jewish nation to reject Jesus, any more than Jesus' foreknowledge that Judas would betray Him compelled Judas to so do. The possibility of the Church being crowded out by the repentance of the Jewish nation did not enter into the "Plan of God," who foresaw the refusal of Israel to accept Jesus as King, and that Israel would not nationally repent until after the Church had been formed and taken out of the world.[4]

God certainly knew the Jewish hardness of heart would cause the majority of the people to ignore or reject Jesus. His mysterious plan would bypass Israel's Old Testament promise of blessings until a future time. And this can certainly be substantiated throughout Scripture.

For example, the Old Testament promises of an earthly kingdom almost always prophesied that the Jews would return from a worldwide dispersement. Those promises also included repentance, an idea repeated often in the book of Acts.

When that day comes, Zephaniah notes, "The LORD has taken away His judgments against you" (3:15) and "the King of Israel, the LORD, is in your midst" and "Do not be afraid, O Zion" (v. 16). In fact, "the LORD your God is in your midst" (v. 17) and

> *"At that time I will bring you in, even at the time when I gather you together; indeed, I will give you renown and praise among all the peoples of the earth, when I restore your fortunes before your eyes," says the LORD. (v. 20)*

Through the prophet Amos, the Lord speaks of the nation, saying, "I will also plant them on their land, and they will not again be rooted out from their land which I have given them" (9:15). The Lord earlier said He would "raise up the fallen booth of David" (v. 11) and rebuild the ruins as in the days of old. And, "I will restore the captivity of My people Israel, and they will rebuild the ruined cities and live in them" (v. 14). Many other references also show the restoration of Israel. Note these verses from Deuteronomy 28–30, for example:

> *The LORD will scatter you among all peoples, from one end of the earth to the other end of the earth. . . . And among those nations you shall find no rest, . . . the LORD will give you a trembling heart, failing of eyes, and despair of soul. . . . And all the nations shall say, "Why has the Lord done thus to this land? Why this great outburst of anger?" . . . "Because they forsook the covenant of the LORD, the God of their fathers," . . . the LORD your God . . . will gather you again from all the peoples where the LORD your God has scattered you. . . . The LORD your God will gather you, and from there He will bring you back. . . . [He] will bring you into the land which your fathers possessed, and you shall possess it; . . . the LORD will again rejoice over you for good, just as He rejoiced over your fathers.*

And these verses from Ezekiel 36–37:

*I scattered them among the nations, and they were dispersed throughout the lands. . . . Thus says the L*ORD *God, "It is not for your sake, O house of Israel, that I am about to act, but for My holy name, which you have profaned among the nations where you went. And I will vindicate the holiness of My great name . . . among the nations . . ." I will take you from the nations, gather you from all the lands, and bring you into your own land. . . . I will put My Spirit within you, and you will come to life, and I will place you on your own land. . . . My servant David will be king over them, and they will have one shepherd. . . . And they shall live on the land that I gave to Jacob My servant, in which your fathers lived; and they will live on it. . . . My dwelling place also will be with them. . . . And the nations will know that I am the L*ORD *who sanctifies Israel, when My sanctuary is in their midst forever.*

When Did the Final Scattering Take Place?

With the destruction of Jerusalem and the temple in A.D. 70, the Jewish people were scattered literally; and they shall return to the land, literally. Then the Lord will restore the kingdom and bring the Messiah to reign and rule. For now, there must be a postponement, and the church, though made up of Jews and peoples from the nations, is prominent with Gentile believers.

If Peter does not speak of a postponement concept in Acts 15, then it is difficult to know what he has in mind. After Peter had addressed the Jerusalem Council about how God was saving Gentiles, James stood up and said, "Simeon [Peter] has related [exegeted, *exageomai*] how God *first* concerned Himself about taking from among the Gentiles a people for His name" (15:14). The word *first* must refer to what James is going to say next: "After these things I will . . . rebuild the tabernacle [tent, the kingdom] of David." In other words, "before he revives Israel's fortunes, He will save Gentiles [through this new thing the church]."

And this is precisely what James does say: "And with this the words of the Prophets agree, just as it is written, 'After these things I will return, and I will rebuild the tabernacle of David which has fallen, and I will rebuild its ruins, and I will restore it, in order that the rest of mankind may seek the Lord, and all the Gentiles who are called by My name,' says the Lord, who makes these things known from of old" (15:15–18).

To make his point, James expanded upon and explained further the context of the verses from Amos. James added, "After these things," which is not in Amos. This must refer to "after God has called out Gentiles for His name" (15:14), i.e., the church. Thus, God will work with the Gentiles before He restores the kingdom to Israel.

James also amplifies after he closes the quote from Amos: "says the Lord, who makes these things known from of old" (15:18). James borrowed that clause from Isaiah 45:21. By this, he emphasized what was well known throughout the Old Testament—that God would first reach the Gentiles prior to the coming kingdom. And James is correct. Many Old Testament passages speak about the worldwide scattering of the Jews, a tribulation, and then a return to the land with a restored kingdom.

In Acts 3, Peter relates a similar theme to the Jewish people. He reminds them that the prophets had written "that Christ should suffer, He has thus fulfilled" (v. 18); following His death and resurrection, the nation should "repent" (v. 19) "in order that times of refreshing may come from the presence of the Lord; and that He may send Jesus, the Christ [Messiah] appointed for you, whom heaven must receive until the period of restoration of all things about which God spoke by the mouth of His holy prophets from ancient time" (vv. 19–21).

Notice the key phrases: "Christ *should* suffer," or "the suffering was certain"; Peter speaks of "you," i.e., the Jewish people, and of a future plan "for them" in contrast to the present salvation of the Gentiles; he refers to the kingdom "times of refreshing," and "the period of restoration of all things"; he reminds the Jews that in the future God will send "Jesus the Christ appointed for you," which can refer only to His kingship.

Other passages imply this concept of the postponement. For instance, when the disciples asked "Is it at this time You are restoring the kingdom to Israel?" (Acts 1:6), the Lord put off their question as if to say "something else is coming along!": "It is not for you to know times or epochs which the Father has fixed by His own authority; but you have received power when the Holy Spirit has come upon you; and you shall be My witnesses" (v. 7–8).

Being pious Jews, the disciples had no other kingdom point of view than the Davidic, earthly reign. When the disciples asked, "Is it at this time . . . ," Jesus should have answered "no" if He meant for the church to replace the prophesied kingdom. But He simply said "that *time* [period] is not for you to know. Instead you have for now something else to do." Toussaint states on Acts 1:7,

Some conclude from the Lord's response that the apostles had a false concept of the kingdom. But this is wrong. Christ did not accuse them of this. If the followers of the Lord Jesus had an incorrect view, this would have been the time for Him to correct it. The fact is, Christ taught the coming of an earthly, literal kingdom (cf. Matt. 19:28; Luke 19:11–27; 22:28–30). Acts 1:3 states that the Lord instructed the disciples about the kingdom; He certainly gave them the right impression as to its character and future coming. What Jesus discussed here (v. 7) was the *time of the coming of the kingdom*.[5]

The writer of the book of Hebrews also reinforces the idea of postponement. He writes, "So Christ also, having been offered once to bear the sins of many, shall appear a second time for salvation without reference to sin, to those who eagerly await Him" (9:28). It already has been established that the suffering had to come before the reign as king. Even the Jewish orthodox rabbis understand those events apart from any New Testament point of reference.

So the author of Hebrews refers to a "second" earthly appearance, labeling this coming a "salvation without reference to sin." He can be referring only to Jesus' messianic reign as the Davidic king. Note also the eager waiting for this event. It follows, then, that the kingdom has been set aside until this present time of personal salvation—the church age, or age of grace—has ended. Pentecost concludes,

John the Baptist had preached that the kingdom of heaven was near (Matt. 3:2). Christ had preached the same message as He began His ministry (4:17), and during His ministry Jesus had offered Israel a kingdom that would be established if the nation would receive Him as Saviour-Sovereign. But the nation had rejected Him and the kingdom had to be postponed. Christ had previously taught that the generation of His day would not see the kingdom (Luke 17:22), because the kingdom would be postponed indefinitely to some future time. The Lord's words did not nullify the genuine offer of the kingdom in His day, nor deny the concept of a literal kingdom in a future day. Rather, this parable was designed to teach the truth concerning *postponement of the kingdom*.[6]

CHAPTER 19

Is the Church Grafted into Israel, as Some Allegorists Believe?

Someone once called the American Civil War "The Great Misunderstanding." Many amillennial and post-millennial commentaries on Romans 9–11 note that God has a future redemption for the Jewish people. On this specific point, amillennialists, postmillennialists, and premillennialists agree. But do premillennialists and amillennialists have a great misunderstanding about the nature of the blessings yet to come upon Israel?

The writings of some non-premillennialists about the conversion of Israel resembles dispensational commentary. Non-premillennialists do not, however, admit to an earthly kingdom reign of Jesus over this restored body of Jewish believers. Thus, the future conversion of Israel is taken literally and historically, but the Davidic kingdom reign is not taken literally. If the Jews' future conversion is literal, why not their kingdom glory, which is described in such literal terms in the Old Testament and in many places in the New Testament?

Before examining various viewpoints, it is appropriate to look at what Romans 9–11 teaches about Israel and her future blessing. The chapters can be outlined as follows:

God's Sovereign Dealing with the Nation of Israel, 9–11

A. Paul's great love for his people (9:1–5)
B. God's sovereignty in Israel's past (9:6–29)
C. Israel's present rejection of the gospel (9:30–10:21)
D. A remnant will be saved (11:1–10)
E. Israel, the natural branches broken off (11:11–24)

F.   The temporary rejection of Israel (11:25–32)
G.   Paul's thanksgiving to God for His wisdom (11:33–36)

What Is Romans 9–11 Teaching?

First, it must be observed that Paul is truly writing about natural Israel in the passage. A normal, literal hermeneutic will lead to no other conclusion. And further, he makes a definite contrast between the nation of Israel and the Gentile nations.

In Romans 9:6–8, Paul emphasizes God's sovereignty in making a division between the children of Abraham—who are part of the promised descendants—and those who are of the seed of Abraham but are not a part of the promise. "For they are not all Israel who are descended from Israel" (9:6), he argues, "but 'through Isaac your descendants will be named'" (v. 7). Thus, even among God's chosen people, He makes a sub-choice.

Paul continues this theme into chapter 11, writing about a further selection in Paul's day; a remnant of Jews "at the present time" (11:5) were being saved. Yet Paul continues to speak of national Israel, contrasting "*you*, Israel," who make *them*, "the Gentiles," jealous (v. 11).

The focal point of Paul's discussion about Israel lies in 11:11–24. Here, Paul speaks of a "rich root of the olive tree" (v. 17) and how the natural branches, Israel, were broken off (v. 19). The Gentiles, the wild olive branches, were grafted in order to be blessed (v. 17).

Paul's reference to the Gentiles being blessed would certainly be this present church age, in which the majority now being added to the body of Christ are from the nations. But the Jews will someday be restored (v. 23) when the fullness of the Gentiles is complete and the national spiritual hardness of Israel has passed: ". . . a partial hardening has happened to Israel until the fullness of the Gentiles has come in; and thus all Israel will be saved" (vv. 25–26a).

Calvin's Views of Romans 9–11

Since Calvin and other amillennialists saw no land and kingdom for the nation of Israel, any restoration for Israel had to do with regaining "faith" only. Calvin interprets *the fullness of the Gentiles* as "the completion of the number among the nations who are to be saved," and interprets *And so all Israel shall be saved* as somehow including national, racial Israel, yes, but also the entire believing people of God. Calvin writes in his commentary,

> Many understand this of the Jewish people, as though Paul had said, that religion would again be restored among them

as before: but I extend the word *Israel* to all the people of God, according to this meaning—"When the Gentiles shall come in, the Jews also shall return from their defection to the obedience of faith; and thus shall be completed the salvation of the whole Israel of God, which must be gathered from both; and yet in such a way that the Jews shall obtain the first place, being as it were the first-born in God's family." . . . Paul intended here to set forth the completion of the kingdom of Christ, which is by no means to be confined to the Jews, but is to include the whole world. The same manner of speaking we find in Gal. vi. 16. The Israel of God is what he calls the Church, gathered alike from Jews and Gentiles.[1]

John Owen, the editor of Calvin's works, does not fully agree. He adds that,

Hammond tells us, that many of the Fathers wholly denied the future restoration of the Jews; and we are told by Pareus, who mentions some of the same Fathers, that they maintained it. But it appears from the quotations made by the first, that the restoration disallowed was that to their own land, and that the restoration referred to by the latter was restoration to the faith; two things wholly distinct. That "Israel" means exclusively the Jewish nation, was almost the unanimous opinion of the Fathers, according to Estius; and that their future restoration to the faith is here foretold was the sentiment of Beza, Pareus, Willet, Mede, and others, and is generally held by modern divines.[2]

Thus, many amillennialists did not mind seeing the Jews come to faith in Christ. They even expected it to take place. But they denied a literal restoration of a Jewish, Davidic kingdom. In fact, the church became the kingdom, replacing a literal reign of Christ over the Jews in Palestine.

Other Views of Romans 9–11

John Gill. Writing from an amillennialist viewpoint, Gill says that *all Israel shall be saved* (11:26) refers to a literal restoration of the Jewish people to their land. He believes, however, that Christ reigns over them before the "wrath to come," thus placing the tribulation after the millennium. Gill writes on *all Israel shall be saved,*

Meaning not the mystical spiritual Israel of God, consisting both of Jews and Gentiles, who shall appear to be saved in the Lord with an everlasting salvation, when all God's elect among the latter are gathered in, which is the sense many give into; but the people of the Jews, the generality of them, the body of that nation, called the fulness of them, ver. 12. And relates to the latter day, when a nation of them shall be born again at once; when, their number being as the sand of the sea, they shall come up out of the lands where they are dispersed, and appoint them one head, Christ, . . . when they as a body, even the far greater part of them that shall be in being, shall return and seek the Lord their God, and David their King; shall acknowledge Jesus to be the true Messiah, and shall look to him, believe on him, and be saved by him from wrath to come.[3]

Albert Barnes. Barnes believes that the Jewish people will be saved, but their redemption will not include a restoration to the land. He sees *this is My covenant with them* (11:27) as something prophetic by which Israel will be restored spiritually. He notes,

It may be remarked, however, that that passage does not mean that the Redeemer shall come personally and preach to them, or re-appear for the purpose of recalling them to himself; nor does it mean that they will be restored to the land of their fathers. Neither of these ideas is contained in the passage. God will doubtless convert the Jews, as he does the Gentiles by human means, . . . so that the Gentiles shall yet repay the toil and care of the ancient Jews in preserving the Scriptures, and preparing the way for the Messiah.[4]

Barnes also sees *the root of the olive tree* in 11:17 as the blessing of Abraham. And although he does not say so, Barnes likely considers the blessings to be from the Abrahamic covenant, a conclusion with which many dispensationalists would agree. Barnes says,

The figure of the apostle [the tree] is a very vivid and beautiful one. The ancient root or stock, that of Abraham, &c. was good. The branches—the Jews in the time of the apostle— had become decayed and unfruitful, and broken off. The Gentiles had been grafted into this stock, and had restored the decayed vigour of the ancient people of God; and a fruitless church had become vigorous and flourishing. . . . The Gentiles derived now the benefit of Abraham's faith and holy labours, and of the promises made to him and to his seed.[5]

William Sanday. Sanday believes also the Lord will restore the Jews to salvation. They will accept their Messiah, but a return to the land is not a part of this blessing. On Romans 11:26 he adds,

When this ingathering of the Gentiles is complete, then the turn of Israel will come round again, and the prophecies of their conversion will be fulfilled.[6]

Sanday recognizes that Paul's quote of Isaiah 59:20–21; 27:9 in Romans 11:26–27 refers to the deliverer, the Messiah, returning literally from the city of Zion in Israel. The passage prophesies of the new covenant, which will be the instrument of the removal of sin from the Jewish people (Jacob).

Just as it is written, "The Deliverer will come from Zion, He will remove ungodliness from Jacob." "And this is My covenant with them, when I take away their sins."

But Sanday believes that although the meaning of the Isaiah quote originated in a literal Jewish restoration, it was changed by Paul to reflect a "spiritualized" meaning. Thus, according to Sanday, Paul changed the meaning from earthly and literal to figurative in order to "broaden the language." Sanday's interpretation destroys what is obvious in the passage. Note his words on Romans 11:26–27:

The passage occurs in the later portion of Isaiah, just where the Prophet dwells most fully on the high spiritual destinies of Israel; and its application to the Messianic kingdom is in accordance with the spirit of the original and with Rabbinic interpretation. St. Paul uses the words to imply that the Redeemer, who is represented by the Prophets as coming from Zion, and is therefore conceived by him as realized in Christ, will in the end redeem the whole of Israel. In these speculations St. Paul was probably strongly influenced, at any rate as to their form, by Jewish thought. The Rabbis connected these passages with the Messiah: . . . Moreover a universal restoration of Israel was part of the current Jewish expectation. All Israel should be collected together. There was to be a kingdom in Palestine, and in order that Israel as a whole might share in this there was to be a general resurrection.[7]

Sanday believes that Paul intended something more spiritual than the rabbinical "purified earthly Jerusalem." ". . . This enables us to see how here also a spiritual conception underlies much of [Paul's] language."[8]

William Plumer. On Romans 11:26 and the phrase *so all Israel shall be saved,* Plumer observes,

> Calvin extends [all Israel] to all the people of God. If this be the correct view, we may understand the "all" in an absolute sense. Then, "all Israel" in this verse embraces all believers, whatever their lineage and nationality may be and that to the end of time. . . . The other view makes "all Israel" to mean the mass of the Jewish nation. In that case the word all must be taken in no absolute sense, as it simply designates the great body of Jacob's descendants, who shall be living when the Jews shall turn to the Lord and accept their own Messiah. This is pretty certain the correct view of the passage.[9]

But again, in Plumer's commentary, there is no mention of the restoration of physical and national Israel to the land.

Charles Hodge. Hodge, also, believes in the future conversion of national Israel. He writes, "The Gentile Christians are not said (ver. 17) to be grafted into the stock of the converted Jews, but as branches with them they are united to a common stock." He says further,

> And the stock into which the branches, now broken off, are to be again grafted, is not the Jewish part of the Christian church, but the original family or household of God.[10]

That original family is the root that goes back to Abraham and the covenant made with him (Gen. 12:1–3). Though he does not say it, Hodge could be implying that both Jew and Gentile are then joined to that covenanted root.

The Plain Sense and Meaning of Romans 11

Looking at the chapter through the lens of a literal hermeneutic, one comes to the following conclusions:

1. God has not permanently rejected the Jewish people, though
    as a national group they are presently in unbelief. "God has
    not rejected His people, has He? May it never be!" (v. 1). The
    word "reject" in Greek is *apotheo* and means to "push aside,
    repudiate."
2. Presently, there is "a remnant [of Jews being saved] according
    to God's gracious choice" (v. 5). But, as Paul continues his
    arguments, he speaks of a future gathering and restoration of
    the nation as a national unit.
3. Though salvation has come to the Gentiles, it is partly to "make
    them jealous" (v. 11). And though (spiritual) riches have now
    come to the Gentiles, "how much more will [the Jews'] fulfill-
    ment be!" (v. 12). Their reconciliation back to God will be like
    "life from the dead" (v. 15).
4. The apostle speaks of a tree with a holy root and holy, natural
    branches (vv. 16–17). He does not say what the root is, but
    there are two choices: (1) It could simply represent God's bless-
    ing, specifically, His blessing of salvation. (2) It could repre-
    sent the Abrahamic covenant, which brings a blessing to the
    Jews (the natural branches, v. 21) and the Gentiles (the en-
    grafted wild branches, v. 24). The second interpretation is the
    most likely because the Gentiles, all families of the earth, are
    blessed through this covenant (Gen. 12:1–3). But whether or
    not officially through the covenant, the root does represent
    blessing in the illustration and context.
5. The Jews, the natural branches, will be grafted in again to
    the root of blessing: "How much more shall these who are
    the natural branches be grafted into their own olive tree?"
    (v. 24).
6. The Jews will be hardened until "the fulness of the Gentiles
    has come in; and thus all Israel will be saved" (vv. 25b–26a).
7. For the whole of the nation of Israel, the change will come
    when "the Deliverer will come from Zion, He will remove un-
    godliness from Jacob" (v. 26b). This of course will be the re-
    turn of Christ, who will gather in Jews to the kingdom. A
    remnant will indeed be saved.
8. The Jews, though in unbelief, are still beloved in God's sight
    because He made irrevocable promises to the nation of Israel
    for the sake of the ancient fathers, Abraham, Isaac, and Jacob
    (vv. 28–29).
9. Finally, because mercy was shown to the Gentiles, it will be
    shown to the Jews (v. 31).

Conclusion Concerning Romans 11

In regard to Romans 11, Pentecost, after arriving at conclusions similar to the plain sense meaning outlined above, summarizes,

> Therefore Paul is showing us that after the rejection of Israel, because of the rejection of the offered kingdom, God brought the Gentiles into the place of blessing, which program continues throughout the present age. When that program is ended, God will inaugurate the theocratic kingdom at the return of the Messiah and fulfill all the covenanted blessings. Thus, throughout the New Testament the kingdom is not preached as having been established, but is still anticipated. In Acts 1:6 the Lord did not rebuke the disciples because their expectation of a yet future kingdom was in error, but only stated that the time of that kingdom, although future, was not to be known by them.[11]

The Reformed scholar Haldane also understands the Romans passage in the same way. He writes,

> The Gentiles, who were a wild olive, having had no place in the good olive tree, are now made the children of Abraham by faith in Christ Jesus, Gal. iii. 26–29. They were grafted into the good olive tree, whose root Abraham was, and were made partakers of his distinguished privileges.
> The Gentile believers become the children of Abraham, and all the blessings they enjoy are in virtue of that relation. Hence the covenant, Jer. xxxi. 31, includes all believers; yet it is said only to be made with the house of Israel and Judah.[12]

Like dispensationalists, Haldane sees the new covenant mentioned in Jeremiah 31:31 as the "gospel covenant." He adds, "After having subdued to Himself the whole of the Gentiles, He will not forget the family of Abraham, His friend, in whom, according to His promise, all the families of the earth were to be blessed."[13] Here, Haldane is referring to the Abrahamic covenant (Gen. 12:1–3). He rightly recognizes the new covenant in Isaiah 59:21, through which God pours out His Spirit upon Israel. Calling the new covenant the "gracious covenant" he notes that it

> . . . is fully developed, Jer. xxxi. 31–34; and again, xxxii. 37–40, where the declaration referred to in the foregoing verse, of

turning away ungodliness from Jacob, is more fully expressed. The Apostle [Paul] grounds his conclusion from the prophecy on the fact that God in these words speaks of a time when He would take away the sins of Israel as a body, and so all Israel shall be saved.[14]

With a normal, natural, and literal hermeneutic, the above conclusions are the natural outcome. An interpreter of Scripture must work hard to rewrite what the Holy Spirit is trying to tell us. Still, many deny the restoration of a separate kingdom that does not include the church.

CHAPTER 20

Why the Church Is *Not* Referenced in the Olivet Discourse

To determine whether or not the church is referenced in the Olivet Discourse one must examine the context in which the discourse was delivered. Thus, we will first look at the larger context of the discourse, then the narrower context, and then the immediate context of the verses in question, Matthew 24:31–36.

The Larger Context of the Discourse

The most complete record of the Olivet Discourse exists in Matthew's gospel. Understanding Matthew's purpose in writing his gospel account gives insight into why he thought it important to include more of the discourse than the other gospel writers, as well as insight for deducing whether the church *is* or *is not* referenced in the Olivet Discourse.

An examination of the overall content of Matthew's gospel discloses that his purpose in writing was to show Jesus' offer of the kingdom to Israel, Israel's rejection of it, and why Jesus did not bring in His kingdom at that time. These purposes relate to Israel and God's program for her.

Preceding the Olivet Discourse, Christ had officially presented Himself to the nation as their King (Matthew 21; the Triumphal Entry) but had been rejected by the nation's leaders. Following this, He had pronounced judgment on them (21:43).

In Matthew 23, the chapter immediately preceding Christ's discourse, He delivers His scathing denunciation of the "scribes and Pharisees" (23:2). In it, He speaks of their hypocrisy of teaching

236

the word but not doing the word (23:3–4) and their evil motives in doing things visibly to be "noticed by men" (23:5) and to be honored verbally (23:7). In 23:13–39, Christ delivers a stinging but accurate account of the spiritual condition of the religious leaders of the nation of Israel, calling them hypocrites seven times (23:13, 14, 15, 23, 25, 27, 29), blind guides, blind men, and blind Pharisees five times (23:16, 17, 19, 24, 26), and fools twice (23:17, 19). He also calls them robbers and self-indulgers (23:25), white-washed tombs (23:27), and serpents (23:33), and He ends His denunciation by proclaiming the rejection of that generation (23:36).

Christ then laments over the nation. He proclaims, "O Jerusalem, Jerusalem, who kills the prophets and stones those who are sent to her! How often I wanted to gather your children together, the way a hen gathers her chicks under her wings, and you were unwilling" (23:37). Notice the larger context here. Christ's denunciation has been toward the leaders of Israel. They had spoken *for* the nation in their rejection of Him. His lament is over "Jerusalem" as the capital of Israel—not just toward the city *per se* but toward the nation it represented. God's chosen people had rejected His Son, and Christ's judgment was, "Behold your house is being left to you desolate" (23:38). The desolation of their house would now last until they recognized Him as their Messiah at His second coming, and they, as a nation, would proclaim, "Blessed is he who comes in the name of the Lord" (Matt. 23:39; Ps. 118:26). But Christ says this will not occur until they see Him again (Zech. 12:10), that is, until Christ returns to set up His millennial reign.

The overall context as traced above, then, leads up to Christ's discourse on the Mount of Olives. Walvoord states,

> In Matthew 24–Matthew 25 the expositor should, therefore, understand that the program of God for the end of the age has in view the period ending with the second coming of Christ to the earth and the establishment of His earthly Kingdom, not the church age specifically ending with the rapture. Both the questions of the disciples and the answers of Christ are therefore, keyed to the Jewish expectation based on Old Testament prophecy, and the program of God for the earth in general rather than the church as the body of Christ.[1]

The Narrower Context of the Discourse

The Questions

Matthew 24 finds Christ leaving the temple, having delivered His condemning words to the Jewish leaders and lamented over their future desolation (Matt. 23). Jesus was apparently departing to the Mount of Olives when His disciples pointed out the temple complex (24:1). One of them stated, "Teacher, behold what wonderful stones and what wonderful buildings!" (Mark 13:1). Pointing out the magnificently beautiful complex was apparently in reaction to Christ's lament over Jerusalem, the point being, perhaps, that Jerusalem was not deteriorating. It was, indeed, a wonderful religious center, but Christ's reaction was, "Do you not see all these things? Truly I say to you, not one stone here shall be left upon another, which will not be torn down" (Matt. 24:2). The nation enjoyed a beautiful place for worship; if only the inside of the people were so beautiful with true worship toward God.

Christ's statement greatly troubled the disciples, so when they arrived on the Mount of Olives, Mark tells us that Peter, James, John, and Andrew came to question Him privately. They asked Him two questions: (1) "When will these things be" (that is, when will the temple complex be destroyed); and (2) "What will be the sign of Your coming, and of the end of the age?" The phrase *the sign of Your coming, and of the end of the age* employs a Granville Sharp construction. Here, the construction is probably what Wallace refers to as the "First Entity [as] Subset of Second."[2] Christ's coming is a part of the end of the age activities along with the resurrections, judgments, etc. Notice again the disciples' concern related to their national place of worship. Their national leaders had rejected Christ, and He had clearly stated that their house would be made desolate, and they would not see Him until they said, "Blessed is He who comes in the name of the Lord!" Now the disciples were concerned about when that event would occur. In other words, what sign would precede His "coming" and the nation's recognition of Him as king (Matt. 23:39)?

Two questions have confused interpreters: Who are the disciples representing? (the church, Israel, or both) and which "age" is being referred to? The answers lie in this narrower context preceding the discourse.

Because the disciples were concerned about the destruction of the temple, their national place of worship, the very nature of their question in Matthew 24 would rule out any reference to the church in the discourse. That the apostles had, at this point, no understanding of the church in its New Testament technical sense would also argue against its mention. Though the word *church* is mentioned in Matthew 16:18 and 18:17, those references could very well mean "assembly," "meeting," or "gathering," in the way the Jews understood the word up until that time. To them, "assembly," coming from the Greek word *ekklesia*, is the translation of the Hebrew word *quhal*, and it is used in that sense in the Septuagint.

However, it remains possible that the Lord in Matthew 16:18 is using the word *church* in an initial reference to the coming new dispensation. If so, there is no interpretive problem here because it is simply a passing mention that the disciples did not fully grasp. (See chapter 16 for a full treatment of Matthew 16.) In Matthew 18:17 there also is no indication that the word *church* is used in its New Testament technical sense—a body of spiritually baptized believers (1 Cor. 12:13). If it is such a reference, the fact remains that the doctrine of the church was a mystery in the Old Testament (Eph. 3:1–12), and Christ was not giving them detailed instructions about this truth. At most it is a quick and cursive mention of this that is recorded in Matthew.

It is reasonable to conclude, then, that the disciples' questions about the temple's destruction were posed as Jews and not as representatives of the church.

> In the common language of the day, which had passed from the schools of the Rabbis into popular use, "this age," or "this world," meant the time up to the coming of the Messiah; the "age or world to come" (chap. xiii. 40; xix. 28; Heb. ii. 5; vi. 5), the glorious time which He was to inaugurate. The disciples had heard their Lord speak in parables of such a coming, and they naturally connected it in their thoughts with the close of the age or period in which they lived.[3]

Insight about what the disciples understood as "the end of the age" clarifies further who the disciples represented. The Jewish understanding of the end of the age is revealed in the question asked of Christ by the Sadducees in Luke 20:28–33 (regarding the widow of the seven brothers) and His answer in Luke 20:34–40. Christ indicated that the end of "this age" and the dawning of "that age" will involve "the resurrection" (Luke 20:35). The Jewish understanding was that *that age* would occur at the coming of the Messiah and the resurrection of the righteous (Dan. 12:2; Ezek. 37:12–14; Isa. 26:19). Therefore, Christ's answer reveals that the Jewish understanding of the end of this age and the dawning of the next involved the resurrection of the Old Testament saints to life in the kingdom (Luke 20:34–36). This is the understanding that the apostles would have had in mind when they asked about the "end of the age." MacArthur sets forth further proof:

> In the parable of the wheat and the tares, Jesus said "The harvest is *the end of the age;* and the reapers are the angels. As, therefore, the tares are gathered and burned in the fire, so shall it be in *the end of this age*" (Matt. 13:39–40). The phrase is used twice in those verses. The end of the age is when God separates the wheat from the tares and sends the tares to hell. Verses 42–43 say He "shall cast them into a furnace of fire; there shall be wailing and gnashing of teeth. Then shall the righteous shine forth as the sun *in the kingdom of their Father.*" The phrase is used again in Matthew 13:49–50: "So shall it be at *the end of the age;* the angels shall come forth, and separate the wicked from among the righteous, and shall cast them into the furnace of fire; there shall be wailing and gnashing of teeth." "The end of the age," then refers to the time when God comes in ultimate, final judgment and sends unbelievers to hell and takes believers into His presence.[4] (italics added)

One must logically conclude that the disciples would have been asking the questions in the context of the future of their nation and not as representatives of the church. Thus, their understanding of Christ's return and the end of the age would have been Jewish and not that of a member of the church. The information contained in the discourse, then, answers the specific questions about the destruction of the temple and the end of the age. And since the disciples were asking questions as Jews with a concern for the future of their nation, the questions had to do with, as Walvoord has stated, "the Jewish expectation based on Old Testament prophecy, and the program of God for the earth in general rather than the Church as the body of Christ."[5] The disciples asked the questions as Jews who awaited Christ's kingdom on earth and were probably still concerned about their place in that kingdom (Matt. 20:20–21).

One last question is worthy of our discussion: "What did the disciples mean by 'your coming'?" MacArthur writes,

The word "coming" in Matthew 24:3 is translated from the Greek word *parousia*. It means "to be around" or "to be present." The best way to translate the verse might be, "What will be the sign of your full presence?" The disciples were referring more to the Lord's permanent presence than to His coming. *Parousia* is also used in verses 27, 37, and 39. Because the Lord used it frequently to refer to His return, the New Testament writers did the same (James 5:8; 2 Pet. 3:4; 1 John 2:28). *Parousia* became synonymous with Christ's arrival to set up His kingdom. However, when the disciples ask about the Lord's coming in Matthew 24:3, they are saying, "When are You going to arrive in Your full messianic revelation? When will You become all that we anticipate You to be?" They didn't think in terms of His leaving and returning; they simply thought the Lord would soon make a transition to setting up His kingdom.[6]

Although Christ later told the disciples that He must leave (John 13:33; 14:2), they still did not grasp this truth, even as late as Christ's ascension (Acts 1:6), where they asked, "Lord, is it at this time that you are restoring the kingdom to Israel?" They anticipated that He would soon reveal Himself in His "full presence."

The Answer

Part 1: The First Half of the Tribulation (Matt. 24:4–14)

Since the first answer relates to the destruction of the temple by the Romans in A.D. 70, it will not be dealt with here. Matthew and Mark (Matt. 24:4–14; Mark 13:5–13) only deal with the answer to the second question, that being, "What will be the sign of Your coming and of the end of the age?" As has already been pointed out, Christ's coming and the end of the age are the same. Many believe that the church is referenced in Matthew 24:4–14. Dr. Walvoord writes,

Taken as a whole, while the order of the predicted events in Matthew 24:4–14 is climatic and increases in intensity and corresponds to the end of the age, the history of the last 1900 years clearly supports the view that all of these things have in large measure characterized the entire age even though these same characteristics may be present in intensified form as the age moves on to its conclusion.[7]

It is because these signs have also characterized the church age, that some believe the Olivet Discourse includes the church age. This can be true only if one denies the context, which has already been explained, and especially the specific questions that the disciples asked. As Benware writes,

> Here is the beginning of God's judgments on the earth—the "birth pangs." These judgments of earthquakes, famines, and wars are not referring to events of the present age; rather, they parallel the seal judgments or Revelation 6. Also, during this time there will be a great rise in false prophets, as well as wickedness in general. But this will be countered by a worldwide preaching of the gospel of the kingdom.[8]

In Matthew 24, Christ answers specific questions from the disciples, and His answers parallel John's revelation of the early stages of the Tribulation. That Christ analogizes these signs as "merely the beginning of birth pangs" (Matt. 24:8) is telling. In pregnancy, true birth pangs (excluding Braxton Hicks contractions) do not occur at conception or during the pregnancy; rather, they come at the end of the pregnancy and are signs of the end of the pregnancy. In the same way, the signs that Christ gave the disciples in Matthew 24:4–14 occur immediately before His coming, not during the church age.

Another key to the end of the age is that "the gospel of the kingdom" (Matt. 24:14) is preached to all nations. The disciples would have understood this statement in only one way. To them, the reference to the "kingdom" would have been to the kingdom of the Messiah and His ruling and reigning on earth. That they still had this understanding is revealed as late as Christ's ascension, as revealed in Acts 1:6, where they asked, "Lord, is it at this time that you are restoring *the kingdom* to Israel." (This statement also shows they had no understanding of the church age even at this late stage.) Walvoord adds this:

> If Christ is going to bring a kingdom to earth in His second coming, it is understandable that before He comes there will be a special heralding of the truth of the coming of the kingdom. This will be the good news that Christ is returning to reign, a message which will encourage those who are afflicted in the great persecution of the end of the age and give them cause to trust in Christ even though they be martyred for their faith. The gospel of salvation will relate them to the

first coming of Christ as the ground of their salvation. The gospel of the kingdom will herald the truth of the future coming Christ when the saints will be delivered from their persecutors and the end of the age of righteousness on earth will be inaugurated.[9]

Matthew 24:13 has caused much confusion because many expositors have misread the context, mistakenly including the church in the passage. Now that we understand the context as occurring in the Tribulation, when the church will be in heaven with Christ, it is clear that Matthew 24:13 does not refer to the loss of personal salvation. Christ is referring to deliverance from persecution and martyrdom. Many during the Tribulation who put their faith in Christ will be martyred (Rev. 7:9–17), but "the one who endures" ("remains under" or "continues") to the end will be rescued at Christ's second coming.

Part 2: The Second Half of the Tribulation—the Great Tribulation (Matt. 24:15–28)

Christ now reveals that at the end of the age, that which the prophet Daniel spoke of—the "abomination of desolation" first mentioned in Daniel 9:27—would be revealed. In the prophecy, Gabriel makes it clear that the information he is giving Daniel is for "your [Daniel's] people" and "your [Daniel's] holy city," Jerusalem (Dan. 9:24). The abomination of desolation was prophesied for the nation of Israel and not the church; thus the context continues to be Jewish in its nature.

When this event occurs, Jewish believers will know that the end of the age is close. Christ's advice for "those who live in Judea" is to flee to the mountains (Matt. 24:16). The flight of some would be impeded by pregnancy, and everyone's flight would be difficult if it occurred on the Sabbath, since the Jews do not travel on the Sabbath. ("If they had to travel on the Sabbath day their flight will be very obvious. It would be very easy to arrest them.")[10]

The abomination of desolation will signal the start of the Great Tribulation, or the second half of the tribulation period, when the Antichrist breaks his covenant with Israel and begins his persecution of the Jewish people (Dan. 9:27; Matt. 24:15–21). The wrath of the tribulation period will intensify and, as revealed in John's Revelation, the majority of the earth's population will be killed through various judgments, including the final great war (Rev. 16:12–16) and the great earthquake of Revelation 16:17–21. The elect who are converted during the Great Tribulation will have the comfort of knowing that this period will not be long, that God will sovereignly end it after just three-and-a-half years, and that many will be preserved through this terrible time.

Christ then contrasts the coming of false christs in the Great Tribulation with His glorious coming. The end of the age will be characterized by false christs (Matt. 24:23–26), but when Christ returns, His coming shall be very clear, like a flash of lightning that is seen from one horizon to another (Matt. 24:27; Rev. 1:7), and when He comes there will be judgment (Matt. 24:28; Rev. 19:17–19).

At this point it is clear that the entire nature of Christ's answer is Jewish and has nothing to do with the church. The discourse is full of terminology that is Jewish in character, and relates events that pertain only to the Jewish nation. Dr. Paul Benware writes,

> As the discourse is interpreted, these questions of the disciples must be kept in mind. The Lord is dealing with issues pertaining to Israel, not to the church. The backdrop of the Olivet Discourse is the rejection of the Messiah and the disciplining of Israel (Matthew 23) and the questions of the disciples pertaining to Jewish concerns. The disciples knew nothing (at this point) of the Church Age, and their questions were not about the Church Age. In Jesus' answer he spoke of things that involved the Jewish people, such as the Sabbath (24:20), those living in Judea (24:16), the abomination of desolation (24:15), the gospel of the kingdom (24:14), and the presence of false prophets (24:11), which would be a problem for Israel (false teachers would be a problem for the church) [I Peter 2:1]. In light of this, we should not see the Church Age in the Olivet Discourse, even as some have in 24:4–8.[11]

One additional note is that the phrase *Son of Man* (Matt. 24:30–31, 37, 39, 44; 25:31) is distinctly Jewish in character and never used by Paul or any of the other writers of the epistles to the church.

Christ seems to have answered the disciples' question by describing events that show the end of the age and His coming were near. In fact, Walvoord believes that the signs are, in fact, the Great Tribulation. He writes:

> The disciples had asked, "What shall be the sign of thy coming, and of the end of the world?" (Matt. 24:3b). What is the specific sign? The sign is the great tribulation. It is an

unmistakable sign. There will be no question about it for anybody who experiences its horrors. It will be a clear sign preceding the second coming of Jesus Christ.

The prospects of a believer in Christ today are entirely different. He is not looking for the great tribulation. He is not looking for the abomination of desolation. His is the blessed hope of the Lord's coming for His own (1 Thess. 4:13–18). *For this there are no signs.*[12] (italics added)

Part 3: The Sign of His Coming—the Second Advent (Matt. 24:29–41)

Jesus then gives more specifics about His return. His return will be preceded by cataclysmic signs (24:29; cf. Isa. 13:10; 34:4; Joel 2:31; 3:15–16) and by "the sign of the Son of Man" (24:30), which will appear in the sky. Very possibly that sign is the visible glory of Christ, the Shekinah glory that will accompany Him as He returns as King. One can not be dogmatic on what the "sign" is, and many suggestions have been offered. Barbieri writes,

> Exactly what the sign of the Son of Man will be is unknown. The sign of the setting aside of the nation of Israel was the departure of the glory from the temple (Ezek. 10:3, 18; 11:23). Perhaps the sign of the Lord's return will again involve the Shekinah glory. Some believe the sign may involve the heavenly city, the New Jerusalem, which may descend at this time and remain as a satellite city suspended over the earthly city Jerusalem throughout the Millennium (Rev. 21:2–3). Or the sign may be the lightning, or perhaps the Lord Himself. Whatever the sign, it will be visible for all to see, for the Lord will return on the clouds . . . with power and great glory (cf. Dan. 7:13).[13]

The Immediate Context of the Verses in Question (Matt. 24:31, 40–41)

From Matthew 24:31, some expositors have tried to make a case for the rapture of the church being described in the Olivet Discourse. Gundry and Reese, both posttribulationalists, are among the major proponents of the view.[14] Their motivation for seeing the Rapture here and in 40–41 is to gain scriptural support for their posttribulational position.

A careful examination of Matthew 24:31 and 40–41, however, clearly reveals what is occurring in these three verses. The larger section of Matthew 24:29–44, as we have observed, follows Christ's descriptions of the tribulation period and of His coming. This "coming" can only be His second coming since it is said to be

1. after the tribulation of those days (v. 29)
2. accompanied by cataclysmic signs (v. 29)
3. a sign visible to "all the tribes of the earth" (v. 30)

As well, the passage clearly states that His coming will involve His visible return with power and great glory (v. 30). That Christ would now include a statement about the rapture of the church would be odd indeed. As we have already discussed, the Rapture has nothing to do with the questions of the disciples. They had no understanding of the doctrine of the church—Christ would not even mention the doctrine until two days later—much less the Rapture. As Benware states,

> The discourse is in answer to questions about the future of Israel and the millennial kingdom, not the church. It would be quite surprising for the Lord to speak about the Rapture because it was a subject that He had never talked about. The first mention of the Rapture (John 14) would be given two days later.[15]

Some expositors claim that the similar terms and phrases mentioned here— "angels," "trumpet call," and "gathering the elect"—as well as in some rapture passages are proof this is a rapture passage (Matt. 24:29, 31; cf. 1 Cor. 15:52; 1 Thess. 4:16–17; 2 Thess. 2:1). Although the passages contain similarities in terminology, arguments can be cited against this being the Rapture. As we have seen, the context is the second coming of Christ to earth. Secondly, the gathering of all the elect will not happen at the Rapture but at the Second Coming. Thirdly, 24:31 mentions neither the translation of the living saints nor the resurrection of deceased saints, two of the most important features of the Rapture. In context, it is clear that the gathering consists of those who have become believers during the Great Tribulation.

Christ continues the discourse elucidating on what He had already taught. He begins with a parable. When the fig tree puts forth its leaves they know winter is passing. In the same way, when they (the generation) see "all these things" (Matt. 24:4–31) taking place, Christ is "at the door." The generation that sees the beginning of these signs will also see their end (v. 34). The certainty of these things occurring is as reliable as Christ's word (v. 35).

But the exact day and hour of His return is uncertain. Only God the Father knows when He will send His Son back to earth (v. 36). But the period will be very much like the days of Noah—although judgment was imminent, life continued as normal with no thought of the wrath to come: "They were marrying and giving in marriage, until the day Noah entered the ark" (v. 38). They did not understand the truth of what would occur until the judgment came on them and "took them away" (v. 39). Christ says that the coming of the Son of Man will be the same (v. 39). Just as in Noah's time, one will be taken away in judgment and the other will be left (to enter the kingdom) (vv. 40–41).

At this point it would be helpful to deal with the arguments of those who believe Matthew 24:31 to be a rapture passage. The first argument relates to the two different Greek words used for "taking away" in verse 39 and in verses 40–41. The word used in verse 39, translated "took them away" in the NASB, is *airō*, and the word used in 40–41, translated "will be taken" in the NASB, is *paralambanō*. Different words are many times significant in exegesis, but one need always consider the context since the Greek language contains many synonyms. Reese argues that the use of *paralamban* in verses 40–41, does not indicate being taken away in judgment: "It is a good word; a word used exclusively in the sense of 'take away' or 'receive,' or 'take home.'"[16] He also notes that *paralambanō* is used in John 14:3 of the Rapture.

In response, an examination of the use of *paralambanō* reveals that Reese is mistaken about it being used always as "a good word." As Walvoord writes, "The same word is used in John 19:16 of taking Christ to Calvary for crucifixion, an express instance of taking one away to judgment."[17] The word is used again in Matthew 27:27 where Christ was taken away by the governor and turned over to the Roman cohort to be mocked and beaten. Clearly the word can also be used perjoratively, and the meaning must be determined by context. The examination also shows that the Greek verbs *airō* and *paralambanō* are virtually synonyms, and the context indicates that they are both used here in the sense of "taken away in judgment."

This passage in Matthew is not dealing with the rapture of the church but with the judgment of the wicked at the time of Christ's return to the earth, a fact made clear by the context of the passage. Verse 39 sets the context as a taking away in judgment, since those that were taken away by the flood were taken away in judgment.

Those left behind, Noah and his family, were left behind to survive. Thus, those taken away in verses 40–41 are taken away in judgment and the ones left are left to enter the kingdom. Christ stated this is how it would be at the "coming of the Son of Man," the same coming of the Son of Man mentioned in verse 30, the Second Coming. If this were His coming to rapture the church, there would be no signs (24:30–31). Thus, Christ links the taking away to judgment of the Flood with the taking away to judgment of Matthew 24:40–41 and offers the first as a parallel to and accurate picture of the second. The context clearly reveals the only accurate interpretation, which is confirmed by a parallel passage in Luke 17:34–37:

> *I tell you, on that night there will be two men in one bed; one will be taken, and the other will be left. There will be two women grinding at the same place; one will be taken, and the other will be left. [Two men will be in the field; one will be taken and the other will be left.] And answering they said to Him, "Where, Lord?" And He said to them, "Where the body is, there also* will the vultures be gathered." *(emphasis added)*

In response to the disciples' question about where they would be taken, Jesus indicated that those taken are taken in judgment. Their lives are taken, and the bodies are fed to the vultures.

Part 4: Parables Stressing Watchfulness, Preparedness, and Faithfulness in Light of Christ's Return (Matt. 24:42–51)

In light of Christ's return and the uncertainty of the exact day and hour, Christ encourages those who will be present during this period, using two parables that stress watchfulness, preparedness, and faithfulness (Matt. 24:42–51). Pentecost writes,

> In these parables the servants represent the people of the nation of Israel who will be God's stewards during the Tribulation. At Christ' return the nation will be judged, the faithful will be received into the kingdom, and the unfaithful will be excluded from the kingdom. Here again the faithfulness is that which springs from faith in Christ, while the unfaithfulness is produced because of lack of faith in Christ. Thus, in view of the signs given to Israel, the people are exhorted to be watchful, prepared, and faithful. The reason is that the signs indicate the coming of a Judge who will separate the saved from the unsaved.[18]

Again, the passages in question, when taken in context with the verse that follows, indicate a taking away in judgment and not a rapture of the church.

Part 5: Parables Dealing with Judgment (Matt. 25)

As Christ continues His discourse, the idea of taking in judgment is also true in the context of Matthew 25. Christ first deals with the coming judgment on Israel in 25:1–30 and then the coming judgment on the Gentiles in 25:31–46. Christ's previous parable about the wise slave (24:45) and the evil slave (v. 48) taught that there would be a severe judgment on those Israelites who were unprepared at His coming. They would be excluded from the Messiah's kingdom. As Pentecost states, "A question then arose concerning this judgment: On what ground would the nation be judged."[19] Christ's parable of the ten virgins shows that the judgment will be based on preparedness when the Bridegroom comes. Is this parable discussing the church as some have believed? Pentecost writes,

> Christ's answer to this question is given first in the parable of the ten virgins (Matt. 25:1–13). The context must be noted at the outset. Christ was dealing here with judgment for the nation of Israel. The church is not in view anywhere in the discourse of Matthew 24–25. Rather, Christ was developing the eschatology of the nation of Israel. Although Paul did refer to the church as a "pure virgin" (2 Cor. 11:2), his use of a similar figure with reference to the church does not prove that the church is in view in this parable.[20]

An interpretive conclusion based simply on similarities and not taking into account differences and context will most often be faulty. The church is not found in this parable since it is a continuation of Christ's discourse in Matthew 24 and thus is still dealing with the nation of Israel. If this parable is dealing with the nation of Israel, so must the following passage, since the context has not changed. Matthew 25:14–30 shows that those Israelites who are faithful will not only be ready to meet Him at His Coming but will be rewarded for their faithfulness (vv. 21, 23), and those not found faithful will be judged (v. 30).

The Old Testament clearly states that Gentiles will also have a part in the Messiah's kingdom. Thus, Christ now turns from dealing with the basis on which the Jews will be judged to explaining the basis on which the nations will be judged (v. 32). The judgment is described as a separation of the sheep and the goats, and will be based on whether the Gentiles extended aid to the believing Jews during the period of the Great Tribulation. Walvoord writes,

> The prominence of works in this situation is derived from the peculiar characteristics of the period before the coming of Christ. In the Great Tribulation there will be worldwide anti-Semitism, and the Jew will be persecuted as he was in the days of Hitler. For a Gentile to befriend a Jew under those circumstances would be most unusual and would indicate his recognition of the Jewish people as the chosen people and would be a by-product of his understanding of God's plan and purpose for the Jew in the Millennium. Accordingly, while kindness to the Jews in most dispensations would not be too significant, in the context of the Great Tribulation, it becomes an unmistakable mark of a person who is in Christ.[21]

Matthew 25, then, continues to discuss events dealing with Christ's second coming and nowhere can the church or the Rapture be seen in this chapter. On the contrary, Christ continues to deal with His answer to the specific questions that the disciples asked; so it is not surprising that the Rapture is not in view.

Conclusion

As has been seen, the larger context, the narrower context, as well as the immediate context of the verses often seen as containing the rapture of the church argue strongly against the concept of the church in general and the doctrine of the rapture of the church in particular from appearing in the Olivet Discourse. If Christ is answering the specific questions asked by the disciples, then the context concerns, as Walvoord has stated, "the Jewish expectation based on Old Testament prophecy, and the program of God for the earth in general rather than the Church as the body of Christ."[22]

Summary: Thirteen Reasons Why the Church (and Thus, the Rapture) Is Not Referenced in the Olivet Discourse

1. The context of the book of Matthew, which contains the most complete account of the Olivet Discourse, was to show Jesus' offer of the kingdom to Israel, Israel's rejection of it, and why Jesus did not bring in His kingdom at that time. All of these

matters relate to Israel—not the church—and God's program for her.

2. Chapter 23, the chapter immediately preceding the Discourse, deals with the denunciation of the Jewish leaders, Christ proclaiming their house was desolate, and the Jewish nation not seeing Him until they recognize Him as Messiah. Again, the context is the Jewish nation.

3. After the disciples had pointed out the temple complex, Christ stated that it would be torn down stone by stone. Their first question was in response to Jesus' statement and showed the disciples' concern for their national place of worship. It again showed the Jewish context.

4. The disciples had no understanding of the church or the Rapture at this point and thus would have been asking the questions as Jews and not representatives of the church.

5. Based on their understanding of Old Testament prophecy as well as Christ's discussion of the "end of the age" in Matthew 13, the disciples' understanding of the "end of the age" would have been the time when Christ comes in final judgment and establishes His kingdom.

6. When the disciples asked about a sign of His coming, they were referring to His full revelation of Himself as Messiah. They would have had no understanding of Him leaving the earth and returning.

7. Christ is answering the specific questions asked by the disciples; thus, the church and the Rapture are excluded in His Discourse.

8. Christ's analogy of the signs as "birth pangs" reveals that these are signs of the "end of the age," since birth pangs do not occur during pregnancy but are signs of the "end" of the pregnancy. Thus, Matthew 24:4–8 cannot be describing the church age.

9. The disciples would certainly have understood "the gospel of the kingdom" as a proclamation that the Messiah was coming to revel Himself fully as Israel's king.

10. The terms used in Christ's answer to the disciples relate to Israel, not the church (i.e., "the Sabbath" [Matt. 24:20], "those living in Judea" [v. 16], "the abomination of desolation" [v. 15], "the gospel of the kingdom" [v. 14], "false prophets" [v. 11], and "Son of Man" [vv. 27, 30, 37, 44; 25:13, 31]).

11. Matthew 24:31 cannot be addressing the Rapture since the entire context is dealing with Christ's second coming.

12. Matthew 24:40–41 cannot be addressing the rapture of the church since the comparison Christ gave was a taking away in judgment, and Christ says the judgment at His return will occur "just like the days of Noah." If Christ were speaking of the Rapture, He would have said those days will be the opposite of the days of Noah. The taking in judgment is confirmed in the parallel passage in Luke 17:34–37, which explicitly states that they will be taken in judgment and their bodies will be fed to the vultures.

13. Since the context of Matthew 24:41 has been Christ's second coming and the end of the age, the context of the remaining portion of the discourse would have to make a radical change in subject to include the church age or the Rapture. But upon careful examination, it can be seen that the context continues to be Christ's answering the disciple's specific questions.

This chapter was adapted from Russell L. Penney, "Why the Church Is Not Referenced in the Olivet Discourse," *The Conservative Theological Journal* 1, no. 1 (April 1997): 47–60.

PART 4

Interpreting Prophecy

CHAPTER 21

Introductory Thoughts on Allegorical Interpretation and the Book of Revelation

The book of Revelation is again in the path of a prophetic storm. There are those who still want to relegate this incredible prophecy to the junk heap of jumbled mysticism, designate it as a strange symbolic allegory of church persecution, or make this letter a mysterious prophecy that was somehow fulfilled in the early church.

Even the secular world speaks of Armageddon, shuddering at the book's descriptions of future terror to come; and even those most skeptical know of the Four Horsemen of the Apocalypse. Unfortunately, many churches have made no clear stand regarding the book, leaving its members in confusion.

Controversy over Revelation

There is no question that Revelation requires effort for even skilled Bible readers to understand its meaning. But some theologians even refuse to believe that God can predict through prophets like John events two thousand years into the future. What follows is a short history of the various views to illustrate how the interpretation of Revelation has fared through the centuries.

The Interpretative Confusion

It was C. I. Scofield who observed that, as we near the time of the events of the book of Revelation, the things prophesied within will become more clear to our understanding. Most premillennialists agree. And most premillennialists hold to a futurist position, whether

255

or not they understand the details of the predictions. But pre-millennialism has not always held the high ground in understanding Revelation. The amillennial view has dominated the history of the interpretation of the book, though Walvoord and others show that this was not the view of the early church. Lange and Walvoord give a short history of how the book has been interpreted through the centuries.

The Second and Third Centuries

Walvoord notes,

> The second century like the first bears a sustained testimony to the premillennial character of the early church. Even the amillenarians claim no adherents whatever by name to their position in the second century except in the allegorizing school of interpretation which arose at the very close of the second century.[1]

Walvoord writes further,

> Justin Martyr (100–168) is quite outspoken. He wrote: "But I and whatsoever Christians are orthodox in all things do know that there will be a resurrection of the flesh, and a thousand years in the city of Jerusalem, built adorned, and enlarged, according as Ezekiel, Isaiah, and other prophets have promised."[2]

Walvoord quotes Herzog's *Cyclopaedia:*

> Chiliasm constituted in the sec[ond] century so decidedly an article of faith that Justin held it up as a criterion of perfect orthodoxy.[3]

Finally, Walvoord observes,

> The third century had its own continued witness to premillennialism, however. Among those who can be cited are Cyprian (200–258), Commodian (200–270), Nepos (230–280), Coracion (230–280), Victorinus (240–303), Methodius (250–311), and Lactantius (240–330). . . . Nepos early recognized the heretical tendencies of the Alexandrian school of theology, which was the first effective opponent of premillennialism, and he attacked it with vigor.[4]

The Old Catholic Period Down to Gregory the Great (Pope, 590–604)

Lange sets forth that many "placed the time of the Millennial Kingdom in the period intervening between the first Coming of Christ in the flesh and the coming of Antichrist."[5] "Jerome interprets allegorically, e.g., he makes the Holy City denote the present world."[6] "Cassiodorus also reckoned the Millennial Kingdom from the birth of Christ; he held the first Resurrection to be significant of Baptism."[7]

Theocratico-Hierarchical Half of the Middle Ages to the Time of Innocent III (Pope, 1198–1216)

Many were certain that the events of Revelation would begin at the year 1000, having calculated the millennial kingdom beginning at the first coming of Christ. Christians expected the speedy coming of Antichrist and the end of the world. When the world did not come to an end at 1000, they modified their views and said the number one thousand symbolically denoted an indefinite period. The mode of interpretation was, as a whole, historico-allegorical.[8]

Second Half of the Middle Ages from Innocent III to the Reformation

Innocent declared Islam to be the Antichrist and Muhammad to be the false prophet. Gregory IX called Frederick II the beast of the abyss, and Frederick retorted by applying the same appellation to the pope. Joachim saw Rome as the carnal church and the new Babylon. Dante felt the papacy was anti-Christian in a secular way. Nicholas de Lyra regarded the Revelation as a prophetic mirror to all of history.

Old Protestant Theology Down to Pietism

Some thought that the one thousand years were past. In the Anabaptist view, the thousand years had just dawned. Many felt Revelation was a prophetic compendium of church history, and it was a settled issue to interpret papal Rome as anti-Christianity. Luther arranged the facts of Revelation to fit his view of church history. He held the one thousand years was from the time of the writing of Revelation down to Gregory VII. Bossuet applied the number 666 to Dioclesian; the loosing of Satan at the end of the thousand years referred to the Turks and Lutheranism.

The Pietistic-Mystical Period

Many continued to see Rome as the Antichrist. Whiston felt Christ's coming should take place in 1715, and then later he said 1766. Isaac Newton said Revelation was written during Nero's time and believed things predicted in chapter 12 had yet to come to pass.

Historico-Critical and Rational Period

With the influence of German rationalism, the meaning of the Apocalypse was nearly destroyed. Semler thought the book was nothing but Jewish chiliastic fanaticism. Many felt it represented enthusiastic idealization and Oriental figurative language. Others looked at the book as a novel, a poem, or an illustration of the fall of Judaism.

More Modern Times

Hengstenberg felt the millennial kingdom had somehow come and gone. But during the modern period, there arose the present fourfold manner of apprehending Revelation:

1. Preterist view. The prophecies contained in the Apocalypse were fulfilled with the destruction of Jerusalem and the fall of Rome.
2. Continuist view. Revelation prophecies are predictive of progressive history, being partly fulfilled, partly unfulfilled. Thus believed Mede, Isaac Newton, Elliot (and many Germans).
3. Simple futurist view. From chapter four on in Revelation, the prophecies relate to an absolute future of Christ's coming, being a prediction of the condition of the Jews after the first resurrection.
4. Extreme futurist view. Even the first three chapters are a prophecy relative to the absolute future of Christ's coming.

Above is only a brief summary of thoughts on Revelation. Are there interpretive tools that will provide firm direction in how Revelation is to be understood? Are there keys within the writing of the prophecy that need more attention and may give clues to approaching the message?

Comparative Language

Is Revelation to be interpreted literally or symbolically? From the Jewish and Christian premillennial perspective, Revelation is interpreted from a *literal* base, taking into account *comparative language* that points to a literal ultimate meaning.

Two words indicate that comparative language is being used: *hos* (ὥς) and *homoios* (ὅμοιος). *Hos* and words related to it are used sixty-eight times in Revelation and approximately 416 elsewhere in the New Testament. *Homoios* is used twenty-two times in Revelation and about twenty-six times in the rest of the New Testament. Both words are used for comparison and should be translated "Like, as, like as, it seemed to be, something like, etc."

In Revelation, the apostle John struggled to describe what he saw. If he was, indeed, spiritually transported into the future, he witnessed things and observed events he had never before seen. Revelation 8:8–9, for example, reads,

And the second angel sounded, and something like a great mountain burning with fire was thrown into the sea; and a third of the sea became blood; and a third of the creatures, which were in the sea and had life, died; and a third of the ships were destroyed.

Something like (*hos*) indicates that John is comparing what he sees (something beyond his own experience or comprehension) to the closest known object with which he is familiar (a mountain on fire). In this case, there is no indication that *burning mountain* is a symbol of anything; it is simply the closest comparison at hand.

We may speculate as to the identity of this future catastrophic event. Could it be an asteroid? An atomic explosion with the signature mushroom cloud of searing heat and radioactive debris that pollutes the oceans with radioactivity? Certainly the destruction that follows (a third of the sea creatures and ships are destroyed) indicates that this is an event of incredible magnitude. The point is, however, that John uses comparative language to describe a literal event, not a symbolic or even figurative event, and certainly not an allegorical event.

The objection could be raised that by *a third of the sea became blood* John did not mean that the sea became actual blood. Therefore, how can one maintain a literal interpretation? Note, however, that John has indicated that he is speaking comparatively: *something like*. If, indeed, John is surveying the aftermath of a devastating ecological event, the water could well have taken on the dark, murky red color of stagnant blood.

While one cannot claim authoritatively that John saw either an asteroid or an atomic explosion, one can say that John saw a literal event, which he described using images drawn from known objects or events of the first century.

Problems of Symbols

Tan says that the patience of Job is required in interpreting biblical symbols. The interpreter has to sift, collect, and collate prophetic data then put it all together.[9] The best possible material for
the interpretation of symbols is the immediate context in which
given symbols are found. Under the guidance of contextual studies,
the guesswork is taken out of many Bible symbols.[10] For example,
the four ferocious beasts of Daniel 7 are explained as four earthly
kingdoms in Daniel 2. "The dragon, that old serpent" in Revelation
20:2 is immediately identified as "the devil and Satan." "Sodom
and Egypt" in Revelation 11:8 is identified at once as the city "where
also our Lord was crucified" (Jerusalem). And the star that fell from
heaven (Rev. 9:1) is identified as symbolic of an actual being (v. 2,
he opened the bottomless pit).[11] Tan continues,

> It must be noted that not every word-picture in prophecy is a
> symbol. Many of these are plain, everyday figures of speech.
> When the angel in Revelation 19 invites the fowls to "the sup-
> per of the great God," figurative language is used. When Isaiah
> exclaims that "in the last days, the mountain of the Lord's
> house shall be established in the top of the mountains . . . and
> all nations shall flow unto it" (Isa. 2:23), the prophecy is not a
> symbol of the Christian church and world evangelization. The
> prophet Isaiah is using figurative language to describe the
> glory of the Jerusalem temple at the millennium.[12]

Milligan demonstrates the extent to which amillennialists go in
denying any literal sense in Revelation. He writes,

> One of the great lessons of the Apocalypse consists in this,
> that it unfolds such a *bright view, not of a world beyond the
> grave, but of this present world,* when we contemplate it with
> the eye of faith. . . . It may be doubted if in this respect there
> is one single picture of the Apocalypse applicable only to
> the future inheritance of the saints. What is set forth in its
> apparent visions of future happiness is rather the *present
> privilege of believers.*[13] (italics added)

If a literate person were somehow unacquainted with the various interpretive approaches and read Revelation for the first time,
would he or she interpret the events of these verses as actual and
literal? The events, taking comparative language into account, would

be taken as literal unless other indicators in the text suggested reading the verses in another way.

Allegorical Confusion

Many Bible scholars look at the Apocalypse through *allegorical interpretation*. The well-known *Ellicott's Commentary on the Whole Bible*, in its introductory remarks on Revelation, represents a prime example of allegorical hedging and confusion. This commentary tries to find common and commendable ground in the three major interpretive views, yet in reality it clouds the waters. At some point the reader of Revelation must ask "What is this book all about, and what is it attempting to communicate?" Because the allegorical interpreter is working from a false starting premise, it's impossible to arrive at an explanation that makes sense. It is difficult to believe that the Holy Spirit is so incapable of clearly imparting revelatory truth. Something is amiss when a key work of inspiration defies explanation. For example, in *Ellicott's* we read,

> We are disposed to view the Apocalypse as the pictorial unfolding of great principles in constant conflict, though under various forms. The Praeterist may, then, be right in finding early fulfillments, and the Futurist in expecting undeveloped ones, and the Historical interpreter is unquestionably right in looking for them along the whole line of history; for the words of God mean more than one man, or one school of thought, can compass. There are depths of truth unexplored which sleep beneath the simplest sentences. Just as we want to say that history repeats itself, so the predictions of the Bible are not exhausted in one or even in many fulfillments. Each prophecy is a single key which unlocks many doors, and the grand and stately drama of the Apocalypse has been played out perchance in one age to be repeated in the next. Its majestic and mysterious teachings indicate the features of a struggle which, be the stage the human soul, with its fluctuations of doubt and fear, of hope and love—or the progress of kingdoms—or the destinies of the world, is the same struggle in all.[14]

Note how the commentator hedges; each interpretive school can be correct. No wonder the layman is confused and runs from the book of Revelation. Nothing could be more unclear than "for the words of God mean more than one man, or one school of thought, can compass." Without question, the full spiritual depth of the Word of God cannot be plumbed, but we're always comprehending more because of personal maturity and Bible study experience. The statement in *Ellicott's*, however, implies hidden meanings, suggesting that the Spirit of God has more than one message secretly tucked away in the grammar and words.

Confusion is compounded with "there are depths of truth unexplored which sleep beneath the simplest sentences." Again, *spiritual depth* and *clarity of written intention* are two different things. All languages and interpretation of languages assumes grammatical keys that unlock meaning. The author in *Ellicott's*, however, implies that all meanings for each language and method of interpretation are equally acceptable!

Ellicott's further clouds interpretation of Revelation in its explanation of the Second Coming. And since the second coming of Christ is a major theme of Revelation, the following excerpt demonstrates that *Ellicott's* utterly fails to see what the book of Revelation is describing:

> The "coming of Christ," viewed from the human side, is a phrase which is not always to be held to one meaning: it is, in this aspect, analogous to the "Kingdom of God." Holy Scripture, beyond all doubt, recognizes potential and spiritual, as well as personal, "comings" of the Lord. There are many comings of Christ. Christ came in the flesh as a mediatorial Presence. Christ came at the destruction of Jerusalem. Christ came, a spiritual Presence, when the Holy Ghost was given. Christ comes now in every signal manifestation of redeeming power. Any great reformation of morals and religion is a coming of Christ. A great revolution, like a thunderstorm, violently sweeping away evil to make way for the good, is a coming of Christ.[15]

It is difficult to understand why Christ's coming and its real and specific meaning is beyond reach for some interpreters. Although all allegorical interpreters may not be confused, most still throw their hands up when attempting to clearly explain meaning in Revelation. Thus, amillennialists, who do not believe in a coming earthly kingdom and who are writing commentary sets, often omit a work on the book of Revelation.

It must be emphasized that both amillennialists and premillennialists may have difficulty grasping the meaning of a specific passage in Revelation, but the amillennialist will claim that the difficulty lies in the spiritual, hidden meanings in the words. The premillennialist will admit difficulty on that same specific passage but will exhaust the interpretive possibilities for finding the one meaning as first inspired by the Holy Spirit.

It is amazing that, when studying the Apocalypse, amillennialists reject the basis of scientific hermeneutics and force a system of allegory on the text. Yet all interpretation must start with literal interpretation. Most Bible scholars understand that, embedded within the literal framework of Revelation, there is room for (1) comparative language ("it seemed to be," "it appeared as") and (2) symbolic language. For example, the scorpions in Revelation 9 represent something very real. Granted, we may not know what that is, but in allegorical interpretation, with prophecy diffused, the hidden spiritual meaning of scorpions may never be discovered. To avoid the risk of confusion, LaHaye urges students of Revelation to interpret by starting at the base—with literal interpretation.

> When the plain sense of Scripture makes common sense, seek no other sense; therefore, take every word at its primary, ordinary, usual, literal meaning unless the facts of the immediate text, studied in the light of related passages and axiomatic and fundamental truths, clearly indicate otherwise. This rule . . . provides basic guidelines for properly interpreting the many signs and symbols in the book.[16]

A premillennialist will start then with the literal base, considering signs, symbols, figures of speech, and comparative language that may convey the prophetic and historical intention of the words.

Ellicott's concludes its *Introduction to Revelation*: "Jerusalem stands as the type of the good cause . . . [and thus is] the Church of Christ. . . . We are thus taught, in this ever-deepening spirituality of the book, to look beneath the phenomena, to trace the subtle and unmasked principles which are at work. . . . The book of Revelation becomes the unfolding of a dream which is from God."

Ellicott's further states, the book "is not a manual of tiresome details." Revelation "is not meant to be a treasure-house of marvels for the prophetical archaeologist: it is a book of living principles."[17]

While it is agreed that Revelation is a book of minute, twisting, and turning details, it is difficult to image why an interpreter would need to be advised that it is not tiresome. Perhaps the allegorical interpretive approach to this work of prophecy renders it so. And

Revelation, being indeed a prophecy book, seems an ideal treasure-house for the prophetical archaeologist. The allegorical interpreter appears to doubt that God can write prophecy in clear terms. Is He not able to give us the plan of the ages? Why does the amillennialist begin with the assumption that distant-future prophecy can not exist? Because Revelation is a treasure house of prophecy, amillennialists have a spiritual problem. They discourage people from learning how God will bring to completion objective and literal earth history.

The Purpose of Revelation

In answering why Revelation was written, the liberal and amillennialist attempt to minimize any possibility that the book is giving distant-future prophetic prediction. To destroy any premillennial possibility, they claim that John wrote the incredible events he saw simply to make martyrdom attractive. *The Interpreter's Bible* propounds that Revelation was written by John

> . . . to sharpen the alternatives open to the Christians, of worshipping either Caesar or God, of being completely loyal to the state or wholly devoted to Christianity. Furthermore, he endeavored to make martyrdom, with its eternal rewards, so attractive, and worship of the emperor, with its eternal punishments, so fearsome, that his readers would quite willingly accept death as martyrs rather than be disloyal to Almighty God and his Christ by worshipping Rome and the emperors.[18]

But if the Old Testament prophets were literal and premillennial in their prophecies, and if Christ was clearly literal and premillennial in His prophecies, the allegorical approach fails in its analysis of the purpose for writing Revelation. It would take a masterful interpreter to derive from Revelation what allegorists would have us see. If however, the base is literal and future, the prophecies fall into place, and fanciful, mystical interpretation is not necessary.

Were the Early Church Fathers Premillennial?

Hal Lindsey does an excellent job in *The Road to Holocaust* in explaining and analyzing the beliefs of the apostolic church fathers. Were they premillennial? Did they take the Tribulation and return of Christ literally as written in Revelation? Were they still looking for His return even after A.D. 70—the destruction of the temple in Jerusalem? Or did they consider the fall of the temple as the Tribulation, which is described in such detail in Revelation?

The Apostolic Fathers are the apostles and those taught directly by them. Lindsey lists at least five beliefs that seem quite common among the early Fathers, as stated by church historian J. L. Neve (who himself, by the way, would not be a premillennialist):

1. They firmly held that Israel would be yet redeemed as a nation and fulfill her unconditional promises as the messianic kingdom. They held that the Second Coming would be the kingdom on earth and that it would last a thousand years.
2. They thought that Christ could come anytime, confirming the rapture doctrine.
3. They saw the coming Tribulation, or great world distress, as maintained by premillennialists today.
4. They held to a personal Antichrist who would come during the terrible period of tribulation.
5. They still held these views long after the destruction of Jerusalem in A.D. 70 and on into the fourth century.

Lindsey notes:

> These prophetic views caused the early Christians to recognize the Jews as a chosen people for whom God will yet fulfill His promises. These views also promoted a compassion for the Jews because the Christians saw them as a demonstration of God's faithfulness to His Word.[19]

The Dating of Revelation

Much of the argument about the interpretation of the Apocalypse turns on the dating of Revelation. The authorship date of 95 or 96 is held by premillennialists, while amillennialists place the date before A.D. 70. The war over dating centers around the amillennialists' struggle to make the prophecies fit a past historical mold. Denying a premillennial position, they attempt to force the book's date of writing to a point before A.D. 70 by lining up certain events in the book to tie into the destruction of Jerusalem. However, *Ellicott's* gives strong internal evidence in Revelation, relating to the seven churches of Asia Minor, that seems to clearly support the late date:

> The advocates of the later date rely much upon the degenerate state of the Asiatic churches, as described in the Epistles to the Seven Churches. The Epistles to the Ephesians,

266 Classical Evangelical Hermeneutics

Colossians, and Philemon were written during the captivity of St. Paul at Rome, about the year A.D. 63. If, then, the Apocalypse was written in A.D. 69 or 70, we have only an interval of six or seven years to account for a striking change in the spiritual condition of the Asiatic churches. Can we believe that a Church which is so forward in love as that of Ephesus (Eph. 3:18) can have in so short a time left its first love? Can it be believed that the Laodicean Church—whose spiritual condition in A.D. 63 can be inferred from that of Colossae (Col. 1:3, 4)—can have, in six brief years, forsaken their "faith in Christ Jesus and their love to all the saints," and become the "lukewarm" church (Rev. 3:15, 16) of the Apocalypse?[20]

An argument against the late date of the book notes that an earthquake destroyed the city of Laodicea in the reign of Tiberius around A.D. 60, about the time of Nero. Therefore, the city could not have been mentioned in Revelation if the book was written in A.D. 96. But Unger points out that "the affluence of the city enabled its citizens to rebuild without help from Rome or the provincial government."[21] If the book was written in A.D. 96, over thirty years would have passed, whereby a thriving metropolis would have been reestablished with a wealthy but spiritually blind church in its place. The well-known and respected New Testament scholar, Theodore Zahn, sums up in strong language the argument for the A.D. 96 date of Revelation:

The correctness of the date is also confirmed by all those traditions which refer the exile of John upon Patmos to his extreme old age, or which describe Revelation as the latest, or one of the latest, writings in the NT. On the other hand, all the differing views as to the date of the composition of Revelation to be found in the literature of the Church are so late and so manifestly confused, that they do not deserve the name of tradition.[22]

Most scholars are certain that the church father Papias was wrong when he wrote that John was killed before A.D. 70. Eusebius and Clement of Alexandria both make the point that on Patmos, John penned the Revelation around A.D. 96. Obviously, there is a conflict of views, but the latter has a greater witness. That witness fits the facts of what the book claims for itself in regard to Patmos and the exile. An objective judgment call would come down on the side of Eusebius and Clement.

Even the renowned church historian Philip Schaff, himself an amillennialist, accepts as genuine the later dating of the book of Revelation, as cited by Irenaeus. He writes,

> The traditional date of composition at the end of Domitian's reign (95–96) rests on the clear and weighty testimony of Irenaeus, is confirmed by Eusebius and Jerome, and has still its learned defenders.[23]

When other arguments prove pointless, attempts are made to sidestep the obvious A.D. 96 dating by denying that the apostle John is the author. Walvoord notes, "It is most significant that in many cases the theological bias against the chiliastic teaching of the book of Revelation seems to be the actual motive in rejecting the apostolic authorship and the late dating of the book."[24] Robertson agrees with the later date when speaking of authorship. He writes,

> The writer calls himself John (1:1, 4, 9; 22:8). . . . The traditional and obvious way to understand the name is the Apostle John. . . . Irenaeus represents the Apostle John as having lived to the time of Trajan, at least to A.D. 98. Most ancient writers agree with this extreme old age of John. Justin Martyr states expressly that the Apostle John wrote the Apocalypse. Irenaeus called it the work of a disciple of John. . . . On the basis of . . . slim evidence some today argue that John did not live to the end of the century and so did not write any of the Johannine books. But a respectable number of modern scholars still hold to the ancient view that the Apocalypse of John is the work of the Apostle and Beloved Disciple, the son of Zebedee.[25]

The testimony of the early church father Irenaeus is of high importance in establishing date and authorship. Ellicott notes,

> The later date was that which was accepted almost uniformly by the older theologians. In favor of this, early tradition has been appealed to. The most important witness (in some respects) is Irenaeus, who says that "the Apocalypse was seen not long ago, but almost in our own age, towards the end of the reign of Domitian." Other writers have been claimed as giving a support to this view by their mention of Patmos as the place of St. John's banishment; and it is plain from the

way in which Eusebius quotes the mention of the Patmos
exile by Clement of Alexandria, that he associated it with
the reign of Domitian.[26]

Concerning Irenaeus, Lindsey further observes,

> Irenaeus was from Asia Minor, the region of the Apostle
> John's last ministry. He was discipled in the area around
> Ephesus where the Apostle John spent his last years. . . . The
> great Polycarp, trained by the Apostle John himself, was
> Irenaeus' spiritual mentor. So there was only one genera-
> tion between Irenaeus and John. Therefore the quality of
> his evidence is as strong and reliable as any we have for any
> book of the New Testament.[27]

Lindsey points out as well that Irenaeus was considered by all a
careful scholar and defender of the faith. His responses against
Gnosticism dealt a death blow to that mystic heresy. Still, he treated
the Gnostics fairly, thus "it is ludicrous to reason that Irenaeus would
be less careful and accurate with facts about the book of Revelation
which he held to be the Word of God."[28]

Without question, the majority of the early church fathers believed Revelation was written after the fall of Jerusalem, and they
looked for Revelation events to take place beyond their own times.
The great amillennial church historian Philip Schaff fairly summarizes the position of the early church fathers and their millennial
beliefs:

> The most striking point in the eschatology of the ante-Nicene
> age is the prominent chiliasm, or millenarianism, that is the
> belief of a visible reign of Christ in glory on earth with the
> risen saints for a thousand years, before the general resurrec-
> tion and judgment. It was indeed not the doctrine of the church
> embodied in any creed or form of devotion, but a widely cur-
> rent opinion of distinguished teachers, such as Barnabas,
> Papias, Justin Martyr, Irenaeus, Tertullian, Methodius, and
> Lactanius. . . . The Jewish chiliasm rested on a carnal misap-
> prehension of the Messianic kingdom, a literal interpretation
> of prophetic figures, and an overestimate of the importance
> of the Jewish people and the holy city as the center of that
> kingdom.[29]

Schaff's analysis of the church fathers' position on Revelation supports a later dating of the book. But with all due respect, it is necessary to question Schaff's judgment regarding "the carnal misapprehension" of the orthodox Jews who held to a physical, earthly reign of the Messiah. How could the Jews be mistaken when a plain literal reading of the Old Testament clearly proclaims just that? Schaff would be forced to admit that the Jews' correct apprehension comes from literal interpretation.

Juggling Interpretations

Schaff shows his own confusion respecting a literal kingdom; he is juggling interpretations to fit his own prejudices against the historical standard interpretation. He says, "The Christian chiliasm [of the early Church] is the Jewish chiliasm spiritualized and fixed upon the second, instead of the first, coming of Christ."[30] Schaff appears to be saying that Christians adopted Jewish "misapprehension." There is, in fact, no misapprehension. The pious orthodox Jews in Old Testament times, during the life of Christ and after, began the interpretation process with a literal, historic, normal hermeneutic. Christ never refuted the orthodox view of prophetic fulfillment—He only complemented it. What does Schaff mean then by "Jewish chiliasm spiritualized"? To the Jews, the Messiah would be born literally and would reign literally. Only with the coming of New Testament events did it all come together, but certainly millennialists do not adopt a Jewish chiliasm *spiritualized.*

Schaff continues,

Justin Martyr represents the transition from the Jewish Christian to the Gentile Christian chiliasm. He speaks repeatedly of the second parousia of Christ in the clouds of heaven, surrounded by the holy angels. It will be preceded by the near manifestation of the man of sin . . . who speaks blasphemies against the most high God, and will rule three and a half years. He is preceded by heresies and false prophets. Christ will then raise the patriarchs, prophets, and pious Jews, establish the millennium, restore Jerusalem, and reign there in the midst of his saints; after which the second and general resurrection and judgment of the world will take place. He regarded this expectation of the earthly perfection of Christ's kingdom as the key-stone of pure doctrine.[31]

Schaff concludes his presentation with the early fathers:

> Irenaeus, on the strength of tradition from St. John and his
> disciples, taught that after the destruction of the Roman
> empire, and the brief raging of antichrist (lasting three and
> a half years or 1,260 days), Christ will visibly appear, will
> bind Satan, will reign at the rebuilt city of Jerusalem . . . will
> celebrate the millennial Sabbath of preparation for the eter-
> nal glory of heaven; then, after a temporary liberation of
> Satan, follows the final victory, the general resurrection, the
> judgment of the world, and the consummation in the new
> heavens and the new earth. [This is virtually what premil-
> lennialists teach today about the book of Revelation. It would
> seem as if they are in good company with the most outstand-
> ing teachers among the early fathers.]

> Tertullian was an enthusiastic Chiliast, and pointed not only
> to the Apocalypse. . . . After Tertullian, . . . chiliasm was
> taught by Commodian toward the close of the third century,
> Lactanius, and Victorinus of Petau, at the beginning of the
> forth. Its last distinguished advocates in the East were
> Methodius (d. a martyr, 311), the opponent of Origen, and
> Apollinaris of Laodicea in Syria.[32]

The Great Departure to Allegorical Amillennialism

Three systems of allegorical interpretation—each of which have
had strong impact on interpreting the book of Revelation—are followed by amillennialists.

Preterist Interpretation

The preterist view holds that in Revelation John was referring to
events of his own day, about A.D. 70. Adhering to this view requires
mental gymnastics that are quite unnecessary if one would apply
the Golden Rule of Interpretation. The Roman emperors Nero or
Domitian could scarcely fulfill the requirements of Revelation for
the Antichrist.

Historical Interpretation

The historical view suggests that John was describing the major
events that would take place during the history of the church. It

therefore suggests that we can see these events as we look back at history. To make historical events fit prophecy, though, calls for the juggling of history, which is historically unsound and tends to distort the plain meaning of prophecy.

Spiritualizing Interpretation

Many believe that everything in Revelation should be taken figuratively or metaphorically, that John was writing about a spiritual conflict and not a physical experience. This view is held by most amillennialists and postmillennialists. Until the turn of the century, postmillennialism gained many followers, proffering the idea that the world was getting better and better and that believers were about to usher in the kingdom. Man's perpetual degeneracy during this century, however, has rendered this a most untenable position.[33]

What, however, brought about the great departure from a literal, millennial position? Did something specific happen in philosophical terms that initiated allegorical, mystical, and nonliteral interpretation?

The history of allegorical interpretation makes a fascinating study. Knowing how these systems of literary study began, however, would likely encourage Christians to reject them outright.

Briefly, in the sixth century B.C., Xenophanes criticized Homer's depiction of the Greek gods. They were too human and too literal in their jealousies and immoral behavior, shocking their followers. Thus, by the time of Plato, the deities and their blatant hedonism were being interpreted symbolically or allegorically. Heraclitus, for example, explained the bedroom scandals of Aphrodite as allegories. Interpreting the stories of the gods as simply symbolic made it safe for children to again read about their deities' escapades.

Later, the Jewish rabbis of Alexandria, Egypt, began teaching with allegory in order to stop Gentile criticism of the Old Testament. Allegorical interpretation softened the harshness of the literal Law, making it more palatable.

It is in this context that the great church father Origen enters. Origen (ca. 185–ca. 254), raised in Alexandria, could not help but absorb the current cultural literary patterns around him, which included allegory—the literary system that promised to yield the hidden, symbolic meaning of Scripture.

Schaff helps us understand the historical and cultural context that led from the prevailing literal interpretation of Revelation to an allegorical one:

In Alexandria, Origen opposed chiliasm as a Jewish dream, and spiritualized the symbolical language of the prophets. . . . But the crushing blow came from the great change in the social condition and prospects of the church in the Nicene age. After Christianity, contrary to all expectation, triumphed in the Roman empire, and was embraced by the Caesars themselves, the millennial reign, instead of being anxiously waited and prayed for, began to be dated either from the first appearance of Christ, or from the conversion of Constantine and the downfall of paganism, and to be regarded as realized in the glory of the dominant imperial state-church. Augustine, who himself had formerly entertained chiliastic hopes, framed the new theory which reflected the social change, and was generally accepted. The apocalyptic millennium he understood to be the present reign of Christ in the Catholic church, and the first resurrection, the translation of the martyrs and saints to heaven, where they participate in Christ's reign. It was consistent with this theory that towards the close of the first millennium of the Christian era there was a wide-spread expectation in Western Europe that the final judgment was at hand.[34]

Thus, Origen, more than anyone else, helped make allegory the key method of interpreting the Bible down through the Middle Ages.

Origen's understanding of biblical inspiration was entirely consistent with a rigorously critical approach to the text. If the Bible is inspired by God but appears in places to be irrelevant to our condition, unworthy of God, or simply banal, we may take it for granted that we have failed to grasp its inner sense. If no spiritual significance is apparent on the surface, we must conclude that this surface meaning, which may or may not be factual, is intended symbolically. . . . It took no genius to recognize that such allegory was a desperate effort to avoid the plain meaning of the text, and that, indeed, is how Origen viewed it.[35]

For example, Origen restated the conquest of Canaan as "Christ's conquest of the fallen human soul."[36] On interpreting the Old Testament as a whole, Origen saw Christ and the individual soul on every page. Regarding the Lord's Prayer, Origen considered the hallowing of God's name and the coming of God's kingdom as referring to our gradual sanctification. Trigg illustrates:

We pray that God's name may be hallowed in our good works and that God's kingdom may come in our well-ordered life. There is not the slightest trace of apocalyptic eschatology, the notion that Christ will in fact reappear to establish God's reign on earth, in Origen's understanding of the kingdom of God.[37]

Trigg gives the clearest explanation of allegorical interpretation and its failure in understanding prophecy—especially the prophecies of the New Testament. Regarding the following quote, one cannot but have in mind the book of Revelation:

One of the most interesting features of the *Commentary on Matthew* (Origen's) is its tendency to psychologize the Gospel's apocalyptic eschatological imagery. Thus, when the Gospel predicts that Christ will come "on the clouds of heaven with power and great glory" (Matt. 24:30), it refers to his appearance to the perfect [or mature] in their reading of the Bible. Likewise, the two comings of Christ, the first in humility and the second in glory, symbolize Christ's coming in the souls of the simple when they receive the rudiments of Christian doctrine and his coming in[to] the perfect [the mature] when they find him in the hidden meanings of the Bible. The trials and tribulations the world must endure before the second coming symbolize the difficulties the soul must overcome before it is worthy of union with the Logos. The imminence of the second coming refers to the imminent possibility, for each individual, of death. Perhaps more radically, the two men laboring in a field, one of whom is taken and the other left when the Messiah comes (Matt. 24:40), represent good and bad influences on a person's will, which fare differently when the Logos is revealed to that person. Although Origen did not openly deny the vivid apocalyptic expectations such passages originally expressed and *still did for many Christians*, he tended by psychologizing them to make them irrelevant. Although that was far from Origen's intention, *the outcome of his work was to make the church feel distinctly more at home in the world.*[38] (italics added)

Note, Origen created interpretation, he did not *seek* interpretation. Though not directly denying prophecy, by rewriting the script and ignoring future prophesied events, he destroyed the truth intended by the passage. Still, many held to the prophetic *"expectations"* that were part of the belief of the early church. But Origen made the *"church feel distinctly more at home in the world."* Premillennialists should not and generally do not ignore passages meant for present day living (an accusation leveled by amillennialists). Likewise, amillennialists should not ignore the great prophetic truths that tell us clearly not to be comfortable in this world because God is bringing it to a definite conclusion.

A Sensual Millennium

Origen as well as Augustine share guilt in throwing the church into the waiting arms of allegorical interpretation. Many from the third century reacted against literal millennialism because of Origen's sensual approach to the one-thousand-year reign of Christ. As he described it in his *De Principiis,* Origen held a very sensuous idea of the kingdom with "marriages and luxuriant feasts."

Though he is called "the father of critical investigation," Origen dealt the church a great blow with his strong leanings into allegory. When this system was fully developed with Augustine, the book of Revelation fell back into a darkness that even persists today. The door was shut on this most profound, inspired prophetic work. It could well be argued that Satan is delighted to render humanity blind to the coming Tribulation, millennial reign, and judgment. Amillennialist Schaff is fair when he describes the great hermeneutical failings of Origen:

> His great defect is the neglect of the grammatical and historical sense and his constant desire to find a hidden mystic meaning. He even goes further in this direction than the Gnostics, who everywhere saw transcendental, unfathomable mysteries. His hermeneutical principle assumes a threefold sense—somatic, psychic, and pneumatic; or literal, moral, and spiritual. His allegorical interpretation is ingenious, but often runs far away from the text and degenerates into the merest caprice.[39]

Without question, Origen's allegorical interpretation is certainly not acceptable for serious students of God's Word.

New Schools of Interpretation

Thus it was that in Alexandria, the North African church developed a new school of interpretation along the lines of pagan and "liberal" Judaism. Mounce explains:

In the Alexandrian church a spiritualizing approach was developing due in part to the influence of Greek thought, the fact that centuries had passed without the establishment of the awaited kingdom, and in reaction to the excessive chiliasm of the Montanist movement. Origen played a major role in the rise of an allegorical method of exegesis. The mysteries of the Apocalypse can be learned only by going beyond the literal and historical to the spiritual. The spiritualizing method was greatly advanced by the work of Tyconius, who interpreted nothing by the historical setting or events of the first century. Augustine followed Tyconius in his capitulation to a totally mystical exegesis. For the next thousand years this allegorical approach was normative for the interpretation of Revelation. . . . A new departure was taken in the twelfth century by Joachim of Floris. Since the rise of the allegorical approach it had been generally thought that the millennial reign had begun with the historic Christ.[40]

It is puzzling that present-day amillennialists, knowing the history of hermeneutics, can still with confidence adhere to the allegorical interpretation system. One would expect that an amillennialist would reexamine his views on prophecy and especially Revelation. Instead, amillennialists continue to utilitze a system of interpretation that is textually and historically at odds with the normal reading understood by the early church.

A Futurist View?

In his *Word Pictures in the New Testament,* after discussing the various interpretive views of Revelation, Robertson addresses the futurist view:

There is the futurist, which keeps the fulfillment all in the future and which can be neither proved nor disproved. There is also the purely spiritual theory which finds no historical allusion anywhere. This again can be neither proved nor disproved. One of the lines of cleavage is the millennium in chapter 20 [of Revelation]. Those who take the thousand years literally are either premillennialists who look for the second coming of Christ to be followed by a thousand years of personal reign here on earth or the postmillennialists who place the thousand years before the second coming. . . . There seems abundant evidence to believe that this apocalypse,

written during the stress and storm of Domitian's persecution, was intended to cheer the persecuted Christians with a
view of certain victory at last, but with no scheme of history
in view.[41]

According to Robertson, then, the purpose of Revelation is rel-
egated to merely cheering up the persecuted Christians in the early
church. The whole maze of description and detail is written off as
impossible to prove or disprove. How can Robertson be so sure
that there is "no scheme of history in view" in the book? It seems
that a barrier arises in the minds of amillennialists when it comes
to distant-future prophecy. It is as if they believe God has nothing
to say about final events for world history.

Interpretive Confusion

It is hard to believe that objections are made against premillennialism while the allegorists grope about for understanding. One
would think that, privately at least, amillennialists would give the
normal, historic, literal hermeneutic another chance. Perhaps they
do not realize how far adrift they are rationally.

Some of the comments on Revelation made by amillennial commentators in *The Preacher's Commentary* border on interpretive
confusion. For example, G. B. Stevens writes,

> The aim of the book [of Revelation] was distinctly practical;
> it was written primarily for its own time. . . . The book is
> obscure because it deals with obscure themes—the program
> of the future and Christ's return to judgment. . . . The lan-
> guage of concealment (which the initiated would be able to
> interpret correctly) consists of Oriental symbols, largely de-
> rived from books like Ezekiel and Daniel, which are neces-
> sarily more or less enigmatic to the Western and modern
> mind.[42]

Although indeed there are certain practical sections in Revelation, especially the first three chapters, the main purpose of the
book is to describe future events. Because Revelation is a panorama
of the future, it should of course influence believers in the way they
live. But Revelation is not first and foremost an instructive epistle.

So what is Stevens's meaning, then, when he says the book is
"distinctly practical"? How is it "primarily" for its own time? No
one yet has been able to show that Revelation's descriptions fully

coincide with specific events in early church history. What is the "language of concealment" that only the initiated can understand? And how does one become initiated? Granted, all Bible study requires research, but why can't *Western* Christians understand Ezekiel, Daniel, and Revelation? Did the Lord hide the meaning of those three books? Or is it hidden from amillennialists who refuse a literal/future hermeneutic when approaching prophecy?

The writer S. Cox, too, exhibits confusion when trying to explain the purpose of the Apocalypse:

> St. John was not a prophet in the ancient and vulgar sense; he was not a mere seer of coming events, a mere student and interpreter of the shadows they cast before them. . . . And, hence, the Apocalypse of St. John is not a series of forecasts, predicting the political weather of the world through the ages of history; it is rather a series of symbols and visions in which the universal principles of the Divine Rule are set forth in forms dear to the heart of a Hebrew Mystic and poet. What is most valuable to us in this book, therefore, is not the letter, the form; not the vials, the seals, the trumpets, over which interpreters, who play the seer rather than the prophet, have been wrangling and perplexing their brains for centuries; but the large general principles which these mystic symbols of Oriental thought are apt to conceal from a Western mind. Whether or not, for example, the vision of an angel flying through heaven to proclaim an impending judgment was taken by St. John's first readers to indicate an approaching event of world-wide moment, is a question of comparatively slight importance to us; it is, indeed, mainly a question of curious antiquarian interest.[43]

How Would John the Apostle Respond?

One wonders how the apostle John might react at being labeled "not a mere seer of coming events," or a "Hebrew Mystic and poet," one who sets forth "symbols and visions" of universal principles of the "Divine Rule." Like Stevens, Cox perceives the value of the book of Revelation as not "the vials, the seals, the trumpets" but rather the mystic symbols of Oriental thought concealed from the Western mind.

Further, it is more than "slightly important" whether or not John is predicting "impending judgment." These are matters to be accorded greater importance than "curious antiquarian interest." What is truly curious is how critics of premillennialism can argue that the literal, normative, prophetic interpretation of Bible prophecy, much less the book of Revelation, can be so foreign. In truth, the interpretive system that Cox creates is unacceptable.

Amillennialists exhibit confusion as to the difference between symbolical language (allegory) and literal language. They fail to comprehend that symbolic language, such as that used in Revelation, may indeed lead to literal concepts.

Symbolic or Literal Interpretation: Where Is the Line Drawn?

W. Milligan proffers the following: "The only question might be whether we are to draw any line between the symbolical and the literal, and if so, where and how? No absolute rule can be laid down. The skill and tact of the interpreter can alone guide him."[44] At this point, premillennialists can somewhat agree.

Skill is needed to interpret the symbolism of Revelation, but the differences between symbolic and literal interpretation are more basic. A premillennialist will argue for a systematic, hermeneutical approach to unlocking Revelation. Signs, symbols, and figures of speech explain literal concepts. It is true that Revelation is very symbolic (though not totally), but there are still literal events embedded behind the figurative language. The typical amillennialist approaches Revelation with a symbolical bias. The premillennialist understands that symbols are used to explain concepts that are difficult to comprehend. The premillennialist approach renders consistent patterns for understanding Revelation.

While the premillennialist leans toward a literal interpretation, the amillennialist spiritualizes the text. Milligan writes, "Everything contained in the Apocalypse is to be understood symbolically and spiritually [or spiritualized]."[45] At this juncture, Milligan misses the point, however, in his illustration of spiritualizing:

> When speaking of the fate of the two witnesses, he [John] says, in ch. xi. 8, And their dead bodies lie in the streets of the great city, which *spiritually* is called Sodom and Egypt— words clearly showing that, in this instance at least, we are not to interpret literally. Apart, however, from these particular words, literal interpretation must be admitted by all to be, at least in the main parts of the book, impossible.[46]

The rest of 11:8 reads ". . . where also their Lord was crucified." The "great city" then is clearly literal Jerusalem. The terms *Sodom* and *Egypt* are used merely to describe the city in a negative, illustrative, *spiritual* way. A spiritual illustration, however, is not the same as spiritualizing. Premillennialists have no problem understanding spiritual language used to describe something distinctly literal. This is not allegorical interpretation. Allegorical interpretation implies there is a hidden, mystical meaning buried beneath the surface. To premillennialists, the terms *Sodom* and *Egypt* vividly describe the future spiritual state of Jerusalem—ungodly, pagan, sensual, idolatrous, and hedonistic—when these events transpire.

The Millennium and the Gospels

In the Gospels, did Jesus abrogate or redefine the promised earthly, historic, literal, and anticipated Davidic kingdom? Jesus taught that the kingdom would have godly and spiritual overtones, yet the Messiah's rule would be literal and worldwide as well, with Jerusalem as the capital city. The kingdom has a blessed and godly agenda but is still a part of the future, coming as an intervention of peace at the end of the horrors of the Tribulation.

Those who *spiritualize* the kingdom in the Gospels argue that the church has either replaced Israel forever in God's plans, or that the prophecies for Israel in the Old Testament were stated symbolically and referred to the church. They claim that God is through with the Jews forever, has totally abandoned that nation, and has inserted the church as a substitute.

Neither John the Baptist nor Jesus redefined the basic structure of the kingdom, though they certainly stressed that it would be spiritual in nature as well as historical.

Mary's Response to the Message of the Angel

The angel announced the coming birth of Jesus to Mary:

And behold, you will conceive in your womb, and bear a son, and you shall name Him Jesus. He will be great, and will be called the Son of the Most High; and the Lord God will give Him the throne of His father David; and He will reign over the house of Jacob forever; and His kingdom will have no end. (Luke 1:31–33)

How did Mary interpret these promises? There is only one answer—literally. (1) Literally and historically, Mary would conceive and bear a son. (2) The child Jesus was indeed called the Son of the Highest. (3) Literally and historically, Jesus will be given, *in the future,* the throne of His father David. (4) Literally and historically, Jesus will *reign* over the house of Jacob forever. (5) The kingdom will have a long engagement; it will have no end. In the Luke passage above, Jesus' first and second coming are prophesied. The language is clear; both His birth and future reign are to be taken literally.

What was the initial message of both John the Baptist *and* Jesus as they began their public ministries? *"Repent, for the kingdom of heaven is at hand"* (Matt. 3:2; 4:17). Was the kingdom of heaven the church, or the anticipated Davidic rule the Jews throughout most of their history had been looking for? And did Jesus ever tell the Jews, "You're looking for the wrong kingdom"? No, He did not, because the Jews did not abandon the literal messianic hope. They were, however, chided for rejecting Jesus as Messiah (the Anointed King). Jesus upbraided the Pharisees for their legalism and hypocrisy but never for their kingdom belief.

What Did the Jewish Rabbis Believe About the Millennium and the Messiah?

Knowing what the Jewish rabbis of Jesus' time believed is important to interpretation. All interpreters know that *context* and *setting* are keys to understanding what is happening in a given story or historical narrative. If the Jews *understood* the millennium as literal, that becomes the *setting* and the *context* for the narration. If Jesus does not refute the belief of the Jews and correct their assumptions, his silence on that matter makes a statement to His listeners, a statement that provides context for the interpreter in understanding the meaning of the Scriptures. Scholars of Jewish history document what the Jews were thinking concerning the kingdom and the Messiah. In Jesus' day,

> There was no departure from the literal interpretation even among the Rabbinical party. . . . The allegorical interpretation of the Sacred Scriptures cannot be historically proved to have prevailed among the Jews from the time of the exile, or to have been common with the Jews of Palestine at the time of Christ and His apostles. . . . The Sanhedrin and the hearers of Jesus . . . give no indication of the allegorical interpretation. Even Josephus has nothing of it. The Platonic Jews of Egypt began, in the first century, in imitation of the heathen Greeks, to interpret the Old Testament allegorically. Philo was distinguished among those in that place who practiced this method and he defends it as something new and

before unheard of, and for that reason opposed by the other Jews. . . . The Jewish method—evidenced by its exclusiveness and Messianic hopes—was adopted by the primitive Church, as witnessed e.g. by its application of prophecy, its Pre-millenarian views, etc. The ideal, presented in the system of Philo, was inaugurated into the Christian Church by the Alexandrian fathers.[47]

Did most of the orthodox Jewish rabbis during the early church period take literally the Old Testament and the book of Revelation in regard to a terrible time of trouble on earth (the Tribulation), the coming of the Messiah, and the establishing of the millennial reign? The answer is yes. Can this be demonstrated by the writings and historic views of most of the rabbis, especially during the Middle Ages? The answer again is yes.

Discussed below are the beliefs of later generations of Jews, which substantiate the orthodoxy of premillennialism, which existed during the time when Jesus lived and ministered. He taught in the context of these beliefs and never once refuted them. Much of the material that follows comes from two valuable works: *Society and Religion in the Second Temple Period*, published in Israel and very incisive as to what the Jews believed during the time of Christ, authored and edited by the great Jewish historian Dr. Michael Avi-Yonah, with Zvi Baras;[48] and *The Messiah Texts* by Raphael Patai.[49]

The Death of the Messiah

Patai in his classic work, *The Messiah Texts,* quotes the ancient rabbinical writings:

Our True Messiah! Even though we are your fathers, you are greater than we, for you suffered because of the sins of our children, and cruel punishments have come upon you the like of which have not come upon the early and the later generations, and you were put to ridicule and held in contempt by the nations of the world because of Israel, . . . your skin cleft to your bones, . . . your strength became like a potsherd [a paraphrase of Psalm 22]. All this because of the sins of our children . . . because of the great sufferings that have come upon you on their account.[50]

In the later, Zoharic . . . legend, the Messiah himself summons all the diseases, pains, and sufferings of Israel to come upon him, in order thus to ease the anguish of Israel, . . . In all this the Messiah becomes heir to the Suffering Servant of God, . . . who suffers undeservedly for the sins of others [Isa. 53]. (From the *Pesiqta Rabbati*)[51]

[In the days of Adam] there was as yet no devastation in the world, but it was then as it will again be in the days of the Messiah, [may he come] quickly in our days. For about those days it is written, *He will swallow up death forever* (Isa. 25:8).[52]

Judaism and Amillennialism

Avi-Yonah notes,

It was inconceivable that the promises should not be fulfilled and that the Kingdom of Heaven upon the earth should not arrive. All Jewish groups believed this implicitly. The disagreement among them concerned only the date of the fulfillment and the means of its accomplishment. Whereas the Sadducees did not carry forward the messianic hope of prophecy.[53]

Even Christianity, essentially messianic . . . is the product of the great messianic promises. By reason of foreign influence, however, it sought the messianic Kingdom of God in a way other than that of Judaism. While Jewish messianism is firmly rooted in this world, in earthly life, even in the "new world" of the days of the Messiah, Christian messianism is a "kingdom not of this world."[54]

Note the statement, *foreign influence,* a clear reference to the pagan allegorical interpretation that was rejected by most orthodox Jewish scholars. *Society and Religion* further elaborates on the "Greek element" [allegorical interpretation] inserted into hermeneutics:

This renewed messianic idea, envisioned by the author of the Book of Daniel, was to be echoed in its essential thrust in the literature that took its clue from it. Its influence on Christianity is unmistakable. Once Christianity, however, introduced a Greek element into Jewish monotheism it changed the basic concept of the Kingdom of Heaven which it had borrowed from Judaism.[55]

Avi-Yonah clearly understood the allegorical influence that makes "the political" difference between amillennial Christian interpretation and Judaism. (The author of this work met professor Avi-Yonah in Israel shortly before his death. I shared with him the premillennial, evangelical enthusiasm and concern for Israel's future. He understood my basic approach to literalism, which he shared, because of his tremendous understanding of hermeneutics.)

The Coming of Elijah

To both premillennialists and orthodox Jews, Elijah is the historic Old Testament personality whom God brings back to earth to herald the coming of the Messiah. Premillennialists speak of Elijah heralding the Messiah's second coming; orthodox Jews speak of Elijah as simply announcing the Messiah's coming to reign for the first time. Patai writes,

> In the Bible, Elijah is depicted as a zealous prophet of God who waged a ruthless war against Canaanite idolatry in Israel, . . . [he] retraced the footsteps of Moses to Mount Horeb . . . and ascended to heaven in a chariot of fire (I Kings 18, 19; II Kings 2) . . . whose return was expected *before the coming of the great and terrible day of the Lord* (Mal. 3:23–24), that is, the day of the Last Judgment. By the first century B.C.E. it was a solidly established tenet that Elijah would be the forerunner of the Messiah.[56]

The New Covenant

Orthodox Jews recognize the importance of the prophesied new covenant given in Jeremiah 31. This passage provides the tenets of the coming new covenant or new testament. To premillennialists, the new covenant was ratified by the sacrificial death of Christ: *"This cup which is poured out for you is the new covenant in My blood"* (Luke 22:20). The church today is a beneficiary of the new covenant, but this sacrificial work of Christ will also have its ultimate fruition and fulfillment for the Jews in the kingdom. It will be applied to believing Jews when they turn to Him at His second coming.

The main features of the new covenant are that (1) all Israel will someday accept the new covenant (Jer. 31:31); (2) it will be unlike the Mosaic covenant, which the Jewish fathers broke (31:32); (3) God will internalize the law and put it in their hearts (31:33); (4) God will indeed be their God, and they shall be His people (31:33); (5) the Jews will all know Him (31:34); (6) they will receive permanent forgiveness for sins; (7) Israel will always be a distinct nation before God forever (31:35–37); (8) God will cleanse the nations of their sins (Ezek. 36:24–25); (9) the Lord will place His Spirit within men, and they will obey Him (36:27); (10) and they will "live in the land that I gave to your forefathers; so you will be My people, and I will be your God" (36:28).

These promises are both spiritual ("I will put My law within") and literal/historical ("you will live in the land"). But these promises are not to be "spiritualized." While it is not the purpose of this chapter to deal extensively with the new covenant and all of its ramifications for Israel and Gentiles or the present church age, suffice it to say that, according to Avi-Yonah, Jews have a certain correct understanding of the spiritual promises of the new covenant.

Premillennialists now understand the covenant in a way similar to that of the orthodox Jews. Avi-Yonah notes,

> The spiritual blessedness of messianic times comprises features no less remarkable. The knowledge of God, the God of Israel, will spread throughout the world. Righteous judgment, good deeds, and rectitude will abound. Men will acquire [a] new heart and new spirit [Ezek. 36:26], a new covenant will be made between God and man [Jer. 31:31].[57]

The Seven-Year Period of Tribulation

Though not often stating so, Jewish scholars interpret from the book of Daniel, as do Christian premillennialists, a seven-year tribulation. Again, looking at the text with a normal reading gives Jews and Christians the same interpretation—a literal/historical understanding of prophecy. Patai, quoting from the rabbinical writings, says, "Things will come to such a head that people will despair of Redemption. This will last seven years. And then, unexpectedly, the Messiah will come."[58] "At the end of the seventh [year] the Son of David will come."[59] Further,

> The pangs of the Messianic times are imagined as having heavenly as well as earthly sources and expressions. . . . awesome cosmic cataclysms will be visited upon the earth: conflagrations, pestilence, famine, earthquakes, . . . These will be paralleled by evils brought by men upon themselves: . . . corruption, oppression, cruel edicts, lack of truth, and no fear of sin. . . . Because of this gloomy picture of the beginnings of the Messianic era, which during Talmudic times

was firmly believed in, some sages expressed the wish not to see the Messiah [because of such judgment coming]. . . . In any case, both the people and its religious leaders continued to hope for the coming of the Messiah . . .[60]

All men, however, will suffer before the days of peace and tranquillity, the days of the Messiah, arrive. The greatest of all tribulations will befall Israel and its land during the period of the "pangs of the Messiah."[61]

The Day of the Lord [will come]. . . . The Kingdom of Heaven will be made manifest over all creation. Satan will then come to an end and with his disappearance sorrow will be banished from the world. God will arise from the throne of His Kingdom to take vengeance. . . . The earth will tremble. . . . The sun will be turned into darkness and the beams of the moon will be broken. The moon itself will be turned into blood.[62]

Here the "pangs of the Messiah" denote "the time of tribulation."[63]

The Kingdom/Millennium

New Testament scholars debate over whether the kingdom of God and the kingdom of heaven mentioned in the Gospels are actually the same. But Avi-Yonah claims, based on rabbinical studies, that the two terms describe the same thing—the earthly, literal kingdom of the Messiah. He notes that the four beasts of Daniel lead to the world dominion of God, i.e., "an everlasting kingdom—'to perfect the world under the Kingdom of God'—a Kingdom of Heaven upon earth."[64]

The rabbis of Christ's day saw in the Old Testament not only the material well-being promised by the prophets but also the spiritual treasures of heavenly blessings that God will open and shower upon the earth. Avi-Yonah further notes,

This description of material plenty agrees with that found both in the Syriac Baruch and in the tradition handed down by one of the Church Fathers, Papias, preserved by Irenaeus. It is this tradition that gave rise to the Christian belief in the Millennial Kingdom of Heaven (Millennium, Chiliasm). One must bear in mind, however, that these descriptions are to be found almost *verbatim* in early Tannaitic and midrashic sources.[65]

The Jews listened for the "Trumpet of the Messiah" that would bring in the blessed kingdom, as described in the Talmud:

> At its sound, the dispersed of Israel will be gathered into their homeland and the tribes of Judah and Ephraim reunited, as in the days of David and Solomon. The land of Israel will attain to a condition of political strength, assuring peace and happiness. . . . The nations . . . will stream in pilgrimage to this land and its [rebuilt] Temple. . . . Swords will be beaten into plowshares, following the final war against Gog and Magog. Even the wild beasts will disappear from the land and those that remain will no longer be injurious. Human beings will live to a ripe old age. The sick and maimed will be healed. The desolate cities will be rebuilt. . . . The boundaries of the land of Israel will be extended. The desert waste will be turned into fertile land. The King Messiah, offspring of the House of David, will rule the world by his holy [s]pirit.[66]

Israel will become the center of the world.

> By the power of his spirit, he expels the nations from Jerusalem and establishes a great kingdom in Zion that serves as the center of the world. The nations serve the God of Israel and the King Messiah. . . . The ingathering of the exiles . . . is a precondition of the coming days of the Messiah. Thus there is a political, national, and territorial aspect to the kingdom of the Messiah. The spiritual aspect, however, remains central.[67]

The Jews looked also for the reconstruction of the temple in Jerusalem.[68] Christian premillennialists are castigated for anticipating the messianic rebuilding of the temple, which has always been a cardinal belief among those who fully understand the entirety of biblical prophecy. "In the Days of the Messiah, a new heaven and a new earth will be created and all creatures will be renewed. The Temple of God will be raised aloft in Jerusalem on Mount Zion."[69]

The Kingdom of Heaven

Because some anticipate a kind of ethereal kingdom, it must be asked, "Just what is the kingdom?" As already pointed out, the Jews view the kingdom of heaven and kingdom of God as the same. Yet the two expressions emphasize a slight difference in source.

Toussaint quotes the excellent summary of Alva J. McClain in his classic work, *The Greatness of the Kingdom:*

> But the question has been raised: Was this Kingdom identical with the Kingdom of Old Testament prophecy? Or was it something different? To these questions the various current answers can be summarized under five heads:
>
> First, the *Liberal-Social* view: that Christ took over from the Old Testament prophets their ethical and social ideals of the kingdom, excluding almost wholly the eschatological element, and made these ideals the program of a present kingdom which it is the responsibility of His followers to establish in human society on earth here and now. . . .
>
> Second, the *Critical-Eschatological* view: that Jesus at first embraced fully the eschatological ideas of the Old Testament prophets regarding the Kingdom, and to some extent the current Jewish ideas; but later in the face of opposition He changed His message; or, at least, there are conflicting elements in the gospel records. As to the precise nature and extent of this change, or the alleged conflicts, the critics are not agreed. . . .
>
> Third, the *Spiritualizing-Anti-Millennial* view: that our Lord appropriated certain spiritual elements from the Old Testament prophetical picture, either omitted or spiritualized the physical elements (excepting the physical details involved in the Messiah's first coming!), and then added some original ideas of His own. . . .
>
> Fourth, the *Dual-Kingdom* view: that Christ at His first coming offered to Israel and established on earth a purely spiritual kingdom; and that at His second coming He will establish on earth a literal Millennial Kingdom. . . .
>
> Fifth, the *One-Kingdom Millennial* view: that the Kingdom announced by our Lord and offered to the nation of Israel at His first coming was identical with the Mediatorial Kingdom of Old Testament prophecy, and will be established on earth at the second coming of the King. This might well be called the *Biblical* view because it is supported by the material in both Testaments taken at its normal or face value.[70] (italics added)

Toussaint clearly spells out the millennial issue as it relates to both Matthew and Revelation. He notes that John had in mind the earthly eschatological kingdom as predicted by the prophets, evident in John and Jesus having no need to explain the kingdom because the Jews already knew from the Old Testament of its literal coming.[71]

> The only conclusion at which one can arrive is that the proclamation of John refers to a literal, earthly kingdom in fulfillment of the Old Testament promises and prophecies. . . .Thus for John the kingdom was near in that the King was near. When Jesus and His disciples heralded the drawing near of the kingdom, the King was there, but the kingdom was still only near. If Israel had accepted its Messiah, the earthly kingdom would have been inaugurated by the King. . . .The kingdom of the heavens was near in a very real sense in that the King was here and it was the Messiah's work to bring the kingdom.[72]

The Coming Judgment

In Jewish rabbinical thinking, putting together various biblical statements, both God and the Son of Man are seen as judging men at the end of days. Toussaint notes,

> The days of the Messiah or, more precisely, the Kingdom of Heaven, will endure forever. Eternal life in the company of the Messiah, close to God . . . is assured for the righteous. As for the sinners and the inciters to sin, they will be judged by the Son of Man from his Throne of Glory.[73]

> The Messiah will be exalted above all. On a command from God, all the heavenly powers will praise him. . . . God will command . . . rulers to acknowledge the Messiah Elect. They behold him sitting on his "Throne of Glory." . . . No falsehood will issue from his lips. . . . [Evil men] will be affrighted by the Son of Man and will prostrate themselves before him, pleading for mercy.[74]

Conclusion

It must be remembered that the preceding discussion is a summation of Jewish thought that was prominent during the time of Christ, Paul, and the New Testament period. The material was compiled by recognized Jewish scholars who are devoted to studying the past culture and history of their own people. Their findings fit exactly into a premillennial pattern.

The amillennial interpretation is an aberration of all reasonable and historic approaches to scriptural hermeneutics. Allegory became a cancer that destroyed understanding of the Old Testament prophecies and mutilated a sound and reasonable understanding of the book of Revelation.

Ironically, from the first, the Jews clearly saw the messianic kingdom in the book of Revelation. In fact, the Jews called the kingdom *the Millennium* in the ancient writing called *Zohar*.[75] In *Zohar* 1:119a we read, "Happy will be all those who will remain in the world at the end of the sixth millennium to enter into the millennium of the Sabbath." In *Zohar* 1:140a, Midrash HaNe'elam, we read, "The total saintly will arise at the rising of the dead of the Land of Israel . . . in the fortieth year of the ingathering of the exiles. And the last ones [will arise] in the . . . sixth millennium [in order to enter the last millennium]."

Interesting, too, is the reaction of the high priest Caiaphas to the words of Jesus. Caiaphas had asked Christ an extremely messianic question, one that would be burning in the minds of all Jews, the common man, and the leadership: "I adjure You by the living God, that You tell us whether You are the Christ, the Son of God" (Matt. 26:63). The Jews well understood both expressions. "Christ" *(Xristos)* was the Hebrew for *HaMaschioch*, "the Anointed One"; and "Son of God" was the common expression of the Messiah taken from Psalm 2, "the Son who has a relationship with God." Jesus answered, "I tell you, hereafter you shall see the Son of Man sitting at the right hand of Power, and coming on the clouds of heaven" (Matt. 26:64). In this statement, Christ referred to the "Son who has a relationship to man" but who also had an eternal position with God the Father in glory. These three key expressions of the Messiah flashed before Caiaphas, and he exploded in rage: "He has blasphemed!" The people agreed: "He is deserving of death!"

This incident tells us the Jews knew the predictions and the prophecies. They also were well aware of the revelations and events that would surround the Messiah's coming to earth to take power. But they failed to see His predicted death, and they misread His love, consideration for sinners, and general care for hurting mankind. In other words, He did not fit the image. Nor were His timing and teaching acceptable.

Norman Cohn explains that, in regard to interpretation, by the time of Augustine (fourth century) the death knell had been tolled on a clear understanding of the book of Revelation. Allegory would cloud its message, and the meaning of the writing would be closed to countless generations. Only in the last one hundred and fifty years has the Revelation prophecy been reexamined. Slowly, as we move further into the end times, the book is being given a new hearing for its full futuristic meaning. Cohn summarizes:

> The third century saw the first attempt to discredit millenarianism, when Origen, perhaps the most influential of all the theologians of the ancient Church, began to present the Kingdom as an event which would take place not in space or time but only in the souls of believers. For a collective, millenarian eschatology Origen substituted an eschatology of the individual soul. What stirred his profoundly Hellenic imagination was the prospect of spiritual progress begun in this world and continued in the next; and to this theme theologians were henceforth to give increasing attention. Such a shift in interest was indeed admirably suited to what was now an organized Church, enjoying almost uninterrupted peace and an acknowledged position in the world. When in the fourth century Christianity attained a position of supremacy in the Mediterranean world and became the official religion of the Empire, ecclesiastical disapproval of millenarianism became emphatic. The Catholic Church was now a powerful and prosperous institution, functioning according to a well-established routine; and the men responsible for governing it had no wish to see Christians clinging to out-dated and inappropriate dreams of a new earthly Paradise. Early in the fifth century St. Augustine propounded the doctrine which the new conditions demanded. According to *The City of God* the book of Revelation was to be understood as a *Spiritual Allegory;* as for the Millennium, that had begun with the birth of Christianity and was fully realized in the Church. This at once became orthodox doctrine.[76] (italics added)

This chapter was adapted from Mal Couch, "Introductory Thoughts on Allegorical Interpretation and the Book of Revelation—Part I," *The Conservative Theological Journal* 1, no. 1 (April 1997): 13–30.

CHAPTER 22

The Kingdom of God

Working from a normal, literal hermeneutic and by simple New Testament observation, one must come to the conclusion that *kingdom of God* and *kingdom of heaven* are two ways of describing the same thing. Because there is disagreement on this issue, a thorough study of both expressions in the Gospels and elsewhere will be enlightening.

Uses of "Kingdom" in Scripture

What does the word *kingdom* mean? The word carries the idea of a rule or reign. The Old Testament word *malkut* and the New Testament word *basileia* are the two most common words to describe the idea of kingdom: "(1) a personage with ruling authority and power, (2) an objective realm of constituents over which to rule, and (3) the actual exercise of that regal authority over that constituency."[1]

The Universal Kingdom

Many Old Testament passages describe the idea of a universal rule of God over His creation.

> The broadest sense of God's rule, His dominion over all of creation at all times, is commonly called the universal kingdom of God. It might be best to speak of God's universal kingdom as His kingdom in macrocosm. This macrocosmic kingdom of God is grounded in His sovereignty as the Creator, Sustainer, and Director of all that exists (Ps. 103:19–22). God's universal rule extends through all eras (Lam. 5:19). It

encompasses every facet of creation (1 Chron. 29:11–12), and
it exists without end (Ps. 10:16). . . . The universal kingdom of
God, then, is God's macrocosmic rule through His exclusive,
sovereign dominion over all of creation, a rule without pause
or end.[2]

The Mediatorial Kingdom

The mediatorial kingdom describes God's rule through an earthly
people or realm. It began with the nation of Israel following the
Exodus from Egypt, when Jehovah dealt with the Jewish people
through His prophet Moses. The Lord established a government, a
Law, and gave to this new nation a land.

In microcosm, the mediatorial kingdom consisted of the Lord
dealing with the Jewish people through Joshua, the various judges,
the elders, King Saul, and finally David's line. With the Babylonian
captivity, the Lord's presence departed from Israel and, in a sense,
God's rule ended. Yet He was neither finished with this kingdom
nor with this earthly people, the children of Israel.

The OT prophets who had forecasted its demise also consistently foretold its consummate restoration (Lev. 26:40–46;
Ezek. 11:14–20; Hos. 1:10–11).

God offered to Israel the restoration of this historic, mediatorial kingdom in the person of the ultimate Davidic
king, Jesus, at His First Advent (Matt. 3:1–2; 4:17; 21:1–9).
Jesus spoke of this kingdom in the Sermon on the Mount
(Matt. 5–7). He preached the Gospel of this kingdom (Matt.
9:35) and sent the disciples to proclaim it to the Jews (Matt.
10:5–7). This is the "kingdom of heaven," the "kingdom of
God," the "kingdom of the Father" to which Christ referred
in the parables (Matt. 13:20, 22), in His discourse on the
Mount of Olives (Matt. 24–25), and in the Upper Room
(Matt. 26:29). With the rejection of the King (Matt. 27:22–25;
John 19:13–15), the restoration of the theocratic kingdom
on earth was deferred until the return of its ruler and His
acceptance by national Israel (Zech. 12:10–13:9; Rev. 1:7).
With the second advent of Christ, the former, historic, me-
diatorial kingdom will be reestablished on earth (Amos 9:11;
Micah 4:8).[3]

Mediatorial means that one is "mediating" or representing for
the Lord on earth. Moses mediated for God with Israel on earth,

and Jesus the Messiah will someday also mediate for God the Father in the future kingdom.

Theocratic reflects the idea that God is reigning with His people, who dwell on earth. During the time of the Exodus, the Lord reigned through the prophet Moses. In the kingdom period, Jesus, who is God the Son, will in a very real and personal sense be "God ruling on earth."

When Jesus the Messiah comes to earth, the theocratic rule of the Lord will be restored, and that worldwide kingdom will last for one thousand years. Though it will be a near-perfect reign, because of the sinful influence of later generations living in that blessed period, even that kingdom will fail.

Kingdom of God/Kingdom of Heaven

Most of the references to *kingdom* in the New Testament refer to the future Messianic reign of Christ that is yet to come. How can we be certain of this meaning?

First, the idea of kingdom was expressed in ancient Jewish writings that certainly predated the time of Jesus. Second, through looking at context within the Gospels and the rest of the New Testament, we can determine how the word was generally used. But what about the specific phrases *kingdom of God* and *kingdom of heaven*? Are they millennial in nature, and do the two phrases mean almost the same thing? Three points must be considered:

1. How is the word *kingdom* used in Acts and the Epistles?
2. How did the ancient Jewish rabbis use the two phrases?
3. Can it be shown that the two phrases are used interchangeably in the Gospels?

1. How is the word kingdom *used in Acts and the Epistles?*

In almost every reference in the Epistles, the context clearly shows that *kingdom* refers to a future earthly inheritance, particularly involving the Jewish people rather than the church only.

After His resurrection, Jesus again taught about the kingdom (Acts 1:3). His disciples must have seen it still as future and relating to Israel, because they asked about its "restoration" (1:6). The kingdom is called "good news" in the Gospels and also in Acts (8:12).

In Paul's epistles, the kingdom again is clearly described as future and is not a reference to the church. If the church were the kingdom, the apostle was certainly not clear in revealing that reference. Paul points out that the wicked *will not* (in the future) inherit the kingdom

(1 Cor. 6:9–10; Gal. 5:21), and he further writes of Christ prophetically appearing in His kingdom (2 Tim. 4:1).

But what about Paul's statement that Christ "will bring me safely
to His heavenly kingdom" (4:18)? Two things stand out in this statement: (1) Paul, being alive, is not existing in the kingdom. He is
living in the church age. Thus, in this reference, the kingdom described here can in no way be this church dispensation. (2) The
apostle is clearly talking about going home to be with the Lord in
heaven. *Heavenly* is an adjective describing the noun *kingdom*. *Kingdom of heaven* has to do with the earthly Davidic kingdom, and its
source is "of" or "from" heaven.

2. How did the ancient Jewish rabbis use the two phrases?

Orthodox Judaism has always seen the "kingdom of God" and
"kingdom of heaven" as messianic. Strong evidence derived from
using historic hermeneutics supports this view, and definitions of
the two phrases can not be changed unless strong evidence to the
contrary suggests that they should be defined in some new way. We
have no such evidence.

In their classic work *Society and Religion in the Second Temple
Period*, editors Michael Avi-Yonah and Zvi Baras shed light on use of
the two phrases. Avi-Yonah and Baras note that Daniel 7:9–18 gave a
clear "messianic vision of the future of the people of Israel."[4] In Daniel
7, He who comes "with the clouds of heaven" as the "Son of Man"
whose kingdom is "an everlasting kingdom" symbolizes "the saints
of the Most High." The Son of Man represents the Messiah.

The Jewish authors of the oldest books of the Pseudepigrapha
similarly understood the prophetic "Son of Man" as referring to the
Messiah.[5] Avi-Yonah and Baras then note,

> [In Daniel] world history in the course of five centuries passes
> before us as links in a single chain whose sole purpose is to
> bring to an end the dominion of the predatory beasts [the four
> great Gentile empires] and to establish the world dominion of
> God, an everlasting kingdom—"to perfect the world under the
> Kingdom of God"—a Kingdom of Heaven upon earth.[6]

Clearly, in historic Jewish usage, the two "kingdoms" are seen as
the same. But another question arises: How did the idea of this
kingdom become spiritualized rather than considered literal and
historic? The authors agree with dispensationalists in their answer—
Greek allegorism. And, as these Jewish authors correctly note, the

amillennialism that was spawned from allegorical interpretation was, by the fourth century, accepted by almost all of Christendom. They write,

> This renewed messianic idea, envisioned by the author of the book of Daniel, was to be echoed in its essential thrust in the literature that took its clue from it. Its influence on Christianity is unmistakable. Once Christianity, however, introduced a Greek element into Jewish monotheism it changed the basic concept of the kingdom of heaven which it had borrowed from Judiasm.[7]

Greek allegory, then, is the connection to false allegorical hermeneutics. It is interesting that Jewish scholars see the historical turning point, but amillennialists in the church do not perceive how literal interpretation evolved into spiritualized interpretation.

Avi-Yonah and Baras show how the early church fathers drew so much of their prophetic theology from the Old Testament and other extra-biblical writings. (Again, present-day premillennialists and dispensationalists are in good rabbinic company.) For example, Avi-Yonah and Baras show that the blessings of the kingdom are

> . . . in the tradition handed down by one of the Church Fathers, Papias, preserved by Iranaeus. It is this tradition that gave rise to the Christian belief in the Millennial Kingdom of Heaven (Millennium, Chiliasm). One must bear in mind, however, that these descriptions are to be found almost verbatim in early Tannaitic and midrashic sourses.[8]

3. Can it be shown that the two phrases are used interchangeably in the Gospels?

It can be shown from the contexts of the Gospels that the terms *kingdom of heaven* and *kingdom of God* are virtually interchangeable, with but a minute shade of difference.

> Most expositors regard the kingdom of heaven as the equivalent of the kingdom of God, and explain it on the grounds that Matthew, like many Jews, did not like to use the word God and used heaven instead.
>
> As normally written, kingdom of God (or heaven) is classified in Greek in a genitive form: "The kingdom of (belonging to) God." But it may be better to translate it in an ablative

form: "The kingdom of (from) God," or, "The kingdom coming down from heaven." There is much disagreement upon this point. Yet most admit the genitive and ablative meanings are actually not far apart. For whatever reasons, Matthew preferred kingdom of heaven and the other writers chose kingdom of God. Matthew may have been focusing on Daniel 2:44, which declares the "God of heaven will set up a kingdom which will never be destroyed. . . . It will itself endure forever."[9]

Studying the harmony of the Gospels will yield the same evidence, as the near-parallel readings below support.[10] As Jesus taught, He apparently used both expressions, or one Gospel author preferred one term over the other; or it is possible that, as our Lord taught the same lessons in different locations, He used slightly different language. For example, as can be seen below, the word *theirs* was used on one occasion, the word *yours* on another.

Matt. 5:3	Blessed are the poor . . . theirs is *the kingdom of heaven.*
Luke 6:20	Blessed are you who are poor, . . . yours is *the kingdom of God.*
Matt. 11:11	He who is least in *the kingdom of heaven* is greater than [John].
Luke 7:28	He who is least in *the kingdom of God* is greater than [John].
Matt. 13:11	The mysteries of *the kingdom of heaven.*
Mark 4:11	The mysteries of *the kingdom of God.*
Luke 8:10	The mysteries of *the kingdom of God.*
Matt. 13:24	*The kingdom of heaven* may be compared to a man. . . .
Mark 4:26	*The kingdom of God* is like a man. . . .
Matt. 13:31	*The kingdom of heaven* is like a mustard seed.
Mark 4:30–31	*The kingdom of God* . . . is like a mustard seed.
Matt. 9:1	Some . . . here . . . shall not taste death until they see *the kingdom of God.*
Luke 9:27	Some . . . here . . . shall not taste death until they see *the kingdom of God.*

Matt. 18:1	Who is greatest in *the kingdom of heaven?*
Matt. 18:3	Unless you . . . become like children, you shall not enter *the kingdom of heaven.*
Matt. 18:4	Whoever . . . humbles himself as this child, he is the greatest in *the kingdom of heaven.*
Mark 10:14	Permit the children to come to Me . . . for *the kingdom of God* belongs to such as these.
Mark 10:15	Whoever does not receive *the kingdom of God* like a child shall not enter it.
Luke 18:16	Do not hinder [the children], for *the kingdom of God* belongs to such as these.
Luke 18:17	Whoever does not receive *the kingdom of God* like a child shall not enter it.

Matt. 19:23	It is easier for a camel to go through the eye of a needle, than for a rich man to enter *the kingdom of heaven.*
Matt. 19:24	I say again, it is easier for a camel to go through the eye if a needle, than for a rich man to enter *the kingdom of God.*
Mark 10:23	How hard it will be for those who are wealthy to enter *the kingdom of God.*
Mark 10:24	How hard it is to enter *the kingdom of God!*
Mark 10:25	It is easier for a camel to go through the eye of a needle than for a rich man to enter *the kingdom of God.*
Luke 18:24	How hard it is for those who are wealthy to enter *the kingdom of God!*
Luke 18:25	It is easier for a camel to go through the eye of a needle, than for a rich man to enter *the kingdom of God.*

Matt. 22:2	*The kingdom of heaven* may be compared to a king, who gave a wedding feast for his son.
Luke 14:15–16	[A man said], "Blessed is everyone who shall eat bread in *the kingdom of God!*" But [Jesus] said to him, "A certain man was giving a big dinner, and he invited many."

Mark 15:43	Joseph of Arimathea . . . was waiting for *the kingdom of God.*
Luke 23:51	A man from Arimathea, . . . who was waiting for *the kingdom of God.*

An important reference in the list above is Matthew 19:23–24. There, in the same context and with parallel sentences, Jesus clearly refers to the kingdom as both "of heaven" and "of God." Joining the two verses with "And again I say to you . . . ," He repeats the identical thought, referring to the same idea with two different descriptions of the kingdom. Surprisingly, no critical analysis has been seen in any commentary to explain the two phrases being used in the same context.

Studying all the references to the kingdom in the Gospels, plus one reference in Acts (1:6), one must conclude that the kingdom is the Davidic reign clearly promised in the Old Testament. Allegorists, of course, deny this and attempt to read *church* into all of the references. Allegorist Hendriksen writes about the word *kingdom* in Matthew:

> [It] indicate[s] God's kingship, rule or sovereignty, recognized in the hearts and operative in the lives of his people, and effecting their complete salvation, their constitution as a church, and finally a redeemed universe.[11]

Other Descriptions of the Kingdom

During Jesus' triumphal entry into Jerusalem, the crowds shouted out Psalm 118:26: "Hosanna! Blessed is He who comes in the name of the Lord" (Mark 11:9). They then added, "Blessed is the coming kingdom of our father David; Hosanna in the highest!" (v. 10). Matthew says that the mob in their cheering also called Jesus the Son of David (21:9, 15). Messianic descriptives are also used abundantly in the kingdom parables in Matthew 13. Jesus is called the Son of Man (v. 37), who sows good seed, meaning "the sons of the kingdom" (v. 38). The kingdom belongs to this Son of Man (v. 41), and the righteous will shine as the sun in the "kingdom of the Father" (v. 43). Jesus also called the kingdom "My Father's kingdom" (26:29).

Following Christ's resurrection, He spent forty days "speaking of the things concerning the kingdom of God" (Acts 1:3). The disciples must have been excited about that promised coming reign, because they asked Him, "Lord, is it at this time You are restoring the kingdom to Israel?" (v. 6). They were not seeking a new definition for or explanation about that kingdom. Christ must have confirmed but expanded on information about that kingdom, much of which the disciples already knew. The doctrinal issue about the kingdom must surely have already been settled, because they ask only about the timetable: "Is it as this time You are restoring. . . ." Notice, this kingdom is called the "kingdom of Israel." Early on in Jesus' ministry, Nathanael says to Him, "You are the Son of God [a reference to Psalm. 2]; You are the King of Israel" (John 1:49–50). These titles are repeated by the crowds at the triumphal entry into Jerusalem: "Hosanna! Blessed is He who comes in the name of the Lord, even the King of Israel" (12:13).

And when Christ was crucified, Pilate, responding to the mood of some of the Jewish mob, had "King of the Jews" placed as an inscription over the cross (Mark 15:25). A king certainly suggests a kingdom; some mocked Jesus on the cross and cried out, "Let this Christ, the King of Israel, now come down from the cross, so that we may see and believe!" (v. 32).

Conclusion

The "kingdom of God" and "kingdom of heaven" both refer to the future Messianic reign of the Messiah. The only point of reference the Jews would have known is the messianic kingdom and the coming rule of peace that would last for one thousand years. Jesus presented Himself as the king who fulfilled the kingship role for that kingdom. He told neither His disciples nor the crowds that they were mistaken in their perceptions.

Feinberg adds this explanation regarding the shades of differences in the two phrases:

> . . . The kingdom is characterized as the kingdom of heaven, because it is patterned after heaven and its perfection. . . . Furthermore, there is involved the thought of the heavenly origin and source of the kingdom; the God of heaven is He who will set it up. The name "kingdom of God" is employed because it points to the spiritual character of the reign and dominion. The glory of God is its chief and sole object.[12]

CHAPTER 23

Is Ezekiel's Temple Literal?

The difference between dispensational the-
ology and reformed theology is largely reflected in their approaches
to interpreting eschatological literature. Dispensational theology
consistently applies a literal hermeneutic to the eschatological and
non-eschatological books of the Bible. Reformed theology frequently
employs the allegorical or spiritualizing method of biblical interpretation when it comes to interpreting prophetic passages of the
Bible. For example, with an allegorical interpretation, Israel does
not have to mean the nation of Israel. It could mean the church. Or
in Revelation 20, the term *thousand years,* used six times, does not
necessarily mean a literal one thousand years. It could mean an
unspecified period of time.

The Reformed view rejects the idea of there being a physical temple
building in Ezekiel 40–48. Instead, they maintain that it refers to
the universal church. Allegorizing the text in this way dismisses the
common, ordinary meaning of words as they were understood in
their historical context.

An old Jewish maxim states, "Jerusalem is in the center of the
world, the Temple Mount is in the center of Jerusalem, and the
Temple is in the center of the Mount."[1] Jerusalem and the temple
are essential to Judaism.

The Bible mentions five temples that play important roles in God's
dealing with Israel and even the nations: (1) The great Solomonic
temple was completed around 960 B.C. and stood until it was destroyed by Nebuchadnezzar in 586 B.C. (2) Zerubbabel built another
temple on the ruins of Solomon's structure. It was completed around

515 B.C. but did not reflect all the glory of the first. (3) Herod built the great gilded temple that stood in the days of Jesus and the apostles. It took years to finish, but it was destroyed, as Jesus prophesied, in A.D. 70. (4) The Scriptures predict another temple standing when the Antichrist enters the Middle East halfway through his seven-year covenant with the regathered Jews living in Palestine. At that time, he comes into the temple and, turning on the Jewish people, proclaims himself as God. (5) The final earthly temple is called the millennial temple. The rabbis see the Messiah as granting permission for its construction.

The First Temple

The tabernacle was a temporary structure, moving from place to place, and housed within a tent until the Israelites were unified spiritually and politically in the land God promised to Abraham. This did not occur until David conquered the Jebusite city of Jerusalem, making it the capital of Israel and the city of God. Scripture records that since the time of the Exodus until that day, God had not chosen a city out of the tribes of Israel in which to build a temple (1 Kings 8:16). Although David desired to build the temple, God refused to allow him to do so because he was a man of war who had shed blood (1 Chron. 28:3). During his last years, David provided for the building of the temple, with resources to be used from the royal treasury as well as a collection taken from the people of Israel (1 Chron. 29:1–9). After his father's death, Solomon completed the temple primarily through forced labor from the Israelites (1 Kings 5:13–16; 2 Chron. 2:2).

Seventy Years for the Sabbath Rests

The temple stood for almost four hundred years (960 B.C.–586 B.C.) before its destruction due to the idolatry and apostasy of the Jewish people. One of God's ordinances, forsaken by Israel, was the sabbatical rest for the land. Therefore, the land of Israel would be desolate for an equivalent period (seventy years for the seventy Sabbath rests, one every seven years for the four hundred and ninety years the commandment was disobeyed). Jeremiah explained God's judgment, and Daniel (in captivity) studied Jeremiah's writings and prayed for his peoples' promised return and restoration of the temple (Jer. 25:10–12; Dan. 6:10; 9:2–19). God encouraged the Jews in Babylonian captivity by demonstrating to them that the sanctity of the temple and its vessels remained. When Belshazzer used the temple vessels for a libation to pagan gods and to boast of his victory over Jerusalem, God's hand appeared and spelled out Babylon's destruction (Dan. 5). That night the city fell to the Persians, the empire God would use to return the Jews to their land and to rebuild the temple (2 Chron. 36:20–21).[2]

The Second Temple

The prophet Isaiah named Cyrus as the Persian king whom God would use to restore Israel to the land and rebuild the temple.

> It is I who says of Cyrus, "He is My shepherd!
> And he will perform all My desire."
> And he declares of Jerusalem, "She will be built,"
> And of the temple, "Your foundation will be laid."
> (Isaiah 44:28)

Conservative scholars date the writing of Isaiah at 740–680 B.C.[3] Cyrus, king of Persia, conquered Babylon in 538 B.C.[4] thus beginning the fulfillment of Isaiah's prophecy given some 142–202 years earlier. With this conquering of Babylon, Israel's dream of returning to Zion was realized. The proclamation was sent throughout the kingdom:

> Thus says Cyrus king of Persia, "The LORD, the God of heaven, has given me all the kingdoms of the earth, and He has appointed me to build Him a house in Jerusalem, which is in Judah. Whoever there is among you of all His people, may the LORD his God be with him, and let him go up!" (2 Chronicles 36:23)

The royal edict of Cyrus included a specific authorization to rebuild the temple on Mount Zion. The first wave of repatriated exiles—headed by Sheshbazzar, prince of Judah, reportedly a descendant of the Davidic dynasty—were not successful in establishing their position firmly in the desolated land, or in carrying out the great plan for a new exodus. They were barely able to lay the foundation of the temple.[5]

What was intended to centralize the temple and Jewish faith—the concept of the *community of Israel*—resulted in religious and political fragmentation, the antagonism of which led at times to mutual persecution and fratricidal war. Thus, paradoxically, the ideology of a centralized unity led to separatist tendencies, taken to an extreme by the Dead Sea sect.[6]

The significance of the temple in Jewish life in the second temple period is clear from the literature of the period. "It can even be said that the Temple was more important in the Second Temple than in the First Temple times, despite the coexistence of other spiritual matters like study of the Torah and living according to the *Halaka*. The honored role of the Temple in disseminating sanctity even beyond its own confines is evidenced by the fact that the laws of ritual purity were taken over from the Temple into daily life."[7]

Desecration of the Second Temple

Judea fell under the reign of Greek rulers—Alexander the Great, Egyptian Greeks (Ptolemies), and Syrian Greeks (Seleucids)— during this time. Alexander the Great and the Ptolemies treated the Jews favorably by allowing continued governorship by the high priests. Under the Syrian Greek, Antiochus IV (Epiphanes), however, conflict erupted as two Jewish factions, Orthodox and Hellenist, contended for the high priesthood. Antiochus IV sided with the Hellenistic party by appointing a high priest who encouraged pagan worship. This conflict continued, ultimately resulting in an invasion of Jerusalem in 170 B.C., during which many Jews were killed and the temple with its treasures was plundered. Antiochus further desecrated the temple by sacrificing a pig (an unclean animal) on the temple altar and erecting a pagan statue in the Holy of Holies.

Further atrocities against the Jews, including the burning of the Torah, forced consumption of pork, and compulsory sacrifice to pagan idols led to the successful Maccabeen revolt. In 164 B.C., Judas Maccabee liberated Jerusalem, purified the temple, and reinstated the daily offerings. That day has been celebrated ever since as Hanukkah or the Feast of Dedication (John 10:22).[8]

Further desecration came to the temple when the independent rule of Judea ended in 63 B.C. with Roman general Pompey's conquest of Jerusalem. Thousands of Jews threw themselves to the ground before Pompey, pleading with him not to desecrate the Holy Place. This convinced Pompey that the temple contained great riches or some hidden secret. Therefore, he entered the Holy Place, tore away the veil, and invaded the Holy of Holies itself. Roman historian Tacitus recorded the event: "By right of conquest [Pompey] entered their Temple. It is a fact well known, that he found no image, no statue, no symbolical representation of the Deity: the whole presented a naked dome; the sanctuary was unadorned and simple."[9]

Building of a Third Temple

In 37 B.C. Rome appointed a self-made man, a former slave of Edomite ancestry by the name of Herod, to rule over the Jews. The Herod dynasty would last for about one hundred years. In 23 B.C. Herod proposed the massive project of completely rebuilding the second temple of Zerubbabel, which had fallen into a state of disrepair. Because Herod's plans involved the demolition of the temple, the people feared that he would not rebuild it. As a result, Herod was forced to prepare and transport all the stones for the project to the temple mount before touching the temple itself.[10]

Herod's temple surpassed anything ever seen on the temple mount in architectural splendor and majesty. Herod devoted a great deal of attention, time, and effort to redesign, renovate, and redecorate the third temple. Vast quantities of building materials and large numbers of skilled masons and stone cutters were required. According to Josephus, ten thousand of these artisans, including a thousand priests, were put to work, and not fewer than a thousand wagons were manufactured to bring stones from the quarries. Josephus stresses that the temple was built *at the top of the mountain* (*Antiquities* 8:430). The plan as a whole was not completed in Herod's lifetime. Josephus further reports (*Antiquities* 20:219) that the work on the temple mount continued as late as the administration of the Roman procurator Albinus (A.D. 62–64) in the last days before the outbreak of the war with Rome.[11]

Destruction of the Third Temple

The turning point of the Jewish revolt came with the defeat of Jewish field armies by Roman commander and future emperor, Vespasian. In A.D. 69, Vespasian was proclaimed emperor and returned to Rome. He left his son Titus to command Roman troops and continue the war, which was now in its last stages. Titus laid siege to Jerusalem in the spring of A.D. 70, commanding an army of four legions plus auxiliaries, eighty thousand men in all. After capturing the city, Titus seems to have deliberated at length as to whether to preserve the temple or destroy it. According to Josephus, he decided against destroying it. A Roman source, however, asserts that he was in favor of its destruction. Josephus records that the matter was ultimately taken out of Titus's hands by a Roman legionaire, who threw a burning brand into the sanctuary, setting it afire.[12]

When the building burned, it is reported that the decorative gold on the walls melted and ran into the seams between the stones. Afterward, in an attempt to recover the gold, Roman soldiers dismantled the stone walls, resulting in the present ruined condition of the esplanade.[13] Thus was fulfilled the prophecy of Christ that one stone would not be left standing one upon another (Matt. 24:1–2).

On June 7, 1967, another event of profound prophetic significance took place. During the Six-Day Arab-Israeli War, Israel repossessed the temple area in the old city of Jerusalem after almost 1900 years of Gentile possession. The Jewish people now possess the ancient city of Jerusalem, including the temple area, and they are determined that no power on earth will remove them from their homeland.[14]

But Will There Be a Fourth *Future* Temple?

A startling possibility is that one may be living in the generation which will see the rebuilding of the Jerusalem temple, the temple predicted for the tribulation era. The fact is that there are serious intentions among a minority of Jews to rebuild the temple.[15]

As indicated, there have been three temples—Solomon's, Zerubbabel's, and Herod's. Scripture, however, speaks of two future temples that will be built in Jerusalem. Four passages in Scripture prophesy that during the seven-year tribulation a temple will be standing, referred to as the tribulation temple. The other future temple is called the millennial temple.

The Tribulation Temple According to the Prophet Daniel

Daniel 9:26–27 foretells the existence of a tribulation temple:

> *Then after the sixty-two weeks the Messiah will be cut off and have nothing, and the people of the prince who is to come will destroy the city and the sanctuary. And its end will come with a flood; even to the end there will be war; desolations are determined. And he will make a firm covenant with the many for one week, but in the middle of the week he will put a stop to sacrifice and grain offering; and on the wing of abominations will come one who makes desolate, even until a complete destruction, one that is decreed, is poured out on the one who makes desolate.*

These two verses reveal a great deal concerning the tribulation temple. A prince will destroy "the city" and "the sanctuary," and ". . . even to the end there will be war." This same prince will make a firm covenant with Israel for a period of seven years. In the middle of the seven-year period—after three and one half years—the evil prince will put a stop to "sacrifice" and "grain offering" and "on the wing of abominations" will come one who makes desolate, until a complete destruction.

Clearly, the prophet Daniel sees the destruction of "the city" (Jerusalem) and the "the sanctuary" (the temple). . . , and also sees that "sacrifices" and "grain offerings" will be stopped, an act of "abomination" will occur, and ". . . even to the end there will be war" that will end in utter destruction. The evil prince, Antichrist, will be at war to the very end of the period. "Commentators who argue that Antiochus Epiphanes fulfilled this prophecy are at a loss to account for the fact that he destroyed neither the Temple nor the city of Jerusalem, though undoubtedly much damage was done (1 Macc. 1:31, 38)."[16]

For Daniel's prophecy to be fulfilled, a tribulation temple must be standing no later than the midpoint of the great seven-year tribulation detailed in Revelation 6–19.

The Tribulation Temple According to the Lord Jesus Christ

In Matthew 24:15–16, the Lord Jesus Christ confirms Daniel's prophecy concerning a tribulation temple:

> Therefore when you see the abomination of desolation which was spoken of through Daniel the prophet, standing in the holy place (let the reader understand), then let those who are in Judea flee to the mountains.

This passage is part of the Olivet discourse wherein the apostles ask Christ the question (Matt. 24:3), "Tell us, when will these things be, and what *will be* the sign of Your coming, and the end of the age?"

> It is Christ's inspired commentary on what Daniel prophesied and is one of the few places in the Bible where the Holy Spirit apprehends one's attention and says, as it were, that one should read this information with understanding.[17]

According to the Lord Jesus, the "abomination" spoken of by Daniel will take place in the Holy Place. As previously discussed in great detail, the Holy Place is one of two rooms within the sanctuary of the temple proper. The Holy Place and the Holy of Holies together make up the sanctuary of the temple. Only the high priest could enter the Holy of Holies, and then only once a year. The Holy Place is that part of the sanctuary that leads to the inner sanctuary, the Holy of Holies. It is in the Holy Place, according to the Lord, that the "abomination" spoken of by Daniel will take place.

This would be "an immediate sign of the second advent of Christ." The prediction is made that those living in that generation will see standing in the Holy Place the abomination of desolation spoken of by Daniel the prophet ("let the reader understand"). This prophecy obviously could not refer to A.D. 70, as it is to immediately precede the second advent of Christ described in Matthew 24:27–31.[18]

The Tribulation Temple According to the Apostle Paul

The apostle's epistle to the Thessalonians also foretells a tribulation temple.

> Let no one in any way deceive you, for it will not come unless the apostasy comes first, and the man of lawlessness is revealed, the son of destruction, who opposes and exalts himself above every so-called god or object of worship, so that he takes his seat in the temple of God, displaying himself as being God. (2 Thessalonians 2:3–4)

The man of lawlessness—Antichrist, the prince to whom Daniel referred, the son of destruction—exalts himself above every so-called god or object of worship so that "he takes his seat in the temple of God." Antichrist opposes God and all that belongs to God. He will demand to be worshiped by humanity as if he were God. "There are two Greek terms in the New Testament translated temple: ἱερός, which means the whole temple area, and ναός, which indicates the temple building proper. Paul states that the man of sin will go into the ναός, the sanctuary, the temple building, and sit down (one will recall that Christ stated that it would be in the Holy Place), and he will claim to be God, and demand worship of humanity."[19] In this passage, the apostle Paul clearly foretells the future tribulation temple.

The Tribulation Temple According to the Apostle John

In Revelation 11:1–2, the apostle John is instructed to measure the tribulation temple:

> And there was given me a measuring rod like a staff; and someone said, "Rise and measure the temple of God, and the altar,

and those who worship in it. And leave out the court which is
outside the temple, and do not measure it, for it has been given
to the nations; and they will tread under foot the holy city for
forty-two months. "

The largest part of the book of Revelation, chapters 4–19, specifically address the tribulation period. It is in this context that the
apostle is instructed to measure the temple.

Ναός (Temple) refers more specifically to the sanctuary here,
because vs. 2 distinguishes the outer precinct of the temple
complex as something separate from it (Johnson). . . . A determination of what this *sanctuary* or *temple* is has received
extensive attention. Considerable effort has gone into proving this to be a figurative reference to the church. The NT
often calls the church the temple of God (1 Cor. 3:16; 2 Cor.
6:16; Eph. 2:21; 1 Pet. 3:5; cf. 1 Cor. 6:19) (Charles, Swete,
Kiddle, Beasley-Murray, Haily). . . . This figurative interpretation fails for a number of reasons, however. The temple as
the dwelling place of God is not in view here. It is the Jewish
temple in Jerusalem which is hardly a suitable picture of
the church which is largely Gentile (Ladd). Further, the outer
court and the entire city experience trampling by the Gentiles (11:2), signifying that the temple and the court stand
for something that best contrasts with the Gentiles, i.e. something Jewish (ibid.). The mention of the sanctuary, the altar,
the court of the Gentiles, and the holy city shows unmistak-
ably that the discussion at this point is on Jewish ground
(Seiss). But most obvious of all is the logical fallacy that if
the sanctuary represents the church of the Messianic community, who are the worshipers that are measured along
with the sanctuary and the altar? This is an unbearable com-
bining of figurative and literal elements connected only by
kai (*kai*, "and"). The non-literal interpretation is woefully
inconsistent and self-contradictory. In addition, this figurative explanation results in a hopeless effort to identity the
outer court and the holy city in 11:2.

The only way out of this entanglement of internal contra-
dictions is to understand this as a literal temple that will
exist in actuality during the future period just before Christ
returns. The false messiah will desecrate it and turn it into a
place for people to worship him (cf. Dan. 9:27; 12:11; 2 Thess.

2:4; Rev. 13:14–15) (Walvoord). This allows for a distinction between the temple and the worshipers in it (Bullinger). Jesus' anticipation of the future abomination of desolation (Matt. 24:15) and Paul's prophecy regarding a future temple (2 Thess. 2:4) require a literal temple in the future (Bullinger, Smith). . . . This requires a re-institution of the national life of this people, including its temple.[20]

The Fifth Temple (The Millennial Temple)

The word *millennium* means "a thousand years." While the word never occurs in the Bible, it refers to the thousand years mentioned six times in Revelation 20. Jews and Christians often identify this period of one thousand years with the many promises in the Old Testament. Those promises speak of a coming kingdom of righteousness and peace on the earth in which the Jews would be leaders and in which all the nations would have great blessing, both spiritual and economic.[21] The Millennium is defined as the literal, one-thousand-year reign of the Lord Jesus Christ on earth beginning with His second advent (Rev. 20).

Symbolic or Literal?

A large portion of Ezekiel's prophecy (40:1–46:24) is devoted to the millennial temple—its structure, its priesthood, its ritual, and its ministry.[22] Some view these chapters in Ezekiel's prophecy to have been fulfilled by the return of the remnant from Babylon. Arno C. Gaebelein refutes this nonliteral view:

> The temple which the remnant built does in no way whatever correspond with the magnificent structure which Ezekiel beheld in his vision. The fact is, if this temple is a literal building (as it assuredly is) it has never yet been erected. Furthermore, it is distinctly stated that the glory of the Lord returned to the temple and made His dwelling place there, the same glory which Ezekiel had seen departing from the temple and from Jerusalem. But the glory did not return to the second temple. No glory filled that house. And furthermore no high priest is mentioned in the worship of the temple Ezekiel describes, but the Jews after their return from Babylon had high priests again. Nor can the stream of healing waters flowing from the temple as seen by Ezekiel be in any way applied to the restoration from the Babylonian captivity.[23]

Others hold one of three alternate views offered by Taylor: the millennial temple (1) symbolizes the church, (2) is literal, (3) symbolically embodies the future age.[24] Taylor notes that older commentators interpret this passage as symbolically representing the Christian church, a view exemplified in John Gill's commentary published in London, 1809:

> Many Christian commentators have omitted the exposition of these chapters; and all acknowledge the difficulties in them. Something however may be got out of them, relating to the Gospel, and Gospel church-state, which I am persuaded is intended by the city and the temple; for that no material building can be designed is clear from this one observation; that not only the whole land of Israel would not be capable of having such a city as is here described built upon it, but even all Europe would not be sufficient; nor the whole world, according to the account of the dimensions which some give of it. The circumference of the city is said to be about eighteen thousand measures, ch. xiviii. 35, but what they are is not certain. Luther makes them to be thirty-six thousand German miles; and a German mile being three of ours, the circuit of this city must be above a hundred thousand English miles; and this is sufficient to set aside all hypothesis of a material building, either of city or temple, the one being in proportion to the other.[25]

Taylor assigns some credibility to this view based on his conclusion that the New Jerusalem in Revelation is based largely on Ezekiel's pattern. Nathaniel West, however, in his classic work, *The Thousand Year Reign of Christ,* soundly refutes the idea that Ezekiel's temple belongs to the New Jerusalem and the new earth.[26] Taylor notes the shortcomings of spiritualizing the text:

> . . . It is overstating the case to refer Ezekiel's vision *directly* to a Christian "fulfillment" [the church], without seeing that it has a real context for the readers of his own day, and this original context must be the prime concern of the Old Testament exegete.[27]

While Taylor acknowledges that spiritualizing the text has problems, he rejects the literal interpretation because of Ezekiel's millennial sacrifices (which I will later address). Taylor offers his own spiritualized interpretation:

> The fourth view is to regard these chapters, not as prophecy, but as apocalyptic, and to interpret them according to the canons of this style of Hebrew writing. Its features are symbolism, numerical symmetry, and futurism. . . . This was Ezekiel's pattern for the Messianic age that was to come. It lay in the future, and yet it grew out of the present. It was expressed in tangible terms and yet these were merely the forms in which the general principles of God's activity were enshrined. The vision of the temple was in fact a kind of incarnation of all that God stood for and all that He required and all that He could do for His people in the age that was about to dawn. On this view, which of all the interpretations seems to take the most realistic view of the literary character of the material with which we are dealing, the message of Ezekiel in these chapters may be summarized as follows:
>
> (a) the perfection of God's plan for His restored people, symbolically expressed in the immaculate symmetry of the temple building;
> (b) the centrality of worship in the new age, its importance being expressed in the scrupulous concern for detail in the observance of its rites;
> (c) the abiding presence of the Lord in the midst of His people;
> (d) the blessings that will flow from God's presence to the barren places of the earth (the river of life);
> (e) the orderly allocation of duties and privileges to all God's people, as shown both in temple duties and in the apportionment of the land (a theme taken in Rev. 7:4–8).[28]

Taylor's interpretation, too, is allegorical in that he takes common, literal terms and assigns to them symbolic meaning not found in or suggested by the text. A careful consideration, then, reveals that the only difference between Taylor's spiritualizing of the text and the spiritualized interpretation that applies this passage to the church (which he rejects) is that Taylor implies an inclusion of the historical Jew. But the church does include Jewish Christians, so those who apply this text to the church will argue their view does in fact offer meaning to the Jewish readers of Ezekiel's day.

Millennial Temple Sacrifices

Paul Lee Tan discusses the millennial temple sacrifices, noting that in Ezekiel chapters 43 to 46 we are given a detailed account of sacrifices and offerings inside the millennial temple. If one interprets Ezekiel's prophecy with a normal reading, it cannot be denied that there will be animal sacrifices during the Millennium.

But if interpreters accept the millennial sacrifices, they face a barrage of ridicule. They are reminded of the New Testament teaching that Christ's one sacrifice on the cross forever superseded the Levitical sacrifices. "It is one of the plainest universal teachings of the New Testament," states Snowden, "that the sacrifices of the Mosaic economy were fulfilled in Christ and were then done away as vanishing shadows."[29] And Archibald Hughes is sarcastic: "To restore all these today, under the New Covenant, would be apostasy. But, in a millennium, under the same New Covenant, it is supposed to be according to prophecy!"[30]

The following observations, however, provide an adequate reply on the issue of the millennial sacrifices:

First, the interpreter who rejects the millennial sacrifices usually also rejects the millennial kingdom. This rejection of an earthly kingdom always goes hand in hand with the rejection of the literal approach to prophecy. Conversely, once the literal approach is upheld, the millennial sacrifices shine under a new light and appear quite logical. As nonliteral interpreter Lorraine Boettner puts it quite aptly, "Only to a literalist does the re-establishment of the sacrificial system and temple ritual seem sensible. To a Post or Amillennialist it is too materialistic."[31]

Second, millennial sacrifices are predicted not only by Ezekiel but also by the Old Testament prophets Isaiah (56:6–7; 60:7), Zechariah (14:16–21), and Jeremiah (33:15–18). In fact, Jeremiah discusses the millennial sacrifices under the context of the Davidic covenant, and so places the sacrifices on a much stronger basis than does Ezekiel.

In the New Testament, Christ Himself certainly foresees the reinstitution of Jewish ritualism when He urges tribulation saints to "pray that your flight be not in the winter, neither on the Sabbath day" (Matt. 24:20), for Jewish ritualistic travel regulations would hinder escape on the Sabbath. Moreover, the abomination of desolation is predicted to stand in the temple (Matt. 24:15, "the holy place") during the Tribulation. The apostle Paul describes the tribulation's Man of Sin as one who "sitteth in the temple of God" (2 Thess. 2:4).

Third, animal sacrifices—whether in the Old Testament, in the present dispensation, or in the kingdom age—can *never* take away sin (cf. Heb. 10:4). The blood of animals is never divinely intended to be efficacious or expiatory for salvation (cf. Heb. 10:1–2). McClain says, "No animal sacrifice in the Bible has ever had any expiatory significance."[32] Yet many nonliteral interpreters say that sacrifices offered during Old Testament times were efficacious. Oswald T. Allis, for instance, affirms that Old Testament sacrifices "were expiatory [and] efficacious in the days of Moses and of David."[33]

By affirming that Old Testament sacrifices were efficacious, amillennialists think that they are able to back premillennialists into a corner, for the latter believe that the millennial sacrifices will be the restoration (albeit in more glorious forms and with fullest significance) of Old Testament sacrifices. Since amillennialists claim that the Old Testament sacrifices were efficacious, then the restored millennial sacrifices would be efficacious too, a state of affairs that would blatantly contradict and minimize the sacrifice that Christ made on the cross. In affirming the efficacious character of Old Testament sacrifices, however, amillennialists themselves minimize the Cross; for if animal sacrifices were really efficacious during Old Testament days, there would have been no necessity for the cross of Christ.

In truth, Old Testament sacrifices served to cover over sins until the cross of Christ, which once and for all perfected the saints. The sacrifice on the cross is the theme of the book of Hebrews, which is addressed to a congregation then made up mostly of Jewish converts who had a tendency to slip back into former practices. The book argues that Christians have no more use for animal sacrifices now that Christ has already come, and that the sin question has been settled by virtue of the death of Christ.

Fourth, while the need for animal sacrifices was nullified by the Cross, there is no reason why some *reminders* of Christ's perfect and final sacrifice should not be allowed, both during the present church age and the millennial age.

During the present age, we have actually been given a reminder of Christ's sacrifice in the bread and wine of the Lord's Supper. Christ commands His disciples to partake "in remembrance of Me" (Luke 22:19). The apostle Paul tells the Corinthian believers that the Lord's Supper is intended to "proclaim the Lord's death until He comes" (1 Cor. 11:26). Why "until He comes"? Because Christians will be in the immortal, resurrected state when the Lord comes again, and they will then need no outward memorials to remind them of the awful sacrifice of Christ on the cross.

But there will be non-resurrected inhabitants of the Millennium who will need *visible* reminders of Christ's sacrifice for them on the cross. According to prophecy, God has chosen to use the millennial sacrifices as reminders of Christ's sacrifice for those mortals in the kingdom.[34] "If the all important subject of converse on the Mount of Transfiguration was 'His decease' which He was to accomplish at Jerusalem, how much more will the merits and benefits of His death be the all-engrossing subject of discussion in that day. . . ."[35]

While engrossing discussion may characterize remembrances of an actual *person*, commemoration does not always apply to the person's works and deeds. As stamps, coins, plaques, etc. bear the names and portraits of *living* personages in commemoration of their works and services, so animal sacrifices may serve the same purpose in regard to the Savior.

Fifth, while the millennial sacrifices will commemorate and be reminders of the sacrifice of Christ, they will not be purely memorial in nature. They will relate to life under the theocracy as well, because in a real sense, the millennial kingdom will be the Jewish theocracy restored. Under the Old Testament economy, sacrifices were brought by the worshiper for two reasons: (1) because of the consciousness or "remembrance" of sin (cf. Heb. 10:3), and (2) for theocratic adjustments. Since Old Testament individuals were corporately related to the theocracy, sins committed by individuals so related would affect their relationship to the theocracy. But as long as the offerings were made, reconciliation and theocratic adjustments were possible. Those who did not participate in the sacrifices were "cut off" from the congregation.

Because of the restoration of the theocracy at the Millennium, the Old Testament theocratic arrangements will remain largely in effect.[36] Just as the sacrifices in the Old Testament serve to effect theocratic adjustments for the offender, the millennial sacrifices will also "make atonement for the house of Israel" (Ezek. 45:17; cf. 44:29), and it will be what God will gladly accept (Ezek. 43:27).

In regard to Ezekiel's temple sacrifices being a commemoration, amillennial interpreters like to cite Ezekiel 44:9:

> *No foreigner, uncircumcised in heart and uncircumcised in flesh, of all the foreigners who are among the sons of Israel, shall enter My sanctuary.*

"And what," they ask, "do our premillennial friends suggest that circumcision would commemorate?"[37]

In reply, it must be noted that during Old Testament days, non-Jews were not barred from participation in the worship of Jehovah; foreigners or non-Jews were allowed to present their offerings in the house of the Lord (cf. Lev. 17:10, 12; Num. 15:14). In the text of Ezekiel cited above, however, the prophet addresses the sacrilegious and unauthorized practice of foreigners officiating in the sanctuary. Although such infringements were probably winked at during the time of Ezekiel (cf. Ezek. 44:7), the prophet predicts that the practice would be strictly banned in the millennial temple (Ezek. 44:9). Only those who are circumcised in heart and flesh may officiate in the millennial temple.[38]

The purpose of the rule of circumcision is to preserve the sanctity of worship in the Millennium and to grant a central position to the chosen people of God inside the millennial temple. The rule thus has practical significance, and to force upon it an obscure interpretation is gratuitous.

The Centrality of the Millennial Temple

The Millennial Temple Will Be the World Center of Worship

The temple is seen as the center of world renewal, drawing all nations and people to the Jewish people and to worship God (Zech. 8:23; 14:16).

> Thus says the LORD of hosts, "In those days ten men from the nations . . . will grasp the garment of a Jew saying, 'Let us go with you, for we have heard that God is with you.'" (Zechariah 8:23)

Zechariah declares ten men will desire to accompany each Jew and so find God. The number ten is used regularly in the Bible as the number of completeness (e.g., Gen. 31:7; Lev. 26:26; Ruth 4:2; 1 Sam. 1:8; Jer. 41:8). Ten men accompanying each Jew represents thousands of thousands, and they will come from all nations of the world. The intensity of their desire for God is indicated by the verb take hold of. Their eagerness demonstrates their faith. Ezekiel saw all the nations recognizing the Lord as God (Ezek. 36:23) when, through renewed Israel, He vindicates His holiness. "The prophecy teaches, then that Israel will be the means of drawing the nations of the Earth to the Lord in time of Messiah's reign upon earth."[39] The temple is the world center of worship, because that is where the Lord Jesus Christ and the *Shekinah* presence of God will be.

> *Then it will come about that any who are left of all the nations that went against Jerusalem will go up from year to year to worship the King, the LORD of hosts, and to celebrate the Feast of Booths. (Zechariah 14:16)*

The Eternal Temple

Following the Millennium is the eternal state described in Revelation 21:1–22:7. Thomas refers to that state as "the future bliss of the saints."[40] Walvoord and Pentecost both refer to this passage from Revelation as "the eternal state."[41]

Conclusion

From eternity to eternity, God's temple has been central in the affairs of Israel and the nations. Moses was given blueprints of the tabernacle. From the pattern of the tabernacle, Solomon built the great temple. The historical centrality of the temple of God in the first two temple periods is a matter of historical record. Even when the physical temple (of the first two temple periods) was destroyed, its centrality did not diminish. It was then and is today the unifying hope of Israel and the scorn of unbelievers. The third temple, the tribulation temple, will be constructed. It will become the focus of the world before the second advent of the Lord Jesus Christ. The temple of God will be central in the eschatological affairs of God, Israel, and the nations in the millennial kingdom. In the eternal state, God is the Temple, filling the new Jerusalem, a perfect cube as seen in the earthly temples of God.

This chapter was adapted from Ron Johnson, "The Centrality of the Jewish Temple in the Affairs of God, Israel, and the Nations—Part I," *The Conservative Theological Journal* 1, no. 1 (April 1997): 61–84; idem, "The Centrality of the Jewish Temple in the Affairs of God, Israel, and the Nations—Part II," *The Conservative Theological Journal* 1, no. 2 (August 1997): 119–39; and Paul Lee Tan, "The Millennial Sacrifices," in *The Interpretation of Prophecy* (Dallas, Tex.: Bible Communications, 1974), 293–98.

A Comparison of Views
Between Covenant Theology
and Dispensational Theology

Looking at crucial passages of Scripture and comparing how covenant theologians and dispensational scholars view them, one can determine which view is more faithful to the clear and normal reading of the verses, and which gravitates to a superficial and artificial theological mind-set that will cloud the meaning of the passages. (Since the orthodox rabbis generally held to literal interpretation, sometimes their views will also be quoted.) By making this comparison, common sense will be able to distinguish more quickly a faulty and inconsistent approach to hermeneutics.

There are, of course, degrees of opinion among both covenant and dispensational theologians as to how to interpret various key passages. Thus, it could be concluded that the following quotes and comparisons are not fully representative of the teachings of the two views. It is hoped, however, that this initial comparison will inspire an examination of other commentaries and theological texts in order to truly understand the approaches to doctrine taken by the two schools of thought.

The "Covenant of Works"

. . . but from the tree of the knowledge of good and evil you [Adam] shall not eat, for in the day that you eat from it you shall surely die. (Genesis 2:17)

Rabbinical View

Unlike the beast, man has also a spiritual life, which demands the subordination of man's desires to the law of God.

The will of God revealed in His Law is the one eternal and unfailing guide as to what constitutes good and evil—and not man's instincts, or even his Reason, which in the hour of temptation often call light darkness and darkness light.[1]

Covenant View

It must be admitted that the term "covenant" is not found in the first three chapters of Genesis, but this is not tantamount to saying that they do not contain the necessary data for the construction of a doctrine of the covenant. . . . It may still be objected that we do not read of the two parties as coming to an agreement, nor of Adam as accepting the terms laid down, but this is not an insuperable objection. . . . There may still be some doubt as to the propriety of the name "Covenant of Works," but there can be no valid objection to the covenant idea.[2]

Dispensational View

As with all God's subsequent commandments, there were positive blessings and negative prohibitions. All earthly goods and pleasures were at man's disposal, except this one tree which was forbidden. . . . Man could eat freely from all the other fruit, but if he ate from the forbidden tree he would surely die.[3]

[Adam] was actually the first man, and his experience took place literally, exactly as described. He and Eve alone, of course, entered the world by creation, rather than by birth; and they alone entered the world with sinless natures, in perfect innocence. . . . Seeing so much evidence of God's love, Adam should naturally assume that any instruction coming from God would likewise evidence His love, and therefore willingly obey it. Thus the one restriction placed by God on Adam (and, a bit later, on Eve) was singularly appropriate for its purpose. There was every reason (based on love, not fear) for man to conform to God's command, and no reason to disobey. If he did disobey, he would be without excuse.[4]

The Protoevangel

And I will put enmity between you [the serpent] and the woman, and between your seed and her seed; he [the Messiah] shall bruise you on the head, and you shall bruise him on the heel. (Genesis 3:15)

Covenant View

The first revelation of the covenant [of grace] is found in the protoevangel, Gen. 3:15. Some deny that this has any reference to the covenant; and it certainly does not refer to any formal establishment of a covenant. The revelation of such an establishment could only follow after the covenant idea had been developed in history. At the same time Gen. 3:15 certainly contains a revelation of the essence of the covenant.[5]

Up to the time of Abraham there was no formal establishment of the covenant of grace. While Gen. 3:15 already contains the elements of this covenant, it does not record a formal transaction by which the covenant was established. It does not even speak explicitly of a covenant.[6]

Dispensational View

God also made gracious provisions. Mankind will die and not live forever in this chaotic state, and children will be born (v. 16) so that the human race will endure and continue. Ultimate victory will come through Christ, the Seed (Gal. 3:16) of the woman (cf. Gal. 4:4, "born of a woman").[7]

The Abrahamic Covenant

Now the LORD said to Abram, "Go forth from your country, and from your relatives and from your father's house, to the land which I will show you; and I will make you a great nation, and I will bless you, and make your name great; and so you shall be a blessing; and I will bless those who bless you, and the one who curses you I will curse, and in you all the families of the earth shall be blessed." (Genesis 12:1–3)

On that day the LORD made a covenant with Abram, saying, "To your descendants I have given this land, from the river of Egypt as far as the great river, the river Euphrates." (Genesis 15:18)

Rabbinical View

Through [Abraham], all men were to be taught the existence of the Most High God, and the love of righteousness, thereby opening for themselves the same treasury of blessings which

he enjoyed. The germ of the idea underlying the fuller conception of a messianic Age was in existence from the time of
the founders of the race of Israel. "In thy seed shall all the
families of the earth be blessed," was the promise given both
to Abraham and Isaac.[8]

Covenant View

The establishment of the covenant [of grace] with Abraham
marked the beginning of an institutional Church. . . . In view
of this establishment of the covenant of grace with Abraham,
he is sometimes considered as the head of the covenant of
grace.[9]

Dispensational View

. . . if the [Abrahamic] covenant promised Israel "permanent existence as a nation," then there must be a future for
Israel and "the Church is not fulfilling Israel's promises."
Second, if the covenant promised Israel "permanent possession of the promised land," then in the future Israel must
possess all of the Promised Land, "for she has never fully
possessed it in her history," and it is not now being fulfilled
in some spiritual way by the Church.[10]

Premillennialism insists that all the provisions of the
Abrahamic Covenant must be fulfilled since the covenant
was made without conditions. Much of the covenant has
already been fulfilled and fulfilled literally; therefore, what
remains to be fulfilled will also be fulfilled literally. This
brings the focus on the yet-unfulfilled land promise. Though
the nation Israel occupied part of the territory promised in
the covenant, she has never yet occupied all of it and certainly not eternally as the covenant promised. Therefore,
there must be a time in the future when Israel will do so,
and for the premillennialist this will be in the coming
millennial kingdom. Thus the Abrahamic Covenant gives
strong support for premillennial eschatology.[11]

The Regathering Back to The Land

. . . then the LORD your God will restore you from captivity,
and have compassion on you, and will gather you again from
all the peoples where the LORD your God has scattered you.
(Deuteronomy 30:3)

Rabbinical View

Punishment is not God's last word unto Israel. If Israel seeks God, Israel will find mercy at the hands of the Lord, and be brought back to the Land of his fathers. . . . [God] will change thy fortune, restore thee to thy former happy state. . . . The Talmud renders it, "And the Lord thy God will return with thy captivity." . . . Though the Israelites be scattered to the four winds of heaven, yet will God reunite them in the Land of the Fathers, and work in Israel a change of heart.[12]

Covenant View

In full analogy with the scheme of prophecy we may add that the return from the Babylonian Captivity has not exhausted their depth. The New Testament takes up the strain (e.g. in Rom. xi.), and foretells the restoration of Israel to the covenanted mercies of God. . . . But whether the general conversion of the Jews shall be accompanied with any "national" restoration, as the chosen people; and further, whether there shall be any local replacement of them in the land of their fathers, may be regarded as of "the secret things" which belong unto God ([Deut.] xxix. 29).[13]

Dispensational View

[This regathering] still awaits realization in any literal sense (cf. Hag. 2:6–9; Zech. 8:1–8; 10:8–12). . . . Israel's restoration to full covenant blessing was described by Jeremiah and Ezekiel as the engraving of the covenant stipulations upon the fleshly tablets of the heart. In the last days, Jeremiah said, the Lord will make a "new covenant with the house of Israel and with the house of Judah," one whose statutes will be put "in their minds" and written "on their hearts." The result will be that he will be their God and they will be his people (Jer. 31:31–33). Ezekiel spoke of this hope as the giving of a new heart and spirit following the return to the land, a return to be marked by prosperity and abundance for the nation (Ezek. 36:24–30). . . . The issue was not whether Israel and/or the Lord would do thus and so but when. Such lack of qualification requires that all of the blessings of restoration promised to Israel be seen as acts of divine initiative and grace, ones reserved for eschatological times and embracing the nation as such.[14]

The Messianic Reign

There will be no end to the increase of His government or of peace, on the throne of David and over his kingdom, to establish it and to uphold it with justice and righteousness from then on and forevermore. The zeal of the LORD of hosts will accomplish this. (Isaiah 9:7)

Rabbinical View

When in God's own good time, the End of Days finally arrives and the Messiah appears, the lore of centuries knows and recounts in remarkable detail what will happen—until the moment, that is, that he ascends the throne of his father David in Jerusalem. The wars, the victories, the resurrection, the ingathering, the judgment, the rebuilding of the Temple—all this is detailed in many sources.[15]

Covenant View

When it is said that he would sit upon the throne of David, it is not to be taken literally. The peculiarity of the reign of David was that he reigned over the people of God. . . . To sit upon the throne of David, therefore, means to reign over the people of God; and in this sense the Messiah sat on his throne. . . . "And upon his kingdom." That is, over the kingdom of the people of God. It does not mean particularly the Jews.

If Jehovah feels this zeal [of establishing the kingdom], and if he will certainly accomplish this, then Christians should be encouraged in their efforts to spread the gospel.[16]

Dispensational View

The Messiah will be the exalted, crucified, risen, glorified Head at His second advent to establish the earthly Kingdom over Israel . . . His government will be perennially prosperous and peaceful. His rule as Prince of Peace will be universal in the earth and perpetual—the millennial Kingdom ultimately merging into the eternal Kingdom . . . He will reign as David's Son (humanity) and Lord (Deity), as the divine-human Redeemer and "King of kings, and Lord of lords" (Rev. 19:16; 20:4–6) in fulfillment of the Davidic Covenant.[17]

The New Covenant

"Behold, days are coming," declares the LORD, "when I will make a new covenant with the house of Israel and with the

*house of Judah, not like the covenant which I made with their
fathers in the day I took them by the hand to bring them out of
the land of Egypt, My covenant which they broke, although I
was a husband to them," declares the Lord. "But this is the
covenant which I will make with the house of Israel after those
days," declares the LORD, . . . "I will put My law within them,
and on their heart I will write it; and I will be their God, and
they shall be My people." (Jeremiah 31:31–33)*

*"If this fixed order [of sun and moon] departs from before Me,"
declares the LORD, "then the offspring of Israel also shall cease
from being a nation before Me forever." (Jeremiah 31:36)*

Rabbinical View

When they return from exile God will make a new covenant
with Israel which, unlike the old, will be permanent, because
it will be inscribed on their hearts. . . . The prophet . . . makes
the assertion that unlike the past, Israel will henceforth remain faithful to God, while He in turn will never reject them.
. . . Permanence is the essence of the new covenant.[18]

Covenant View

Necessarily therefore the Mosaic Church was temporary, but
the sanctions of Jeremiah's Church are spiritual—written in
the heart—and therefore it must take the place of the former
Covenant (Heb. viii.13), and must last for ever. The prophecy was fulfilled when those Jews who accepted Jesus of
Nazareth as the Messiah, expanded the Jewish into the Christian Church. . . . In Matt. xxviii. 19, 20 Jeremiah's prophecy
receives its Christian application, and Israel becomes the
Church, with the promise of perpetual existence.[19]

Dispensational View

[The new covenant] is to be made with the whole united
Israelite nation (Israel and Judah), not with the Christian
church, except secondarily and as grafted into the stock of
spiritual privilege (Rom. 11:16–27). This is evident from the
fact that the context (Jer. 31–32) is strictly the restoration of
the literal nation Israel. . . . [The new covenant] stands in
contrast to the (old) Mosaic Covenant (33–34). It is based
upon the full atonement to be secured by Christ's death, even-
tuating in forgiveness of sins (Zech. 12:10–13:1). . . . Although

an earnest of that salvation is mediated to the church (see Heb. 8:7–13), the promise here to Israel is national and universal and to be effected by a phenomenal outpouring of the Spirit upon the restored nation at the beginning of the Kingdom age.[20]

The Prophecy of the Spirit
Coming upon Regathered Israel

For I will take you [Israel] from the nations, gather you from the lands, and bring you into your own land. Then I will [slosh] clean water on you, and you will be clean; I will cleanse you from all your filthiness and from all your idols. Moreover, I will give you a new heart and put a new spirit within you; and I will remove the heart of stone from your flesh and give you a heart of flesh. And I will put My Spirit within you. (Ezekiel 36:24–27a)

Rabbinical View

Since Israel's evil ways were compared to the uncleanness of a woman in her impurity (verse 17), the forgiveness of [Israel's] sins is characterized as purification by cleansing water. . . . "My spirit." i.e. the [H]oly [S]pirit of God. . . . By restoring the exiled Israelites to their homeland, that will be a demonstration that the captivity was not the effect of God's weakness. . . . As the consequence of spiritual regeneration, Israel will remain in possession of the land (cf. xxviii. 25, xxxvii. 25). . . . The nation's tendency to lapse into sin will be overcome by the power of the new spirit [i.e., the Holy Spirit].[21]

Covenant View

The dispersion [of Israel] yet continues, the reunion will be in those days when Israel shall be gathered into the Church of God. . . . As Israel throughout the prophecy of Ezekiel prefigures the visible Church of Christ, needing from time to time trial or purification—so does the renovated Israel represent Christ's mystical Church (Eph. v. 26).[22]

Dispensational View

Whenever the Old Testament prophets spoke about the new covenant, they viewed it as something yet future. . . . The fulfilling of this covenant was inseparably tied to Israel's future restoration back to the land (Ezek. 36:24–25; 37:11–14).

The nation has never experienced this promised restoration to the land (the Palestinian covenant) and therefore has not experienced their spiritual restoration as a nation.[23]

Israel will be regathered from her present worldwide Diaspora to her homeland. . . . Israel will be forgiven her sin and receive inner cleansing. "Then will I sprinkle [slosh] clean water upon you, and ye shall be clean." . . . [The passage] points to the sacrifice of Christ applied by faith to the heart . . . , which in that day will be a reality, accomplished by Christ at His first advent and applied to the nation Israel at His second advent . . . The forgiveness and cleansing will be deep and thorough, from all of Israel's filthiness and idolatry. . . . Spiritual regeneration will result in "a new heart" . . . and "a new spirit," that is, taking away the "stony heart" . . . and giving "an heart of flesh." . . . The Spirit will indwell [the redeemed Jews]. "I will put my Spirit within you . . . as an abiding presence to enable Israelites in the Millennium to 'walk in' . . . God's Word."[24]

Daniel's Seventy Weeks Prophecy

[Author's note: After Daniel relates his seventy-week vision (which represents 490 years), he omits one week in his calculation as a period yet to be fulfilled. That one week represents a seven-year period that seems to clearly correspond with the seven-year tribulation period described in the book of Revelation. In other words, God's countdown in His dealing with Israel is presently stopped as He now reaches the world with the gospel during this dispensation of grace. He will begin anew His work with Israel when the "prince," the Antichrist (Dan. 9:26), makes a covenant with the Jews for one week (a seven-year "peace" covenant, v. 27). Dispensationalists believe the period of the Antichrist's covenant will be the tribulation. Only limited space can be given to this issue here.]

Seventy weeks have been decreed for your people and your holy city, to finish the transgression, to make an end of sin, to make atonement for iniquity, to bring in everlasting righteousness, to seal up vision and prophecy, and to anoint the most holy place. So you are to know and discern that from the issuing of a decree to restore and rebuild Jerusalem until Messiah the Prince there will be seven weeks and sixty-two weeks [69 weeks = 483 years]. (Daniel 9:24–25)

Covenant View

And he [the prince of v. 26] will make a firm covenant with the many for one week [seven years]. (Daniel 9:27)

The meaning of the expression here cannot be mistaken, that during the time specified, "he" (whoever may be referred to) would, for "one week"—pursue such a course as would tend to establish the true religion; to render it more stable and firm; to give it higher sanctions in the approbation of the "many," and to bring it to bear more decidedly and powerfully on the heart. Whether this would be by some law enacted in its favour; or by protection extended over the nation; or by present example; or by instruction; or by some work of a new kind, and new influences which he would set forth, is not mentioned.[25]

. . . but in the middle of the week [three and a half years] he will put a stop to sacrifice and grain offering. (Daniel 9:27b)

The word "he," in this place, refers to the Messiah, if the interpretation of the former part of the verse is correct, for there can be no doubt that it is the same person who is mentioned in the phrase "he shall confirm the covenant with many." . . . So far as the Divine intention in the appointment of these sacrifices and offerings was concerned, they ceased at the death of Christ—in the middle of the "week."[26]

Dispensational View

It is far more plausible to see the sixty-nine weeks fulfilled historically and the seventieth week as yet unfulfilled. The reasons are as follows: First, to view the six things in Daniel 9:24—to finish the transgressions, to make an end of sin, to make atonement for iniquity, to bring in everlasting righteousness, to seal up vision and prophecy, and to anoint the most holy place—as having been fulfilled in Christ's death at His first advent is impossible. All these have reference to the nation of Israel and none of these has been fulfilled to that nation. Israel has not yet finished her transgression, nor been purged of her iniquity. Nor has she experienced the everlasting righteousness promised her. Paul sees this still in the future for Israel (Rom. 11:25–27). . . . The person who confirms the covenant in Daniel 9:27 cannot refer to

Christ. (1) The nearest antecedent is "the prince who is to come," in verse 26. (2) At no time in Christ's ministry did He confirm an already-existing covenant. . . . The abomination of desolation has not yet been fulfilled. In Matthew 24:15 Jesus said that it would occur after His ministry on earth. He spoke of the appearance of the abomination of desolation in the Jerusalem temple as a signal of the great tribulation which is immediately followed by Christ's second advent. It is true that Jerusalem suffered destruction in A.D. 66–70 but Christ did not return in A.D. 70. In fact, the book of Revelation speaks of Jerusalem's desolation as yet future and not as having been fulfilled nearly a quarter century before its composition. . . . The seventieth week (the final seven years) is yet to be fulfilled. The sixty-nine weeks have been fulfilled.[27]

The Birth of the Messiah

And behold, you [Mary] will conceive in your womb, and bear a son, and you shall name Him Jesus. He will be great, and will be called the Son of the Most High; and the Lord God will give Him the throne of His father David; and He will reign over the house of Jacob forever; and His kingdom will have no end. (Luke 1:31–33)

Covenant View

It should be unnecessary to state that according to our Lord's own explanation it is not an earthly or political kingdom that is in view here, but rather the kingdom or rule of grace and truth established in the hearts and lives of all those who have the God of Jacob as their refuge (Ps. 46:7, 11).[28]

. . . the apparent promise is that of a kingdom restored to Israel such as the disciples expected even after the Resurrection (Acts i. 6). It needed to be interpreted by events before men could see that it was fulfilled in the history of Christendom as the true Israel of God.[29]

Dispensational View

Jesus, as David's descendant, will sit on David's throne when He reigns in the Millennium (2 Sam. 7:16; Ps. 89:3–4, 28–29). . . . Jesus' reign over the nation Israel as her King will begin in the Millennium and continue on into the eternal state. . . . Mary would have understood that the angel was speaking to

her of the Messiah who had been promised for so long. . . .
Mary did not seem surprised that the Messiah was to come.
Rather, she was surprised that she would be His mother since
she was a virgin (lit., "since I do not know a man").[30]

The Throne of the Son of Man

*And Jesus said to [His disciples], "Truly I say to you, that you
who have followed Me, in the regeneration when the Son of
Man will sit on His glorious throne, you also shall sit upon
twelve thrones, judging the twelve tribes of Israel." (Matthew
19:28)*

Covenant View

What is meant by these "twelve tribes of Israel"? In all prob-
ability the term refers to the restored new Israel. Whether,
as such, it indicated the total number of the elect gathered
out of the twelve tribes of the Jews from the beginning to
the end of the world's history (cf. Rom. 11:26), or even all
the chosen ones of both the Jews and the Gentiles (cf. Gal.
6:16), in either case it must refer to those who have been
regenerated.[31]

Dispensational View

The twelve disciples will govern the twelve tribes of Israel in
the messianic kingdom. This is not allegory or parable or
symbolism but a promise of future reward for faithful ser-
vice. Barnes attempts to relegate this promise only to an
honorable title, but his understanding flows from a theological bent away from an actual millennial kingdom rather
than from any normative interpretation of the text.[32]

The Gathering of the Elect into the Kingdom

*[The Son of Man] will send forth His angels with a great trum-
pet and they will gather together His elect from the four winds,
from one end of the sky to the other. (Matthew 24:31)*

Rabbinical View

[The dead of Israel] will rise from the dust and each man will
recognize his fellow man, [and so will] husband and wife,
father and son, brother and brother. All will come to the Messiah from the four corners of the earth, from east and from
west, from north and from south. The Children of Israel will

fly on the wings of eagles and come to the Messiah. . . . And the Temple will appear as Ezekiel prophesied it.[33]

Covenant View

It is not certain, however, that [Christ meant this gathering] would be literally so, but it may be designed only to denote the certainty that the world would be assembled together. . . . Elect. The word means Christians—the chosen of God.[34]

Dispensational View

When He comes the King will send forth His angels to re-gather His people Israel from the extremities of the earth. Many expositors take this to be a reference not to Israel but to the gathering of the church. For several important reasons it is evident that the faithful of Israel are in view. . . . When He comes again, the believing remnant of Israel will be regathered from the corners of the earth to be placed in the land. This is prophesied clearly in the Old Testament (Jeremiah 16:14–15; Isaiah 11:11–16; 27:13). . . . Such terms as the gospel of the kingdom (24:14), the holy place (24:15), the Sabbath (24:20), and the Messiah (24:23–24) indicate that Israel as a nation is in view. . . . The discourse relates to the end time described in Daniel's prophecy of the seventy weeks (Matthew 24:15). Finally, the church cannot be in view since it will not go through the tribulation period . . . It may be concluded then that Christ will come in glory with His church (Colossians 3:4) and with His angels (Matthew 16:27) at the close of the tribulation period. At that time He will send forth His angels to regather faithful Israel to its land (Matthew 24:31).[35]

The Disciples' Question About the Kingdom

"Lord, is it at this time You are restoring the kingdom to Israel?" He said to them, "It is not for you to know times or epochs which the Father has fixed by His own authority; but you shall receive power when the Holy Spirit has come upon you; and you shall be My witnesses." (Acts 1:6b–8a)

Covenant View

Before [the death of Christ] the disciples had thought that "the kingdom of God should immediately appear" (Luke xix. 11). Then had come the seeming failure of those hopes.

. . . Now they were revived by the Resurrection, but were still predominantly national. Even the Twelve were thinking, not of a kingdom of God, embracing all mankind, but of a sovereignty restored to Israel. . . . [The disciples] are left to the teaching of the Spirit and of Time to re-mold and purify their expectations of the restoration of Israel.[36]

Dispensational View

Some conclude from the Lord's response that the apostles had a false concept of the kingdom. But this is wrong. Christ did not accuse them of this. If the followers of the Lord Jesus had an incorrect view, this would have been the time for Him to correct it. The fact is, Christ taught the coming of an earthly, literal kingdom. . . . Acts 1:3 states that the Lord instructed the disciples about the kingdom; He certainly gave them the right impression as to its character and future coming. What Jesus discussed here (v. 7) was the time of the coming of the kingdom.[37]

However, a time is coming, commonly called the Millennium, when God will burst into human history in a spectacular way to establish His rule on earth. This is what is meant by the term "kingdom of God."[38]

The One-Thousand-Year Millennial Reign of Christ

. . . *those who had not worshiped the beast or his image, and had not received the mark upon their forehead and upon their hand; and they came to life and reigned with Christ for a thousand years. . . . They will be priests of God and of Christ and will reign with Him for a thousand years. And when the thousand years are completed . . . (Revelation 20:4b, 6b, 7a)*

Covenant View

The vision [of the Millennium] has its approximate fulfillment as the Church of Christ, in the faith of the reality of her Lord's victory, carries on her warfare against the prince of this world and spiritual wickedness in high places. That this approximate fulfillment is not unreal may be seen in the fact that Christendom has replaced heathendom, Christ has taken the throne of the world, the prince of this world has been judged, the ascendancy of Christian thought and Christian principles has marvelously humanized and purified the world. . . . A thousand years was the length at which Rabbis fixed the duration of Messiah's kingdom. The period is not to be understood literally. . . . The same applies to the duration of the imprisonment [of Satan]; it is not to be understood literally any more than the other numbers in the book; it symbolizes a lengthened period.[39]

Dispensational View

The expositor is not free to spiritualize the interpretation of the vision [of the Millennium] but must accept the interpretation in its ordinary and literal meaning. It this is done, there is no other alternative than the premillennial interpretation which holds that at the second coming of Christ, Satan will be bound for a thousand years. This will constitute one of the major features of Christ's righteous rule upon the earth and in fact will make possible the peace and tranquillity and absence of spiritual warfare predicted for the millennial kingdom. The period before Satan is bound, that is, the great tribulation, and the period at the close of the millennium, when Satan is again loosed, stand in sharp contrast to the tranquillity of the thousand years in between. The fact is that the only period in all human history in which Satan will not execute his work of deception will be the thousand years in which Christ will reign.[40]

Endnotes

Chapter 1

1. Mal Couch, "Amillennialism," in *Dictionary of Premillennial Theology*, ed. Mal Couch (Grand Rapids: Kregel, 1996), 37.
2. Louis Berkhof, *Principles of Biblical Interpretation* (Grand Rapids: Baker, 1990), 152.
3. A. A. Hodge, *Outlines of Theology* (Grand Rapids: Eerdmans, 1957), 570–73.
4. Bobby Hayes, "Premillennialism," in *Dictionary of Premillennial Theology*, 311.

Chapter 2

1. James Draper, *Authority: The Critical Issue for Southern Baptists* (Old Tappan, N.J.: Revell, 1984), 15.
2. Francis A. Schaeffer, *The Great Evangelical Disaster* (Westchester, Ill.: Crossway, 1984), 51.
3. Ibid., 60.
4. Ibid., 44–45.
5. Norman L. Geisler and William E. Nix, *A General Introduction to the Bible*, rev. ed. (Chicago: Moody, 1986), 39.
6. E. J. Young, *Thy Word Is Truth* (Grand Rapids: Eerdmans, 1957), 113.
7. Paul D. Feinberg, "Bible, Inerrancy and Infallibility of," in *The Evangelical Dictionary of Theology*, ed. Walter A. Elwell (Grand Rapids: Baker, 1984), 142.
8. Geisler and Nix, *General Introduction to the Bible*, 156.

9. John M. Lewis, *Layman's Library of Christian Doctrine* (Nashville: Broadman, 1985), 57.

10. Schaeffer, *Great Evangelical Disaster,* 60.

11. Geisler and Nix, *General Introduction to the Bible,* 156–60.

12. Ibid., 162–63.

13. Ibid., 156–60.

14. A. S. Van Der Woude, *The World of the Old Testament* (Grand Rapids: Eerdmans, 1985), 166–67.

15. Ibid., 187.

16. Ibid., 230, 232–33.

17. Bruce Wilkinson and Kenneth Boa, *Talk Thru the Bible* (Nashville: Nelson, 1983), 190–91.

18. Charles C. Ryrie, *The Ryrie Study Bible* (Chicago: Moody, 1978), 1012.

19. Mansoor Menahem, *The Dead Sea Scroll* (Grand Rapids: Eerdmans, 1964), 70.

20. J. Randall Price, *Secrets of the Dead Sea Scrolls* (Eugene, Ore.: Harvest, 1996), 154, 155.

21. Feinberg, "Bible, Inerrancy and Infallibility of," 173.

22. Geisler and Nix, *General Introduction to the Bible,* 53.

23. Roy B. Zuck, *Basic Bible Interpretation* (Wheaton, Ill.: Victor, 1991), 70.

24. Kenneth O. Gangel, "2 Peter," in *The Bible Knowledge Commentary, New Testament,* ed. John F. Walvoord and Roy B. Zuck (Wheaton, Ill.: Victor, 1983), 878.

25. Cited in Grant Jeffrey, *The Signature of God* (Toronto, Ont.: Frontier Research, 1996), 141.

26. Ibid., 144–45.

27. C. W. Ceram, *The Secret of the Hittites* (New York: Knopf, 1955), 24–25.

28. Merrill F. Unger, *The New Unger's Bible Dictionary* (Chicago: Moody, 1988), 576–80.

29. Schaeffer, *Great Evangelical Disaster,* 44–45.

Chapter 3

1. J. I. Packer, *Scripture and Truth: The Centrality of Hermeneutics Today,* ed. D. A. Carson and John D. Woodbridge (Grand Rapids: Academie, 1983), 345.

2. Millard J. Erickson, *Christian Theology* (Grand Rapids: Baker, 1985), 24.

3. Ibid., 25.

4. Walter A. Elwell, ed., *Evangelical Dictionary of Theology* (Grand Rapids: Baker, 1986), 1064–65.

5. Packer, *Scripture and Truth*, 325.
6. Bernard Ramm, *Protestant Biblical Interpretation*, 3d rev. ed. (Grand Rapids: Baker, 1970), 121.
7. Leon Morris, *The Revelation of St. John* (Grand Rapids: Eerdmans, 1981), 235.
8. Paul Lee Tan, *The Interpretation of Prophecy* (Dallas: Bible Communications, 1993), 137–38.
9. Ibid., 138.
10. Ramm, *Protestant Biblical Interpretation*, 24.
11. F. F. Bruce, *Commentary on Galatians* (Grand Rapids: Eerdmans, 1982), 214.
12. Elwell, *Evangelical Dictionary of Theology*, 33.
13. Morris, *Revelation of St. John*, 235.
14. Charles C. Ryrie, *Dispensationalism* (Chicago: Moody, 1995), 79.
15. Ibid., 25.
16. Ibid., 23.
17. Louis Berkhof, *Systematic Theology* (Grand Rapids: Eerdmans, 1938), 293.
18. Ibid., 211.
19. Ibid.
20. Packer, *Scripture and Truth*, 328.
21. Cited in J. Dwight Pentecost, *Things to Come* (Grand Rapids: Zondervan, 1964), 372, 373.
22. Cited in Ryrie, *Dispensationalism*, 83.
23. Berkhof, *Systematic Theology*, 713.
24. Ibid.
25. Ibid.
26. Walter C. Kaiser Jr., "Legitimate Hermeneutics," in *Inerrancy*, ed. Norman L. Geisler (Grand Rapids: Academie, 1980), 127–28.
27. Packer, *Scripture and Truth*, 325.

Chapter 4

1. Paul N. Benware, *Understanding End Times Prophecy: A Comprehensive Approach* (Chicago: Moody, 1995), 132.
2. Ibid., 83.

Chapter 5

1. Charles Hodge, *Systematic Theology*, 3 vols. (reprint, Grand Rapids: Eerdmans, 1977), 1:186–87.
2. Ibid., 1:187.
3. Ibid., 1:187–88.
4. Ibid., 1:186–87.

5. Bernard Ramm, *Protestant Biblical Interpretation*, 3d rev. ed. (Grand Rapids: Baker, 1970), 115.

6. Ibid., 164.

7. Ibid.

8. Ibid., 54–55.

9. Merrill F. Unger, *Unger's Commentary on the Old Testament*, 2 vols. (Chicago: Moody, 1981), 1:647.

10. Ramm, *Protestant Biblical Interpretation*, 51.

11. Hodge, *Systematic Theology*, 1:187.

12. Ramm, *Protestant Biblical Interpretation*, 58–59.

13. Hodge, *Systematic Theology*, 1:187.

14. David K. Lowery, "1 Corinthians," in *The Bible Knowledge Commentary*, ed. John F. Walvoord and Roy B. Zuck (Wheaton, Ill.: Victor Books, 1983), 544.

15. R. C. H. Lenski, *The Interpretation of St. Luke's Gospel* (Minneapolis: Augsburg, 1961), 67–69.

16. Ramm, *Protestant Biblical Interpretation*, 119, 122–23.

17. Ibid., 54, 58.

18. Ibid., 108.

19. Ibid., 55.

20. Ibid., 128.

21. Ibid., 129.

22. Ibid., 131–32.

23. Ibid., 134.

24. Ibid., 135.

25. Ibid., 137.

26. Paul Lee Tan, *The Interpretation of Prophecy* (Dallas: Bible Communications, 1974), 119.

27. Ibid., 121.

28. Ibid., 124.

29. Ibid.

30. Ibid.

31. David L. Cooper, *The God of Israel* (Los Angeles: Biblical Research Society, 1945), iii.

32. Unger, *Unger's Commentary on the Old Testament*, 2:1174–75.

33. Roy B. Zuck, *Basic Bible Interpretation* (Wheaton, Ill.: Victor, 1993), 184–85.

34. Clinton Lockhart, *Principles of Interpretation* (Ft. Worth, Tex.: S. H. Taylor, 1915), 49, 156.

35. Unger, *Unger's Commentary on the Old Testament*, 2:1173.

36. Ramm, *Protestant Biblical Interpretation*, 170–71.

Chapter 6

1. For a discussion on "Elijah," see Paul Lee Tan, "Repeated Foreshadowing," in *The Interpretation of Prophecy* . . . (Dallas: Bible Communications, 1974), 185–87.

2. E. W. Hengstenberg, *Christology of the Old Testament*, 4 vols. (Grand Rapids: Kregel, 1956), 4:394.

3. Patrick Fairbairn, *The Interpretation of Prophecy* (reprint, London: Banner of Truth Trust, 1964), 122.

4. Thomas Hartwell Horne, *An Introduction to the Critical Study and Knowledge of the Holy Scriptures*, 4 vols. (Boston, Mass.: Littell and Gay, 1868), 1:378.

5. Fairbairn, *Interpretation of Prophecy*, 128.

6. Floyd E. Hamilton, *The Basis of Millennial Faith* (Grand Rapids: Eerdmans, 1942), 144.

7. William Kelly, *An Exposition of the Book of Isaiah* (London: C. A. Hammond, 1947), 46.

8. Louis Berkhof, *Principles of Biblical Interpretation* (Grand Rapids: Baker, 1966), 150.

9. Lewis Sperry Chafer, *Systematic Theology*, 8 vols. (Dallas: Dallas Seminary Press, 1948), 4:259.

10. Fairbairn, *Interpretation of Prophecy*, 147–48.

11. Shirley Jackson Case, *The Millennial Hope* (Chicago: University of Chicago Press, 1918), 78.

12. Berkhof, *Principles of Biblical Interpretation*, 153.

13. Loraine Boettner, *The Millennium* (Philadelphia: Presbyterian and Reformed, 1964), 90.

14. Ibid.

15. John C. Whitcomb Jr. and Henry M. Morris, *The Genesis Flood* (Grand Rapids: Baker, 1961), 461. For a detailed discussion of the vegetarian diet of animals before the Fall, see pages 461–64 in the same book.

16. Adam Clarke, "The Epistles and Revelation," in *The New Testament with a Commentary and Critical Notes*, ed. Daniel Curry (New York: Eaton and Mains, 1883), 6:630.

17. Herman Hoeksema, *Reformed Dogmatics* (Grand Rapids: Reformed Free Pub., 1966), 819.

18. Citing James Oliver Buswell, *A Systematic Theology of the Christian Religion*, 2 vols. (Grand Rapids: Zondervan, 1963), 2:502.

19. F. Gardiner, "Ezekiel," in *Ellicott's Commentary on the Whole Bible*, ed. Charles John Ellicott (Grand Rapids: Zondervan, 1959), 5:315.

20. Milton S. Terry, *Biblical Hermeneutics* (New York: Eaton and Mains, 1911), 262.

21. Gerald B. Stanton, *Kept from the Hour* (London: Marshall, Morgan and Scott, 1964), 311.

22. Charles Caldwell Ryrie, *The Bible and Tomorrow's News* (Wheaton, Ill.: Scripture Press, 1969), 22.

23. Nathaniel West, *The Thousand Years in Both Testaments* (Chicago, Ill.: Revell, 1880), 96.

24. Herman A. Hoyt, *The Revelation of the Lord Jesus Christ* (Winona Lake, Ind.: Brethren Missionary Herald, 1966), 104–5.

25. John J. Davis, *Biblical Numerology* (Winona Lake, Ind.: BMH Books, 1968), 124.

26. Charles Lee Feinberg, *Premillennialism or Amillennialism?* (Wheaton, Ill.: Van Kampen, 1954), 21.

27. Patrick Fairbairn, *The Typology of Scripture* (Grand Rapids: Zondervan, n.d.), 1.

28. Oswald T. Allis, *Prophecy and the Church* (Philadelphia: Presbyterian and Reformed, 1964), 23.

29. Donald K. Campbell, "The Interpretation of Types," *Bibliotheca Sacra* 112, no. 447 (July 1955): 250.

30. E. Schuyler English, *The New Scofield Reference Bible* (New York: Oxford University Press, 1967), 994.

31. John Wick Bowman, "Dispensationalism," *Interpretation* 10, no. 2 (April 1956): 184.

32. Charles Caldwell Ryrie, *The Basis of Premillennial Faith* (New York: Loizeaux Brothers, 1953), 43.

33. Cited by Patrick Fairbairn, *The Typology of Scripture* (Grand Rapids: Zondervan, n.d.), 20.

34. C. I. Scofield, *The Scofield Bible Correspondence School*, 3 vols. (Los Angeles: Bible Institute of Los Angeles, 1907), 1:46.

35. Berkhof, *Principles of Biblical Interpretation*, 262.

36. Bernard Ramm, *Protestant Biblical Interpretation*, 3d rev. ed. (Grand Rapids: Baker, 1970), 262.

37. Other examples are Psalms 2 and 45.

38. Fairbairn, *Typology of Scripture*, 135.

Chapter 7

1. Millard J. Erickson, *Contemporary Options in Eschatology* (Grand Rapids: Baker, 1977), 111.

2. Clarence B. Bass, *Backgrounds to Dispensationalism* (Grand Rapids: Baker, 1960), 14.

3. Walter A. Elwell, review of *Progressive Dispensationalism*, by Craig A. Blaising and Darrell L. Bock, in *Christianity Today*, 12 September 1994, 28.

4. For statements of their respective positions see Charles C. Ryrie, *Dispensationalism,* revised and expanded (Chicago: Moody, 1995), 61–77; and Arnold D. Ehlert, *A Bibliographic History of Dispensationalism* (Grand Rapids: Baker, 1965), 5–30.

5. For a full discussion of Darby's dispensational theology and its relationship to that of C. I. Scofield, see Larry V. Crutchfield, *The Origins of Dispensationalism: The Darby Factor* (Lanham, Md.: University Press of America, 1992).

6. For treatments of the *sine qua non* of dispensationalism, that which one must believe in order to be rightfully called a dispensationalist, see Ryrie, *Dispensationalism,* 38–41; Robert P. Lightner, "Theological Perspectives on Theonomy, Part 1: Theonomy and Dispensationalism," *Bibliotheca Sacra* 143 (January–March 1986): 34; and Renald E. Showers, *There Really Is a Difference* (Bellmawr, N.J.: The Friends of Israel Gospel Ministry, 1990), 52–53.

7. Lightner, "Theological Perspectives on Theonomy, Part 1," 33.

8. Ryrie, *Dispensationalism,* 18–19.

9. Ibid., 146–49.

10. F. W. Farrar, *History of Interpretation* (New York: E. P. Dutton and Co., 1886), 164–65.

11. See Eusebius *Church History* VII, 24.

12. See J. N. D. Kelly, *Early Christian Doctrines,* rev. ed. (New York: Harper and Row, 1978), 469. Here, Kelly says that in *Caput contra Caius* (or *Chapters Against Caius*), Hippolytus abandoned Irenaeus's interpretation of the thousand years in Revelation 20 as the literal duration of the kingdom, and rather explained it as "a symbolical number which should be interpreted as pointing to its splendour" (see Kelly's note: *Cap. c. Caium* [GCS I, Pt. 2, 246f.]). The "evidence" for this supposed reversal by Hippolytus is weak and unsubstantiated.

13. For a fuller discussion of the relationship between Israel and the church in the ante-Nicene age, see Larry V. Crutchfield, "Israel and the Church in the Ante-Nicene Fathers: Part 1 of Rudiments of Dispensationalism in the Ante-Nicene Period," *Bibliotheca Sacra* 146 (July–September 1987): 254–76.

14. For documentation on "The Early Patristic Concept of the Seed of Abraham and the Relationship Between Israel and the Church" see the appendix to this article.

15. Peters observes that "in the earliest writings, there is not a decisive passage which teaches the prevailing modern view. While the fathers insisted on the universal government of God, the Headship of Christ over the church, yet they do not designate the church the Kingdom of God, or profess to be in the Kingdom, but represent

themselves as looking for it still future" (George N. H. Peters, *The Theocratic Kingdom* [Grand Rapids: Kregel, 1952], 1:643).

16. See Larry V. Crutchfield, "Ages and Dispensations in the Ante-Nicene Fathers: Part 2 of 'Rudiments of Dispensationalism in the Ante-Nicene Period,'" *Bibliotheca Sacra* 147 (October–December 1987): 377–401.

17. C. Norman Kraus, *Dispensationalism in America* (Richmond: John Knox, 1958), 43.

18. Ibid., 25.

19. See Crutchfield, "Ages and Dispensations in the Ante-Nicene Fathers," 401.

20. Ibid., 400.

21. Clarence E. Mason, "A Review of 'Dispensationalism' by John Wick Bowman," *Bibliotheca Sacra* 114 (January 1957): 16. Mason's concluding point here directly contradicts Kraus's assertion that one of the essential assumptions held in common by the early fathers "is that there is only one basic dispensational division. This is the division between the Old Covenant and the New" (Kraus, *Dispensationalism in America,* 23).

    Naturally the early fathers made a distinction between the old and new covenants, between God's dealings with His people Israel in the Old Testament and His people the Church in the New. They firmly believed that Christ was alive and active in the Old Testament, but beginning with the incarnation in the New Testament, that activity took on distinctly new importance and reached far greater proportions. Yet these fathers also maintained that there were differing arrangements of God within the two major divisions of biblical history. They regularly drew dispensational boundaries around Adam, Noah, Abraham, and Moses in the Old Testament, and around Christ, and to a large extent, the millennial kingdom in the New. It is simply untrue to say, as Kraus does, that the fathers held to only one basic dispensational division.

22. Mason, "A Review of 'Dispensationalism' by John Wick Bowman," 19–20.

23. John F. Walvoord, review of *Backgrounds to Dispensationalism,* by Clarence B. Bass, *Bibliotheca Sacra* 118 (January 1961): 69.

24. Ibid., 5–6.

25. Philip Schaff, *History of the Christian Church,* 8 vols. (Grand Rapids: Eerdmans, 1960), 2:614.

26. For a detailed account of the various phases of and participants in the two resurrections, see J. Dwight Pentecost, *Things to Come* (Grand Rapids: Zondervan, 1958), 395–411.

27. Henry C. Thiessen, *Introductory Lectures in Systematic Theology* (Grand Rapids: Eerdmans, 1949), 477. For the Hermas reference, see *The Shepherd: Visions* IV, II. It will become apparent in our examination of the Hermas material that this is not an unqualified pretribulational reference.

28. Thiessen, *Introductory Lectures in Systematic Theology*, 477.

29. John F. Walvoord, *The Rapture Question*, revised and enlarged (Grand Rapids: Zondervan, 1979), 51.

30. Ibid., 50–54.

31. Millard J. Erickson, who is himself a posttribulationist, says, "To be sure, the premillennialism of the church's first centuries may have included belief in a pretribulational rapture of the church." But he avers elsewhere that "while there are in the writings of the early fathers seeds from which the doctrine of the pretribulational rapture could be developed, it is difficult to find in them an unequivocal statement of the type of imminency usually believed in by pretribulationists" (Erickson, *Contemporary Options in Eschatology*, 112, 131). This in essence is the position for which we are contending. We do not say that the early fathers were pretribulationists in the modern sense, only that the seeds were indeed there but were crushed under the allegorist's foot before they could sprout and bear early fruit.

32. Ryrie, *Dispensationalism*, 65.

Chapter 8

1. Joseph Wilson Trigg, *Origen* (Atlanta, Ga.: John Knox, 1983), 33.

2. Paul Lee Tan, *The Interpretation of Prophecy* (Rockville, Md.: Assurance, 1988), 45.

3. Ibid., 46.

4. Ibid., 47.

5. Ibid.

6. Bernard Ramm, *Protestant Biblical Interpretation* (Grand Rapids: Baker, 1986), 27.

7. C. D. Yonge, trans., *The Works of Philo* (Peabody, Mass.: Hendrickson, 1993), 42.

8. Ibid., 43.

9. William Varner, "Philo Judaeus," in *Dictionary of Premillennial Theology*, ed. Mal Couch (Grand Rapids: Kregel, 1996), 305.

10. J. Dwight Pentecost, *Things to Come* (Findlay, Ohio: Dunham, 1961), 23–24.

11. Trigg, *Origen*, 121.

12. Ibid., 124.

13. Ibid., 246.
14. Ibid., 212–13.
15. Larry V. Crutchfield, "Origen," in *Dictionary of Premillennial Theology*, 289.
16. Tan, *Interpretation of Prophecy*, 50–51.
17. Ramm, *Protestant Biblical Interpretation*, 36–37.
18. John F. Walvoord, *The Revelation of Jesus Christ* (Chicago: Moody, 1966), 37.
19. John Peter Lange, *Revelation* (Grand Rapids: Zondervan, n.d.), 345.
20. Ibid.
21. Norman Cohn, *The Pursuit of the Millennium* (New York: Oxford University Press, 1970), 29.
22. Larry V. Crutchfield, "Augustine," in *Dictionary of Premillennial Theology*, 59.

Chapter 9

1. George Mardsen, "Introduction: Reformed and American," in *Reformed Theology in America: A History of Its Modern Development*, ed. David F. Wells (Grand Rapids: Baker, 1997), 8–9.
2. Ibid., 9.
3. Edward Hindson, "John Bale," in *Dictionary of Premillennial Theology (DPT)*, ed. Mal Couch (Grand Rapids: Kregel, 1996), 62–63.
4. Edward Hindson, "Joseph Mede," in *DPT*, 250–51.
5. Edward Hindson, "The Mathers," in *DPT*, 249–50.
6. Lonnie L. Shipman, "Isaac Watts," in *DPT*, 422–23.
7. Timothy George and David Dockery, eds., *Baptist Theologians* (Nashville: Broadman, 1990), 78.
8. John Gill, *A Complete Body of Doctrinal and Practical Divinity*, 2 vols. (Grand Rapids: Baker, 1978), 2:278.
9. John Gill, *Exposition of the Old and New Testaments*, 9 vols. (Paris, Ark.: Baptist Standard Bearer, 1989), 8:538, 540.
10. Kevin Stilley, "Jonathan Edwards," in *DPT*, 100–1.
11. Thomas Ice, "Morgan Edwards," in *DPT*, 100–2.
12. Robert Haldane, *Commentary on Romans* (Grand Rapids: Kregel, 1996), 550–54.
13. Floyd Elmore, "John Nelson Darby," in *DPT*, 82–84.
14. Steven McAvoy, "John Charles Ryle," in *DPT*, 383–85.
15. Mal Couch, "James Robinson Graves," in *DPT*, 128.
16. Mal Couch, "Joseph A. Seiss," in *DPT*, 394.
17. Thomas Ice, "Elijah Richardson Craven," in *DPT*, 74.
18. George N. H. Peters, *The Theocratic Kingdom*, 3 vols. (Grand Rapids: Kregel, 1952, 1972); in the preface to vol. 1 by Wilbur M. Smith.

19. Mal Couch, "George N. H. Peters," in *DPT*, 302.
20. Mal Couch, "Nathaniel West," in *DPT*, 423–24.
21. Timothy Demy, "James Hall Brookes," in *DPT*, 64–65.
22. Brian K. Richards, "E. W. Bullinger," in *DPT*, 65–66.
23. Harold D. Foos, "Dwight Lyman Moody," in *DPT*, 272–73.
24. Thomas Ice, "Samuel H. Kellogg," in *DPT*, 228–29.
25. Mal Couch, "Sir Robert Anderson," in *DPT*, 42–43.
26. John Hannah, "Cyrus Ingerson Scofield," in *DPT*, 389–93.
27. Thomas Ice, "Clarence Larkin," in *DPT*, 239–40.
28. Steven McAvoy, "James Martin Gray," in *DPT*, 128–30.
29. Mal Couch, "David Baron," in *DPT*, 63.
30. Mal Couch, "William Bell Riley," in *DPT*, 379.
31. Mal Couch, "Arno Gaebelein," in *DPT*, 120–21.
32. Lonnie L. Shipman, "W. H. Griffith Thomas," in *DPT*, 407–8.
33. Lonnie L. Shipman, "William T. Pettingill," in *DPT*, 302–3.
34. Michael D. Stallard, "Henry Allan Ironside," in *DPT*, 183–84.
35. Mal Couch, "John Fredrick Strombeck," in *DPT*, 400–1.
36. Mal Couch, "Harry Bultema," in *DPT*, 66.
37. Mal Couch, "M. R. DeHaan," in *DPT*, 88–89.
38. Steven L. McAvoy, "René Pache," in *DPT*, 290–91.

Chapter 10

1. Bruce L. Shelley, "Hodge, Charles," in *The New International Dictionary of the Christian Church*, ed. J. D. Douglas (Grand Rapids: Zondervan, 1974, 1978), 473–74.
2. Charles Hodge, *Systematic Theology*, 3 vols. (reprint, Grand Rapids: Eerdmans, 1977), 3:373–74.
3. Ibid., 3:374.
4. Ibid.
5. Ibid., 3:375.
6. Ibid.
7. Ibid., 3:376.
8. Ibid., 3:377.
9. Ibid.
10. Ibid., 1:187–88.
11. *The Preacher's Homiletic Commentary*, 31 vols. (1891; reprint, Grand Rapids: Baker, 1981), 18:402.
12. Ibid., 403.
13. Paul N. Benware, *Understanding End Times Prophecy: A Comprehensive Approach* (Chicago: Moody, 1995), 19–29.
14. Ibid., 21.
15. Ibid., 23.

16. Ibid., 24.
17. Ibid., 26.
18. Ibid.
19. Ibid., 27.
20. Ibid.
21. Ibid., 28.
22. Ibid., 29.

Chapter 11

1. Louis Berkhof, *Systematic Theology* (Grand Rapids: Eerdmans, n.d.), 293.
2. Ibid.
3. Ibid., 297.
4. Ibid., 299–300.
5. Earl D. Radmacher, ed., *The Nelson Study Bible* (Nashville: Nelson, 1997), 20.
6. Paul N. Benware, *Understanding End Times Prophecy: A Comprehensive Approach* (Chicago: Moody, 1995), 130.
7. Ibid., 131.
8. John McLean, "Law and Grace," in *Dictionary of Premillennial Theology*, ed. Mal Couch (Grand Rapids: Kregel, 1996), 241.
9. Ibid.
10. Steve McAvoy, "Abrahamic Covenant," in *Dictionary of Premillennial Theology*, 27.
11. Ibid.
12. Ibid.
13. Ibid.
14. Mal Couch, "Genesis, Eschatology of," in *Dictionary of Premillennial Theology*, 2.
15. Ibid.
16. J. Dwight Pentecost, *Things to Come* (Grand Rapids: Dunham, 1961), 95.
17. Ibid., 98–99.
18. Paul Enns, *The Moody Handbook of Theology* (Chicago: Moody, 1989), 61.
19. Ibid., 67.
20. Berkhof, *Systematic Theology*, 277.
21. Rodney Decker, "New Covenant, Dispensational Views of the," in *Dictionary of Premillennial Theology*, 281.
22. Ibid.
23. Ibid., 282.
24. Ibid.

25. Hal Lindsey, *The Road to Holocaust* (New York: Bantam, 1989), 114–15.
26. Benware, *Understanding End Times Prophecy*, 72–73.

Chapter 12

1. James Orr, *The Progress of Dogma* (Grand Rapids: Eerdmans, n.d.), 303–4.
2. Louis Berkhof, *Systematic Theology* (Grand Rapids: Eerdmans, 1994), 213.
3. Ibid.
4. Ibid.
5. Ibid., 214.
6. Ibid., 216.
7. Ibid., 217.
8. Ibid., 218.
9. Ibid., 266.
10. Charles Hodge, *Systematic Theology*, 3 vols. (Grand Rapids: Eerdmans, 1981), 2:117.
11. Ibid.
12. James Oliver Buswell, *A Systematic Theology of the Christian Religion*, 2 vols. (Grand Rapids: Zondervan, 1963), 1:122.
13. Berkhof, *Systematic Theology*, 217.
14. Charles C. Ryrie, *Dispensationalism Today* (Chicago: Moody, 1965), 184.
15. Ibid., 185.
16. Berkhof, *Systematic Theology*, 265.
17. Hodge, *Systematic Theology*, 2:358.
18. Ibid.
19. Ibid., 359.
20. Ibid.
21. Ibid., 364.
22. Charles C. Ryrie, *Dispensationalism*, rev. ed. (Chicago: Moody, 1995), 190.
23. Ibid.

Chapter 13

1. Bernard Ramm, *Protestant Biblical Interpretation* (Grand Rapids: Baker, 1982), 11.
2. Roy Zuck, *Basic Bible Interpretation* (Wheaton, Ill.: Victor Books, 1991), 19.
3. A. A. Hodge, *Outlines of Theology* (Grand Rapids: Eerdmans, 1957), 21.

4. Paul Lee Tan, *The Interpretation of Prophecy* (Rockville, Mass.: Assurance, 1988), 29.
5. Zuck, *Basic Bible Interpretation,* 19.
6. James Oliver Buswell, *A Systematic Theology of the Christian Religion* (Grand Rapids: Zondervan, 1977), 24–26.
7. Walter C. Kaiser, *Toward an Exegetical Theology* (Grand Rapids: Baker, 1981), 44–45.
8. Ramm, *Protestant Biblical Interpretation,* 12–16.
9. Zuck, *Basic Bible Interpretation,* 25.
10. Kaiser, *Toward an Exegetical Theology,* 45.
11. Ramm, *Protestant Biblical Interpretation,* 14.
12. Charles C. Ryrie, *Dispensationalism* (Chicago: Moody, 1995), 25.
13. Ibid., 28.
14. Clarence E. Mason, *Dispensationalism Made Simple* (Arnold, Mo.: Shield, 1976), 19.
15. Mal Couch, *God's Plan of the Ages* (Ft. Worth: Seminary Press, n.d.), 17.
16. Paul N. Benware, *Understanding End Times Prophecy: A Comprehensive Approach* (Chicago: Moody, 1995), 84.
17. Paul Enns, *The Moody Handbook of Theology* (Chicago: Moody, 1989), 389.
18. W. Robert Nicoll, *The Expositor's Greek Testament,* 5 vols. (Grand Rapids: Eerdmans, 1988), 3:259–60.
19. Ryrie, *Dispensationalism,* 142.
20. Enns, *The Moody Handbook of Theology,* 520–21.
21. Lewis S. Chafer, *Major Bible Themes,* rev. John F. Walvoord (Grand Rapids: Zondervan, 1974), 236.
22. Ibid., 240–41.

Chapter 14

1. Simon J. Kistemaker, *Acts,* New Testament Commentary (Grand Rapids: Baker, 1995), 90–91.
2. J. A. Alexander, *Commentary on the Acts of the Apostles* (Grand Rapids: Zondervan, 1956), 61–63.
3. Horatio B. Hackett, *Commentary on Acts* (Grand Rapids: Kregel, 1992), 46–47.
4. Stanley D. Toussaint, "Acts," in *The Bible Knowledge Commentary, New Testament,* ed. John F. Walvoord and Roy B. Zuck (Wheaton, Ill.: Victor Books, 1978), 358.
5. John Eadie, *Commentary on the Epistle to the Galatians* (Grand Rapids: Zondervan, 1894), 470–71.
6. William Ames, *The Marrow of Theology* (Grand Rapids: Baker, 1997), 204–5.

7. Louis Berkhof, *Systematic Theology* (Grand Rapids: Eerdmans, 1994), 568.
8. Ibid., 569.
9. Ibid.
10. Ibid.
11. Ibid.
12. W. Robert Nicoll, *The Expositor's Greek Testament*, 5 vols. (reprint, Grand Rapids: Eerdmans, 1990), 3:293.
13. Charles Hodge, *Commentary on the Epistle to the Ephesians* (Grand Rapids: Eerdmans, 1994), 131–39.

Chapter 15

1. Charles C. Ryrie, *Dispensationalism*, revised and expanded (Chicago: Moody, 1995), 105. This volume was formerly titled *Dispensationalism Today* (Chicago: Moody, 1965).
2. C. I. Scofield, *The Scofield Reference Bible* (New York: Oxford University Press, 1917), 1115.
3. Ibid., 1124.
4. O. T. Allis, *Prophecy and the Church* (Philadelphia: Presbyterian and Reformed, 1945), 42.
5. Ibid., 248.
6. Charles C. Ryrie, *Dispensationalism Today*, 123.
7. L. S. Chafer, "Inventing Heretics Through Misunderstanding," *Bibliotheca Sacra* 101 (July 1944): 259.
8. L. S. Chafer, *Grace* (Findlay, Ohio: Dunham, 1922), 113.
9. Ryrie, *Dispensationalism*, rev., 109. For a more in-depth discussion of the relationship of Law and grace in the dispensation of Law see Ryrie's discussion in the this excellent volume cited.
10. Ibid., 117.
11. Paul Enns, *The Moody Handbook of Theology* (Chicago: Moody, 1989), 522.
12. Lewis S. Chafer, *Systematic Theology*, 8 vols. in 4 (reprint, Grand Rapids: Kregel, 1993), 7:175–76, quoting Scofield, *Scofield Reference Bible*, 1343.
13. Ryrie, *Dispensationalism Today*, 123.
14. Ryrie, *Dispensationalism*, rev., 120–21.

Chapter 16

1. William Hendriksen, *The Gospel of Matthew* (Grand Rapids: Baker, 1982), 651.
2. A. T. Robertson, *Word Pictures in the New Testament*, 6 vols. (Nashville: Broadman, 1930), 1:133–34.

3. R. C. H. Lenski, *The Interpretation of Matthew* (Minneapolis, Minn.: Augsburg, 1961), 628–29.
4. D. A. Carson, "Matthew," in *The Expositor's Bible Commentary,* 12 vols., ed. Frank E. Gaebelein (Grand Rapids: Zondervan, 1984), 8:369.
5. Hendriksen, *Gospel of Matthew,* 646.
6. Edward Denny, *Papalism* (London: Rivingtons, 1912), 11.
7. Ibid., 13, 15, 17.
8. Carson, "Matthew," 8:370–71.
9. Denny, *Papalism,* 30.
10. Ibid., 41.
11. Joseph Deharbe, *A Complete Catechism of the Catholic Religion* (New York: Schwartz, Kirwin & Fauss, 1912), 134.
12. Ibid.
13. Ibid., 135–36.
14. Ibid., 139.
15. Ibid., 141.
16. Ibid., 141–42.
17. Ibid., 142.
18. Ibid., 145.
19. Ibid., 146.
20. Ibid., 148–49.
21. Ibid., 149.
22. Ibid., 148.
23. Richard P. McBrien, *Catholicism,* revised (New York: Harper Collins, 1994), 673.
24. Ibid., 692.
25. Ibid., 694.
26. Ibid.
27. Ibid., 730.
28. Ibid., 1180.
29. Ibid.
30. Ibid., 1181.

Chapter 17

1. Charles Hodge, *Systematic Theology,* 3 vols. (reprint, Grand Rapids: Eerdmans, 1977), 1:187.
2. Charles John Ellicott, ed., *Commentary on the Whole Bible,* 7 vols. (Grand Rapids: Zondervan, 1959), 6:81.
3. Ibid.
4. Ibid., 82.
5. Ibid.

6. J. Dwight Pentecost, *Thy Kingdom Come* (Wheaton, Ill.: Victor, 1990), 220.
7. Arnold G. Fruchtenbaum, *Israelology: The Missing Link in Systematic Theology* (Tustin, Calif.: Ariel Ministries, 1993), 612.
8. Stanley Toussaint, *Behold the King* (Portland, Ore.: Multnomah, 1980), 175–76.
9. Ed Glasscock, *Matthew* (Chicago: Moody, 1997), 281.
10. Roy Beacham, "Kingdom, Parables of the," in *Dictionary of Premillennial Theology*, ed. Mal Couch (Grand Rapids: Kregel, 1996), 233.
11. William Hendriksen, *The Gospel of Matthew* (Grand Rapids: Baker, 1982), 576.
12. Beacham, "Kingdom, Parables of the," 234.

Chapter 18

1. J. Dwight Pentecost, *Thy Kingdom Come* (Grand Rapids: Kregel, 1995), 293.
2. J. W. McGarvey, *New Commentary on Acts of Apostles* (Delight, Ark.: Gospel Light, 1892), 5.
3. Clarence Larkin, *Rightly Dividing the Word* (Glenside, Pa.: Rev. Clarence Larkin Est., 1920), 55, 57.
4. Ibid., 57.
5. Stanley D. Toussaint, "Acts," in *The Bible Knowledge Commentary, New Testament*, ed. John F. Walvoord and Roy B. Zuck (Wheaton, Ill.: Victor, 1983), 354.
6. Pentecost, *Thy Kingdom Come*, 226.

Chapter 19

1. John Calvin, *Romans*, ed. John Owen (Grand Rapids: Baker, 1989), 437.
2. Ibid.
3. John Gill, *Exposition of the Old and New Testaments*, 9 vols. (Paris, Ark.: The Baptist Standard Bearer, 1989), 8:538.
4. Albert Barnes, *Notes on the New Testament*, 14 vols. (Grand Rapids: Baker, 1996), 10:254.
5. Ibid., 250.
6. William Sanday, "Romans," in *Ellicott's Commentary on the Whole Bible*, ed. Charles John Ellicott (Grand Rapids: Zondervan, 1959), 7:250.
7. William Sanday, "The Epistle to the Romans," in *International Critical Commentary* (New York: Charles Scribner's Sons, 1911), 336.
8. Ibid., 337.

9. William Plumer, *Commentary on Romans* (Grand Rapids: Kregel, 1993), 553.

10. Charles Hodge, *Commentary on the Epistle to the Romans* (Grand Rapids: Eerdmans, 1994), 367.

11. J. Dwight Pentecost, *Things to Come* (Findlay, Ohio: Dunham, 1961), 468.

12. Robert Haldane, *Commentary on Romans* (reprint, Grand Rapids: Kregel, 1996), 545, 547.

13. Ibid., 550.

14. Ibid., 551.

Chapter 20

1. John F. Walvoord, "Christ's Olivet Discourse on the End of the Age—Part I," *Bibliotheca Sacra* 128, no. 510 (April 1971): 116.

2. Daniel B. Wallace, *Greek Grammar Beyond the Basics: An Exegetical Syntax of the New Testament* (Grand Rapids: Zondervan, 1996), 287.

3. Charles John Ellicott, *Ellicott's Commentary on the Whole Bible* (Grand Rapids: Zondervan, 1957), 6:145.

4. John F. MacArthur Jr., *Signs of Christ's Return: Matthew 24–25* (Chicago: Moody, 1987), 22.

5. Walvoord, "Christ's Olivet Discourse on the End of the Age—Part I," 116.

6. MacArthur, *Signs of Christ's Return*, 21–22.

7. John F. Walvoord, "Christ's Olivet Discourse on the Time of the End—Part II: Prophecies Fulfilled in the Present Age," *Bibliotheca Sacra* 128, no. 511 (July 1971): 208–9.

8. Paul N. Benware, *Understanding End Times Prophecy: A Comprehensive Approach* (Chicago: Moody, 1995), 318.

9. Walvoord, "Christ's Olivet Discourse on the Time of the End—Part II," 212–13.

10. John F. Walvoord, "Christ's Olivet Discourse on End of the Age—Part III: Signs of the End of the Age," *Bibliotheca Sacra* 128, no. 512 (October 1971): 321.

11. Benware, *Understanding End Times Prophecy*, 317–18.

12. Walvoord, "Christ's Olivet Discourse on End of the Age—Part III," 322.

13. Louis A. Barbieri Jr., "Matthew," in *The Bible Knowledge Commentary, New Testament*, ed. John F. Walvoord and Roy B. Zuck (Wheaton, Ill.: Victor, 1983), 78.

14. Robert H. Gundry's view is presented in his book *The Church and the Tribulation* (Grand Rapids: Zondervan, 1973); and Alexander

Reese's view in his book *The Approaching Advent of Christ* (London: Marshall, Morgan and Scott, 1932).

15. Benware, *Understanding End Times Prophecy*, 209.

16. John F. Walvoord, *The Rapture Question* (Grand Rapids: Zondervan, 1979), 189, quoting Reese, *Approaching Advent of Christ*.

17. John F Walvoord, *The Blessed Hope and the Tribulation* (Grand Rapids: Zondervan, 1976), 90–91.

18. J. Dwight Pentecost, *The Parables of Jesus* (Grand Rapids: Zondervan, 1982), 151.

19. Ibid., 152.

20. Ibid.

21. Walvoord, *Rapture Question*, 191.

22. Walvoord, "Christ's Olivet Discourse on the End of the Age—Part I," 116.

Chapter 21

1. John F. Walvoord, *The Millennial Kingdom* (Findlay, Ohio: Dunham, 1959), 120.

2. Ibid.

3. Ibid., 121.

4. Ibid., 123.

5. John Peter Lange, *Revelation* (Grand Rapids: Zondervan, n.d.), 65.

6. Ibid.

7. Ibid.

8. Ibid.

9. Paul Lee Tan, *The Interpretation of Prophecy* (Rockville, Mass.: Assurance, 1988), 162.

10. Ibid.

11. Ibid., 163.

12. Ibid., 164.

13. *The Preacher's Homiletic Commentary*, 31 vols. (Grand Rapids: Baker, 1996), 18:402.406–7.

14. Charles John Ellicott, *Ellicott's Commentary on the Whole Bible* (Grand Rapids: Zondervan, 1957), 4:529.

15. Ibid., 529.

16. Tim LaHaye, *Revelation* (Grand Rapids: Zondervan, 1980), 3.

17. Ellicott, *Ellicott's Commentary on the Whole Bible*, 4:531–32.

18. George A. Buttrick, gen. ed., *The Interpreter's Bible*, 12 vols. (New York: Abingdon, 1957), 12:354.

19. Hal Lindsey, *The Road to Holocaust* (New York: Bantam, 1989), 10–11.

20. Ellicott, *Ellicott's Commentary on the Whole Bible*, 8:526.

21. Merrill F. Unger, *Archaeology and the New Testament* (Grand Rapids: Zondervan, 1962), 267.

22. Theodore Zahn, *Introduction to the New Testament* (Minneapolis: Klock and Klock, 1909), 3:183–84.

23. Philip Schaff, *History of the Christian Church*, 8 vols. (Grand Rapids: Eerdmans, 1960), 1:834s.

24. John Walvoord, *The Revelation of Jesus Christ* (Chicago: Moody, 1966), 14.

25. Archibald T. Robertson, *Word Pictures in the New Testament* (Nashville: Broadman, 1933), 6:272–73.

26. Ellicott, *Ellicott's Commentary on the Whole Bible*, 4:526.

27. Lindsey, *Road to Holocaust*, 242.

28. Ibid., 243.

29. Schaff, *History of the Christian Church*, 2:614.

30. Ibid.

31. Ibid., 2:616.

32. Ibid., 2:617–18.

33. Ibid., 2:4.

34. Ibid., 2:618–19.

35. Joseph Wilson Trigg, *Origen* (Atlanta: John Knox, 1983), 121.

36. Ibid., 122.

37. Ibid., 162.

38. Ibid., 212–13.

39. Schaff, *History of the Christian Church*, 2:792.

40. Robert H. Mounce, *The Book of Revelation*, in The New International Commentary on the New Testament (Grand Rapids: Eerdmans, 1977), 39.

41. Robertson, *Word Pictures in the New Testament*, 6:277.

42. *The Preacher's Homiletic Commentary*, 31 vols. (Grand Rapids: Baker, 1996), 30:404–5.

43. Ibid., 30:405.

44. Ibid., 30:406.

45. Ibid.

46. Ibid.

47. George N. H. Peters, *The Theocratic Kingdom*, 3 vols. (Grand Rapids: Kregel, 1988), 1:50–51.

48. Michael Avi-Yonah and Zvi Baras, eds., *The World History of the Jewish People: Society and Religion in the Second Temple Period Jewish History* (Jerusalem: Massada, 1977).

49. Raphael Patai, *The Messiah Texts* (Detroit: Wayne State University Press, 1979).

50. Ibid., 113.

51. Ibid., 104–5.
52. Ibid., 49.
53. Avi-Yonah and Baras, *Society and Religion,* 185.
54. Ibid., 186.
55. Ibid., 159.
56. Patai, *Messiah Texts,* 96.
57. Avi-Yonah and Baras, *Society and Religion,* 154.
58. Patai, *Messiah Texts,* 96.
59. Ibid., 97.
60. Ibid., 95–96.
61. Ibid., 165.
62. Ibid., 172.
63. Ibid., 173.
64. Avi-Yonah and Baras, *Society and Religion,* 159.
65. Ibid., 161.
66. Ibid., 154.
67. Ibid., 171.
68. Ibid., 168.
69. Ibid.
70. Stanley D. Toussaint, *Behold the King* (Portland, Ore.: Multnomah, 1981), 61, quoting Alva J. McClain, *The Greatness of the Kingdom: An Inductive Study of the Kingdom of God* (Winona Lake, Ind.: BMH Books, 1959), 274–76.
71. Ibid., 62.
72. Ibid., 62–63.
73. Ibid., 167.
74. Ibid., 166.
75. Moses de Leon, ed., *Zohar,* 3 vols. (Rome: n.p., 1894). The central work in Kabbalistic literature, written in Aramaic between 1270–1300 in Spain.
76. Norman Cohn, *The Pursuit of the Millennium* (New York: Oxford University Press, 1970), 29.

Chapter 22

1. Roy E. Beacham, "Kingdoms, Universal and Mediatorial," in *Dictionary of Premillennial Theology,* ed. Mal Couch (Grand Rapids: Kregel, 1996), 235.
2. Ibid.
3. Ibid., 236.
4. Michael Avi-Yonah and Zvi Baras, eds., *The World History of the Jewish People: Society and Religion in the Second Temple Period Jewish History* (Jerusalem: Massada, 1977), 158.

5. Ibid.

6. Ibid., 159.

7. Ibid.

8. Ibid., 161.

9. Mal Couch, "Kingdom of God, of Heaven," in *Dictionary of Premillennial Theology,* 231.

10. A. T. Robertson, *A Harmony of the Gospels for Students of the Life of Christ* (New York: Harper & Row, 1950).

11. William Hendriksen, *The Gospel of Matthew,* New Testament Commentary (Grand Rapids: Baker, 1982), 249.

12. Charles L. Feinberg, *Millennialism,* The Two Major Views (Winona Lake, Ind.: BMH Books, 1985), 203.

Chapter 23

1. J. Randall Price, *In Search of Temple Treasures* (Eugene, Ore.: Harvest House, 1994), 37.

2. J. Randall Price, *The Desecration and Restoration of the Temple in the Old Testament, Jewish Apocalyptic Literature, and The New Testament* (San Marcos, Tex.: World of the Bible Ministries, 1993), 113.

3. Stanley A. Ellisen, *Knowing God's Word* (New York: Nelson, 1984), 173–76.

4. Benjamin Marzar, *The Mountain of the Lord* (New York: Doubleday, 1975), 104.

5. Ibid., 61.

6. Michael Avi-Yonah and Zvi Baras, *The World History of the Jewish People: Society and Religion in the Second Temple Period Jewish History* (Jerusalem: Massada, 1977), 5.

7. Ibid., 18.

8. Ibid., 116–17.

9. Ibid., 117.

10. Ibid., 118.

11. Marzar, *Mountain of the Lord,* 105.

12. Ibid., 89–91.

13. Price, *The Desecration and Restoration of the Temple,* 123.

14. Thomas McCall, "How Soon the Tribulation Temple—Part I," *Bibliotheca Sacra* 128, no. 510 (April 1971): 341.

15. Ibid., 342.

16. Joyce Baldwin, "Daniel," in *Tyndale Old Testament Commentaries* (Downers Grove, Ill.: InterVarsity, 1978), 171.

17. McCall, "How Soon the Tribulation Temple—Part I," 346.

18. John F. Walvoord, "Will Israel Build a Temple In Jerusalem?" *Bibliotheca Sacra* 125, no. 497 (April 1968): 103.

19. McCall, "How Soon the Tribulation Temple—Part I," 347.

20. Robert L. Thomas, *Revelation 8–22: An Exegetical Commentary* (Chicago: Moody, 1995), 81.

21. John F. Walvoord, *The Millennial Kingdom* (Grand Rapids: Zondervan, 1959), 4.

22. J. Dwight Pentecost, *Things to Come* (Grand Rapids: Zondervan, 1958), 512.

23. Ibid., 513, quoting Arno C. Gaebelin, *The Prophet Ezekiel* (New York, N.Y.: Our Hope, 1918), 272.

24. J. B. Taylor, "Ezekiel," in *Tyndale Old Testament Commentaries*, 250–54.

25. John Gill, *Ezekiel–Malachi: Exposition of the Old and New Testaments*, vol. 6 (reprint, Paris, Ark.: Baptist Standard Bearer, 1989), 218.

26. Nathaniel West, *The Thousand Year Reign of Christ* (reprint, Grand Rapids: Kregel, 1993), 432–33.

27. Taylor, "Ezekiel," 252.

28. Ibid.

29. James H. Snowden, *The Coming of the Lord* (New York: Macmillan, 1919), 206.

30. Archibald Hughes, *A New Heaven and a New Earth* (Philadelphia: Presbyterian and Reformed, 1958), 157.

31. Loraine Boettner, *The Millennium* (Philadelphia: Presbyterian and Reformed, 1964), 95.

32. Alva J. McClain, *The Greatness of the Kingdom* (Grand Rapids: Zondervan, 1959), 250.

33. Oswald T. Allis, *Prophecy and the Church* (Philadelphia: Presbyterian and Reformed, 1964), 246.

34. Floyd E. Hamilton replies that ". . . any memorials are unnecessary when the one to be memorialized is present in person, as Christ would be after His Second Coming" (*The Basis of Millennial Faith* [Grand Rapids: Eerdmans, 1942)], 40).

    While this may be true in most cases when the person himself is to be remembered, it certainly does not apply when one's works and deeds are to be commemorated. Thus, stamps, coins, plaques, etc., bear the names and portraits of living personages in commemoration of their works and services.

35. Merrill F. Unger, *Great Neglected Prophecies* (Chicago: Scripture Press, 1955), 75.

36. A *theocracy* is the government of a state by the immediate direction of God.

37. Hamilton, *Basis of Millennial Faith*, 43.

38. In the last verse of his book, Zechariah again prophesied that "in

that day there shall be no more a Canaanite in the house of the Lord of hosts" (Zech. 14:21; cf. Ezra 8:20; Josh. 9).

39. Ibid., quoting Charles L. Feinberg, *God Remembers: A Study of the Book of Zechariah* (New York: American Board of Missions to the Jews, 1965), 156.

40. Thomas, *Revelation 8–22*, 437.

41. John F. Walvoord, *The Revelation of Jesus Christ* (Chicago: Moody, 1966), 312; and Pentecost, *Things to Come*, 568.

Appendix

1. J. H. Hertz, ed., *The Pentateuch and Haftorahs* (London: Soncino, 1971), 8.

2. Louis Berkhof, *Systematic Theology*, 4th ed. (Grand Rapids: Eerdmans, 1939, 1941), 213–14.

3. John F. Walvoord and Roy B. Zuck, eds., *The Bible Knowledge Commentary, New Testament* (Wheaton, Ill.: Victor, 1983), 31.

4. Henry M. Morris, *The Genesis Record* (Grand Rapids: Baker, 1994), 92–93.

5. Berkhof, *Systematic Theology*, 293.

6. Ibid., 295.

7. Walvoord and Zuck, *Bible Knowledge Commentary, New Testament*, 33.

8. Hertz, *Pentateuch and Haftorahs*, 45.

9. Berkhof, *Systematic Theology*, 295–96.

10. Arnold Fruchtenbaum, *Israelology: The Missing Link in Systematic Theology* (Tustin, Calif.: Ariel Ministries, 1992), 338.

11. Charles C. Ryrie, *Basic Theology* (Wheaton, Ill.: Victor Books, 1986), 453–54.

12. Hertz, *Pentateuch and Haftorahs*, 880–81.

13. Albert Barnes, "Deuteronomy," in *Barnes' Notes* (Grand Rapids: Baker, 1996), 2:329.

14. Eugene H. Merrill, "Deuteronomy," in *The New American Commentary* (Nashville: Broadman & Holman, 1994), 388–89.

15. Raphael Patai, *The Messiah Texts* (Detroit: Wayne State University Press, 1979), xxxv–xxxvi.

16. Albert Barnes, "Isaiah," in *Barnes' Notes*, 6:194–95.

17. Merrill Unger, *Old Testament Commentary* (Chicago: Moody, 1981), 1:1168.

18. A. Cohen, *Jeremiah* (London: Soncino, 1970), 211–12.

19. Albert Barnes, "Jeremiah," in *Barnes' Notes*, 5:226.

20. Unger, *Old Testament Commentary*, 2:1424.

21. A. Cohen, *Ezekiel* (London: Soncino, 1970), 243–44.

22. Albert Barnes, "Ezekiel," in *Barnes' Notes*, 5:386–87.

23. Paul N. Benware, *Understanding End Times Prophecy: A Comprehensive Approach* (Chicago: Moody, 1995), 69.
24. Unger, *Old Testament Commentary*, 2:1571–72.
25. Albert Barnes, "Daniel," in *Barnes' Notes*, 7:181.
26. Ibid., 186.
27. Harold W. Hoehner, *Chronological Aspects of the Life of Christ* (Grand Rapids: Zondervan, 1977), 131–33.
28. William Hendriksen, *The Gospel of Luke* (Grand Rapids: Baker, 1981), 87.
29. Charles John Ellicott, ed., *Commentary on the Whole Bible*, 8 vols. (Grand Rapids: Zondervan, 1959), 6:247.
30. Walvoord and Zuck, *Bible Knowledge Commentary, New Testament*, 205.
31. William Hendriksen, *The Gospel of Matthew* (Grand Rapids: Baker, 1982), 730.
32. Ed Glasscock, *Matthew* (Chicago: Moody, 1997), 394.
33. Patai, *Messiah Texts*, 143–44.
34. Albert Barnes, "Matthew," in *Barnes' Notes*, 9:260.
35. Stanley D. Toussaint, *Behold the King* (Portland, Ore.: Multnomah, 1981), 277–78.
36. Ellicott, *Commentary on the Whole Bible*, 7:2.
37. Walvoord and Zuck, *Bible Knowledge Commentary, New Testament*, 354.
38. Ibid., 353.
39. Ellicott, *Commentary on the Whole Bible*, 8:623.
40. John F. Walvoord, *The Revelation of Jesus Christ* (Chicago: Moody, 1966), 293–94.

Scripture Index

Subject Index

Also by Kregel Publications

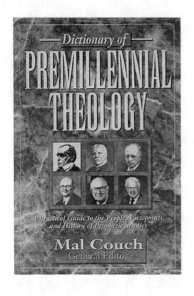

Dictionary of Premillennial Theology

Mal Couch, general editor

More than fifty scholars, authors, and Bible teachers have combined their expertise to present a historical and topical dictionary of premillennial theology. Included are articles on the major figures in prophetic studies such as Darby, Scofield, Chafer, Ladd, and Walvoord, as well as historical figures such as Augustine, Edwards, and Spurgeon. Additional articles cover major terms and concepts in premillennial theology as well as the eschatology of individual Bible books, Scripture passages, and extra-canonical writings.

Contributors include Robert Gromacki, Tommy Ice, Edward Hindson, John Hannah, Robert Lightner, Charles Ryrie, Tim LaHaye, and H. Wayne House.

Comprehensive in scope yet concise in its entries, *Dictionary of Premillennial Theology* will serve the needs of both the academic and lay reader as a practical reference book for prophetic studies.

448 pages
0-8254-2351-1 / hardcover